Fundamenta... on

An Explor...

Sam Jackson

Edited by Jonathan Curtis

With thanks to Tom Sharp

Published by Artificer Productions
Printed in the United Kingdom

ISBN: 978-0-9957273-4-2

www.JonathanCurtis.co.uk
© Artificer Productions 2022
All rights reserved

The moral rights of the author have been asserted.

Contents

1: Rhythm and Meter — 14

2: Pitch and Harmony — 23

3: Establishing Tonality — 45

4: IV and Back Again — 59

5: Turnarounds and Cycles — 66

6: Changing Key — 80

7: The Blues — 92

Interlude I — 102

8: Melody and Song — 108

9: Chord Tones and Non-Chord Tones — 114

10: Harmonising Melodies — 128

11: Melodic Phrases — 138

Interlude II — 147

12: The Chorus — 152

13: Arrangement — 164

Interlude III — 186

14: Substitutions for V and II-V — 198

15: Elaborations of I — 212

16: Modes and Modal Jazz — 218

17: Non-Functional Harmony — 231

18: More Scales — 237

19: More Melodic Techniques — 248

20: More Harmonic Techniques — 266

21: Chord Voicings — 271

22: Writing for Rhythm Section — 288

23: Writing for Melodic Instruments — 297

Closing Thoughts — 310

Index — 312

Introduction

Jazz musicians are necessarily improvisers, and must spontaneously manipulate rhythms, melodies, and chords, effectively composing in real time every time they perform. All great jazz composers have been performers, and virtually all great jazz performers have developed unique and compelling compositional styles of their own. The history of jazz is a story of the interplay between these two crafts, as improvised material is assimilated into new compositions which, in turn, inspire new improvisational approaches.

Though there is a great deal of literature focusing on jazz from the perspective of improvisation, far less has been written on how that same musical language might be used to compose music. This is perhaps partly due to a general de-emphasis on the study of composition within the culture. For many musicians, opportunities to perform original music are limited. Many musicians compose only infrequently if at all, and rely on vague and inconsistent notions of trial and error or intuition rather than on well-defined processes and techniques to guide their compositional practice.

There is a tendency in wider culture to romanticise the creative process. The musical composer in particular is often characterised as being at the mercy of a fickle and intermittent muse. This is not a useful way for a musician to approach the craft of composition, and has probably inhibited many latent composers who were not immediately struck with inspiration as soon as they picked up a pencil. As an alternative, let us try to conceptualise writing music as a process of trouble-shooting and problem-solving. Whatever stage we are at in an incomplete work, our immediate task is to identify the next hurdle. We proceed by asking ourselves 'which chord should go here?', 'could this melody be improved?', 'which key should the next section be in?', or simply 'what should happen next?'.

This book aims to lay out in a clear and coherent manner the fundamentals that guide harmony, melody, and form in jazz music. These are the tools that jazz composers use to solve their compositional problems. This book's aim is to present a metaphorical toolbox, collating and categorising the concepts and techniques found in the music of the canon in a logical format that may either be read in sequence or used as a reference.

If you have picked up this book, you probably either already write music or have done so in the past. It must be stressed that nothing in your current process is incorrect and that there are no right or wrong ways to create music. This book will not attempt to prescribe any particular procedure for writing. Instead, it suggests that we should look at what we currently have, and ask what it needs.

It is not our purpose within these pages to explore specific compositional styles in real depth. Instead, this volume is intended to be a study of the fundamentals, and we shall primarily focus on the common language that unites the music's significant practitioners. Writing in the style of a particular composer is a process that must begin with studying their music and identifying the tropes and techniques present. Although this practice is highly encouraged, pastiche has not historically had a large role in the output of jazz composers. Ultimately most of us will discover and develop our own unique aesthetic sensibility. On the other hand, innovation is not generally a path that is deliberately pursued by artistically successful musicians. We need not actively pursue or invent our own style, because it will find us in its own time over the course of practising, gaining experience, being persistent, and staying open to a healthy degree of trial and error.

The best jazz invariably emphasises improvisation, spontaneous interplay, individual expression, and personal style. All of these elements require that the composer does not obstruct those who are to perform their music. The role of a jazz performer is not to realise a composer's intentions accurately so much as it is to manipulate the written material to their own ends, using the piece as a medium for their own personal expression.

Although many musicians have found or invented alternative ways to graphically represent their ideas, conventional music notation is the most direct way to communicate most mainstream jazz. Some composers have deliberately eschewed any kind of notation, preferring to transmit ideas aurally to their performers. Such a method is probably more time consuming than notation, but might encourage musicians to be more aurally receptive in performances, and to personalise their contributions.

There are various software options for producing notation, and the advantages of these over handwriting are broadly the same as the advantages of a word processor as opposed to pen and paper in producing text. Music notated in software can be manipulated very easily, duplicated, and backed up, and there is little risk of illegibility. Some musicians do prefer to handwrite their music, particularly in casual and spontaneous circumstances, or if they wish to notate in unconventional ways.

Traditionally, a composer working in the western tradition might expand their initial drafts or sketches into a score: a document consisting of systems of vertically aligned staves, with one stave for each instrument. From the score, parts are produced to be read by the performers, each showing only what is to be played by a single instrument. When a prescribed instrumentation is required to perform a specific arrangement, this remains the best process, but in many situations, composers working within the jazz idiom may instead produce what is called a lead sheet.

A lead sheet is effectively a multi-use part for all instruments, consisting of only a single stave of melody with chord symbols above it. This enables a composer to show the chord progression, melody, form, style, and tempo of a piece in a manner that enables interpretation by any combination of instruments, and with little preparation or rehearsal. Although it cannot be said that all composers necessarily conceive of their music in this form – though many certainly do – the lead sheet is also an ideal format for us to begin thinking about and writing music. A lead sheet is a complete and performable jazz piece, but can also serve as the basis from which we might flesh out specific details of instrumentation and arrangement.

The only prerequisite skill strictly necessary to study from this book is familiarity with standard stave notation. In addition to this, basic keyboard facility is surely one of the best tools for aspiring composers, as the piano is the only instrument that enables us to play music with multiple parts easily. Composing at the piano is by no means a necessity, but it is worth bearing in mind that the overwhelming majority of jazz composers have worked in this way.

Each of the musical excerpts included here are invented by the author to demonstrate a specific principle, and most are presented in lead sheet format. Neither tempo nor performance style are specified when these details do not affect the issue in discussion. Excerpts that introduce harmonic concepts are always presented in relation to the keys of C major and C minor. This is to facilitate easy cross-comparison, and it is expected that the student makes themselves familiar with all of this material in all keys.

Learning to compose music from a book alone is like painting landscapes whilst blindfolded; results may be highly idiosyncratic and inconsistent. Recordings and live performances are the primary sources for jazz composition. Original scores are excellent resources where they are available, but transcriptions made by anyone other than the composer, such as anything found in a fake book, should be assumed to be inaccurate. Listen to as much music as you can, and learn as much as you can from it, whether by active transcription or casual absorption of the sounds. Write as much music as you can, and experiment with all of the techniques described in these pages.

The Jazz Tradition

In the first decade of the twentieth century, musicians in New Orleans began to synthesise African-American forms, such as ragtime and blues, with European harmony and brass band instrumentation. The music of these anonymous pioneers was to become the central hub in a vast web of interrelated styles that, together, were to become a defining American art form in a century where America dominated global culture.

Many of jazz music's greatest practitioners – the likes of Charles Mingus, Max Roach, Duke Ellington, Art Blakey, John Coltrane, Miles Davis, and Charlie Parker – have explicitly and publicly repudiated the word 'jazz', considering it to be irrelevant, inappropriate, or racist. Suggested alternatives have included New Orleans music, American music, black American music, modern music, and simply The Music. With some hesitation, and with no disrespect intended toward those that are uncomfortable with it, the J-word will be used throughout this book. In these pages, 'Jazz' is intended to serve as a shorthand for 'the music of Pops, Duke, Bird, Trane, and of their musical antecedents and descendants'.

Early jazz, sometimes called traditional jazz, Dixieland, or New Orleans jazz, is a style most associated with the late 1910s and the 1920s. Compositions of this era are often based around simple forms such as the twelve-bar blues, but may have rather complex arrangements featuring collective improvisations and passages in which the band drops out to feature a single soloist. A typical ensemble might consist of a singer, trumpet, trombone, and/or clarinet, and a rhythm section of piano, double bass, drums, and optional guitar. Practically any of the music made by Louis Armstrong, Jelly Roll Morton, or Sidney Bechet in the 1920s represents this style well.

During the early 1930s jazz bands were becoming increasingly popular in dance halls, and the need for greater volume led to bands taking on more and more musicians. Having ten or fifteen musicians on stage rather than five or six was a new challenge for jazz composers, and the music of this era placed a little less emphasis on improvisation and a little more on orchestration and arrangement. The preeminent style from early 1930s to the mid '40s is often called 'swing', and is most typically associated with the Big Band, an ensemble which became standardised to feature four trumpets, four trombones, five saxophones, and a rhythm section of piano, bass, drums, and, sometimes, guitar.

Duke Ellington – along with his in-house composer and arranger Billy Strayhorn – and Count Basie are perhaps the most significant composer/performers of this era.

The repertoire of jazz musicians in this period began to incorporate and take influence from the music of the Great American Songbook. This term refers broadly to the popular music written between the 1930s and 1950s as part of a thriving industry centred on New York's Tin Pan Alley. Professional songwriters such as George Gershwin, Jerome Kern, Irving Berlin, and Cole Porter produced hundreds of songs in a uniquely American style for musical theatre, film, and for recording by popular singers. The assimilation of these songs brought new material into the jazz language in the form of melodies that were perhaps descended a little more directly from older European music, an extended harmonic vocabulary, and the 'song form', which was to become practically ubiquitous in jazz practice.

The next clear stylistic leap came in the mid-1940s. In response to an economic need for smaller bands, a group of brilliantly innovative New York-centric musicians spearheaded by Charlie Parker, Bud Powell, Thelonious Monk, and Dizzy Gillespie began to play and write in a style that later become known as bebop. This music returned the emphasis to small groups and to improvisation, with a renewed insistence on instrumental virtuosity. Like the word 'jazz', the word 'bebop' is exonymic, and was explicitly rejected by virtually all of its originators.

Bebop compositions typically feature complex and asymmetric melodies, often performed in unison and at high tempos. Ensembles typically retained the swing-era rhythm section of piano, double bass, and drums but reduced the front line to just two or three horns. Much of the best bebop has the feel of a jam session; it is loose, freewheeling, and passionate rather than cool and controlled. The role of the rhythm section also evolved significantly during this era. Drummers in particular began to free themselves from background timekeeping roles, and started interacting with the melodic material much more actively.

One type of compositional characteristic of bebop is the contrafact, in which a melody is composed to fit a pre-existing chord progression, usually a popular songbook tune. The chord changes of George Gershwin's *I Got Rhythm*, the 'rhythm changes' (page 153), in particular were the basis for a huge swath of bebop repertoire.

Another growing trend of the 1940s was the integration of Latin American rhythms, in particular the music of Cuba and Brazil. Dizzy Gillespie's collaborations with Cuban musicians were early contributions to this trend, which provided jazz rhythm sections with alternatives to 4/4 swing time. After the enormous popularity of Stan Getz's early 60s work with guitarist João Gilberto, Brazilian styles such as bossa nova and samba were enthusiastically assimilated.

By the mid-1950s the prevailing aesthetic had transformed into what is now called 'hard bop'. This music cooled the boiling intensity of bebop with a little blues, gospel, and soul music. Any of the recordings made between about 1955 and 1965 by Art Blakey's Jazz Messengers or Horace Silver's bands are great examples of this style, as is virtually any of the other music released on the Blue Note label during that decade.

Typically, a hard bop ensemble might feature two or three horns and a rhythm section. This music places a little more emphasis on horn harmonies, orchestration, and arrangement than is found in bebop, and makes more frequent use of rhythm section ostinatos – repetitive patterns – than in any earlier styles. Popular Tin Pan Alley songs were also incorporated into the repertoire of most musicians by this time, where they mixed freely with bebop, swing, and hard bop style compositions.

Much has been written about modal jazz, particularly with reference to Miles Davis' enormously popular and influential 1959 album *Kind of Blue*, which more or less laid out a manifesto for this new style. This said, for most musicians, modal music has only ever made up a small portion of repertoire, so it does not quite seem accurate to describe it as a genre. Modal jazz is perhaps better understood as a series of interrelated compositional techniques. A modal piece might utilise long durations of a single chord, and the structures of harmonies themselves might be unusual, such that they might have no relation to the major and minor triads that are integral in tonal music.

Furthermore, the harmonic sequences within a piece might not be 'functional', in that chords might not relate to one another in obvious ways. In this regard, modal jazz represented a major deviation from the conventions that jazz harmony had inherited from pre-twentieth century European traditions. The 1960s albums of Herbie Hancock and Wayne Shorter, and their work with Miles Davis during the same period, feature many seminal compositions that demonstrate this gradual movement towards abstraction in harmony.

From the early 1960s onwards, musicians such as Ornette Coleman, Albert Ayler, Cecil Taylor, and John Coltrane began to discard conventional melody, form, harmony, rhythm, or all of the above in favour of more spontaneous musical expression.

Coleman's 1961 album *Free Jazz* was to give its name to a movement that had previously been called 'The New Thing'. Although this music heavily emphasised improvisation over pre-composed material, all of the free jazz movement's pre-eminent artists did develop powerful compositional techniques and styles of their own. A free jazz composition might consist of approximate sketches of the contour or texture that a piece is to have. A composed melody might be combined with improvised backing, or the reverse. Many free jazz performances are completely improvised without any preconceived material at all, and free jazz ensembles may consist of virtually any instrumentation.

The harmonic innovations of Herbie Hancock and Wayne Shorter, and the free jazz of Ornette Coleman and Cecil Taylor were, in reality, not particularly distinct movements. These were interrelated aspects with an increased emphasis on improvisation and a general movement towards abstraction, and were accompanied by a gradual emancipation of the rhythm section from their historic roles of anonymous accompaniment.

It would be egregious to talk about jazz composition in the 1950s and 60s without mentioning the charismatic and prolific bassist Charles Mingus, though his music does not fit easily into any category. By referencing early jazz, free jazz, bebop, hard bop, and classical music simultaneously in his work, Mingus was perhaps the first significantly postmodern jazz composer.

As the 1960s came to an end, Miles Davis was once again found at the forefront of stylistic revolution. Albums such as *In a Silent Way* and *Bitches Brew*, released in 1969 and 1970 respectively, are often held to represent the inception of jazz fusion. It is difficult to describe the compositional techniques of jazz fusion in anything other than extremely general terms. Davis' fusion music combined funk and rock with modal harmony and free jazz, but other jazz fusion statements have also incorporated R&B, free jazz, electronica, and the music of Cuba, Brazil, or India in practically any combination. The most consistent element in jazz fusion is the incorporation of electric instruments into the jazz ensemble: electric guitars, bass guitars, synthesisers, and electric keyboards are all characteristic elements of the fusion sound.

From this point onward, the proliferation of aesthetic threads frustrates any attempt to identify a single narrative in the development of jazz style, though a few very general trends may still be identified. From the mid-1980s many musicians became interested in a return to pre-fusion styles and acoustic instrumentation. A loose collective emerged, centred on the Marsalis brothers, Wynton and Branford, whose ostensible aim was to pick up exactly where acoustic jazz had left off in 1969. Whilst there were musicians playing acoustic music through the 1970s, all of the major stylistic innovations during that period had been within fusion genres. The generation that played this 'neo-bop' music (or, as Miles Davis described it, 'warmed-over turkey') are often referred to as The Young Lions.

In response to the Young Lions, a brilliant wave of young musicians and composers appeared in the early 1990s. Musicians such as Mark Turner, Brad Mehldau, Kurt Rosenwinkel, Christian McBride, and Joshua Redman assimilated Marsalis-style neo-classicism with fusion, earlier jazz styles, and a newfound openness to pop music. Musicians of this era might open a set swinging like Art Blakey, then combine Wayne Shorter-style harmony with a J-Dilla beat, or adapt a Beatles song to fit a 7/4 time signature.

The new millennium is too close at hand for us to clearly identify the important new trends in jazz style. The music is more vital than ever, but also more divided, and there are composers working at the highest levels in almost any style. The assimilation of jazz with electronica and/or hip hop is one major branch, as is the exploration of increasingly complex rhythms. There is also ongoing work on the synthesis of jazz with rhythmic patterns from other cultures. Acoustic small-group jazz continues to evolve towards greater levels of abstraction and group interplay, and elsewhere, large ensemble music is being made that references electronica and twentieth century orchestral music.

Although polystylism abounds in all twenty-first century music making, contemporary jazz musicians generally engage in neither pastiche of older styles nor ironic references to the past. Styles are assimilated and referenced in a spirit of reverence and affection, and contemporary jazz musicians are expected to have a deep knowledge and love for the entirety of the jazz tradition. Even the most avant-garde and forward-thinking jazz composers would benefit from a deep understanding of the fundamentals outlined in the following chapters, rather than simply casting them aside, as may be popularly conceived. As with the old aphorism, one must first learn the rules in order to break them.

From the canon emerges a shared repertoire of jazz standards. These are the pieces that jazz players are expected to commit to memory in order to perform spontaneously with other musicians. There can be no strict definition to what constitutes a jazz standard, and shared repertoire may vary hugely depending on time and place. Many would only consider those pieces that were adapted from the Great American Songbook to be standards, but there are also a great number of jazz compositions in the common repertoire.

Below is a list of musicians who have made significant aesthetic contributions in the field, either as performers or interpreters of jazz composition. They may all be heard on recordings under their own names, and as sidemen or women, and most of them have written compositions that have been performed and recorded by others:

Aaron Parks
Abdullah Ibrahim
Ahmad Jamal
Albert Ayler
Alice Coltrane
Allan Holdsworth
Ambrose Akinmusire
Andrew Hill
Anthony Braxton
Antonio Carlos Jobim
Art Blakey
Benny Golson
Bill Evans
Bill Frisell
Billie Holiday
Bobby Hutcherson
Brad Mehldau
Bud Powell
Cannonball Adderley
Carla Bley
Cecil Taylor
Cedar Walton
Charles Mingus
Charlie Parker
Chick Corea
Chris Potter
Christian McBride
Clifford Brown
Coleman Hawkins
Count Basie
Dave Holland
Derek Bailey
Dizzy Gillespie
Django Reinhardt
Don Cherry
Duke Ellington
Earl Hines
Eric Dolphy
Erroll Garner
Fats Waller
Fred Hersch
Freddie Hubbard
Gary Burton
Gil Evans
Gilad Hekselman
Henry Threadgill
Herbie Hancock
Horace Silver
Jackie McLean
Jakob Bro
Jan Garbarek
Jelly Roll Morton
Jim Hall
Jimmy Giuffre
Joe Henderson
John Abercrombie
John Coltrane
John Lewis
John McLaughlin
John Scofield

John Taylor	Mark Turner	Stan Kenton
Joshua Redman	Mary Halvorson	Steve Coleman
Julian Lage	Mary Lou Williams	Steve Swallow
Keith Jarrett	Masabumi Kikuchi	Tadd Dameron
Kenny Wheeler	McCoy Tyner	Thad Jones
Kurt Rosenwinkel	Miles Davis	Thelonious Monk
Lee Konitz	Ornette Coleman	Tony Williams
Lee Morgan	Pat Metheny	Tyshawn Sorey
Lennie Tristano	Paul Bley	Vijay Iyer
Lester Young	Paul Motian	Wayne Shorter
Louis Armstrong	Peter Brötzmann	Wes Montgomery
Mal Waldron	Robert Glasper	Wynton Marsalis
Maria Schneider	Ron Carter	
Mark Guiliana	Sonny Rollins	

Chapter 1
Rhythm and Meter

Duke Ellington's iconic *It Don't Mean a Thing (If It Ain't Got That Swing)* is more than simply a masterpiece of a popular song, it is a sincere manifesto for jazz performance. The jazz tradition places rhythm at the very highest level of importance. Rhythmic nuance is a medium of expression for the jazz performer, with musicians being free to place their notes behind or ahead of the prevailing tempo. The musicians within an ensemble have a dynamic relationship with the underlying pulse and with each other's rhythms. They may lock in, or push and pull against each other, generally or within individual passages.

Though the rhythmic minutiae that bring jazz to life are in the hands of performers, there are various aspects of jazz rhythm of which composers should be aware. In most music, events are spaced at regular intervals through time. At the surface level of this phenomenon is the steady implicit pulse that we call the beat. The frequency of the beat usually falls somewhere between 40 and 300 cycles per minute, and this tempo defines how fast or slow we perceive a piece of music to be. Other musical events are understood in relation to this fundamental pulse. They may begin on or in-between beats, and their durations can be measured in terms of how many beats they cover.

Some beats are more important than others. In most jazz, and western music generally, the most common meter – or time signature – is 4/4, where the first of every four beats receives emphasis. Much of the rhythmic language used by jazz performers has complex or subtle relationships with the underlying meter. Musicians may deemphasise the obvious rhythmic landmarks in favour of upbeats, deemphasised beats, and off-beats, the points between beats. Rhythmic phrases that imply alternative emphases or meters over the underlying pulse are said to be syncopated, and its application is so ubiquitous in the rhythmic language of jazz that non-syncopated rhythms often sound out of place.

Swing Time

Whilst not strictly a necessary component of jazz performance (entire genres exist without it), swing time is undeniably a crucial aspect of jazz rhythm. Rather than subdivide each beat exactly in half to produce eighth notes, swing time delays the off-beat eighth note, resulting in a rhythm that implies an underlying triplet subdivision.

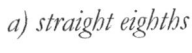

a) straight eighths

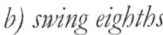

b) swing eighths

In jazz performance, the placement of these inter-beat events is highly flexible. They may fall exactly half way between beats, or be very delayed, implying a triplet or even a sixteenth note subdivision. These minute details of rhythmic expression fall outside the responsibility of the composer, and are an aspect of an individual player's style that should be left in the hands of performers. Some musicians play very straight eighths, some very swung, some play ahead of the beat or behind the beat, and all of these parameters may vary at different tempos, on different pieces, or even within a single phrase of music.

A triplet subdivision can suggest the partition of a bar of 4/4 into two groups of quarter note triplets. This creates an implied polyrhythm against the underlying meter of quarter notes, comprising two simultaneous pulses interrelated by the ratio 2:3. This consists of two quarter notes on the one hand, and the three notes of a quarter note triplet on the other. This is implied polyrhythm is a defining feature of jazz rhythm, and one which harks back to its rhythmic roots in West Africa. The 2:3 relationship is often implicit in swing time:

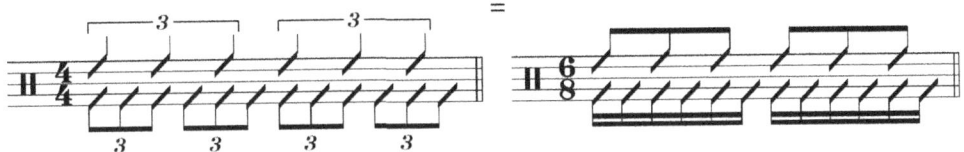

Straight eighths have also been present in jazz for most of its history, initially inspired by the music of Cuba and Brazil. Later, pop and rock music adopted straight eighths, an influence which transferred back into some contemporary jazz via numerous strains of jazz-rock and fusion.

Emphasis Within Meter

Beat one is, by definition, a moment of emphasis. In 4/4 time, we find a moment of lesser emphasis on beat three, because this is half way between beat one and the first beat of the subsequent bar. Half way between these points we find a further point of lesser emphasis, and so on in a steadily diminishing way. If we rank these points of emphases numerically, with 1 possessing the most importance, we might visualise an entire bar thus:

These numbers should not be taken to be related to the dynamics with which notes in these positions should be played. Performers do not necessarily play beat one louder than beat two, and much of the language used by jazz performers actually emphasises beats two, four, and the off-beat eighth notes. It is perhaps more accurate to say that, with all other things being equal, we *perceive* events that take place on beat one to be more significant than those taking place on beat two, because they are inherently emphasised by the meter.

That 4/4 time can be divided in half, and in half again, to produce whole beats likely accounts for its omnipresence in western music, but other meters are regularly used in jazz. Older music in 3/4 time generally accents beats one and three, as in a waltz or minuet, but jazz musicians are also likely to divide the 3/4 bar equally, placing an accent halfway through the second beat. Once again, this produces the 2:3 coincidence, the same implicit polyrhythm, characteristic of West African-influenced music:

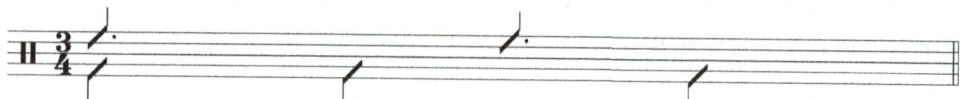

5/4 is also used extensively in modern jazz, stretching back to the innovations of Max Roach and Dave Brubeck in the late 1950s, but becoming far more commonplace from the 1990s. A bar of 5/4 generally has an implicit secondary accent on either the third beat or the second, dividing the bar either into three and two, or two and three. A performance may switch between these variants, or even employ both simultaneously across the ensemble:

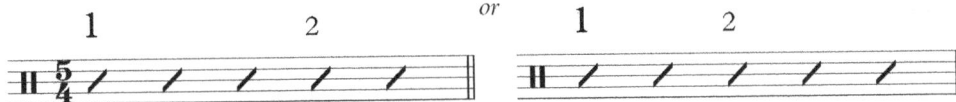

Additionally, a secondary accent might be present at the halfway point of the bar, producing a 2:5 polyrhythm:

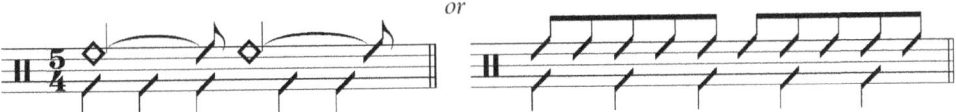

A so-called 'long five' may also be implicit or present alongside the primary pulse, consisting of five half notes spread over two bars:

All of the same principles may be applied to other time signatures. 7/4 is reasonably common in contemporary jazz performance, typically being implicitly subdivided as either four and three, or three and four, the accented moments therefore being thus:

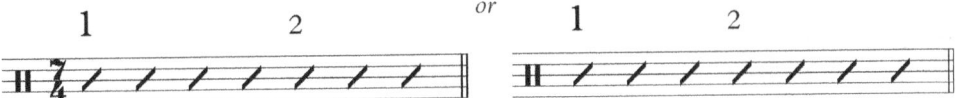

Once again, the 'long seven' may be present, either implicitly or explicitly, here consisting of seven half notes over two bars:

This is by no means an exhaustive list of the time signatures used in jazz. It is safe to assume that any time signature of manageable length has been employed by jazz musicians at some point. 4/4, 3/4, 5/4, and 7/4 are perhaps the only meters popular and simple enough to have particular conventions associated with them. When any of the numerous other possible time signatures are used, they are invariably subdivided into combinations of groups of twos, threes, and fours. Musicians sometimes refer to the particular sequence of divisions within an unusual rhythm as its clave, in analogy to the repetitive rhythmic figure present in much Afro-Cuban music. As an example, here are some of the numerous clave permutations that can be used to divide points of emphasis in a bar of 9/8:

a) 3+3+3   b) 2+2+3+2   c) 3+4+2

d) 2+3+2+2   e) 2+2+2+3   f) 3+2+4

Each has its own distinct character, with points of emphasis generally falling on the first note of each group. Though these variations may be overlaid or heard alongside each other within the same piece, some consistency is necessary if the effect of regular meter is required. When writing music in an unconventional time signature, it is best to make sure that the beaming of the notes is consistent throughout a piece and reflects the rhythmic phrasing found in the music.

If the required pattern of metric emphases long, it may be better expressed as combinations of shorter bars. This reflects how longer meters appear in practice, and is more digestible for performers. For example, a bar of 13/4 with emphases on the fifth, eighth, and eleventh beats…

…will be easier for musicians to read and comprehend as four shorted bars, utilising a change of meter:

There are no definite rules about how to divide bars in such situations, but the aim of notating music is to express compositional ideas to musicians with clarity, even if this means notating the idea in different way to how it was conceived.

Mixed meter – music with changing time signatures – was a relatively late addition to the rhythmic language of jazz, not appearing until the more progressive music of the late 1960s. The possibilities of mixed meter music are infinite, but perhaps the most common usage of irregular changes in time signature is the addition of one or more beats at the end of a passage in regular time, which produces the sensation of delaying the end of the phrase:

Conversely, the subtraction of one or more beats at the end of a passage, which truncates the phrase by adding a sense of urgency, makes it feel as though the next passage begins too early:

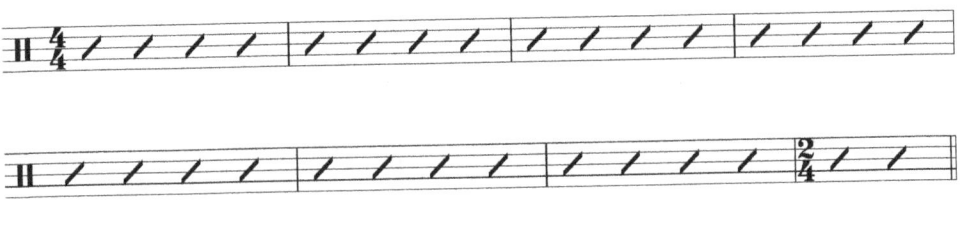

Hypermeter

Just as we group individual pulses into bars, the meter, we group the bars themselves into larger phrases in a practice called hypermeter. The pattern of emphases within a bar – lesser points of emphasis found at nodes halfway between the greater ones – repeats on this larger scale.

Below is an example of hypermeter. First we see a single bar of 4/4 showing typical points of emphasis. Following it is a four-bar passage employing the same pattern of relative accents:

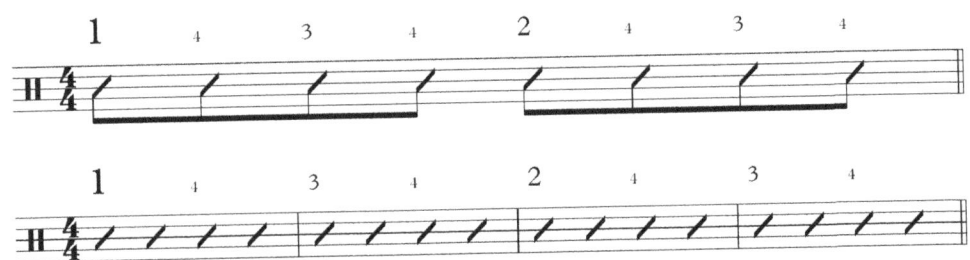

The same sequence of emphases can likewise exist across a sixteen-bar passage of music thus:

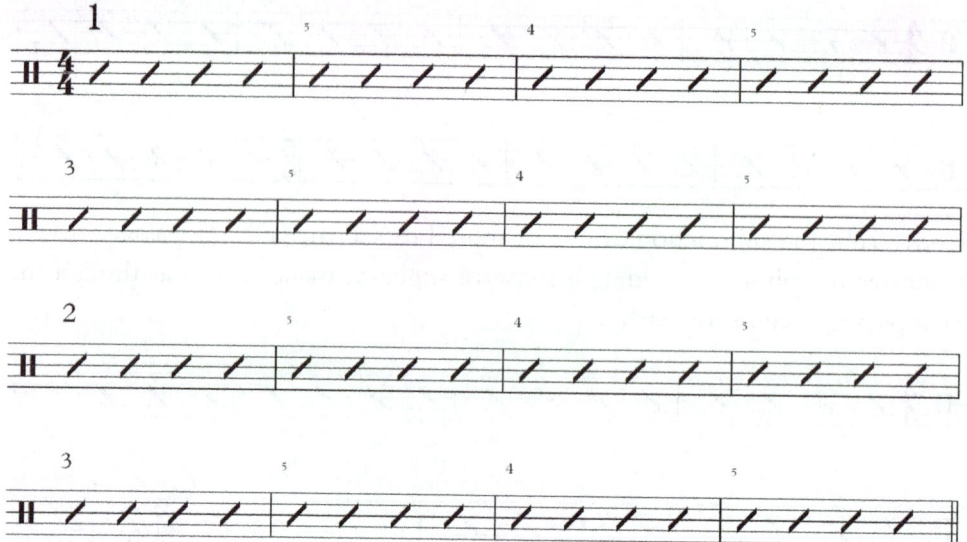

All other things being equal, events taking place at the beginning of bars one or nine of a sixteen bar passage feel more significant than those taking place in bars five or seven.

Phrase, Period, and Chorus

A musical phrase is a short fragment of material, often existing as a discrete idea. There is no strict definition of a phrase, but for our purposes, we can define it as the amount of music that would accompany a single line of lyrics, or the amount of melody that could be sung with a single breath, two concepts influenced by Tin Pan Alley.

More tangibly, we might define a melodic phrase as a fragment of melody, typically two or four bars in length, preceded and separated by rests. However, this definition is somewhat contingent on the tempo of the piece.

Because of the inherent symmetry in conventional hypermeter, chord progressions tend to begin the first and last bar of every four, eight, and sixteen-bar segment of music with a harmonically significant moment. Melodic phrases tend to roughly align with the harmonic phrases that underlie them.

The phrases within a piece must relate to each other in order to create a coherent musical statement. A melodic phrase may be followed by a repetition of the same phrase or a variation upon it, ideas that will be further explored in Chapter 11.

A passage of music consisting of two or four phrases might constitute a coherent musical statement, having a sense of journey, destination, and complete resolution. Jazz musicians might casually refer to this type of subdivision as a section, but the term period will be used throughout this book because its meaning is far more specific.

A period might be eight measures long, twelve, as in a twelve-bar blues, or, at particularly fast tempos, sixteen. Just like the individual beats in a bar, the bars within a period greater than five or six bars in length tend to subdivide themselves into smaller phrases: a nine-bar period, for example, will usually sound like a four bar phrase followed by a five bar phrase or its inverse, depending on the content and context.

In this book, periods will be denoted with double bar lines, and, wherever practical, new periods will begin with a new system on a new line of stave. It is a good idea to implement this formatting style in any parts or lead sheets that are produced, as this communicates to performers how the piece is to be subdivided

Just as phrases are compiled into periods, musical periods are combined into larger structures, sometimes repeating themselves with or without alteration. A typical jazz performance consist of a head, in which the composed melody is accompanied by the harmonic and rhythmic backing of the rhythm section, followed by a series of solos, where each soloist improvises over the same chord progression; the head melody will be recapitulated after the solos. The head at the beginning of a piece is sometimes called the in-head, and the head at the end of a piece the out-head.

This extended chord sequence is called a chorus, because it developed from the chorus section of early twentieth century popular song. Thirty-two bar choruses are typical, often consisting of four eight-bar periods structured *A-A-B-A* or *A-B-A-C*, but sixteen-bar *A-B* pieces and the single-period twelve-bar blues are also very common. These ideas are further discussed in Chapter 12.

A majority of jazz performances are based upon on this 'head-solos-head' format, but there is much flexibility within it. Typical variations include the addition of an introduction before the first head, a coda after the last, or an interlude between solos, all of which are described more fully in Chapter 13.

Chapter Summary

Music tends to be based on a fundamental pulse or beat in relation to which the timing of musical events can be understood.

The subdivision of the pulse in swing time may suggest the first and third note of an eighth note triplet, but is often highly flexible in its rhythmic placement.

Certain moments within a bar receive more inherent emphasis than others. Beat one is, by definition, the point of most inherent emphasis.

Longer meters such as 5/4 and 7/4 tend to be explicitly or implicitly subdivided into shorter periods.

A phrase is a fragment of material lasting for a few seconds.

A period is a discrete passage of music usually eight to sixteen measures in length.

A chorus is a large-scale chord progression that repeats without alteration.

Certain moments within a phrase, period, or chorus receive more inherent emphasis than others, a phenomenon that can be referred to as hypermeter.

Chapter 2
Pitch and Harmony

This chapter serves as a primer on the pitched content of jazz – harmonies and melodies – and their derivation from earlier styles, and from basic physical principles. Much of the content of jazz harmony is heavily influenced by pre-twentieth century European music. The term 'common practice music' will be used throughout this book whenever it is necessary to refer collectively to the Baroque, Classical, and Romantic styles predominant in European art music between about 1600 and 1900.

Pitches and Intervals

Sound is our perception of pressure waves travelling through the air at different frequencies. When one frequency predominates, we perceive the sound to have a pitch. We perceive it to be high or low relative to other sounds, and based on whether the fundamental frequency that we hear is high or low. In this book the words 'tone' and 'note' are used interchangeably with 'pitch'.

We perceive pitches whose frequencies are related by simple mathematical ratios to be consonant with each other. Those whose frequencies are related by more complex ratios are perceived to be dissonant with each other. For example, pitches whose ratio is 1:2 (or 2:1, 1:4, 1:8, and so on) sound so similar that we assign them all the same name, and consider them to be functionally identical. 220Hz, 440Hz, and 880Hz are all given the name of 'A'. We name the band of frequencies that separates each A an octave, and from the eighteenth century onwards common practice musicians have divided each octave into twelve bands of equal width, in a system called equal temperament. The set of twelve pitches produced by this equal division is the chromatic scale.

The distances between pitches we call intervals, with the interval between any two adjacent pitches of the chromatic scale being called a half step, and the distance between pitches, two half steps apart being a whole step. We may construct our full musical alphabet from A-G by beginning from any A, and ascending in the following sequence: whole step, half step, whole step, whole step, half step, whole step:

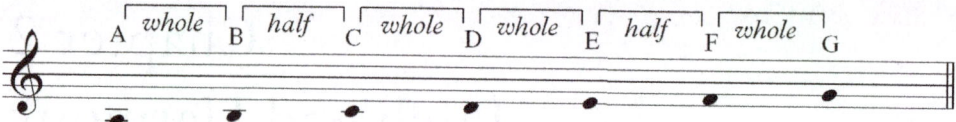

This collection of seven pitches is most associated with music that implies resolution to the pitch of C, so they are typically reordered into a sequence which begins with C: the C major scale:

The five pitches that fall in-between these seven are described in terms of being either raised (sharp, denoted ♯) or lowered (flat, denoted ♭) by a half step relative to the pitches of the C major scale. Pitches that are neither raised nor lowed are called natural, denoted ♮. Identical pitches with two alternative names. C-sharp and D-flat are said to be enharmonic equivalents:

The major scale is a pattern that can be built from any of the twelve pitches of the chromatic scale by ascending in the following sequence: whole step, whole step, half step, whole step, whole step, whole step. We always name these seven pitches alphabetically, which means that each major scale has exactly one pitch for each of the seven letters from A to G. This is why enharmonic pitches occur: the pitch used as C-sharp in an A major scale must be repurposed to function as D-flat in an A-flat major scale:

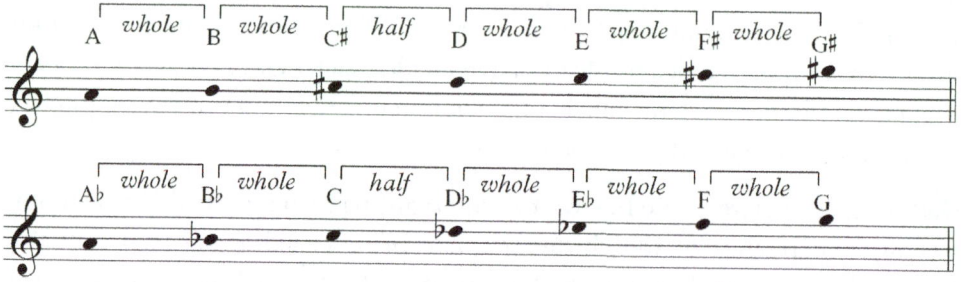

Almost all of the world's music is tonal, which is to say the pitched material is arranged so that one pitch in particular becomes the axis around which the others revolve.

This central pitch, known as the tonic or tonal centre, is the implied destination of a piece or passage of music. The music sounds as though it is heading there, even though it need never actually arrive. When we discuss the use of pitches in tonal music, we compare them to the major scale of the tonic. If the tonic of a piece is E-flat, we say that E-flat is the root, and we discuss its other pitches in relation to the E-flat major scale. We can do this by numbering the pitches of the major scale 1-7:

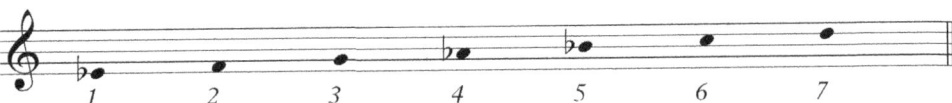

Now, we can use ordinal numbers to describe these pitches. We are also able to describe other pitches that occur in the piece in relation to these seven:

This system allows us to describe any pitch in terms of its function by its relationship to the tonic. We might say that C-flat is the flattened sixth of E-flat, or that B is the raised fifth of E-flat. This parlance enables us to discuss and think about music in terms that are entirely abstracted from alphabetically named pitches, and thereby relate the same material to different tonics. In other words, we can discuss general harmony without being tied to a specific key. Below is an example of how an idea might be transposed. The pitches themselves are changed, but their numerical relationships to the tonic are the same:

Tonic is E♭:   *Tonic is G:*

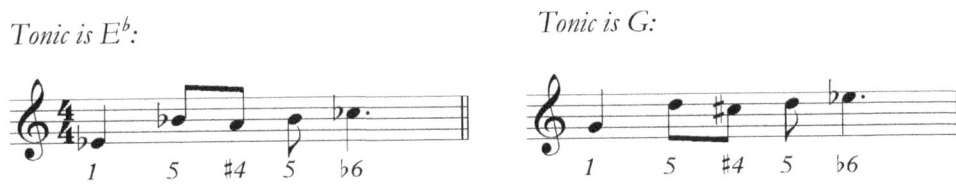

More broadly, we use ordinal numbers to describe the intervallic relationship between any two notes, specifically to describe how far apart they are. Again, the major scale is the reference with which other intervals are compared. We might describe an A-flat as being a natural third below a given C, and a D-flat as being a flattened ninth above it:

The following table names all of the intervals that we will encounter most frequently. Intervals of greater than an octave can be labelled as compound, such that a thirteenth could be described as a compound sixth:

Name(s)	Half steps from Root	Above C	Below C
Unison	0	C	C
Half step, flattened second, minor second	1	D^b	B
Whole step, major second	2	D	B^b
Flattened third, minor third	3	E^b	A
Natural third, major third	4	E	A^b
Natural fourth, perfect fourth	5	F	G
Tritone, raised fourth/flattened fifth*	6	F♯/G^b	F♯/G^b
Natural fifth, perfect fifth	7	G	F
Flattened sixth/raised fifth*, minor sixth	8	G♯/A^b	E
Natural sixth, major sixth	9	A	E^b
Flattened seventh, minor seventh	10	B^b	D
Seventh, major seventh	11	B	D^b
Octave	12	C	C
Flattened ninth	13	D^b	B
Natural ninth, ninth	14	D	B^b
Flattened tenth, minor tenth	15	E^b	A
Tenth, major tenth	16	E	A^b
Natural eleventh, eleventh	17	F	G
Raised eleventh/flattened twelfth*	18	F♯/G^b	F♯/G^b
Natural twelfth, perfect twelfth	19	G	F
Flattened thirteenth	20	A^b	E
Natural thirteenth, thirteenth	21	A	E^b
-	22	B^b	D
-	23	B	D^b
Compound octave	24	C	C

*Dependent on context

Building Triads

Multiple pitches may be sounded simultaneously as chords. In this book the words 'chord' and 'harmony' are used interchangeably as nouns to describe these sonic structures, and the word 'harmony' is also used to describe the general concept of combining pitches simultaneously.

Major and minor triads are the most consonant three-note harmonies possible within equal temperament. The major triad consists of a root, a third, and a fifth. The frequencies of these pitches are interrelated by the ratio 4:5:6, a relatively simple formula which produces the most consonant three-note chord possible:

C major triad

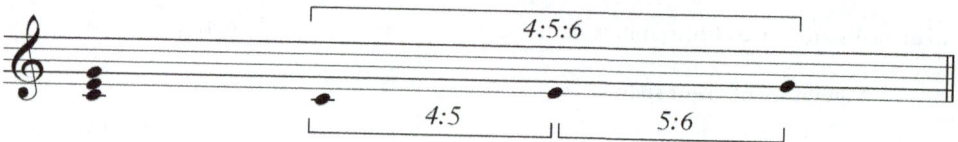

The minor triad consists of a root, a flattened third, and a fifth. Again, in terms of the frequencies involved, it can be expressed as a ratio 10:12:15, a more complex structure that we perceive to be slightly more dissonant:

C minor triad

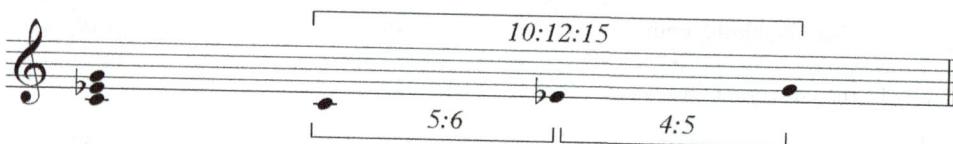

A major triad consists of a major third (4:5) under a minor third (5:6), while a minor triad consists of a minor third (5:6) under a major third (4:5). There are two more triads, both of which can be built by stacking thirds in this way.

Firstly, stacking a major third above a major third gives us the slightly more dissonant augmented triad:

C augmented triad

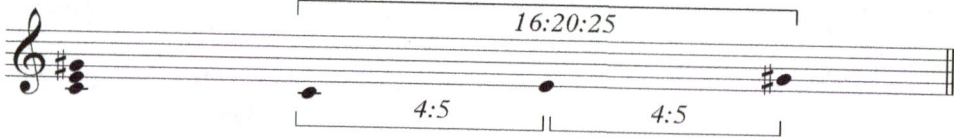

Secondly, stacking a minor third above a minor third gives us a harsh-sounding diminished triad, whose dissonant sound reflects the complexity of the 45:54:64 interrelationship:

C diminished triad

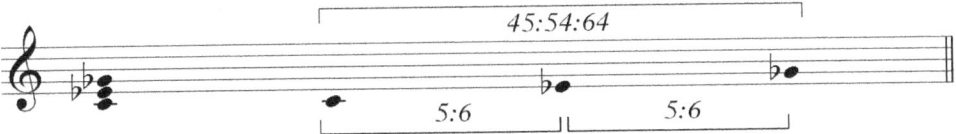

In equal temperament, all of these ratios are only approximated, and therefore slightly out of tune. Because we have divided each octave into twelve, an equal tempered major third is in fact only 4:5 to the nearest twelfth of an octave.

The practice of building chords from stacked thirds in this manner is sometimes called tertiary harmony, and is the basis of how we construct chords in tonal music. These tertiary structures may not occur literally. Any of the three pitches of a triad may be displaced into different octaves, duplicated, or both. All that is required for a chord to be a C major triad is that it contains any C, any E, and any G. The precise structure of a chord is known as its voicing. The following are all voicings of a C major chord; all three structures contain only the pitches C, E, and G:

The table below shows these four triads alongside each other, allowing us to see how the structure of each relates to the major scale. The rightmost column shows how, by replacing 'X' with the relevant root note, we could express each triad with a chord symbol:

Major	1	3	5	X
Minor	1	♭3	5	X^m, X^-
Augmented	1	3	♯5	X^+
Diminished	1	♭3	♭5	$X^°$

These triads are shown below in standard notation, with C as the root note:

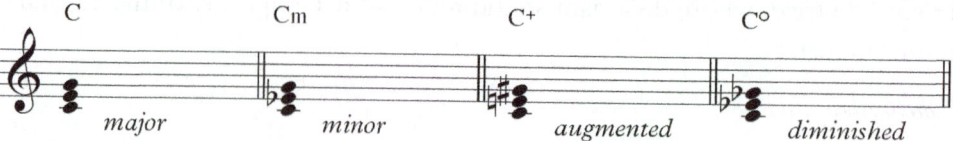

In jazz, the precise voicing of a chord is one of the many details usually left to the discretion of the performer. Pianists and guitarists, for example, are usually provided with just a chord symbol, and given autonomy to voice each chord however they deem appropriate.

Keys and Key Signatures

In common practice music and its harmonic descendants, major and minor triads are considered to be so consonant that they function as the target of a piece of tonal music. Rather than seeking resolution to a target tonic pitch, a tonal passage may seek resolution to a target major or minor triad. The tonic pitch can be said to have been elaborated into a tonic chord. We describe a passage whose tonic is elaborated by a major triad as being a in a major key, and a piece whose tonic is elaborated by a minor triad as being a in a minor key. We name the tonality, or key, of a passage of music after its tonic chord. Music in G major has an implied destination of a G major triad, and music in E-flat minor has an implied destination of an E-flat minor triad. For major keys, this terminology can be abbreviated, allowing a piece of music in G major to be described as being 'in G'.

It important to note that in modern harmony, key is often subjective and ambiguous. Key may be present, absent, or nebulous at various points within a piece, and to varying degrees. We might liken a sense of key in music to harmonic gravity: in some situations, we feel a strong pull towards a particular tonic, or the attraction of two or more tonal bodies. If the chords do not suggest any particular destination, the harmony might feel as though it is floating freely.

Chords, chord progressions, and melodies that establish or confirm a sense of key are said to be functional, in that they perform a function within the tonal framework of the passage. Material that does not have any obvious relationship to key or tonality can be said to be non-functional, but again these categories are rather subjective, and functionality is best thought of as a quality that music may have by degree, rather than simply in presence or absence. Most of the discussion of harmony in this book will relate initially to functional – or tonal – material, but non-functional harmony will addressed specifically in Chapter 17.

Music in major keys primarily utilises the pitches of the major scale, so in order to simplify notation, it is written with a key signature. At the beginning of the stave, those pitches that must be sharpened or flattened in order to construct a major scale based on the tonic are pre-emptively sharpened or flattened.

This shorthand relieves the composer from having to denote every A-flat with a ♭ symbol, and also enables the performer to see at a glance which key the passage is in. Being able to recognise the following key signatures, and knowing their associated major scales, is an essential skill for any composer:

When pitches occur that are not part of the tonic major scale, we alter them with accidentals: sharps, flats, or natural signs. When enharmonic options are present, the key signature with the fewest accidentals is preferred. For example, the following scales are sonically identical in even tempered music:

In this example, E-flat major would be the preferred option because it only requires three flats, as opposed to the five sharps and two double sharps (𝄪) required by the key of D-sharp major. The enharmonic keys of F-sharp and G-flat both require six accidentals, and so are completely interchangeable.

Minor key music uses a set of pitches closely related to the major scale three half steps above its root. For example, C is three half steps above A, and music in the key of A minor uses a similar set of pitches to music in C major.

We describe major and minor scales that are related in this way as relative, such that A minor is the relative minor of C major, and C major is the relative major of A minor.

This is also reflected in the key signature. Music in both A minor and C major is written with a key signature that contains no accidentals, and music in both B-flat minor and its relative major D-flat major is written with a key signature with five flats. Minor scales always begin three half steps below their relative majors. Familiarity with the key signatures of minor keys is also essential:

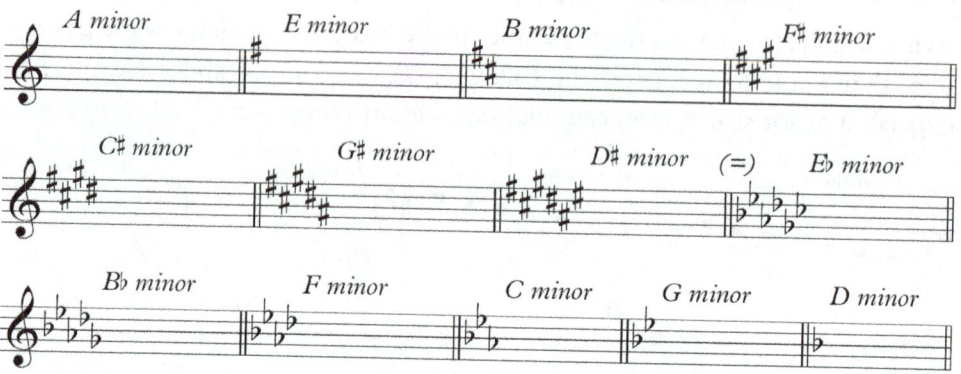

Minor Scales

The use of a key signature based on the major scale to denote the key of a passage can be misleading, because tonal music is ultimately defined by how its pitches function, rather than which pitches are used. The major scale contains only some of the pitches that might found in a piece of music written in a major key. Tonal music invariably uses both diatonic material, pitches native to the key signature, and chromatic material, pitches that must be denoted with accidentals.

Minor keys are illustrative of this. Traditionally minor tonality has been described in terms of three scales that must work in conjunction to produce minor key music.

Firstly, the natural minor scale, which is a permutation of the major scale. The C natural minor scale uses the same set of pitches as the E-flat major scale, but in a context where the tonic is C rather than E-flat.

The natural minor scale best reflects the pitches likely to be used alongside chords other than the tonic and dominant of a minor key, and demonstrates effectively the close relationship between a major key and its relative minor. The two keys

aug. 2nd

use many of the same pitches and are therefore often used together within the same piece.

The harmonic minor scale represents an attempt to explain all minor key harmony as being derived from a single scale. From its seven notes, all of the most typical chords of the minor key, namely I^m, IV^m, and V^7, can be created.

The downside of the harmonic minor scale is that it creates a conspicuous augmented second between the flattened sixth and the natural seventh. Common practice composers deemed this interval to be ugly when occurring in melodies.

In the following instances, *(a)* shows an example of a flattened seventh that clashes with the underlying harmony. Using the harmonic minor to solve this by using a raised seventh of the that scale, as in *(b)*, would create an undesirable augmented second interval in the melody. A possible solution is shown in *(c)*:

(a) B♭ clashes with B♮ *(b) Augmented second between A♭ and B♮* *(c) Issue solved with A♮ and B♮*

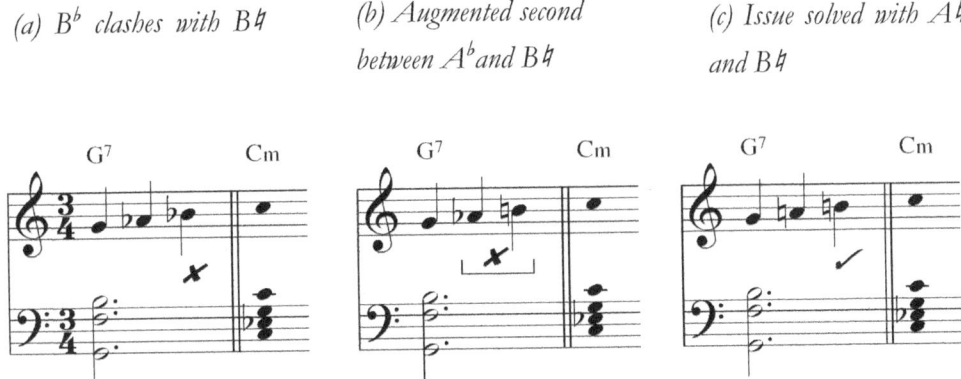

The solution in *(c)* uses both an A-natural and a B-natural. A-natural does not appear in either the natural or harmonic minor scales, and the presence of the B natural in the harmonic minor produces the undesirable augmented second, as shown in *(b)*. By raising the A-flat to an A-natural, the melody can proceed without clashing with the key signature, or producing the augmented second.

To allow for the presence of both an A-natural and B-natural, music theorists extrapolate the existance of a third type of minor scale, dubbed the melodic minor scale, which must consist of different pitches on the ascent and descent:

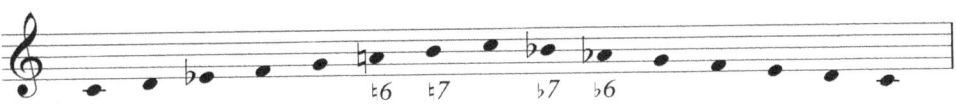

33

In the above rendition of the melodic minor scale, the natural sixth and seventh are both flattened on the descent.

This three-minor-scale system was intended to represent the subtleties of common practice writing, but has instead caused confused for two centuries of music students. Minor keys are not more complicated than major keys, and it is not useful to think of chords or keys as simply based on scales.

Beyond Triads

Major, minor, augmented, and diminished triads may be expanded to include more notes. These extra pitches, called extensions, are generated by stacking additional major and minor thirds beyond the fifth of the chord.

Since a triad consists of a root, third, and fifth, the first extension to be added is the seventh. Any of the four triads might have a natural seventh or a flattened seventh, and a diminished triad also frequently appears with a double flattened seventh ($\flat\flat$), which is enharmonically equivalent to a natural sixth. This gives us nine possible seventh chords, some of which are used far more frequently than others:

Major seventh	1	3	5	7	$X^{maj7}, X^{\Delta7}$
Minor seventh	1	$\flat 3$	5	$\flat 7$	X^{m7}, X^{-7}
Dominant seventh*	1	3	5	$\flat 7$	X^{7}
Minor seventh flat five**	1	$\flat 3$	$\flat 5$	$\flat 7$	$X^{m7\flat5}, X^{-7\flat5}, X^{\varnothing7}$
Diminished seventh	1	$\flat 3$	$\flat 5$	$\flat\flat 7$	$X^{\circ 7}, X^{dim7}$
Diminished major seventh	1	$\flat 3$	$\flat 5$	7	$X^{\circ\Delta 7}, X^{\circ maj7}, X^{dim\Delta 7}$
Minor-major seventh	1	$\flat 3$	$\flat 5$	$\flat 7$	$X^{m\Delta 7}, X^{-\Delta 7}$
Augmented seventh	1	3	$\sharp 5$	$\flat 7$	$X^{+7}, X^{7\sharp 5}$
Augmented major seventh	1	3	$\sharp 5$	7	$X^{+maj7}, X^{maj7\sharp 5}, X^{\Delta\sharp 5}$

*Or just 'Seventh'. The word 'dominant' may also be applied to chords with a specific function within a key. This definition is explored further on page 46.

**Or: 'Half-Diminished'

Here are the chords from the table, written with a root note of C:

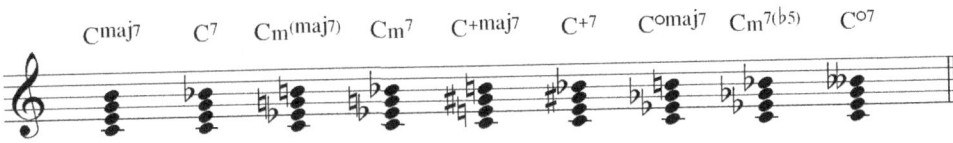

There are a few other four-note structures which frequently occur in tonal jazz. The natural sixth may be added to major or minor triads instead of a seventh to produce major sixth and minor sixth chords.

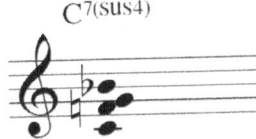

The third of a major triad may be replaced with a fourth to produce a suspended chord. In jazz, this chord invariably appears with a flattened seventh.

Suspended seventh	1	4	5	7	X^{7sus4}
Major sixth	1	3	5	6	X^6
Minor sixth	1	$\flat 3$	5	6	X^{m6}, X^{-6}

We may continue stacking thirds beyond the octave, which gives access to ninths, elevenths, and thirteenths. The thirteenth is the highest extension available; by ascending a third beyond this we arrive back at the root:

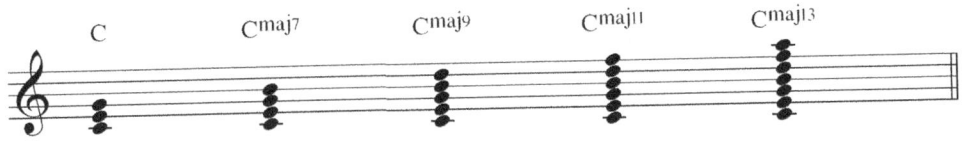

Seventh, ninth, eleventh, and thirteenth chords are all theoretically constructed entirely from consecutive thirds, and each extension included in a chord symbol assumes the presence of the seventh, and of those beneath it. All ninth chords include sevenths, all eleventh chords may include ninths, and all thirteenth chords may include elevenths, ninths, and thirteenths.

In the reality of jazz practice, pitches from these tertiary structures may be duplicated or displaced into different octaves, and pitches deemed inessential may be omitted from voicings. Some general guidelines for how this works are found on page 273. The omission of an extension below the topmost note does not affect the chord symbol. A thirteenth chord may omit the fifth, ninth, and eleventh and still qualify as a thirteenth chord. The following are all possible interpretations of the chord symbol F^{13}:

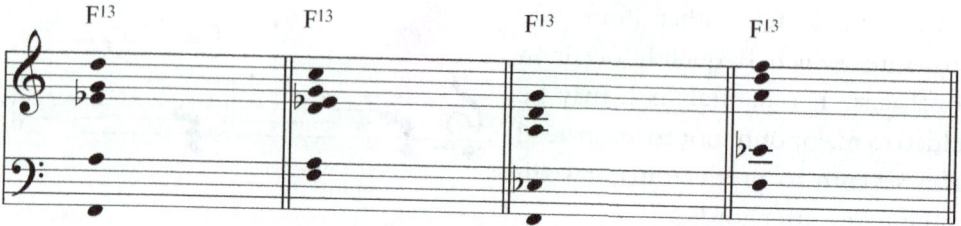

Ninths, elevenths, and thirteenths are named in terms of the major scale, and again may be raised or lowered relative to it. The following are the most common extensions that occur in relation to a root note of C:

Altered extensions may be specified by chord symbols. Convention dictates that unaltered chord extensions are placed before altered extensions. This prevents, for example, E^7 with a flattened thirteenth from being written as E^{b13}, which is actually a completely different chord. The formula for chord symbols is:

(root)(triad type)(highest unaltered extension)(altered extensions in numerical order)

The following ninth chords are all found in jazz:

Major ninth	1	3	5	7	9	$X^{maj9}, X^{\Delta 9}$
Minor ninth	1	$\flat 3$	5	$\flat 7$	9	X^{m9}, X^{-9}
Dominant ninth	1	3	5	$\flat 7$	9	X^{9}
Dominant sharp ninth	1	3	5	$\flat 7$	$\sharp 9$	$X^{7\sharp 9}$
Dominant flat ninth	1	3	5	$\flat 7$	$\flat 9$	$X^{7\flat 9}$
Minor ninth flat five	1	$\flat 3$	$\flat 5$	$\flat 7$	9	$X^{m9\flat 5}, X^{-9\flat 5}, X^{\o 9}$
Diminished ninth	1	$\flat 3$	$\flat 5$	$\flat\flat 7$	9	$X^{\circ 9}, X^{dim9}$
Minor-major ninth	1	$\flat 3$	5	7	9	$X^{m\Delta 9}, X^{-\Delta 9}$
Suspended ninth	1	4	5	7	9	X^{9sus4}
Sus flat ninth	1	4	5	7	$\flat 9$	$X^{7sus4\flat 9}$
Six-nine	1	3	5	6	9	$X^{6/9}$
Minor six-nine	1	$\flat 3$	5	6	9	$X^{m6/9}, X^{-6/9}$

In chords that contain a natural third, the natural eleventh is typically omitted due to its dissonance. These are the most common eleventh chords that are often encountered:

Major seventh sharp eleven	1	3	5	7	(9)	$\sharp 11$	$X^{maj7\sharp 11}, X^{\Delta 7\sharp 11}$
Minor eleventh	1	$\flat 3$	5	$\flat 7$	(9)	11	X^{m11}, X^{-11}
Dominant seventh sharp eleventh	1	3	5	$\flat 7$	(9)	$\sharp 11$	$X^{7\sharp 11}$
Minor eleventh flat five	1	$\flat 3$	$\flat 5$	$\flat 7$	(9)	11	$X^{m11\flat 5}, X^{-11\flat 5}, X^{\o 11}$
Minor-major eleventh	1	$\flat 3$	5	7	(9)	11	$X^{m\Delta 11}, X^{-\Delta 11}$

Fundamentals of Jazz Composition

The flattened thirteenth is dissonant against the fifth of the chord, and is not found in many of the commonly employed thirteenth chords. For the reasons laid out above, the eleventh is omitted from all chords that contain a major third:

Major thirteenth	1	3	5	7	(9)	-	13	X^{maj13}, $X^{\Delta 13}$
Minor thirteenth	1	$\flat 3$	5	$\flat 7$	(9)	(11)	13	X^{m13}, X^{-13}
Dominant thirteenth	1	3	5	$\flat 7$	(9)	-	13	X^{13}
Dominant seventh flat thirteenth	1	3	5	$\flat 7$	(9)	-	$\flat 13$	$X^{7\flat 13}$
Minor-major thirteenth	1	$\flat 3$	5	7	(9)	(11)	13	$X^{m\Delta 13}$, $X^{-\Delta 13}$

There are four altered extensions available for dominant chords: the flattened ninth, raised ninth, raised eleventh, and flattened thirteenth. Because none of these clash with each other, they may all be used interchangeably. A dominant seventh which uses only altered extensions may include any or all of them. Such a structure is referred to as an altered seventh or altered chord:

Altered seventh	1	3	-	$\flat 7$	$\flat 9$ and/or $\sharp 9$	$\sharp 11$ and/or $\flat 13$	$X^{7alt.}$

There are many chord symbols possible other than those shown above. Once the structure of seventh chords are known, the less common chord symbols become self-explanatory. $C^{maj7\sharp 5\flat 9}$, for example, is a highly unusual chord symbol, but contains all of the instructions needed to build it: raise the fifth of a C major seventh chord, and add a flattened ninth:

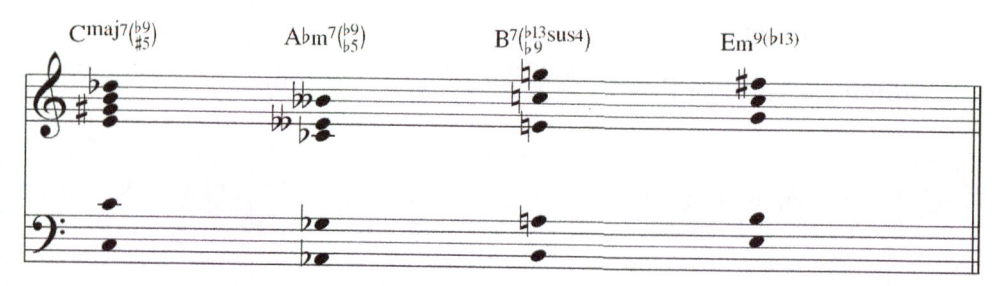

Because competent jazz musicians typically include extensions in their voicings according to taste and style, it is recommended that chord symbols be written in the simplest terms possible. This generally means writing chords as sevenths rather than ninths, elevenths, and thirteenths.

There are conventions that dictate which extensions might be included in the interpretation of a seventh chord. Pitches that are a whole step rather than a half step above the root, third, or fifth of a chord are the least dissonant and most popular, particularly when those pitches are found within the key signature. In accordance with this rule, below is a full list of the ninth, eleventh, and thirteenth chords available within the scale of C:

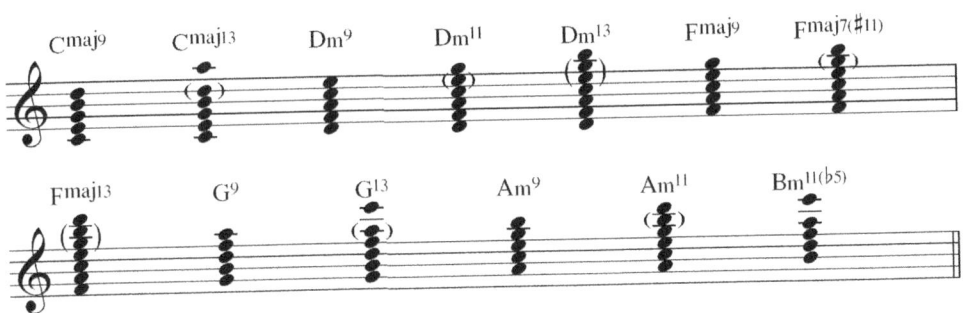

The eleventh of a major seventh or seventh chord, the flattened thirteenth of a minor seventh chord, and the flattened ninth over a minor or minor seven flat five chord are all possible within a key signature, but are generally avoided due to their dissonance. All of those extensions disagree strongly with the chord tone one half step (or a half step and an octave) below:

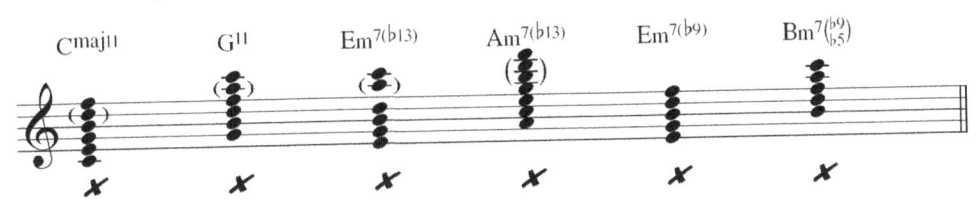

Other than simply omitting the offending tones from voicings, one possible solution is to raise them by a half step, thereby violating the key signature to produce more consonant harmonies. The following amended harmonies are more likely to occur in the key of C than those above, particularly in more progressive styles:

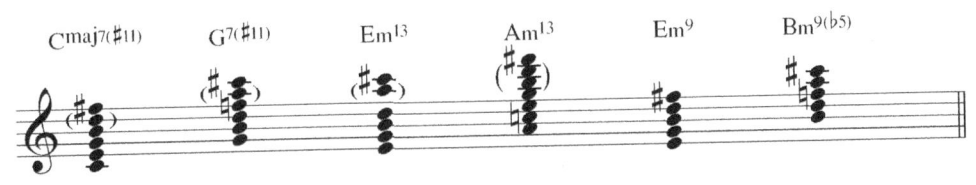

Any chord may appear with a pitch other than the root in the bass. When written as a chord symbol, such chords are best expressed as a slash chord: a chord symbol followed by a slash (/), followed by the bass note. The most common type of slash chord puts a pitch from the triad in the bass. Such structures are called inversions:

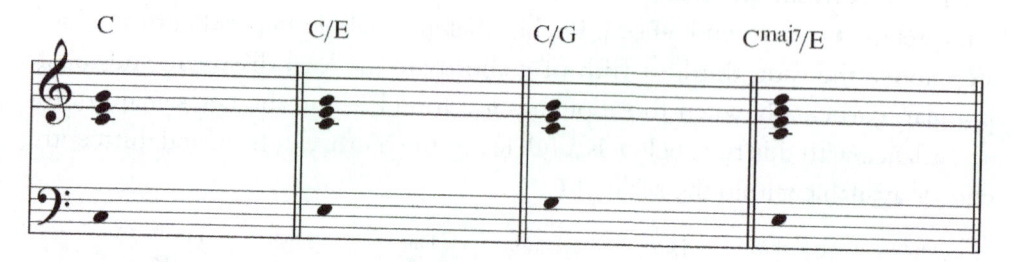

However, the altered bass note might be any pitch at all:

Many more applications of slash chords will be explored in what follows, but some general comments may be found on page 266.

Chord Progressions and Roman Numerals

Chords appear in sequences or chord progressions. Like individual pitches, chord progressions can be analysed with reference to the major scale. Roman rather than Arabic numerals are used for this type of analysis. Whenever chords are discussed like this, the root note of the chord symbol is replaced with a capitalised Roman numeral denoting the position of that root relative to the tonic. For example:

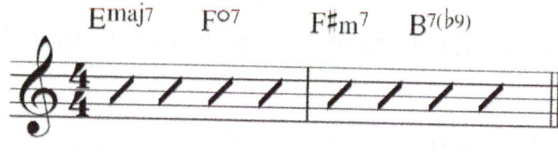

If this chord sequence occurs in the key of E, we would analyse its root notes relative to the E major scale, and find that E, F, F♯, and B are respectively 1, ♭2, 2 and 5.

The Roman numeral notation for this chord sequence is therefore: I^{maj7}, $^{b}II^{o7}$, II^{m7}, V^{7b9}. We are now able to understand these chords in terms of function, and may easily transpose them into different keys:

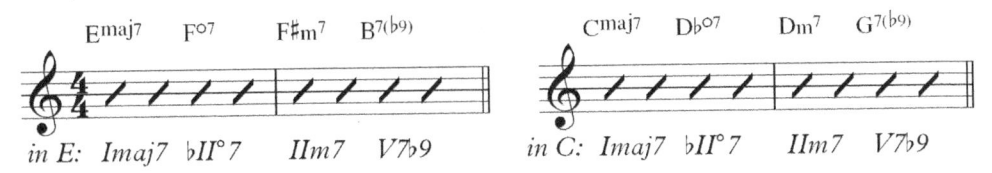

[Musical notation: in E: E^{maj7} F^{o7} $F\sharp^{m7}$ $B^{7(b9)}$ — Imaj7 bII°7 IIm7 V7b9; in C: C^{maj7} $D\flat^{o7}$ D^{m7} $G^{7(b9)}$ — Imaj7 bII°7 IIm7 V7b9]

Some systems of Roman numeral analysis use small case numerals to denote a chord with a flattened third. In what follows, capitalised numerals followed by full chord symbols will be used throughout.

Unfortunately, there is no generally accepted way to notate slash chords in Roman numeral analysis, but in this book, we shall denote the bass note with an Arabic numeral showing its relationship to the root of the chord.

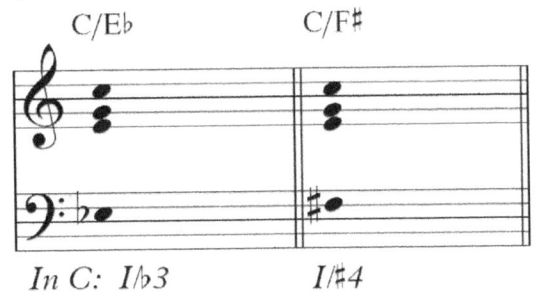

[Musical notation: C/E♭, C/F♯; In C: I/♭3, I/♯4]

Voice Leading

Common practice harmony descends from the vocal music of the European Middle Ages and Renaissance, in which two or more largely autonomous melodies would interact rhythmically, melodically, and harmonically. Elements of this polyphonic style were retained into the common practice period, so that when performed on a single instrument, each pitch of a chord must lead to a pitch in the following chord. This practice is called voice leading, and ensures melodic continuity between adjacent harmonies.

Both examples below consist of the same three chords, and have the same rhythmic values. In the first, the chords contain different numbers of notes and appear in different registers with different levels of density. In the second, each pitch leads smoothly into a pitch in the next chord. This second passage mimics the sound of four singers performing four simple melodies simultaneously.

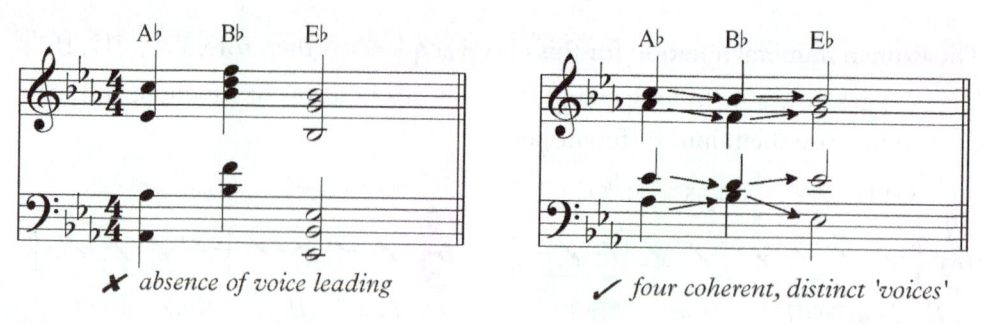

✗ *absence of voice leading*   ✓ *four coherent, distinct 'voices'*

Voice leading in jazz is rarely as literal or tangible as in the example above, and may be implicit, heavily obscured, or deliberately disregarded, but the principle that harmonies may be connected to each other in continuous textures nonetheless underlies our harmonic language.

Harmony and the Rhythm Section

In a sense, chords and chord changes are only theoretical events in jazz performance. Because the details of voicings, bass lines, and comping rhythms are mostly left to the rhythm section players themselves, there is a great deal of room for interpretation and alteration of a written part. Musicians may spontaneously add or remove pitches from the suggested harmonies, insert or omit interstitial harmonies, or completely replace the written chords with alternatives. Moreover, the rhythmic position of a chord change may be altered: a chord might be introduced earlier, or have its arrival delayed.

As a general rule in writing swing time jazz, chord changes typically occur up to twice per bar, and chords generally do not last for more than two bars without some kind of embellishment. Sometimes a new chord might be introduced on each beat of the bar in a 4/4 ballad, but this level of activity is best kept brief. By the same logic, very fast pieces tend to have fewer chord changes to avoid a sense of overcrowding. New chords are generally introduced in a metrically strong position such as the first beat of a new bar:

(a) new harmonies introduced in metrically weak positions

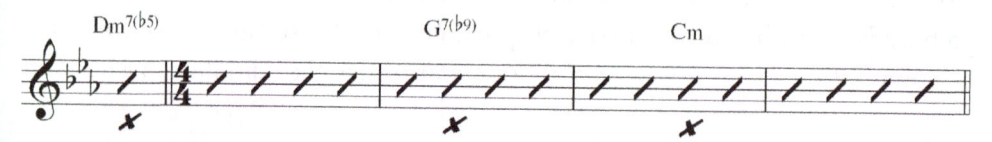

$Dm^{7(b5)}$ $G^{7(b9)}$ Cm

(b) new harmonies introduced in metrically strong positions

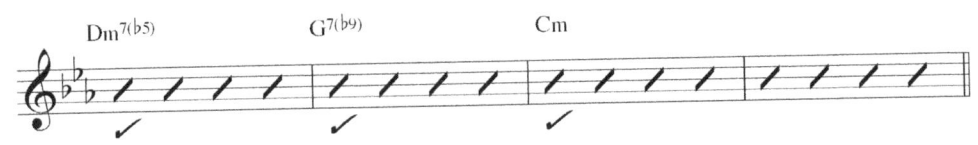

[musical notation: Dm⁷⁽♭⁵⁾ | G⁷⁽♭⁹⁾ | Cm |]

Where there are two chords within the same bar of 4/4, the second will begin on beat three, thus agreeing with the implicit half-measure emphasis:

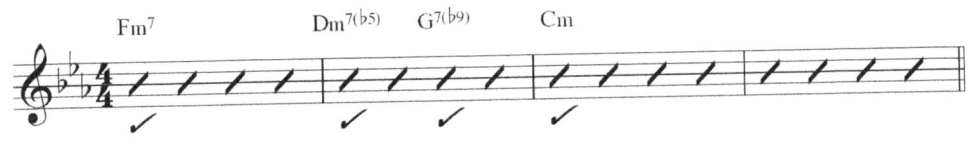

[musical notation: Fm⁷ | Dm⁷⁽♭⁵⁾ G⁷⁽♭⁹⁾ | Cm |]

The duration of a chord rarely carries it into to a stronger hypermetric position than its starting point. Below, $G^{7♭9}$ begins on beat two of the first bar of a phrase, and is sustained into the metrically stronger beat one of bar two, contradicting the implicit hypermeter:

[musical notation: Dm⁷⁽♭⁵⁾ G⁷⁽♭⁹⁾ | Cm |]

Introducing this chord on the first beat of the second bar of the phrase, and sustaining it for two bars is also unconventional. Again, the harmonic rhythm is at odds with the hypermeter:

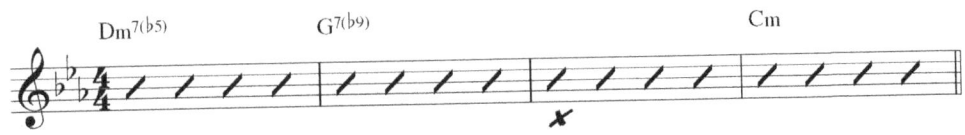

[musical notation: Dm⁷⁽♭⁵⁾ | G⁷⁽♭⁹⁾ | | Cm |]

Both are unusual effects, and should be used sparingly. They draw attention to themselves and disrupt the sense of flow.

Chapter Summary

The equal tempered system divides each octave equally into twelve pitches.

In tonal music, pitched material is used in a manner that implies a destination pitch: the tonic.

Pitches in tonal music may be described with ordinal numbers that describe their relationship to a major scale, with its root on the tonic.

When pitches are sounded simultaneously, we hear their combined frequencies as a chord. The dissonance or consonance of a chord is determined by the mathematical relationships between the pitches present. The most consonant structures available are major and minor triads.

The key of a piece or passage may be explicit, ambiguous, or even subjective.

The pitch content of a scale describes the pitch content of a piece of tonal music only imperfectly.

Pitches may be added to triads to create numerous different types of seventh, ninth, eleventh, and thirteenth chords. These extensions are highly prevalent in jazz performance, particularly when they are a whole step rather than a half step above a pitch in the underlying triad.

Chords in tonal music may be denoted with Roman numerals that describe their relationship to the tonic.

Chord changes should be introduced in strong metric positions such as the first beat of a bar, and should not be sustained into a stronger metric position than their starting point.

Chapter 3
Establishing Tonality

In this chapter we shall begin to explore some of the most important chords and chord progressions found in jazz music. Of primary importance is the tonic, or I chord, the implicit destination of any tonal passage, but another essential element in tonal music is chord V, which defines the tonic by suggesting resolution into it. In jazz styles, V is often preceded by chord II, which resolves to V as V does to I, forming a chain of resolutions that signpost the position of the tonic chord. These relationships are fundamental to tonal music.

Chord I

Early jazz accompanists sometimes played the tonic chord of a major key as a triad, but the major sixth chord soon became a more common tonic harmony in most styles. By the 1950s, the major seventh chord was also regularly used in the tonic position. I^6 and I^{maj7} chord symbols are interchangeable in most contexts.

A contemporary pianist, guitarist, or arranger might choose to include a natural ninth and/or a natural thirteenth in a tonic major seventh chord. However, the natural eleventh is typically avoided because it is a compound half step above the third. The fifth is also likely to be omitted from a major seventh voicing, though it must be included in a major sixth chord as its omission would produce an inversion of the VI minor triad, undermining any sense of tonic function.

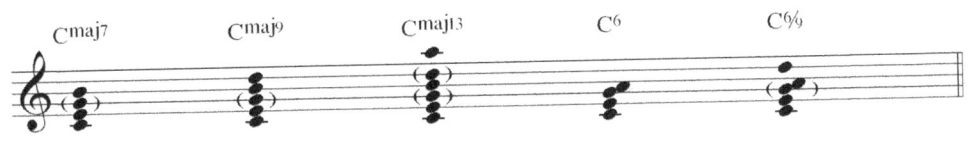

Since, in practice, the I^6, I^{maj7}, I^{maj9}, and I^{maj13} chord symbols are essentially interchangeable, the I^{maj7} chord symbol will generally suffice. The delta symbol is sometimes used for this chord in place of the letters ^{maj}: $C^{\Delta7}$ instead of C^{maj7}. Both are clear and in common usage, but it is important to be consistent within a single work. C^{Δ} and C^{maj} are ambiguous and should be avoided, as it is not clear whether or not a seventh should be included.

Chord V

Because it resolves very strongly to I, the V chord has an essential role in establishing the key of a passage. Below is an idealised diagram of how a V-I chord progression might be considered to function: the movement from V to V^7 introduces a highly dissonant raised fourth interval between the seventh and third of the V chord, which then resolves very strongly into the consonant third and root of the I chord.

This movement is at the heart of the European tradition from which jazz draws its harmony, and is responsible in one way or another for much of the sense of movement within tonal chord progressions.

Because of its essential role within a key, music theory traditionally names a chord with its root on the fifth of the key the dominant chord. However, jazz musicians use the term dominant far more liberally, applying it to any chord with a flattened seventh and a natural third, regardless of its position within or without a key.

For example, $F^{7\sharp 11}$, $A^{7\flat 9}$, and D^9 might all occur in a passage of music in the key of C, and could all be referred to as dominant chords. This definition will be used throughout the rest of this book. The resolution of V^7 to I is so persuasive that some of these non-V dominant chords might be perceived as momentary suggestions of alternative keys. The presence of a D^9 chord within a passage of music in C, for example, hints at the key of G without fully destabilising the overarching sense of C major tonality.

In jazz styles, the V chord is rarely heard without its flattened seventh, and is usually notated as V^7. Again, the natural ninth and/or a natural thirteenth are available as extensions, though the natural eleventh is typically omitted because it is a compound half step above the third. V^9 and V^{13} chord symbols are therefore somewhat redundant, and the V^7 chord symbol is recommended in most situations. We will discuss some specific situations where unaltered extensions might be included in chord symbols on page 123.

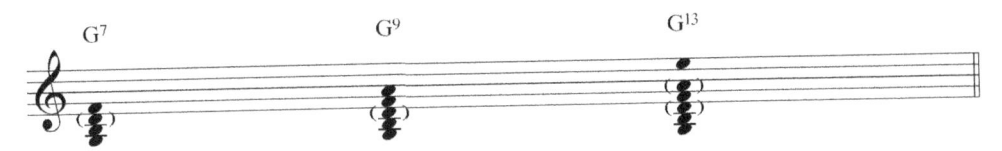

[G⁷   G⁹   G¹³ chord voicings shown on staff]

Chord I may move directly to chord V, and V resolves back to I. Working, for now, in full bars of 4/4 time, this gives us the following available phrases:

(a) chord I metrically accented

[Cmaj7 | G7 | Cmaj7]
  I   V   I

(b) chord V metrically accented

[G7 | Cmaj7]
 V   I

(c) chord I metrically accented

[Cmaj7 | | G7 | | Cmaj7]
  I   V   I

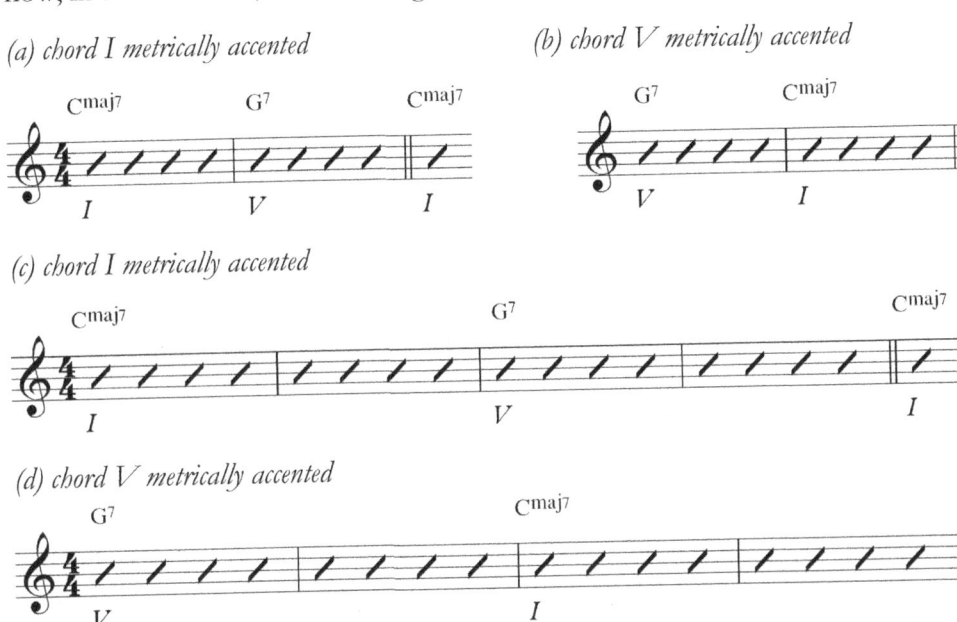

(d) chord V metrically accented

[G7 | | Cmaj7 | |]
 V   I

Chord II

In major key jazz, chord II typically appears as a minor seventh, and functions like a V of V, leading to the V^7 chord that leads to I. The bass movement of an ascending fourth (or descending fifth) from II to V mimics the bass movement from V to I, as does the voice leading of a flattened seventh, moving downwards to the natural third of the following chord.

[Dm⁷ G⁷ C shown on staff]
IIm7 V7   I

Note that II is not actually the V of V. The true V chord of G would be one from the key of G itself: a D major triad, or a D^7 chord. D^{m7} is only *similar* to this chord. Progression from D^{m7} to G^7 uses the same root movement as D^7 to G, and retains most of the same voice leading, but since it does not contain any pitches from outside the prevailing C major key signature, D^{m7} is less disruptive to the key than

D^7 would be. II^7 – the true V of V – is sometimes used as a kind of intensified II^{m7}, the usage of which is further discussed on page 55.

Typically written as II^{m7}, the II chord may be interpreted to include the natural ninth, the natural eleventh, and/or the natural thirteenth. Again, there is usually no reason to write II^{m9}, II^{m11}, or II^{m13} for a jazz rhythm section.

Minor seventh chords are sometimes written as D^{-7} or D^{min7} rather than D^{m7}. All three symbols are clear and in common usage, but it is again best to be consistent.

The II-V-I Progression

The II^{m7} chord was not such a ubiquitous part of the vocabulary of early jazz musicians, but by the end of the 1930s almost any V^7 was liable to be preceded by II^{m7}. In practice, II^{m7}-V^7 is compatible and interchangeable with V^7, and even from chorus to chorus within a tune, musicians may change V to II-V, or II-V to V. These two harmonies are so similar in sound that it is even possible for musicians within an ensemble to simultaneously imply different chords without contradiction.

Here is an invented excerpt demonstrating how two musicians might simultaneously interpret the same chord chart in quite different ways:

• Chapter 3: Establishing Tonality

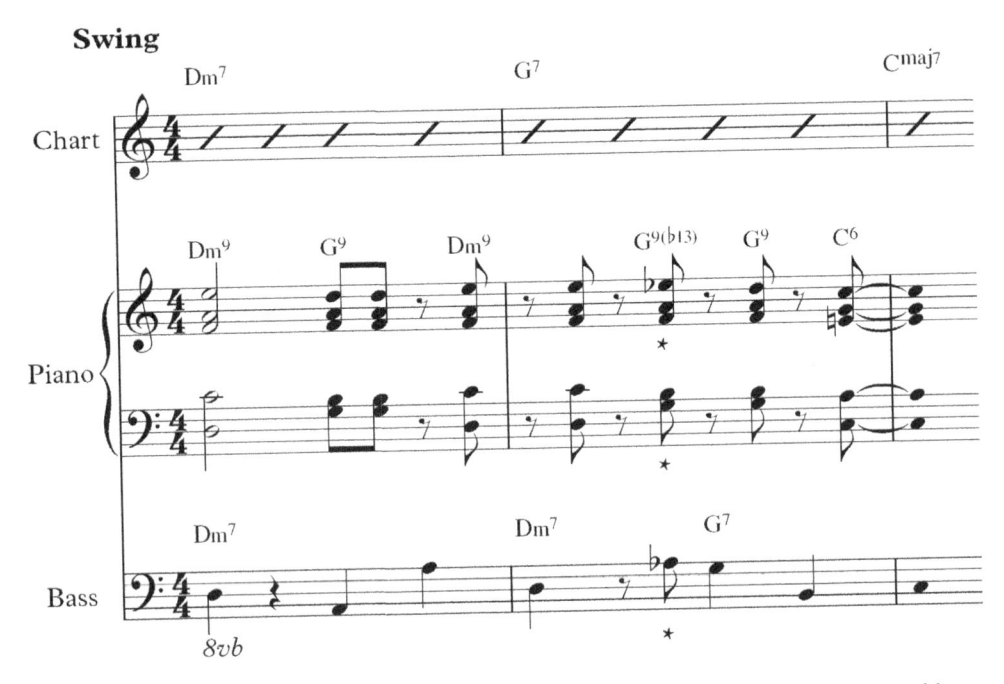

Swing

[Musical score with Chart, Piano, and Bass parts. Chord symbols: Dm7, G7, Cmaj7 (Chart); Dm9, G9, Dm9, G9(♭13), G9, C6 (Piano); Dm7, Dm7, G7 (Bass, 8vb)]

There are moments of great disparity and dissonance between the piano and bass, especially at the asterisk, but because both instruments begin the passage on II and move through V to I, the dissonance is acceptable within the context, and the harmony is functional. The logic of the underlying II-V-I triumphs over the temporary dissonance.

In the context of the II-V-I progression, II is almost always metrically emphasised relative to V^7. Perhaps the simplest way to think of this is that II generally replaces the first half of a region of V:

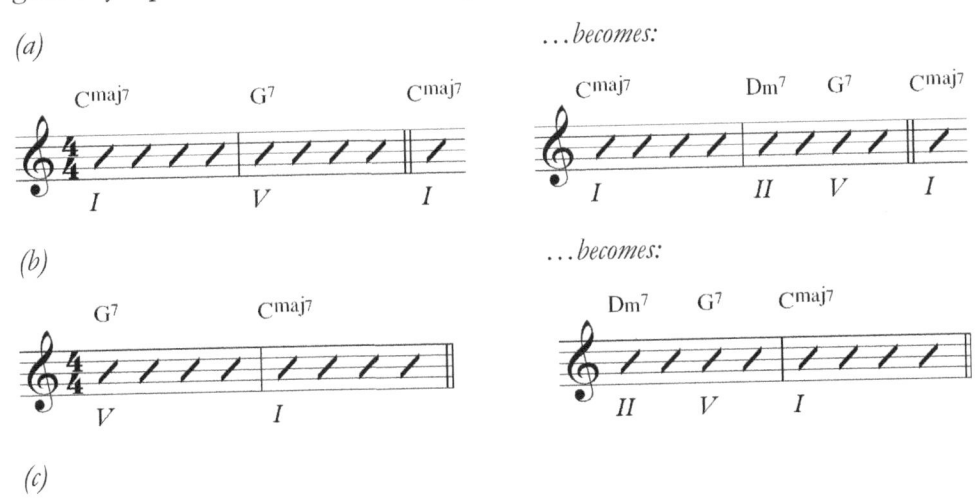

(a)

[Musical example: Cmaj7 | G7 | Cmaj7 with roman numerals I V I]

...becomes:

[Musical example: Cmaj7 | Dm7 G7 | Cmaj7 with roman numerals I II V I]

(b)

[Musical example: G7 | Cmaj7 with roman numerals V I]

...becomes:

[Musical example: Dm7 G7 | Cmaj7 with roman numerals II V I]

(c)

49

Fundamentals of Jazz Composition •

Cmaj7	G7		Cmaj7
I	V		I

...becomes:

Cmaj7	Dm7	G7	Cmaj7
I	II	V	I

(d)

G7	Cmaj7		
V	I		

...becomes:

Dm7	G7	Cmaj7	
II	V	I	

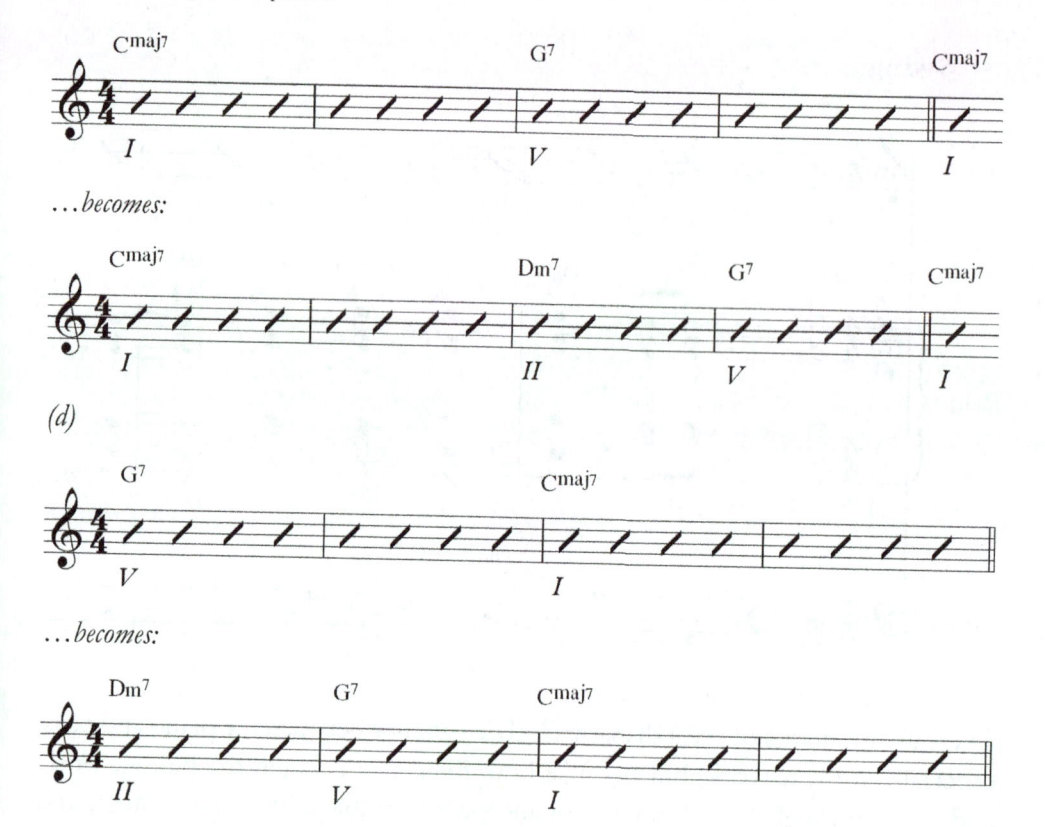

Because of the central importance of the II-V-I sequence to jazz harmony, it is recommended that all performers and composers learn to recall, recognise, and play these three chords in all keys as high priority.

II^{m7}	V^7	I^{maj7}
D^{m7}	G^7	C^{maj7}
A^{m7}	D^7	G^{maj7}
E^{m7}	A^7	D^{maj7}
B^{m7}	E^7	A^{maj7}
$F\sharp^{m7}$	B^7	E^{maj7}
$C\sharp^{m7}$	$F\sharp^7$	B^{maj7}
$G\sharp^{m7}$	$C\sharp^7$	$F\sharp^{maj7}$
$A\flat^{m7}$	$D\flat^7$	$G\flat^{maj7}$
$E\flat^{m7}$	$A\flat^7$	$D\flat^{maj7}$
$B\flat^{m7}$	$E\flat^7$	$A\flat^{maj7}$
F^{m7}	$B\flat^7$	$E\flat^{maj7}$
C^{m7}	F^7	$B\flat^{maj7}$
G^{m7}	C^7	F^{maj7}

Minor Keys

I, V, and II function identically in minor keys, although the structures of the three chords change slightly. As in the major key, early jazz accompanists usually played the tonic chord of a minor key as a triad, but the natural sixth and natural ninth might also be included in voicings, the former of which is not native to the key signature.

Minor seventh chords are sometimes used in more progressive styles, particularly when the duration of the chord is more than a bar or two, and where chord V is absent. Although not particularly dissonant, the natural eleventh is rarely included in tonic minor chords, as it undermines the stability of the tonic triad.

The minor chord with a major seventh is very popular as a sustained final chord of a minor piece, but less so in normal accompaniment.

As with tonic major chords, the fifth might be omitted from a voicing if the seventh is present, but a minor sixth chord with no fifth is unbalanced. A tonic minor sixth chord with no fifth is, in fact, a VI diminished triad.

The chord symbols I⁻, I^min, and I^m are interchangeable, and are both appropriate for a tonic minor chord, as are I⁻⁶, I^min6, and I^m6. Here are some possible realisations of a tonic minor chord:

The V chord in a minor key usually appears as a dominant with a flattened ninth. This pitch a compound half step above the root is the most common exception to the previously mentioned rule of thumb that extensions one half step above a chord tone are to be avoided. An interesting feature of the dominant seven flat nine structure is that it contains the entirety of a diminished seventh chord.

The flattened thirteenth is also available as an extension of V chords in minor keys, where it invariably replaces the fifth of the chord. The raised ninth, present in the key signature, is available as an alternative to the flattened ninth.

V⁷♭⁹ is the recommended chord symbol for the V chord in a minor key.

The voice leading from V⁷ to I^m functions in exactly the same way as its major key equivalent. The dissonance between the flattened seventh and natural third of V⁷ is resolved by movement downward to the third and upward to the root. The addition of a flattened ninth over the V⁷ acts as a further dissonance requiring resolution, in this case downward to the fifth of the tonic triad:

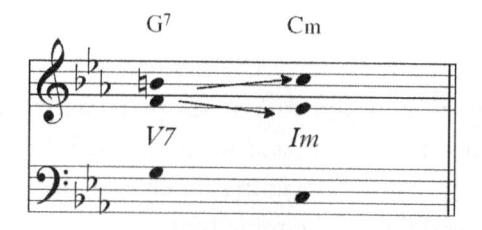

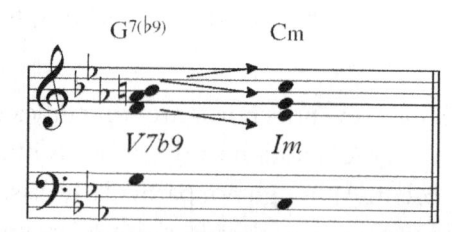

The II chord in a minor key again has more or less identical functionality to its major key parallel, delaying the arrival of V, and resolving into it in a manner analogous to V-I movement. In minor keys, II generally appears as a minor seventh chord with a flattened fifth, a structure also called half-diminished due to its similarity to the diminished seventh chord.

When this chord came into common usage in jazz, musicians conceptualised and notated it as IV^m over its sixth: $D^{m7b5} = F^m/D$. This idea remains valuable as a mental shorthand for the chord, as voicings of D^{m7b5} and F^m are interchangeable.

The voice leading from II to V to I in a minor key is essentially the same as its major key equivalent, though the flattened sixth native to the key (A-flat relative to C) is usually included in both the II and V chords. As in major, the II functions as a V of V, setting up the dominant chord which in turn leads to the tonic.

The minor seventh flat five chord may include a natural eleventh, but, of the other extensions present in the key signature, neither the flattened ninth nor flattened thirteenth are commonly used; the former is dissonant with the root, and the latter unbalances the structure, as it sounds more like $^bVII^7/3$ than as a II chord.

Since the 1960s, musicians have sometimes included the natural ninth in minor seven flat five chords, which violates the key signature, but is far more consonant than the flattened ninth. Possible chord symbols for a II chord in minor are II^{m7b5}, II^{-7b5}, or the half-diminished symbol $II^{ø7}$. All are clear and in common usage but, as always, consistency within a work is essential for clarity.

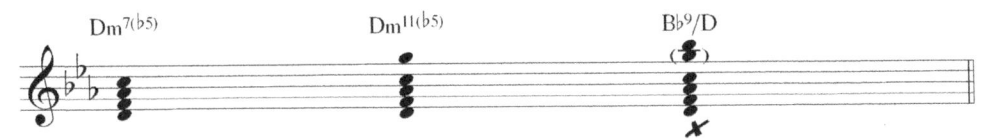

II-V-I in Minor

As in major tonalities, II is compatible and interchangeable with V. V can usually be changed to II-V, or II-V changed to V with minimal disruption. The II-V-I progression also follows the same hypermetric conventions as in major, such that II is almost invariably rhythmically emphasised in comparison with the V that follows. All of the typical major key chord progressions that appeared on page 49 may be transposed directly to the minor key:

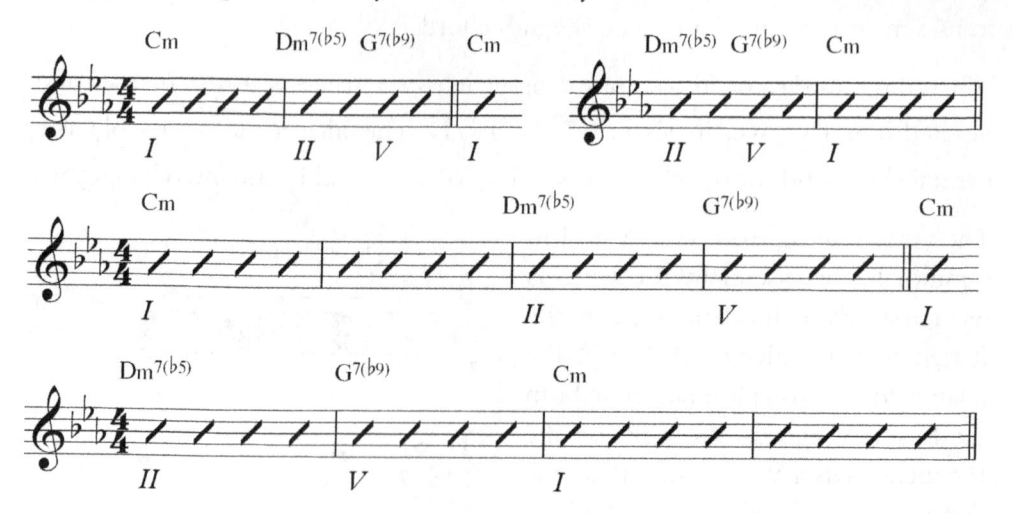

Once again, learning to write, play and recognise them in every key is essential for any jazz musician.

II^{m7b5}	V^{7b9}	I^m
D^{m7b5}	G^{7b9}	C^m
A^{m7b5}	D^{7b9}	G^m
E^{m7b5}	A^{7b9}	D^m
B^{m7b5}	E^{7b9}	A^m
F♯^{m7b5}	B^{7b9}	E^m
C♯^{m7b5}	F♯^{7b9}	B^m
G♯^{m7b5}	C♯^{7b9}	F♯^{m}
A^{bm7b5}	D^{b7b9}	G^{bm}
E^{bm7b5}	A^{b7b9}	D^{bm}
B^{bm7b5}	E^{b7b9}	A^{bm}
F^{m7b5}	B^{b7b9}	E^{bm}
C^{m7b5}	F^{7b9}	B^{bm}
G^{m7b5}	C^{7b9}	F^m

II^7: The Secondary Dominant

We have previously stated that, within the jazz idiom, any chord with a flattened seventh and natural third may be referred to as a dominant seventh chord, regardless of its position within or without a key (page 46). Sometimes, dominant seventh chords that do not occur as chord V of the key suggest the key in which they would be chord V. A chord operating in this way is said to function as a secondary dominant.

An important instance of a secondary dominant occurs when chord II in a II-V-I progression appears as a dominant chord rather than as a minor seventh. Here, the increased dissonance of II^7 and its foreignness to the prevailing key make this chord a kind of intensified version of the native II, as it demands movement to V more urgently. This is an example of a secondary dominant, because II^7 can be understood as chord V from the key of V, borrowed and transplanted into our home key. In the key of C for instance, the dominant seventh chord D^7 might replace D^m as a secondary dominant, momentarily suggesting the key of G, in which it would be chord V.

In major keys, the raised eleventh is a highly typical extension on II^7, dating back to its prominent use in the melody of Billy Strayhorn's iconic *Take the 'A' Train*:

The II^7 chord enables a few important variations on the II-V progression:

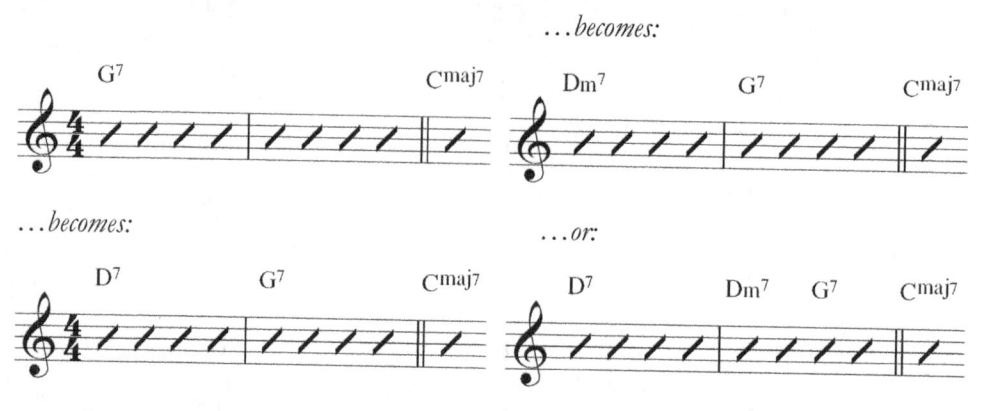

Or, II^7 may be further elaborated with a II chord of its own: the V of V becomes the II-V of V. This momentary sidestep to another key is arguably too brief to be considered a true key change. We might think of it as a borrowed chord that references a nearby key:

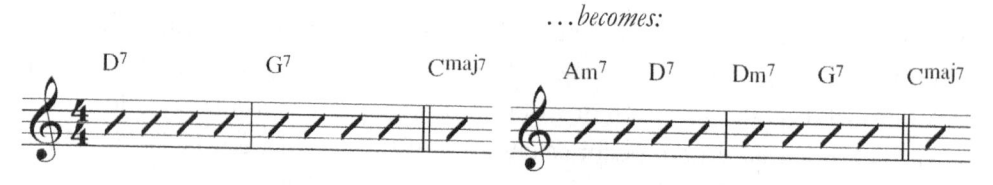

II^7 is perhaps less common in minor keys, but still occurs with some frequency. Available extensions within the key signature are the flattened ninth, raised ninth, raised eleventh, and the flattened thirteenth:

Because every extension is altered in this chord, this structure is called an altered chord, and may be more simply denoted with the X^{7alt} chord symbol. Altered seventh chords are described in more detail on page 201. As in the major key, this chord might replace the native II:

...becomes:

| Dm7(♭5) G7(♭9) Cm | D7alt. G7(♭9) Cm |

Chapter Summary

Tonic major chords are typically written as X^{maj7}.

V chords in major keys are typically written as X^7.

II chords in major keys are typically written as II^{m7}.

Tonic minor chords are typically written as X^m or X^{m6}.

V chords in minor keys are typically written as X^{7b9}.

II chords in minor keys are typically written as II^{m7b5}.

II leads to V and V leads to I in both major and minor keys.

II is almost always metrically emphasised relative to V^7.

II^7 may replace II^{m7} in major keys and $II^{7alt.}$ may replace II^{m7b5} in minor keys.

Whichever style is chosen, chord symbol usage should be employed consistently.

Chapter 4
IV and Back Again

The IV chord has an important function in the harmonic language of the American Songbook, and thereby the jazz tradition. It is a secondary destination within a key, and a temporary resting place on the journey to the tonic because it has neither the pull to the tonic of V, nor the pull to V of II. A great many chord sequences in all styles of jazz, and popular music generally, feature direct or indirect movement from I to IV and back again.

From I to IV

In a major key, chord IV is a major seventh chord with the natural ninth, raised eleventh, and natural thirteenth available as extensions. This is the only chord which has a raised eleventh native to the key signature, making this particular pitch a fingerprint of the IV chord in major keys. Essentially, adding a raised eleventh to any major seventh chord will make it sound more like a IV chord.

X^{maj7} is sufficient as a chord symbol because musicians can recognise when a major seventh chord is functioning as a IV, and include the raised eleventh if they wish.

IV is such a common destination that several conventional routes to it from I. Firstly, we may simply borrow the II-V from the key of IV. The IV chord may be in a metrically accented or unaccented position relative to its II-V:

(a) chord IV metrically accented:

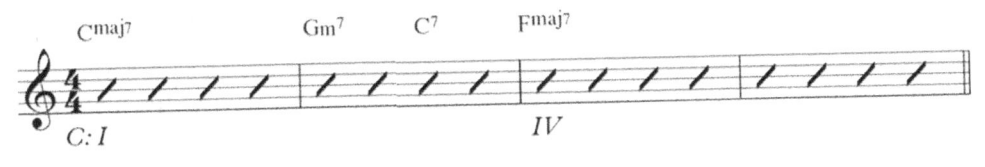

(b) chord IV metrically unaccented:

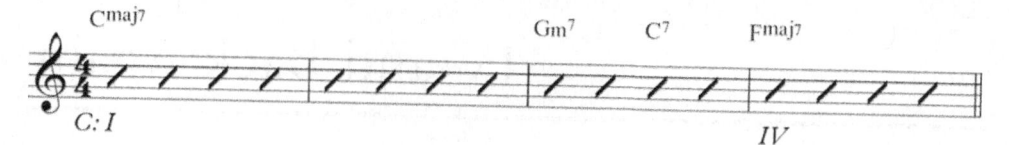

[Cmaj7 | / / / / | / / / / | Gm7 C7 / / / / | Fmaj7 / / / /]
C: I   IV

The progression from I through I⁷ to IV implies a chromatic line that descends from the root of the tonic to the third of the IV. This internal voice leading brings coherence to the progression, and is frequently referenced in melodies and accompaniments over these chords.

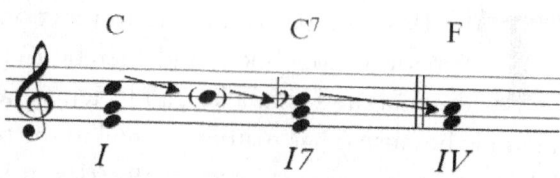

[musical example: C (I) → C7 (I7) → F (IV)]

It is worth restating the convention that a chord is rarely carried over into a stronger rhythmic position than its starting point. Because the F^{maj7} chord in the following passage carries over from bar four to five, the harmony contradicts the expected hypermeter and suggests a three-bar phrase followed by a five-bar phrase, rather than two four-bar phrases.

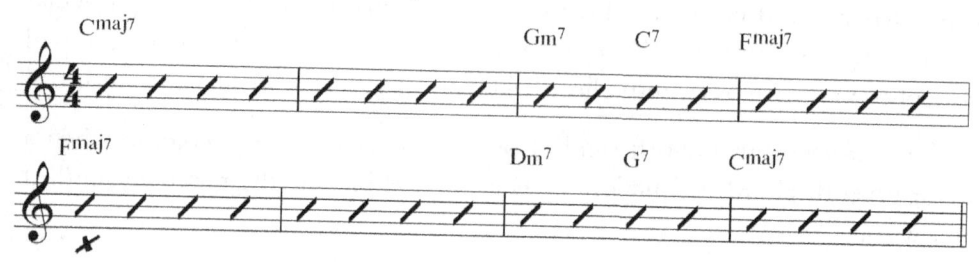

[Cmaj7 | / / / / | / / / / | Gm7 C7 / / / / | Fmaj7 / / / /]
[Fmaj7 / / / / | / / / / | Dm7 G7 / / / / | Cmaj7 / / / /]

Another typical way to get from I to IV is via III⁷. This movement is effective because III⁷ is the V of VI, and the essential voice leading of this resolution remains intact if III⁷ instead moves to IV:

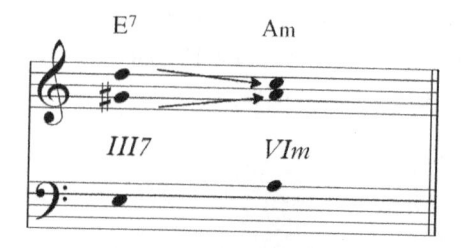

[E7 → Am : III7 → VIm]   [E7 → F : III7 → IV]

Typical extensions of III⁷ are found within the key signature, namely the flattened ninth and the flattened thirteenth. Since III⁷ behaves like a V of VI, a II-V to VI has the same functionality:

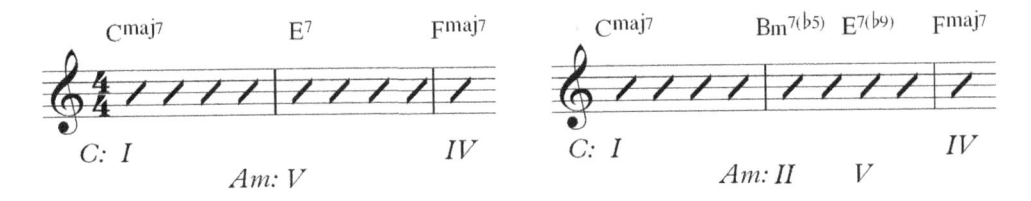

[Musical notation: Cmaj7 | E7 Fmaj7 || Cmaj7 | Bm7(b5) E7(b9) Fmaj7
C: I — IV ; Am: V
C: I — IV ; Am: II V]

From IV to I in Major

Just as there are conventions for moving from I to IV within a key, there are established routes back to I. The most obvious way to get home is to insert a II-V back to the tonic. Skipping the II is an option, but the resulting movement from IV directly to V is perhaps more typical of common practice music or rock harmony than classic jazz.

[Musical notation: Fmaj7 | Dm7 G7 | Cmaj7
IV — II V — I]

A less obvious but perhaps more common route from IV to I in songbook-style harmony is the backdoor cadence: IV^{maj7} is transformed into IV^{min7}, which is followed by $\flat VII^7$ and then I. This creates a II-V in the key of $\flat III$ major.

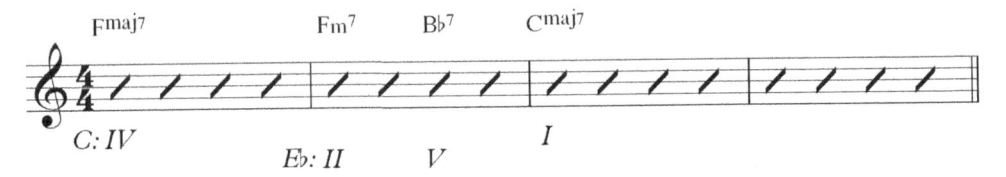

[Musical notation: Fmaj7 | Fm7 Bb7 | Cmaj7
C: IV ; Eb: II V ; I]

Explaining why any musical technique works is always a dubious task. Ultimately, the reason that the backdoor cadence leads convincingly to I is because it is an established convention and we expect it to. We could see this cadence as being borrowed from the relative major of the parallel minor (E-flat major is the relative major of C minor, and C minor is the parallel minor of C major). If this seems far-fetched, observe the similarity between V-I in C minor and $\flat VII^7$ to I in C major. The upper structure remains unaffected by a change in bass note:

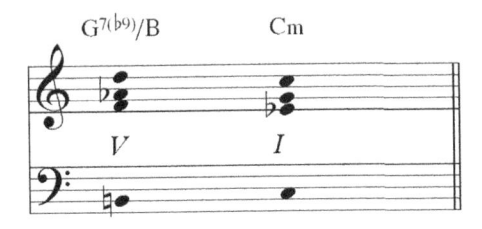

[Musical notation: G7(b9)/B Cm || Bb7   C
V   I   bVII   I]

The backdoor cadence could simultaneously be understood as a relative of the minor II-V (page 53), with which it shares the same upper structure:

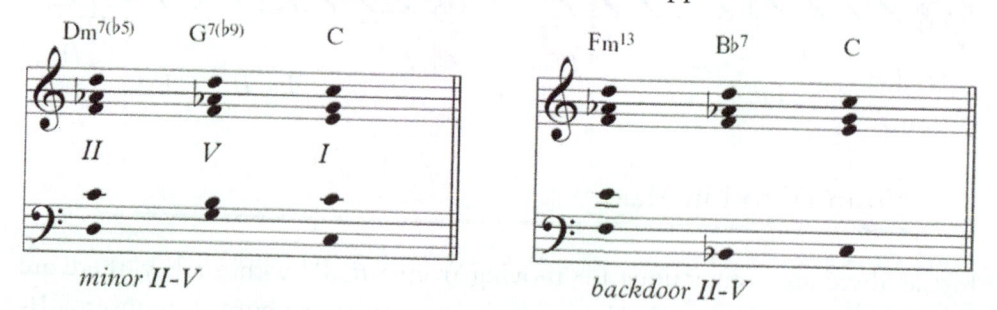

minor II-V — Dm7(b5) G7(b9) C — II V I

backdoor II-V — Fm13 Bb7 C

Furthermore, the backdoor cadence continues the implicit descending chromatic voice that was initiated as I moved to IV. Again, melodies and accompaniments over this chord progression often refer to this line, or to part of it:

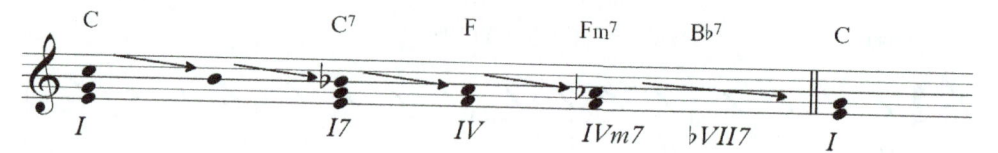

C — C7 — F — Fm7 — Bb7 — C
I — I7 — IV — IVm7 — bVII7 — I

IV^{m7} may be omitted from the backdoor cadence, in which case $^{b}VII^{7}$ is particularly likely to include its raised eleventh, a pitch now common to the entire progression:

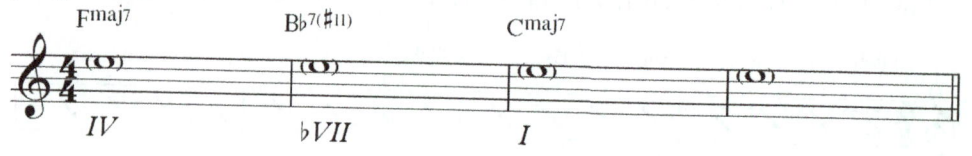

Fmaj7 — Bb7(#11) — Cmaj7
IV — bVII — I

IV^{m} can also lead directly to I. When not followed by $^{b}VII^{7}$, IV^{m} is often voiced as a minor sixth chord, which gives it an identical upper structure to $^{b}VII^{7}$:

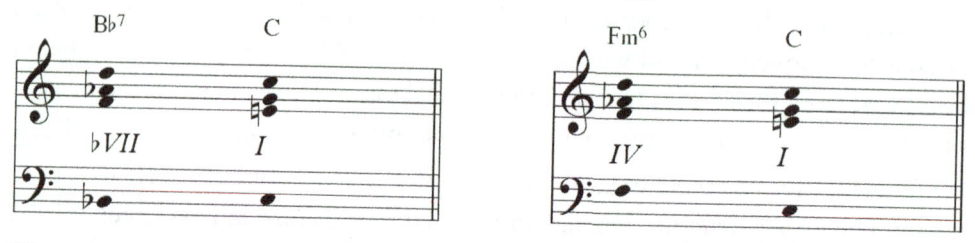

Bb7 C — bVII I

Fm6 C — IV I

There is one final conventional route from IV to I: we may pass from IV through $\sharp IV^{\circ 7}$ to I over its fifth. This produces a chromatically ascending bass line that builds inevitably towards the V chord:

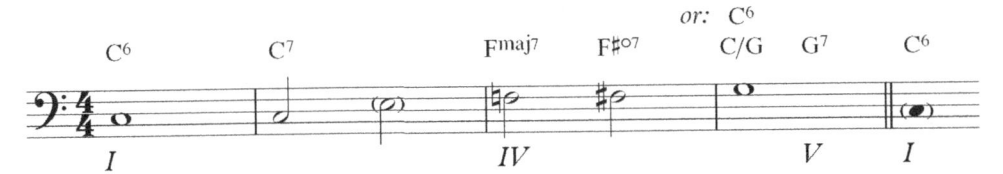

It might be more useful to think of the I/5 chord in this sequence as a kind of V chord whose fourth and sixth resolve downwards into its third and fifth.

In this analysis, $\sharp IV^{\circ 7}$ could be seen as a V of V, ($F\sharp^{\circ 7} = D^{7\flat 9}$ with no root), which resolves to G, and finally to C. Unlike the backdoor progression which may be initiated in a metrically accented position, $\sharp IV^{\circ 7}$ is invariably in a weaker metric position than the IV that it follows.

From I to IV and Back Again in Minor

The IV chord is equally important in minor keys, where it has the same function as a secondary destination within the key. In minor keys, IV is usually a minor seventh chord, with extensions from the key signature, namely the natural ninth, natural eleventh, and natural thirteenth. X^{m7} is the most appropriate chord symbol for any of these variations:

$V^{m7\flat 5}$ followed by $I^{7\flat 9}$ gives us a minor II-V from the key of IV, the only standard route from I to IV in a minor key:

(a) chord IV metrically accented:

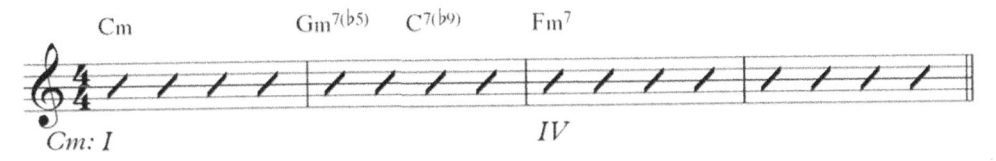

(b) chord IV metrically unaccented:

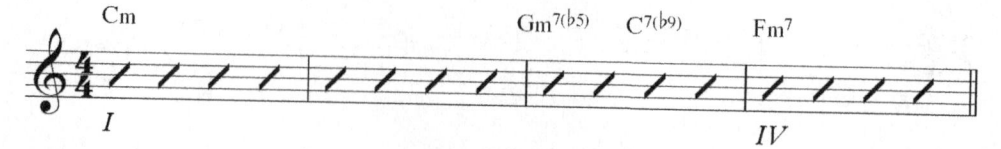

[Musical notation: Cm | (rest) | Gm⁷⁽♭⁵⁾ C⁷⁽♭⁹⁾ | Fm⁷ — labeled I ... IV]

There is also only one commonly utilised route back from IV to I in minor keys: through a minor II-V. The implicit descending bass from IV^{m7} through $IV^{m7}/{^\flat}7$ to $II^{m7\flat5}$ is often written into chord charts, but is potentially redundant as musicians are likely to play this progression regardless:

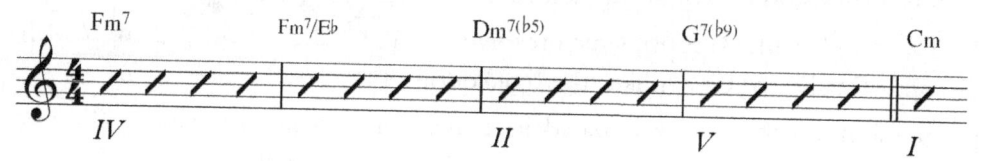

[Musical notation: Fm⁷ | Fm⁷/E♭ | Dm⁷⁽♭⁵⁾ | G⁷⁽♭⁹⁾ | Cm — labeled IV ... II V I]

Chapter Summary

Chord IV is important as a destination chord in both major and minor keys.

In major keys, IV is a major seventh chord, and may be approached from the V or II-V of IV, or from the V or II-V of VI.

In major keys, we may get from chord IV to I via II-V, the backdoor cadence, or through $^\sharp IV^{\circ 7}$

In minor keys, IV is a minor seventh chord, and may be approached from the V or II-V of IV.

In minor keys, we may get from chord IV to I via II-V.

Chapter 5
Turnarounds and Cycles

So far, we have discussed major and minor tonic chords, the V chords that lead to them, the II chords which lead to those, and IV chords in their capacity as temporary destinations within a key. These are the primary harmonic milestones within a key. They function as home (I), take us home (V or II-V), or take us momentarily away from home whilst remaining within the same key (IV). In a great deal of tonal jazz, one of these four chords will be present at the beginning of each phrase or period.

To a large extent, many of the remaining chord progressions that are found within the pre-1960 harmonic vocabulary can be understood either as modulations – changes of key – or as elaborations and variations on these fundamentals. In this chapter we shall cover some of the conventional ways that we might elaborate our chord progressions through the use of turnarounds.

Chord VI and the I-VI-II-V Progression

Until the advent of modal jazz in the 1960s, jazz music rarely utilised extended periods of tonic harmony. A tonic chord would rarely last more than two measures without some kind of movement. Jazz musicians of the mid-50s generally did not deal with passages of harmony such as the following:

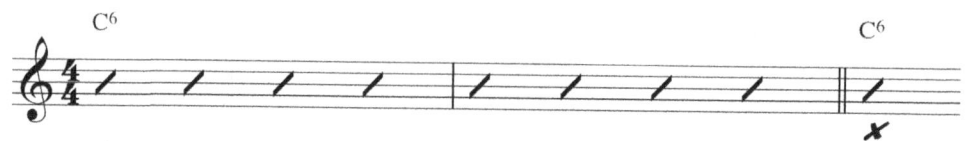

The stasis is usually broken up, often elaborated with movement to V and back:

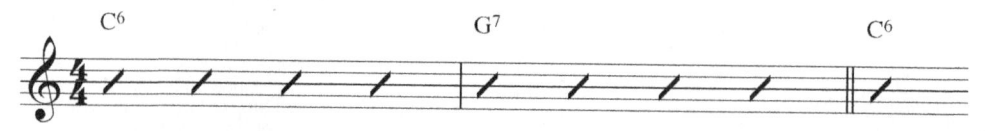

Since II-V is compatible and interchangeable with V, this might be further elaborated:

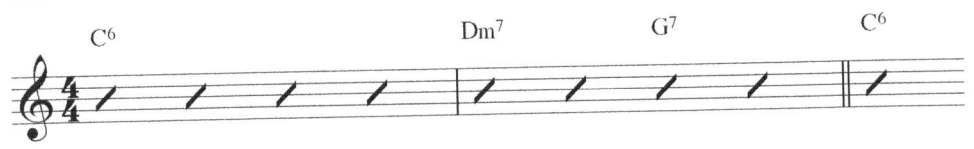

$$C^6 \quad\quad\quad Dm^7 \quad G^7 \quad\quad C^6$$

Not content with this, we might also introduce a new chord. Having approached our target tonic from V, with its root a fifth above the destination chord, and V from II, with its root a fifth above *that* destination chord, we could also approach II from the chord with its root a fifth above that. This gives us the sixth of the key as a bass note, on which we can build a chord that will function like a V to II, or the V of V of V.

When we first introduced the II chord (page 47), we saw that it is in fact a stand-in for the true V of V, having the same bass movement, and maintaining most of the same voice leading. It also reduces the harmonic friction of a true V of V by remaining wholly within the prevailing key signature.

By building a chord from the sixth of a major key, we can create a stand-in for the V of II: a VI^{m7} chord with the natural ninth and eleventh available as extensions. The flattened thirteenth, though available within the key signature, is invariably omitted because it lies a half step above the fifth.

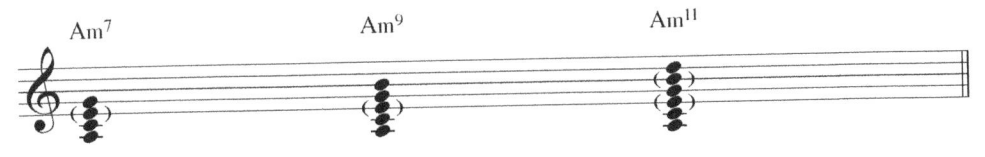

$$Am^7 \quad\quad\quad Am^9 \quad\quad\quad Am^{11}$$

This gives us a structure that can be inserted into our elaboration of the static tonic to form a constant stream of chords:

$$C^6 \quad Am^7 \quad Dm^7 \quad G^7 \quad C^6$$
$$I \quad\;\; VI \quad\;\; II \quad\;\; V \quad\;\; I$$

As they consist of the same pitches over different bass notes, I^6 and VI^{m7} are compatible and interchangeable. This means that there is no contradiction or aural disparity between any of the following variations:

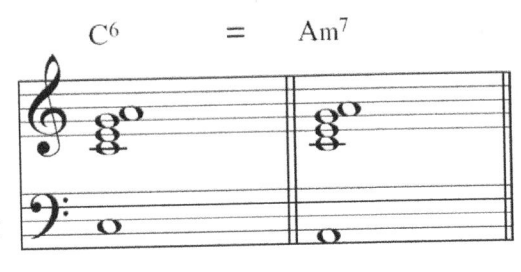

$$C^6 \quad = \quad Am^7$$

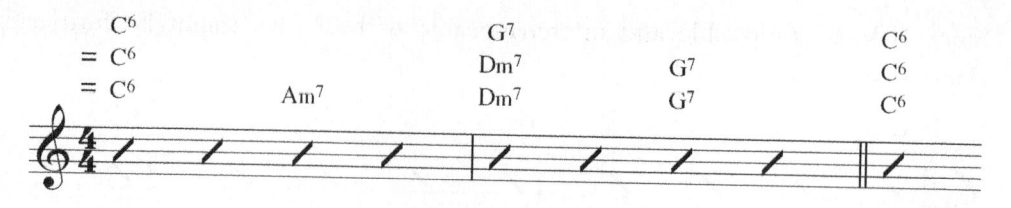

[Musical notation: C6 | = C6 ... = C6 Am7 Dm7 G7 G7 Dm7 G7 C6 C6 C6]

The final chord of the I-VI-II-V progression leads into the first, which means that it can be looped indefinitely, a feature that makes the sequence useful whenever we wish keep the harmony in a piece active without travelling away from the tonic; this is the harmonic equivalent of treading water. Jazz musicians often call a short chord sequence that loops in this way a turnaround, and the I-VI-II-V turnaround in particular is prevalent in swing-time jazz. It may occur wherever a harmonic phrase begins and ends on I:

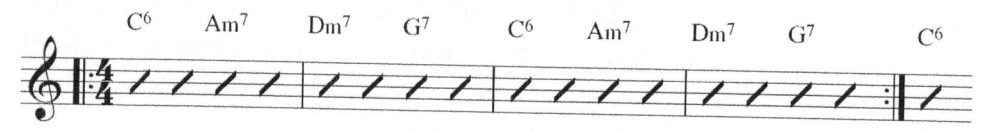

[Musical notation: C6 Am7 Dm7 G7 | C6 Am7 Dm7 G7 | C6 (repeated)]

The I-VI-II-V progression can also appear at half the harmonic rhythm, with each chord lasting an entire bar:

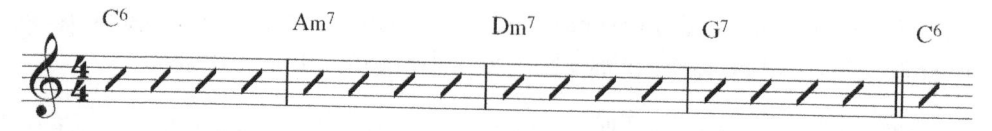

[Musical notation: C6 | Am7 | Dm7 | G7 | C6]

This cycle may also elaborate a V-I movement, which is to say that the same chord progression may appear with II-V metrically accented over I-VI. The following passage:

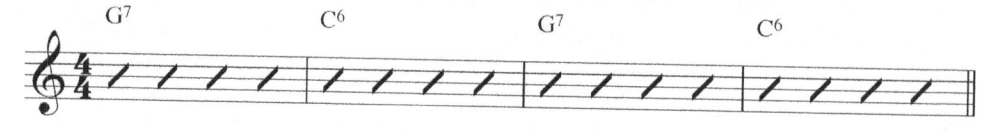

[Musical notation: G7 | C6 | G7 | C6]

...may be elaborated to:

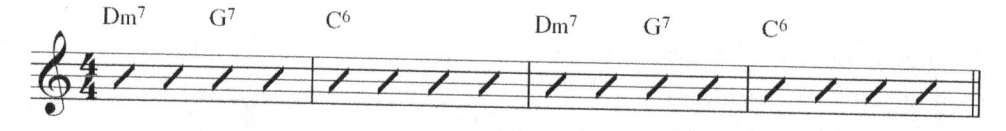

[Musical notation: Dm7 G7 C6 | Dm7 G7 C6]

...and therefore, further elaborated:

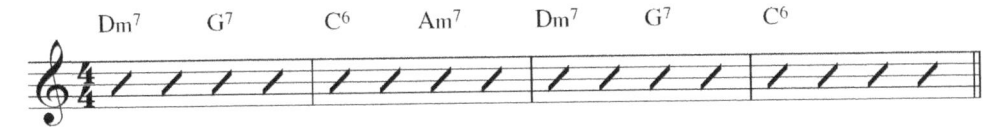

| Dm⁷ | G⁷ | C⁶ | Am⁷ | Dm⁷ | G⁷ | C⁶ |

And again, this phrase may occur with the chord durations doubled:

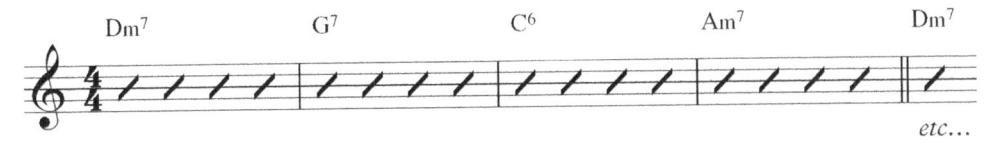

| Dm⁷ | G⁷ | C⁶ | Am⁷ | Dm⁷ |

etc...

The V of II

Rather than approach the II chord from IV^{m7}, which mimics the root movement of its dominant, we can insert the actual dominant of II: chord V from the key of II. Since II is a minor triad, we use the V chord from the key of II minor. Relative to the key of C:

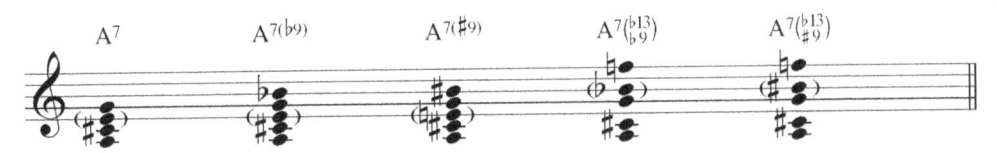

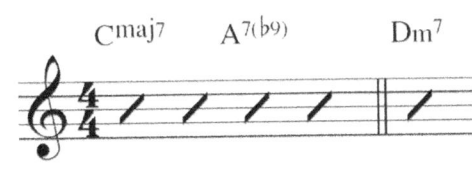

A⁷   A⁷(♭9)   A⁷(♯9)   A⁷(♭13/♭9)   A⁷(♭13/♯9)

| Cmaj7 | A⁷(♭9) | Dm⁷ |

This is another example of a secondary dominant chord, and like the II⁷ chord previously explored (page 55), VI⁷ has a stronger sense of resolution to its target chord, but is more disruptive to the prevailing key than VI^{m7} is. X⁷ or X$^{7♭9}$ are both chord symbols for a dominant VI chord that is followed by II.

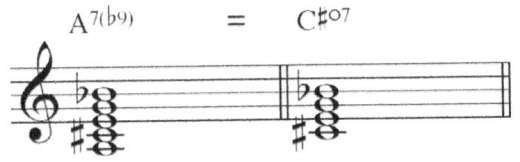

A⁷(♭9) = C♯°7

A popular variation on VI$^{7♭9}$ places its third in the bass, thereby connecting I to II via a chromatically ascending bass line. The structure of a seventh chord with a flattened ninth contains the entirety of a diminished seventh chord within it. This means that VI$^{7♭9/3}$ is, in practice, identical to ♯I$^{°7}$. ♯I$^{°7}$ is a preferable chord symbol due to its comparative simplicity.

Cmaj7	A7(b9)	Dm7		Cmaj7	C#°7	Dm7
I	VI7b9	II		I	#I°7	II

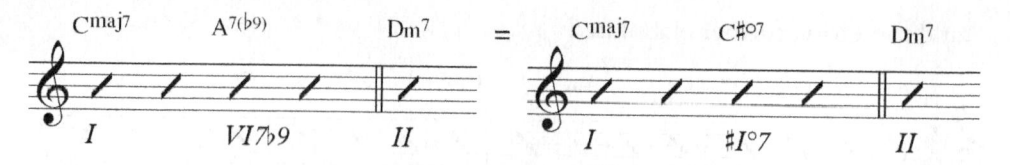

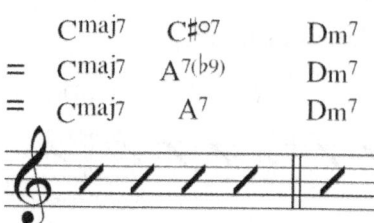

	Cmaj7	C#°7	Dm7
=	Cmaj7	A7(b9)	Dm7
=	Cmaj7	A7	Dm7

These three possible chord symbols are all essentially different names for the same thing. They are all interchangeable and may be used whenever I is followed directly by II in a major key.

At slow tempos, or when I appears two measures before II, there is space for further elaboration. The V of II may be preceded by the II of II, again borrowed from the key of II minor. This is III^{m7b5} relative to the home key:

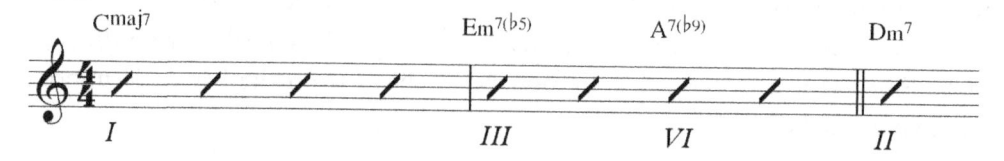

Cmaj7	Em7(b5)	A7(b9)	Dm7
I	III	VI	II

This progression may be further elaborated by the use of a chord connecting I to III^{m7b5}. IV^{maj7} and IV^7 are both options, and the movement from I to IV echoes the ascending fourth/descending fifth bass movement characteristic of functional chord progressions:

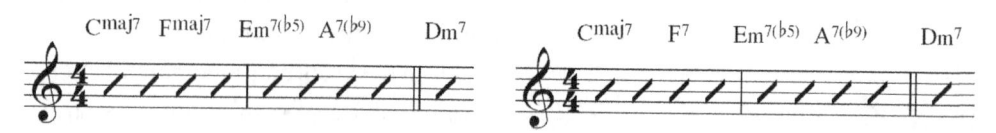

| Cmaj7 Fmaj7 | Em7(b5) A7(b9) | Dm7 | | Cmaj7 F7 | Em7(b5) A7(b9) | Dm7 |

IV^7 is a new chord to us. It typically includes extensions from the key signature:

F7   F9   F7(#11)   F13(#11)

III^{m7} may replace I in a turnaround to produce III-VI-II-V. This could be thought of as a II-V into II, followed by a II-V into I.

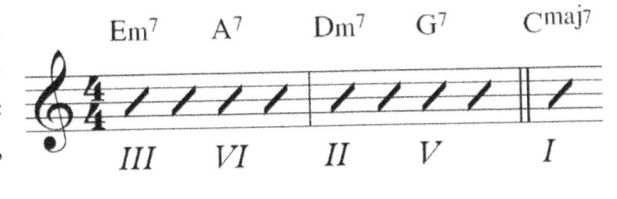

This sequence works because III^{m7} is very similar in structure to I, and leads into chord VI because its root is a fifth higher.

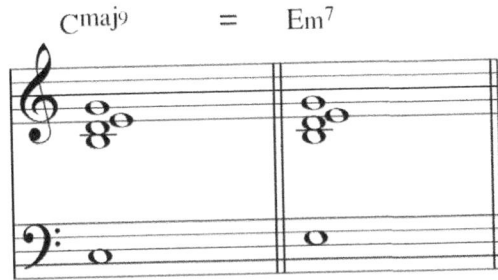

III^{m7} is therefore simultaneously both a substitute for I, and for the V of V of V of V. Because they consist of the same structure over a different bass note, III^{m7} and I^{maj7} are compatible and interchangeable.

In a repeating turnaround, III^{m7} may replace every second occurrence of I:

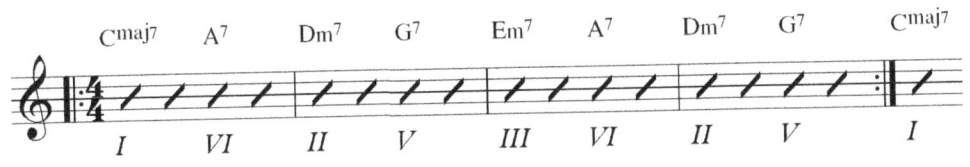

This sequence is significantly less common with the hypermetric accents inverted, in which III^{m7} is accented relative to I:

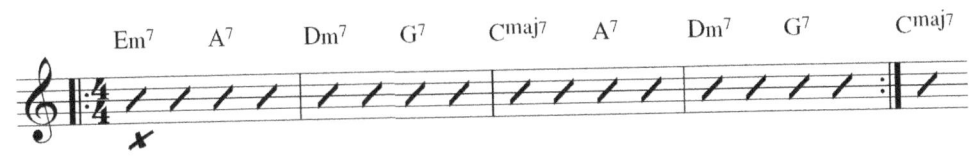

III^{m7b5} is a common substitute for this usage of III^{m7}, giving us a minor II-V into II, followed by a major II-V into I.

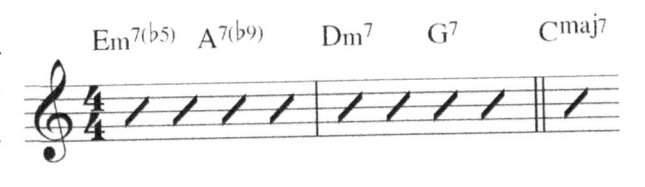

Any of the preceding progressions are available at half the harmonic rhythm, particularly at higher tempos where a decent pace of harmonic movement will be retained:

[Chord chart: Em7 | A7 | Dm7 | G7 | Cmaj7 — III VI II V I]

or:

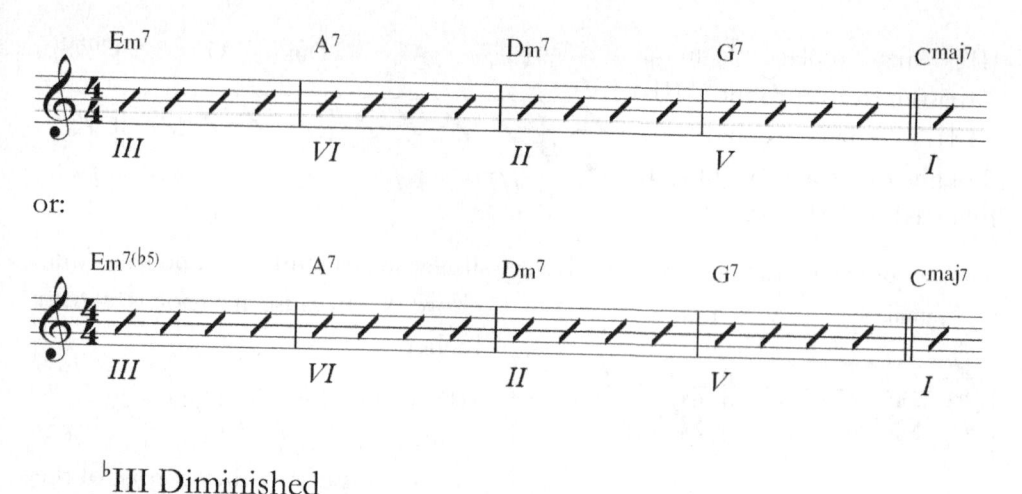

[Chord chart: Em7(b5) | A7 | Dm7 | G7 | Cmaj7 — III VI II V I]

♭III Diminished

A further variation on the major key turnaround is that we may move from I to II through a diminished seventh chord with its root on the flattened third of the key.

Below, I^6 is intensified. Two tones remain stationary, but two move downward by a half step, transforming the chord into a dissonant diminished seventh structure. This tension can be resolved in two ways.

Firstly, in *(a)* the voices return to their initial positions, thus resolving the dissonance over a static bass note, a function that will be further explored later (page 208).

Secondly, by resolving downward, the same upper structure may lead us from I to II, as in *(b)*. The change of bass note from C to E-flat further strengthens this sense of resolution, as the bass may now also resolve as $^{\flat}III^{\circ7}$ moves to II^{m7}:

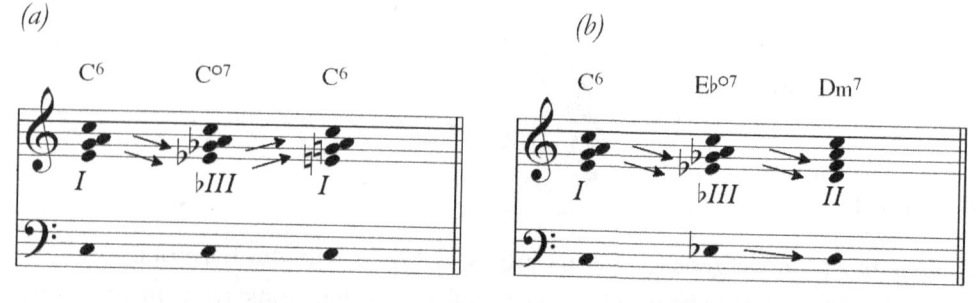

(a) [C6 – C°7 – C6 : I – ♭III – I] *(b)* [C6 – E♭°7 – Dm7 : I – ♭III – II]

This common tone diminished chord may be inserted into a turnaround as an alternative to VI. It connects I or III to II. Notice that movement from III to $^{\flat}III^{\circ7}$ extends the descending bass movement. $^{\flat}III^{\circ7}$ must be de-emphasised relative to the I or III chord that it follows:

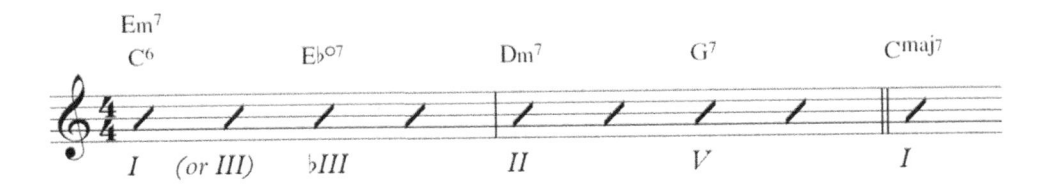

[Musical notation: Measures showing chords Em7/C6, Eb°7, Dm7, G7, Cmaj7 with Roman numerals I (or III), bIII, II, V, I]

[Musical notation: Dm7, G7, Cmaj7, Eb°7, Dm7 with Roman numerals II, V, I, bIII, II]

The use of $^{\flat}III^{\circ 7}$ in this context is perhaps more associated with pre-war styles. Musicians of the bebop era onward generally prefer VI^{m7} or VI^7 to connect I to II in major tonalities.

Cycling Home

The cycle of ascending fourths/descending fifths in a chord progression like III-VI-II-V-I is particularly compelling in producing the forward motion that defines tonal harmony. Each chord functions as a dominant to the next, implying an inexorable sequence of successive V-I resolutions. The qualities of these chords can be altered without disrupting the effect. We have already seen that III-VI-II-V-I might appear as a two successive major II-V progressions:

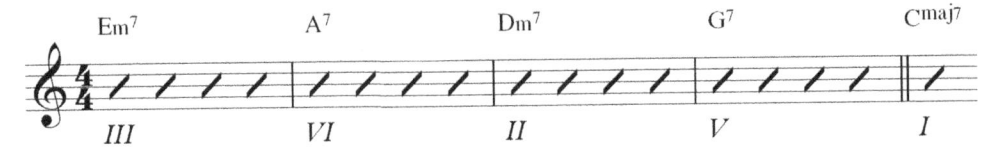

[Musical notation: Em7, A7, Dm7, G7, Cmaj7 with Roman numerals III, VI, II, V, I]

...or a minor II-V followed by a major II-V:

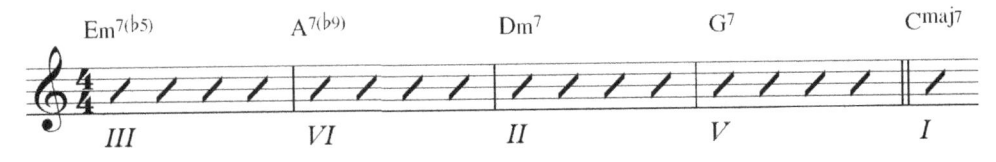

[Musical notation: Em7(b5), A7(b9), Dm7, G7, Cmaj7 with Roman numerals III, VI, II, V, I]

All four might be transformed into seventh chords, producing a sequence where each chord functions as the secondary dominant to the next:

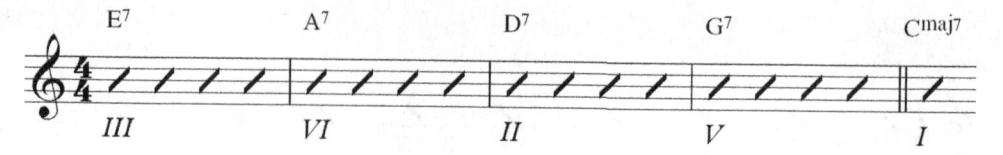

[Musical example: E7 | A7 | D7 | G7 | Cmaj7, labeled III VI II V I]

In a further elaboration, any of these dominants may be preceded with a II, producing a distinctive pattern where each V chord is transformed into the II of the next cadence, for example:

...*becomes*:

[Musical example: D7 | G7 | Cmaj7 (II V I) becomes Am7 D7 | Dm7 G7 | Cmaj7]

The preceding pattern is also very common with the harmonic rhythm halved:

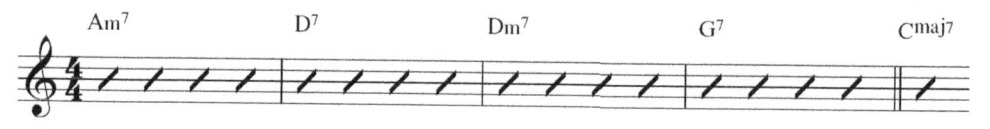

[Musical example: Am7 | D7 | Dm7 | G7 | Cmaj7]

A cycle may be extended further so that it begins on a chord with its root on the raised fourth of the key. ♯IV and VII typically appear as a minor II-V, and contain the root of the prevailing key:

[Musical example: F♯m7(♭9) B7(♭9) | Em7 A7 | Dm7 G7 | Cmaj7, labeled ♯IV VII III VI II V I]

This sequence also appears with the second chord exchanged for IV^{m6} and the fourth chord exchanged for ♭III°7, which facilitates a continuously descending bass line:

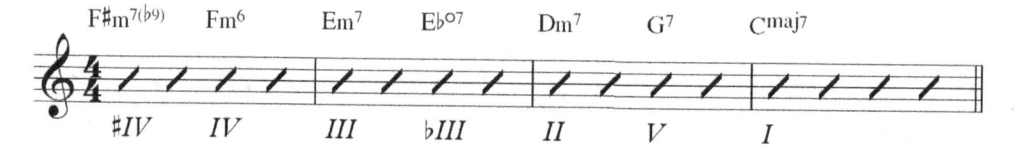

[Musical example: F♯m7(♭9) Fm6 | Em7 E♭°7 | Dm7 G7 | Cmaj7, labeled ♯IV IV III ♭III II V I]

I-VI-II-V in Minor

As in major keys, extended tonic minor harmony lasting more than two consecutive bars is rare in pre-1960 jazz:

[Cm | Cm]

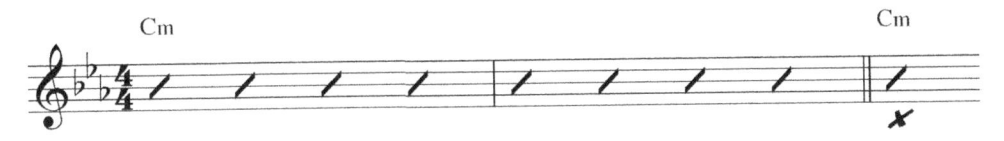

The same solutions apply as in major keys, namely the interjection of V:

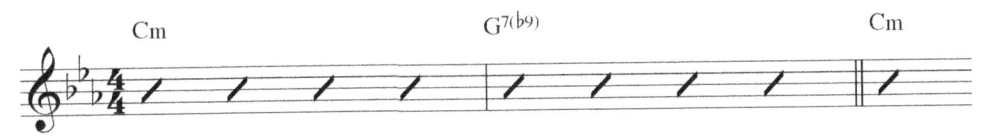

[Cm | G7(b9) | Cm]

...or the elaboration of V with II:

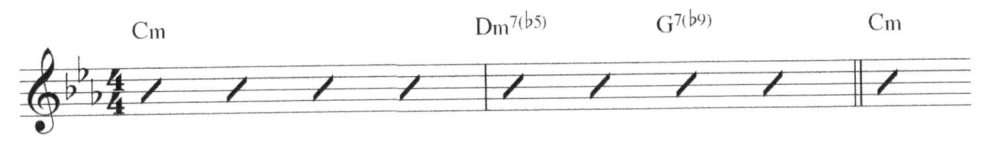

[Cm | Dm7(b5) G7(b9) | Cm]

We might further elaborate the II-V-I in minor just as we did in major, with a chord leading to II. The most obvious way to approach II would be from a chord with its root a fifth above, which, in the case of chord II, is the sixth of the key.

Stacking diatonic thirds from this root note gives us the flattened third, the flattened fifth, and the flattened seventh, with the natural eleventh available as an extension. This structure is identical to the II chord in the key of V minor: A^{m7b5}, for example, occurs as both VI in the key of C minor, and II in the key of G major:

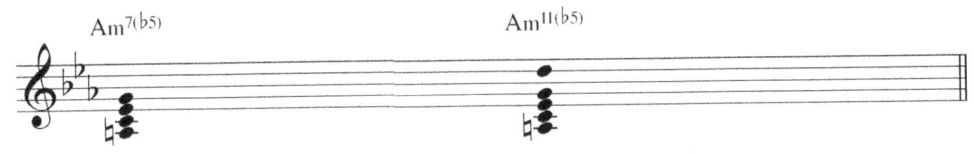

[Am7(b5) | Am11(b5)]

Because the natural sixth is not native to the key signature in a minor key, the bass note of the VI chord in minor will require an accidental. To use the native flattened sixth as a bass note would result in a $^{b}VI^{maj7}$ chord, which, whilst a pleasant sonority in itself, fails our requirement for a bass line that ascends a perfect fourth. $^{b}VI^{maj7}$ does not mimic the V of II closely enough to convincingly resolve into II:

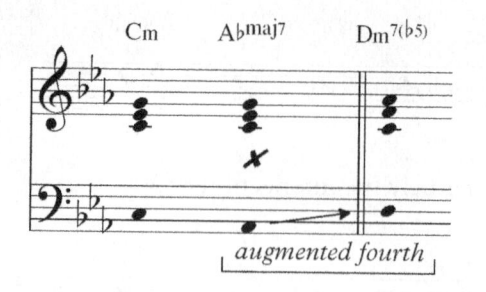

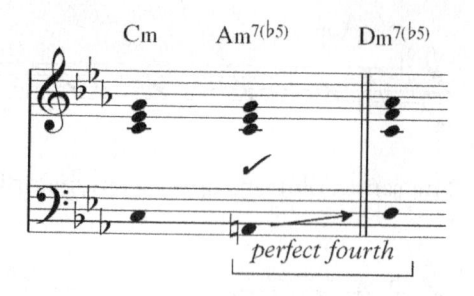

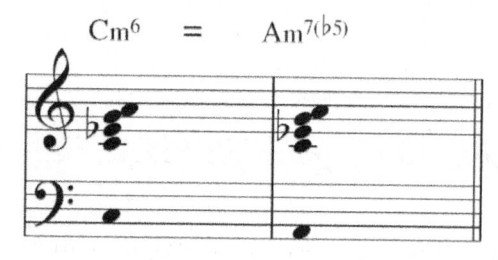

[Musical example: Cm — A♭maj7 — Dm7(♭5), marked "augmented fourth" with an ✗]

[Musical example: Cm — Am7(♭5) — Dm7(♭5), marked "perfect fourth" with a ✓]

[Musical example: Cm6 = Am7(♭5)]

The root, flattened third, fifth, and sixth of I^{m6} are the flattened third, flattened fifth, flattened seventh, and root of $VI^{m7♭5}$ respectively. These two chords are the same structure over a different bass note. This means that all of the following progressions are compatible and interchangeable:

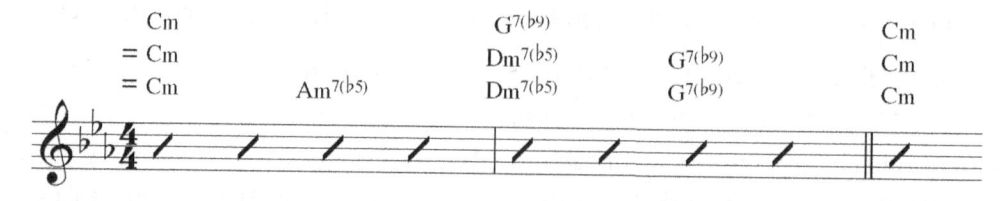

```
   Cm                    G7(♭9)                    Cm
 = Cm                    Dm7(♭5)    G7(♭9)         Cm
 = Cm       Am7(♭5)      Dm7(♭5)    G7(♭9)         Cm
```

As in major, the minor I-VI-II-V may appear at half the rate of the harmonic change:

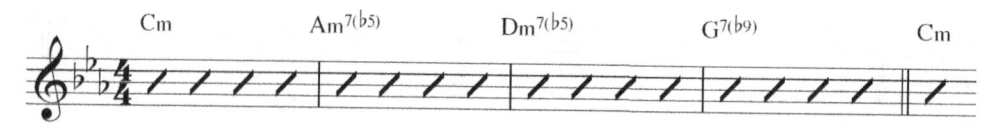

```
 Cm        Am7(♭5)       Dm7(♭5)    G7(♭9)         Cm
```

It may also be metrically inverted, replacing a V-I cycle:

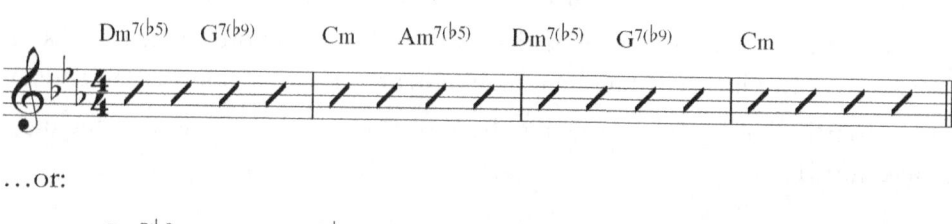

```
 Dm7(♭5)   G7(♭9)   Cm   Am7(♭5)    Dm7(♭5)  G7(♭9)   Cm
```

…or:

```
 Dm7(♭5)   G7(♭9)        Cm         Am7(♭5)       Dm7(♭5)
```

VI^{m7b5} in minor is a little less common than its major key equivalent, possibly because the non-native natural sixth in the bass makes the chord more disruptive to the prevailing tonality.

Whilst extremely common in major keys, VI^7 is rare in minor. When it does occur, it usually appears with extensions from the key signature, namely the flattened ninth or raised ninth, raised eleventh, and flattened thirteenth. Because all of the available extensions are altered, this chord is usually notated as an altered chord VI$^{7alt.}$:

VI$^{7alt.}$ is a more dissonant alternative to VI^{m7b5} in a minor key, and it intensifies the movement from VI to II. In this context the altered chord was a fairly late addition to the harmonic palette:

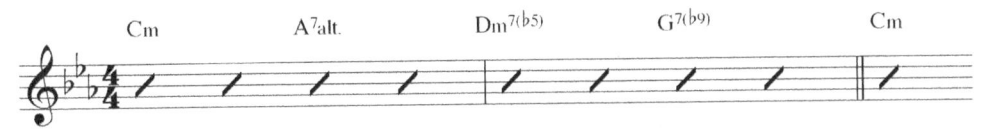

More Minor Turnarounds

There are fewer conventional variations of the turnaround in minor keys, partly due to the unavailability of a III chord to lead to VI. A natural third in the bass undermines minor tonality, whilst a native flattened third in the bass lacks the ascending fourth/descending fifth bass movement to II necessary to imply V functionality:

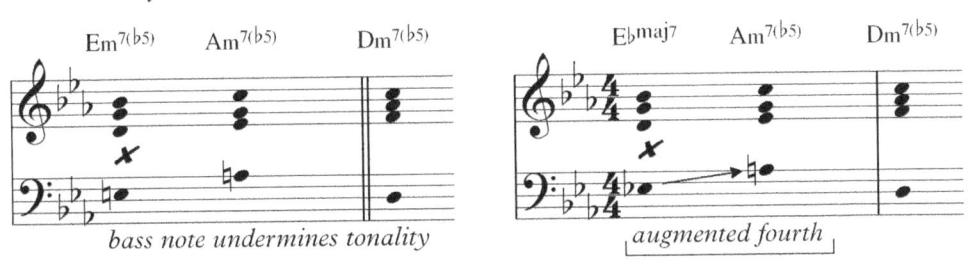

bass note undermines tonality   *augmented fourth*

There are a few alternative options for minor key turnarounds. A diatonically descending bass line can take us through ^{b}VI to V in a progression usually heard with I accented over ^{b}VI:

[Musical example: Cm | Cm/Bb | Abmaj7 (or: Ab7) G7(b9) | Cm]

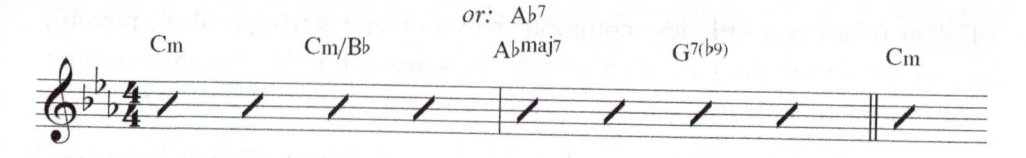

♭VI is a new chord to us. It may appear with the natural seventh native to the key signature, but more often appears as a dominant chord, particularly when it is followed by V⁷. It is most typically furnished with extensions from the key signature, namely the natural ninth, raised eleventh, and natural thirteenth. ♭VI⁷ could be seen as a tritone substitution of II⁷, a technique that will be addressed later (page 198):

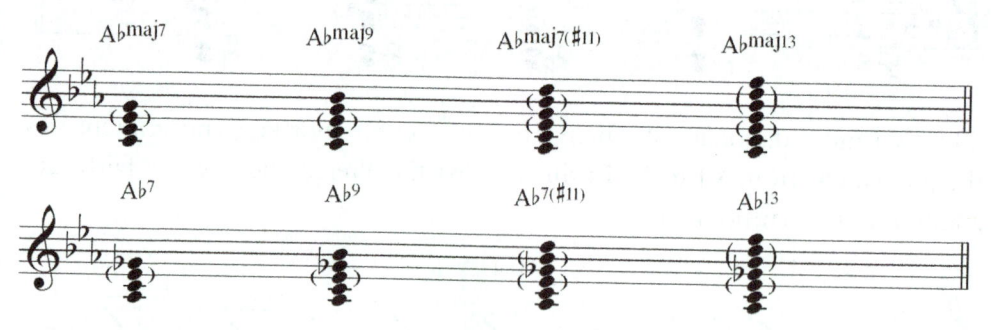

[Musical example showing chord voicings: Abmaj7, Abmaj9, Abmaj7(#11), Abmaj13; and Ab7, Ab9, Ab7(#11), Ab13]

♭VI invariably precedes V, and is, in many contexts, interchangeable with II. This is particularly the case in minor keys, as it shares several pitches with II^(m7b5). The more distinctive ♭VI⁷ is generally the more popular choice:

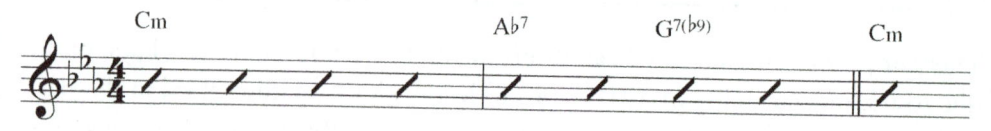

[Musical example: Cm | Ab7 G7(b9) | Cm]

The example below is less common, but has the advantage of a pleasing chromatic bass descent:

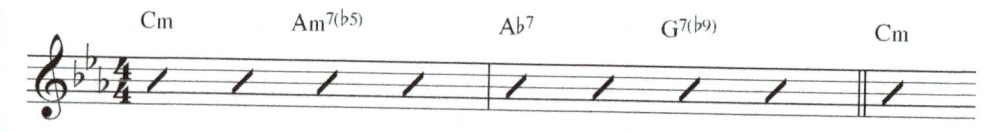

[Musical example: Cm | Am7(b5) | Ab7 G7(b9) | Cm]

When writing tonal jazz, we often wish to remain in the tonic area for an extended period. Older jazz styles in particular demand constant harmonic movement, and the cyclical chord progressions in this chapter provide the language for us to tread water, elaborating the tonic without the need for modulation or harmonic digression.

Chapter Summary

Static tonic harmony may be elaborated with V, II-V, or VI-II-V.

In major keys, VI^7, $^{\sharp}I^{°7}$, or $^{\flat}III^{°7}$ may be used to connect I to II.

In major keys, I-VI-II-V may be replaced with III-VI-II-V.

Any chord that is followed by a chord with its root a fourth above/fifth below is liable to be intensified into a dominant chord type.

In minor keys, VI^{m7b5} or $VI^{7alt.}$ may be used to connect I to II.

In minor keys, $^{\flat}VI^7$ may replace II^{m7b5} to precede V.

Chapter 6
Changing Key

In Chapter 4 we found that, because chord IV does not lead directly to either I or V, it is particularly useful as a temporary destination for our harmonic schemes. Chord VI can be constructed entirely within the key signature, which means that its presence has a relatively mild effect as a stopping-off point within the key, rather than as a key change.

True key changes are found in a huge proportion of jazz repertoire. The key change, or modulation, is an essential tool for retaining interest. It gives us access to new and refreshing harmonic palettes, and may serve to demarcate different periods within a piece. Arrival in a new key might be a significant harmonic event, but a key change might also be transient, or even disputable.

The circle of fifths is a very useful tool for understanding the relationships between keys. By arranging the twelve keys in clockwise order of ascending fifths, we position the tonally related keys adjacent to each other. Relative major and minor keys are the most closely related since they share much of the same tonal material, which is reflected in the fact that they share a key signature.

Beyond this, modulation upwards by a fourth, a fifth, or to the relative minor/major of either of those keys takes us to a tonality with a key signature that differs by only one pitch. From any given key, the five most closely related tonalities are those adjacent on the diagram below. From C major, these are the keys of F major, G major, A minor, E minor, and D minor:

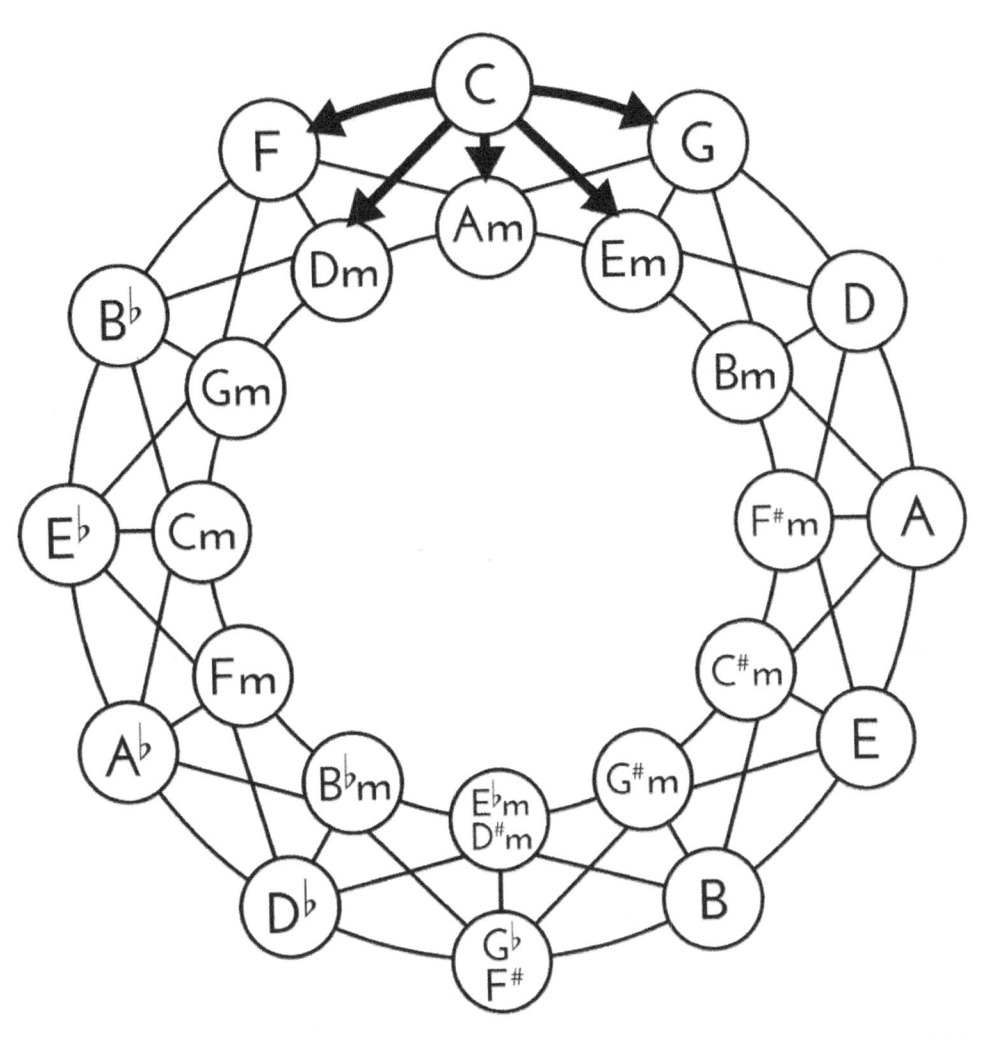

The tonic triads of all five of these tonally adjacent keys are wholly present within the key signature of our starting key, C major:

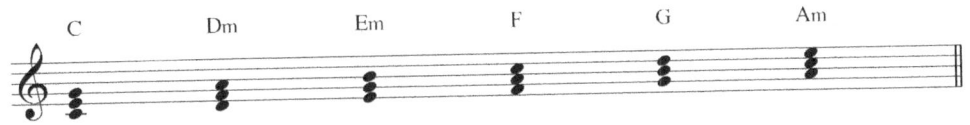

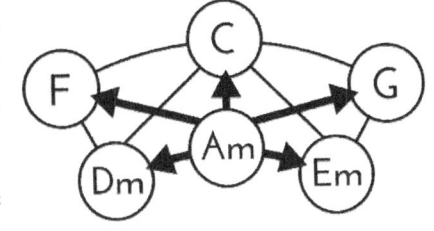

The same principle applies to minor keys. A modulation to the relative major, or any key adjacent on the circle of fifths, takes us to a closely related tonality.

Because most of the pitches in any of these five adjacent keys are present in the home key, modulations to these areas are the least disruptive. In many situations, the entire reason for changing key is that we actively wish to disrupt the previous tonality with a radical shift; the further that we travel around the circle of fifths to find our new key, the more drastic that change in sonority.

In common practice music, key changes to neighbouring keys were the most popular, and more radical modulations were relatively rare. Key changes were typically disguised by the use of pivot notes or pivot chords, material that functions both within the old key and the destination key.

The passage that follows shows a modulation from A minor to G major, in which the asterisked A minor chord functions simultaneously in both keys, dovetailing the transition. Because there is no single moment of modulation, the effect is rather subtle:

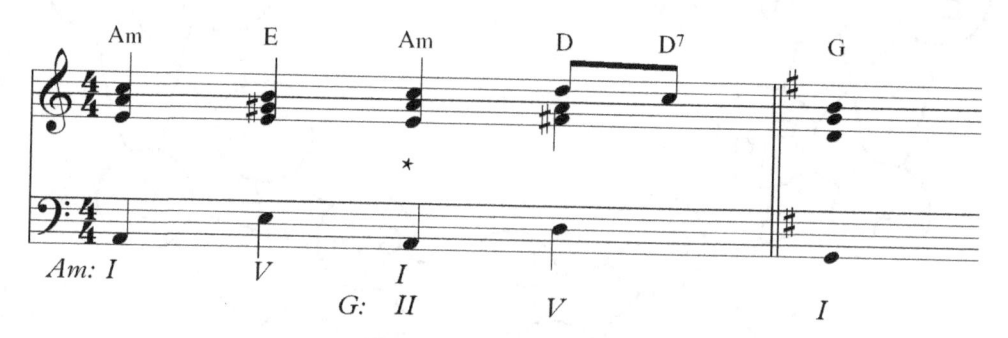

Although the use of pivot harmonies and melodies were virtually compulsory in the key changes found in common practice music, much of the popular music of the twentieth century made little attempt to avoid abrupt tonal shifts, and examples can be found in the jazz and songbook repertoire of modulations to almost any relative key.

Furthermore, the use of pivot chords is no longer obligatory. Even in more conservative songbook style pieces, a new key might be introduced with nothing more than its V chord, or a II-V movement in its place.

Here are some excerpts showing chord progressions that a jazz composer might use to connect a passage in G major to a new period in F major, with the new period represented by a double bar line. The modulation can either be set up by a II-V cadence in the new key to appear in bar one of the new period, or the II-V can begin in bar one of the new period. All three examples are highly typical:

(a) new tonic on bar one of the new period:

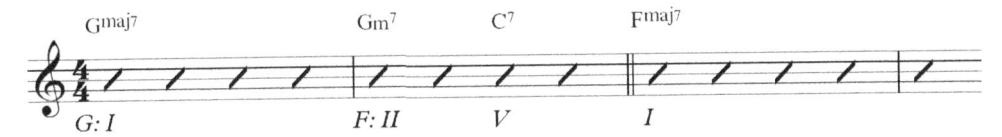

[Music notation: Gmaj7 | Gm7 C7 | Fmaj7]
G: I   F: II   V   I

(b) cadence to new tonic begins on bar one of the new period:

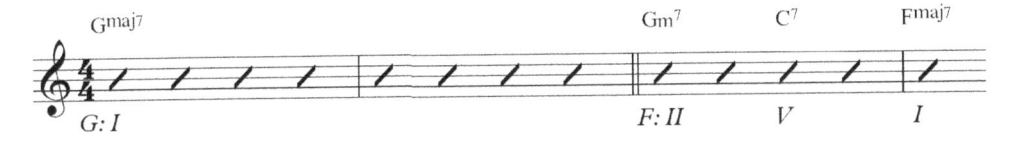

[Music notation: Gmaj7 | | Gm7 C7 | Fmaj7]
G: I   F: II V   I

...or:

[Music notation: Gmaj7 | | Gm7 | C7 | Fmaj7]
G: I   F: II   V   I

Key changes are particularly likely to occur at the start of a new period, but they might also be fleeting.

As an example of this, here is an eight-bar passage which briefly modulates from the prevailing key of G major to a distant key of E-flat, four steps removed around the circle of fifths, before returning to G major on its way to a more closely related B minor tonality:

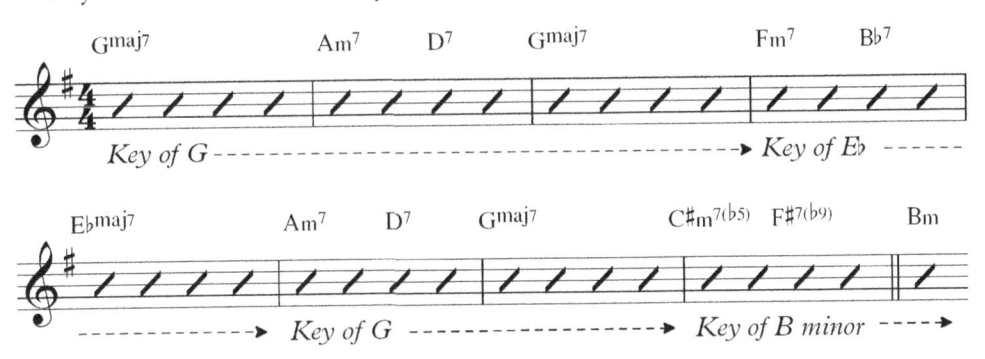

[Music notation: Gmaj7 | Am7 D7 | Gmaj7 | Fm7 Bb7]
Key of G ----------------------------→ Key of Eb ------

[Music notation: Ebmaj7 | Am7 D7 | Gmaj7 | C#m7(b5) F#7(b9) | Bm]
---------→ Key of G ----------------→ Key of B minor ---→

Any major or minor key could, in theory, modulate to any of the twenty-three other possible keys.

Although examples of almost any of these can be found somewhere in the canon, certain destination tonalities are common enough to jazz repertoire to earn specific mention.

Modulation to the Parallel I

In a major key, one possibility is to *minorise* the tonic chord, thereby modulating to the key of I minor; the effect of a I minor chord in a major key is harmonically dramatic. Because I minor is approached from the same chord as I major, V^7, the listener is unprepared for the sudden appearance of a minorised tonic:

The inverse, a modulation from a minor key to its parallel major, is more common. A minor key piece might feature a period in the parallel major, and another popular practice is to end a minor-key period with a surprising cadence to I major. Here, I major is approached with a minor II-V, which complies better with the signature of the prevailing minor key:

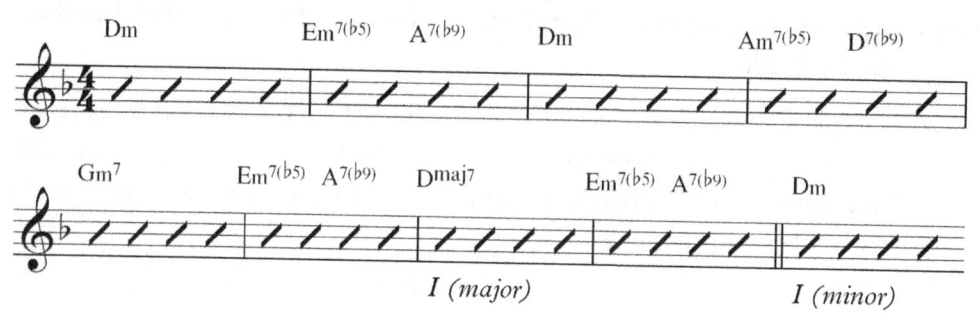

This effect is a relative of the Picardy cadence that was popular in European music of the Baroque era, wherein a minor-key piece ends with a cadence to a tonic major triad.

Modulation to the Key of IV

As discussed in Chapter 4, tonal jazz that stays within a key for any length of time tends to arrive at chord IV at some point. Actual modulation to the key of IV is also common, particularly at the beginning of the second period of the piece, but it can sometimes be ambiguous as to whether a piece has modulated to the key of IV or merely moved to chord IV:

[musical example: Cmaj7 | Gm7 C7 | Fmaj7 | etc.
C: I   F: I? IV?]

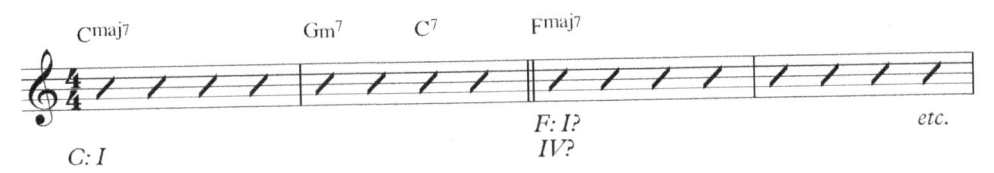

Such ambiguity can be eliminated by reaffirming the IV key centre with key of IV-specific material. More chords from the key of IV will achieve this. For example:

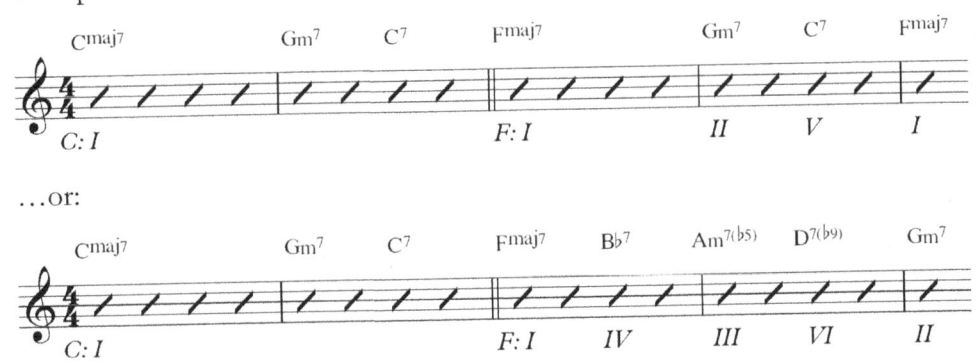

[musical example: Cmaj7 | Gm7 C7 | Fmaj7 | Gm7 C7 | Fmaj7
C: I   F: I   II   V   I]

...or:

[musical example: Cmaj7 | Gm7 C7 | Fmaj7 Bb7 | Am7(b5) D7(b9) | Gm7
C: I   F: I   IV   III   VI   II]

Two things change in a modulation to the key of IV: the tonal centre shifts up a fourth (or down a fifth), and the seventh of the old key is lowered to become the fourth of the new one. The key of IV-specific harmonies demonstrated above reinforce the sense of modulation by including this new pitch, but melody also plays an important part in making this distinction.

We can compare the following examples, in which an ambiguous movement from I to chord IV is followed by two contrasting phrases, the first of which implies a return to the tonic, and the second confirms a modulation:

(a) chord IV appears in the key of C:

[musical example: Cmaj7 Gm7 C7 Fmaj7 Fm6 Cmaj7
ambiguous | B♮ confirms C major *]

(b) modulation from key of C to key of F:

[musical example: Cmaj7 Gm7 C7 Fmaj7 Gm7 C7 Fmaj7
ambiguous | B♭ confirms F major *]

Modulation to IV major is the most common key change for major key songbook-style harmony. Minor pieces are more likely to modulate to more closely related key of IV minor than they are to IV major.

Modulation to the Key of V

Music of the common practice period almost always modulates directly to the key of V, expanding and extending an unresolved V chord to the point that it becomes a new key in itself, before invariably being resolved back to the original key. This is surprisingly rare in jazz and songbook repertoire, perhaps because it sounds too much like common practice music.

Although modulation *directly* to the key of V is relatively uncommon, the key of V is often arrived at indirectly via other keys. One prominent example an eight-bar connecting passage found in countless early twentieth century songs, which consists of four bars in the key of IV, and four bars in the key of V:

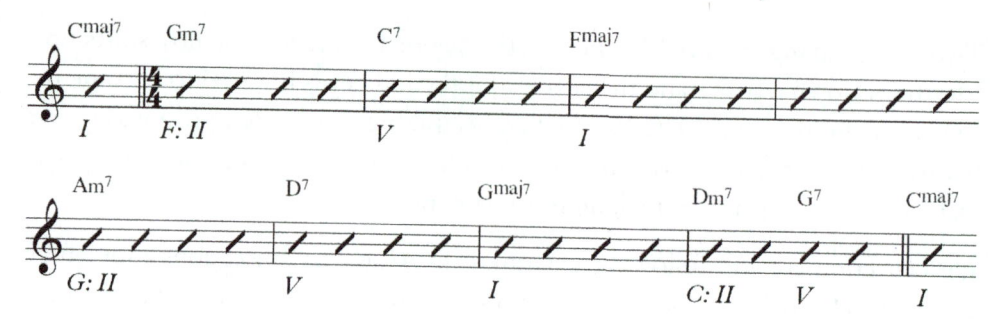

```
Cmaj7    Gm7         C7          Fmaj7
 I       F: II       V           I

Am7      D7          Gmaj7       Dm7      G7       Cmaj7
G: II    V           I           C: II    V        I
```

Modulation to the Key of ♭III

Minor key music has a strong tendency to modulate up to the key of ♭III major, its relative major. As discussed earlier, these two keys are the most closely related to each other, and even share a key signature.

The arrival at the new tonic is frequently preceded by a II-V. In the songbook style this particular modulation is also popular in the major key, another example of the tendency of keys to refer to their parallel tonality. In terms of bass movement, the old tonic momentarily resembles a V to II in the new key as the bass ascends a fourth:

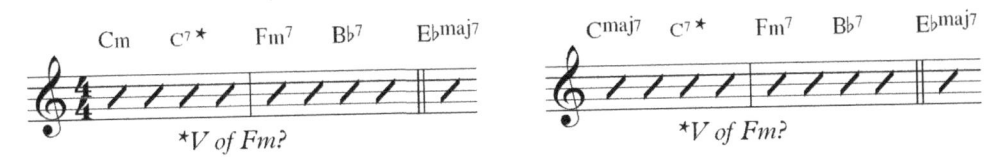

[Musical notation: Cm | C7* | Fm7 Bb7 | Ebmaj7 || Cmaj7 | C7* | Fm7 Bb7 | Ebmaj7 ||
*V of Fm?   *V of Fm?]

The II-V in the progression above also occurs as a backdoor to chord I (page 61), further linking a major key with the key of III major. In other words, the chord progression IV^{m7}-♭VII^7 might occur in a major key either as a precursor to ♭III or to the tonic:

[Musical notation: Cmaj7 | Fm7 Bb7 | Ebmaj7 || Cmaj7 | Fm7 Bb7 | Cmaj7 ||
'front door' to ♭III   'back door' to I]

Modulation to the Key of III

The key of III minor is a popular destination for major key pieces. It is a closely related key with a contrasting tonality, whose tonic chord is native to the old key. The E minor chord, for example, is possible within a C major key signature. The obvious route to the key of III is via a connecting II-V into the new key.

Another popular variation found in the songbook style *majorises* the destination key, moving from I to III major. This rather radical leap in tonality, four steps around the circle of fifths, is smoothed out by retaining the minor style II-V, in which the old tonic pitch is still present, as both F♯^{m7b5} and B^{7b9} include the pitch of C:

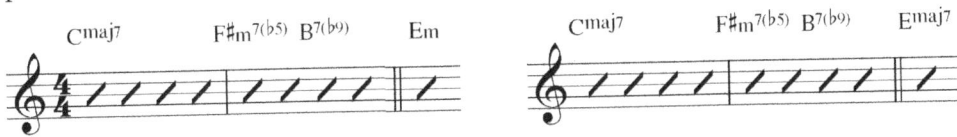

[Musical notation: Cmaj7 | F♯m7(b5) B7(b9) | Em || Cmaj7 | F♯m7(b5) B7(b9) | Emaj7 ||]

Modulation to the Key of VI

Short term modulation to the relative minor is very common, but it is a rather conservative destination for an entire period within a major key piece. VI minor is most frequently preceded by a minor II-V. An interesting alternative is to modulate to the key of VI major, the parallel major of the relative minor.

There is an uplifting sensation as a cadence prepares us for a modulation to a relative minor, which turns out to be major after all. A minor style II-V bridges the transition to the key of VI smoothly because it conforms more closely to the key signature:

[Musical notation: Cmaj7 | Bm7(b5) E7(b9) | Am ‖ Cmaj7 | Bm7(b5) E7(b9) | Amaj7]

Another option is to resolve the V of a major key up a step to the VI^m chord. In jazz styles, this is usually done through a connective diminished chord that allows chromatic bass movement. Much like the #I°7 introduced earlier (page 69), this chord is functioning as a secondary dominant. The G#°7 below is essentially the V of VI, an E7b9 over its third:

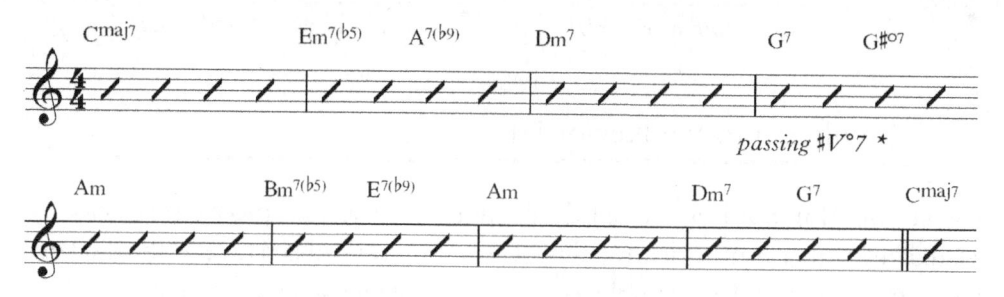

[Musical notation: Cmaj7 | Em7(b5) A7(b9) | Dm7 | G7 | G#°7]

*passing #V°7 **

[Musical notation: Am | Bm7(b5) E7(b9) | Am | Dm7 | G7 | Cmaj7]

Transitional Passages and Pivot Pitches

The examples in this chapter have all demonstrated modulation in terms of unprepared II-Vs to the new key, but more subtle and complex conjoining material is also possible. An intermediary key may be used to connect one key to another.

In the following example, we move from a tonic C major chord to a brief suggestion of F minor tonality. This connective key of F minor is only briefly glimpsed before its tonic is revealed to be a pivot chord, bridging the way to the distant key of D-flat major:

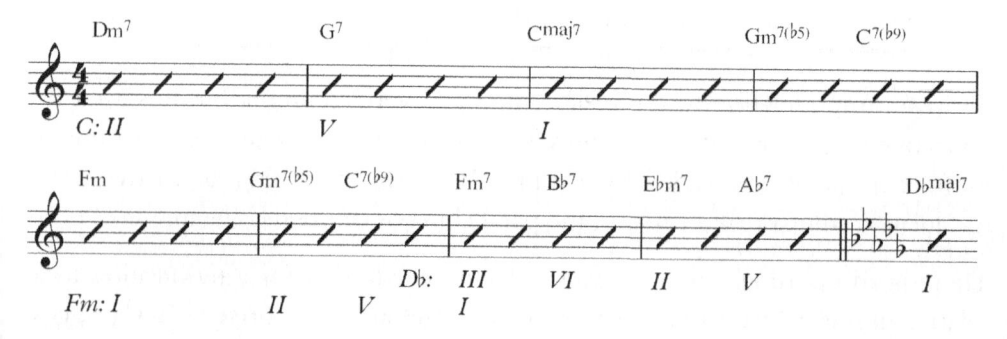

[Musical notation:
Dm7 | G7 | Cmaj7 | Gm7(b5) C7(b9)
C: II   V   I

Fm | Gm7(b5) C7(b9) | Fm7 Bb7 | Ebm7 Ab7 | Dbmaj7
Fm: I   II   V   Db: III VI   II   V   I
]

88

Alternatively, from the same opening sequence, the key of E-flat serves as a bridging tonality to its own IV, connecting the key of C major to a distant A-flat major:

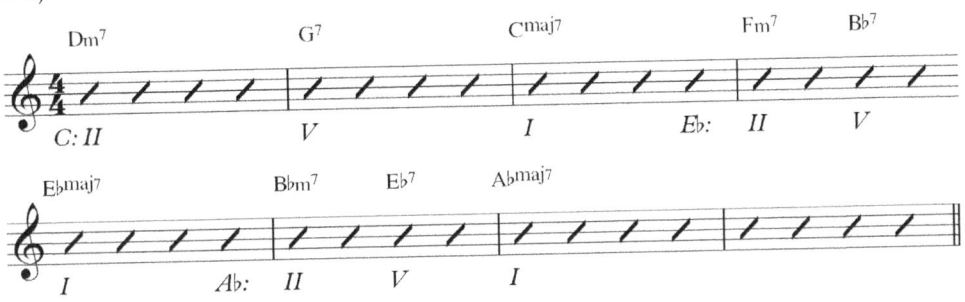

[Musical notation: Dm7 | G7 | Cmaj7 | Fm7 Bb7]
[C: II   V   I   Eb: II   V]

[Musical notation: Ebmaj7 | Bbm7 Eb7 | Abmaj7]
[I   Ab: II   V   I]

All of the examples that we have examined so far have used V chords or II-Vs to establish the new key, but a new key may also arrive completely unannounced. Such a radical effect is particularly appropriate at the beginning of a new period:

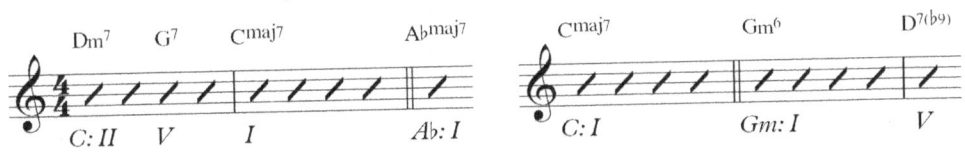

[Musical notation: Dm7 G7 Cmaj7 | Abmaj7 | Cmaj7 | Gm6 D7(b9)]
[C: II V I   Ab: I   C: I   Gm: I   V]

Melody is another important factor in connecting radical modulations. A common melody pitch can bridge two very different keys, functioning as a pivot around which the harmony revolves. Here, the repeated pitch F connects a phrase in D minor to a very distant G-flat major:

[Musical notation: Em7(b5) | A7(b9) | Dm6 | Db7 | Gbmaj7]

The effect is slightly disguised here, as the repeated pivot pitch E is interrupted with embellishing material as it connects C major to the unlikely destination of B major:

[Musical notation: Cmaj7 | C#m7 F#7 | Bmaj7]
[*   embellishment   *]

In common practice music, pieces may modulate multiple times to distant tonalities, but they invariably begin and end on the tonic chord of the same key. This makes the key of a given piece quite easily discernible and definable. We may say with confidence that Beethoven's first symphony is in the key of C, despite the numerous temporary key centres that are featured throughout its duration. The popular music and jazz of the twentieth century follows no such conventions. Even the highly tonal chord progressions of Tin Pan Alley-style songs might begin and end in different keys. Jazz musicians, for example, will not hesitate to write a chorus in C that cadences to D-flat major at the end, such as in Thelonious Monk's *Bemsha Swing*, or which alternates between G and D-flat major, like in Steve Swallow's *Ladies in Mercedes*, or which contains no root position major or minor chords at all, such as in Herbie Hancock's *Maiden Voyage*.

Such harmonic schemes lie at various points along the functional to non-functional continuum, and demonstrate the maxim that key is present or absent only by degrees.

If a piece modulates only temporarily, jazz composers generally notate the foreign material with accidentals rather than temporarily changing the key signature. There is no defined rule regarding when to change key signature for a modulatory passage, and we must use our own discretion. Eight or twelve bars is a reasonable amount of time to spend in a new key without introducing a new key signature. If a piece modulates many times, does not favour any particular key, or is not in any key, it is probably best notated without a key signature at all.

Chapter Summary

Modulation to closely related keys is less disruptive than modulation to distant keys.

Major key pieces most often feature modulation to the key of IV major, ♭III major, III minor, III major, VI minor and VI major.

Minor key pieces most often feature modulation to the key of I major, IV minor and ♭III major.

Connective passages featuring pivot pitches or chords may disguise even radical modulations, but key changes might also be entirely unprepared.

Chapter 7
The Blues

Though they grew from the same roots and share many characteristics, blues music and jazz have long been separate branches of African-American music. Despite this bifurcation of style, the blues remains a constant presence in the jazz idiom as an undefined and undefinable aesthetic. The most tangible (and prosaic) expression of the blues in jazz is the ubiquitous twelve-bar blues chord progression, which introduces several essential idiomatic exceptions to the harmonic conventions that we have already explored. Here, in the key of C, is the twelve-bar blues chord progression in its simplest form:

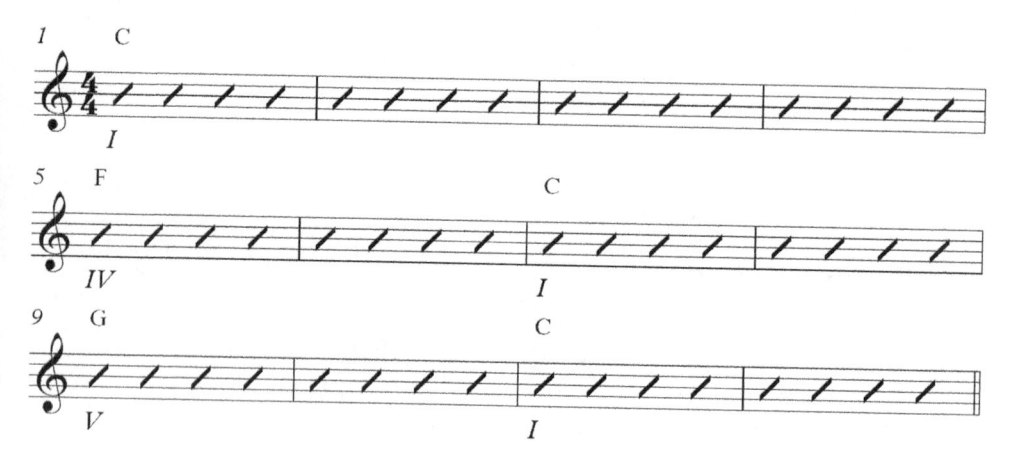

This simple sequence is the basis for countless variations and alterations, and accounts for an enormous proportion of jazz repertoire. It is also by far the most common deviation from the omnipresence of eight- and sixteen-bar periods.

I^7 and IV^7

Within twelve-bar blues and blues-derived material, both jazz and blues musicians often add flattened sevenths to tonic and IV chords, expanding them into dominant chord types rather than the major sevenths native to the key. This I^7 chord is identical in structure to a V chord from the key of IV. The C^7 which appears as a tonic chord in a blues piece is the same chord as the C^7 that appears in the key of F major, with the ninth and thirteenth as optional extensions, and the eleventh typically eschewed:

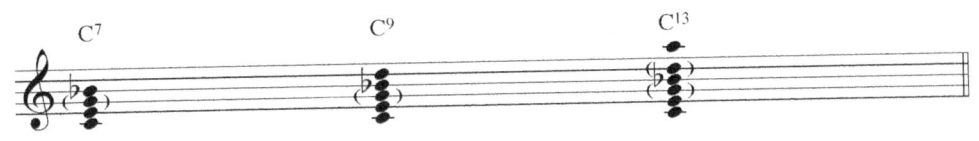

[Musical notation: C⁷, C⁹, C¹³]

The IV⁷ chord (page 70) is particularly likely to include the raised eleventh native to the key signature:

[Musical notation: F⁷, F⁹, F⁷(♯11), F¹³(♯11)]

This inclusion of the flattened seventh in chords I and IV of an ostensibly major key piece is a significant deviation from common practice harmony. In pre-twentieth century styles, the dominant chord was invariably a moment of harmonic tension. It often demanded resolution to a more consonant harmony, preferably a major or minor triad with a root a fourth above/fifth below that of the dominant chord. In fact, this kind of functionality describes every dominant chord to have been so far described.

In the context of what might be called blues harmony, the dominant seventh structure has no such implications, and functions as a static, tonic harmony. This leads us to our first elaboration on the blues:

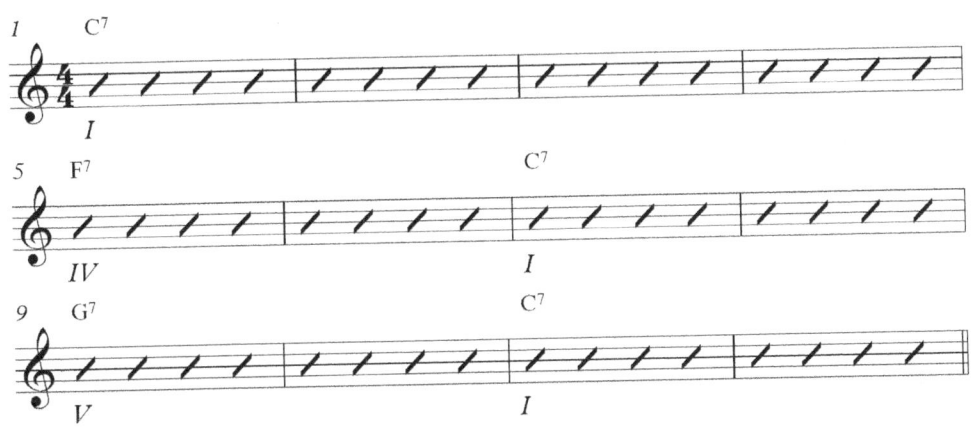

[Musical notation: 12-bar blues progression
Bars 1–4: C⁷ (I)
Bars 5–6: F⁷ (IV); Bars 7–8: C⁷ (I)
Bars 9–10: G⁷ (V); Bars 11–12: C⁷ (I)]

Above, all of the chords in this progression are now dominant-type chords. The distinctive flavour of this harmonic style is reflected in blues melodies, which tend to accent the flattened seventh, rarely referencing the natural sevenths native to both chords I and IV.

Another melodic deviation from common practice is that blues melodies often prominently feature the flattened third of the key, such as E-flat in the key of C, despite the pitch being apparently at odds with the underlying major or dominant chord. This rather intense dissonance suggests another possibility for a blues tonic chord: a dominant seventh sharp nine, which incorporates both the natural and flattened thirds, re-spelling the latter as a raised ninth for clarity:

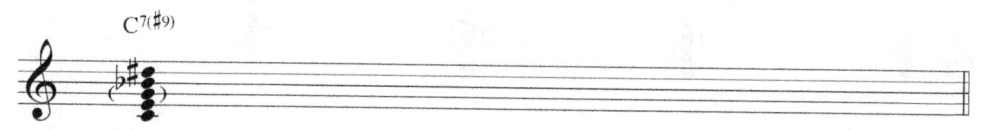

The idiomatic conventions of blues melody are explored further in later sections (page 255).

The Blues in Jazz

Blues music often introduces one or more of the following elaborations to the basic twelve-bar sequence. Chord IV may appear in bar two for one bar; chord IV may appear in bar ten for two bars; chord V may occur in the final bar.

Below, the twelve-bar sequence is presented with these three changes incorporated:

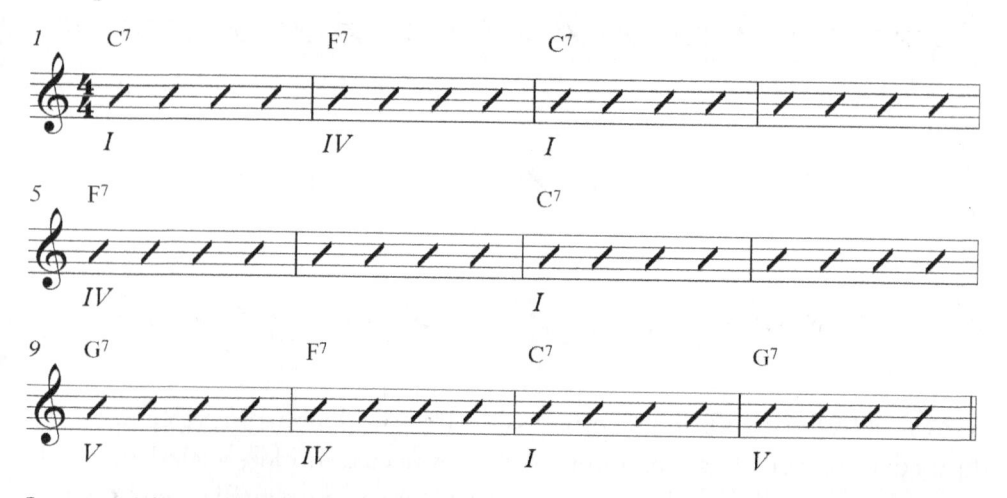

Jazz musicians tend to elaborate further the initial sequence thus: chord IV may appear in the second bar for one bar; a $\sharp IV^{\circ 7}$ chord may appear in bar six, thereby connecting IV to I (page 62); the V chord in bars nine and ten may be replaced with a II-V, which allows the II^{m7}, now in bar nine, to be approach with VI^7, functioning as the V of II (page 69); a II-V may appear in the final bar to cadence back to the beginning of the progression. This gives us the more elaborate twelve-bar blues sequence most typical to jazz practice:

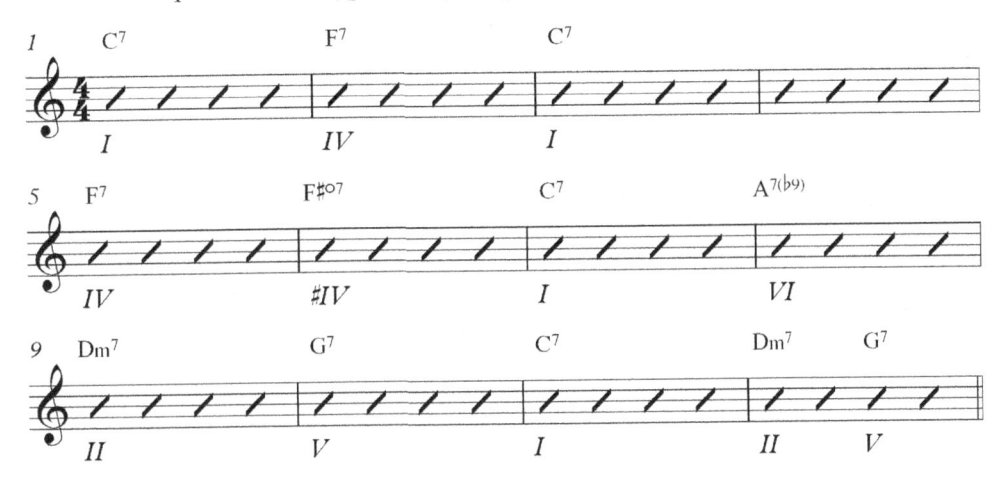

```
1   C7            F7            C7            C7
    I             IV            I

5   F7            F#o7          C7            A7(b9)
    IV            #IV           I             VI

9   Dm7           G7            C7            Dm7    G7
    II            V             I             II     V
```

Like all tonal progressions, jazz musicians are likely to elaborate these chords *ad libitum*. All of the following are common elaborations, and all are chord progressions that have already been described in this book: a #IV^{o7} may appear in chord in bar two to connect IV to I; the II-V from the key of IV may appear in bar four to lead into chord IV; the II^{m7} chord in bar nine may be approached with its own II-V, which may be connected to the I chord in bar seven via IV; the II-V in bar twelve may be approached from VI.

Below is the full twelve-bar blues progression integrating all of ideas. These substitutions are largely compatible and interchangeable with the chords in the previous example, and performers can be expected to interchange them freely:

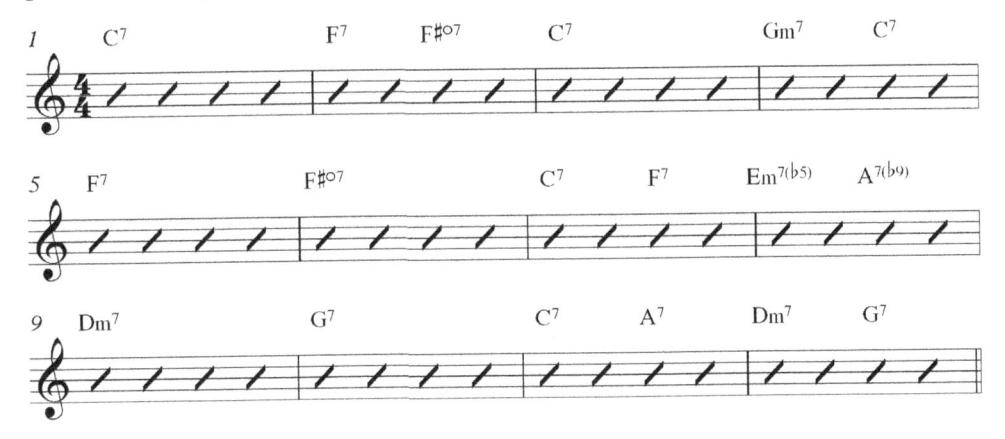

```
1   C7            F7    F#o7    C7            Gm7    C7

5   F7            F#o7          C7     F7     Em7(b5)  A7(b9)

9   Dm7           G7            C7     A7     Dm7    G7
```

The Minor Blues

Despite the peculiarities of their tonic chords, all of the blues forms previously described are more easily understood as relating to the major key rather than the minor. By minorising the tonic and IV chords of a major blues, we produce the following basic minor blues sequence:

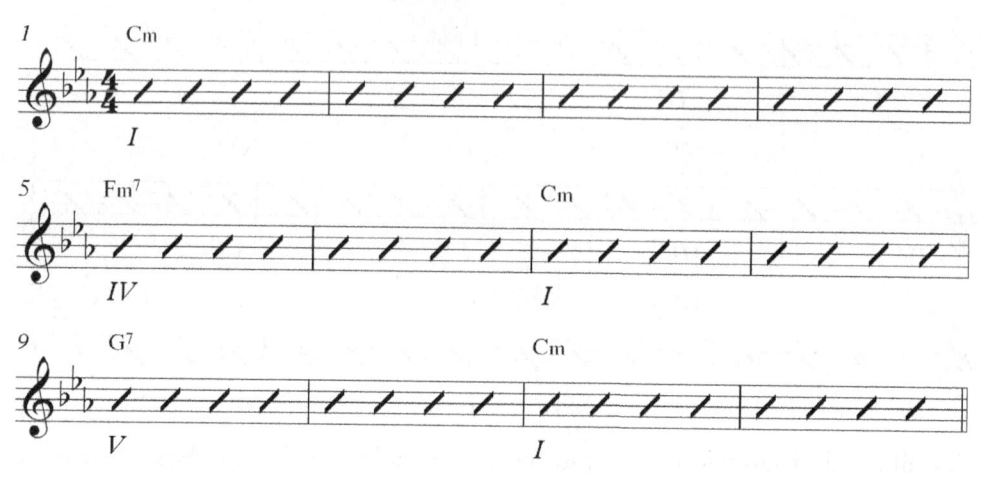

[Musical notation: bars 1–4, Cm (I); bars 5–6 Fm⁷ (IV), bars 7–8 Cm (I); bars 9–10 G⁷ (V), bars 11–12 Cm (I)]

Various substitutions can be expected in a jazz performance, particularly the insertion of chord IV into the second bar, and preceding metrically significant I and IV chords with their respective II-Vs.

Rather than placing chord II into bar nine, most jazz performances use the ♭VI⁷ substitution described previously (page 78). The following is a more typical jazz style interpretation of the minor blues sequence:

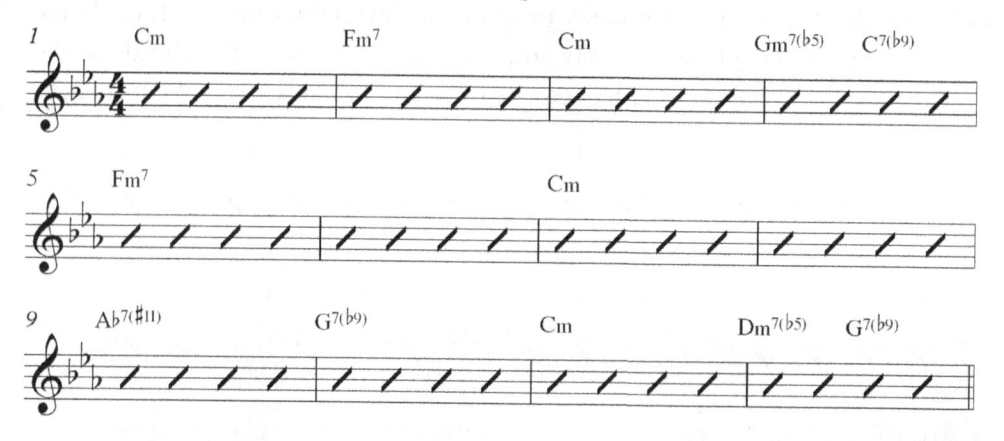

[Musical notation: bar 1 Cm, bar 2 Fm⁷, bar 3 Cm, bar 4 Gm⁷⁽♭⁵⁾ C⁷⁽♭⁹⁾; bar 5 Fm⁷, bars 6–7 Cm; bar 9 A♭⁷⁽♯¹¹⁾, bar 10 G⁷⁽♭⁹⁾, bar 11 Cm, bar 12 Dm⁷⁽♭⁵⁾ G⁷⁽♭⁹⁾]

♭VI⁷ is popular in this context because it supports the bluesy flattened fifth of the key, asterisked, as a melody pitch. A discussion of the blues scale on page 245 explores the implications and usages of this so-called blue note:

[Bar 9:] A♭7(♯11) | G7(♭9) | Cm

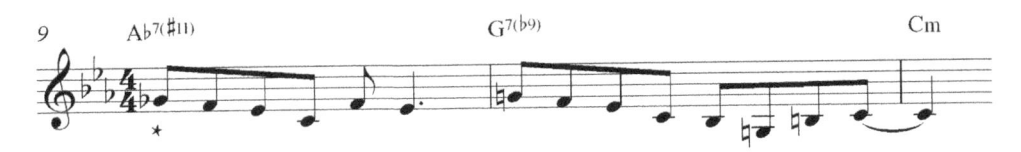

There are many possibilities for elaboration and re-harmonisation. The following is a more detailed interpretation of the minor blues, and elaborates the basic form with chord progressions already described:

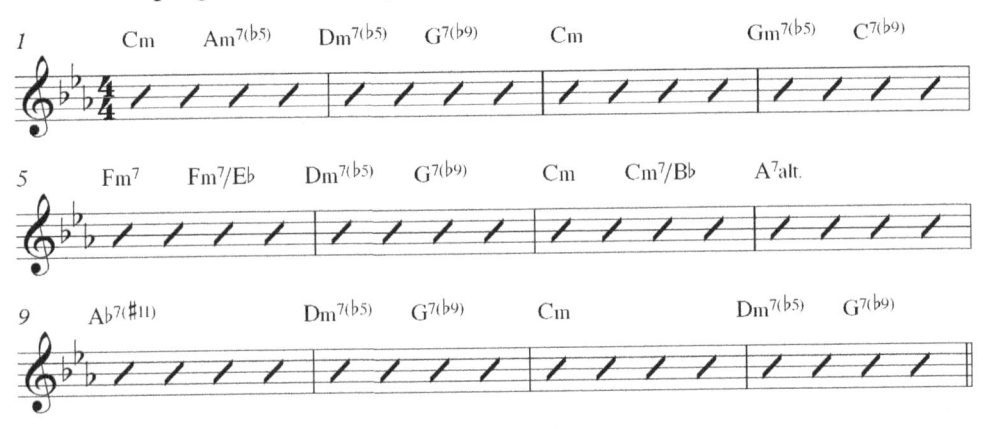

[Bar 1:] Cm Am7(♭5) Dm7(♭5) G7(♭9) | Cm | Gm7(♭5) C7(♭9) |
[Bar 5:] Fm7 Fm7/E♭ | Dm7(♭5) G7(♭9) | Cm Cm7/B♭ | A7alt. |
[Bar 9:] A♭7(♯11) | Dm7(♭5) G7(♭9) | Cm | Dm7(♭5) G7(♭9) |

Not the Twelve-Bar Blues

In addition to the many elaborations available for the basic blues form, a chord sequence might reference the twelve-bar progression in a passage of a different duration. Sixteen- and eight-bar variants such as the following are typical. Here, the II-V cadence is repeated two more times, delaying resolution to the tonic:

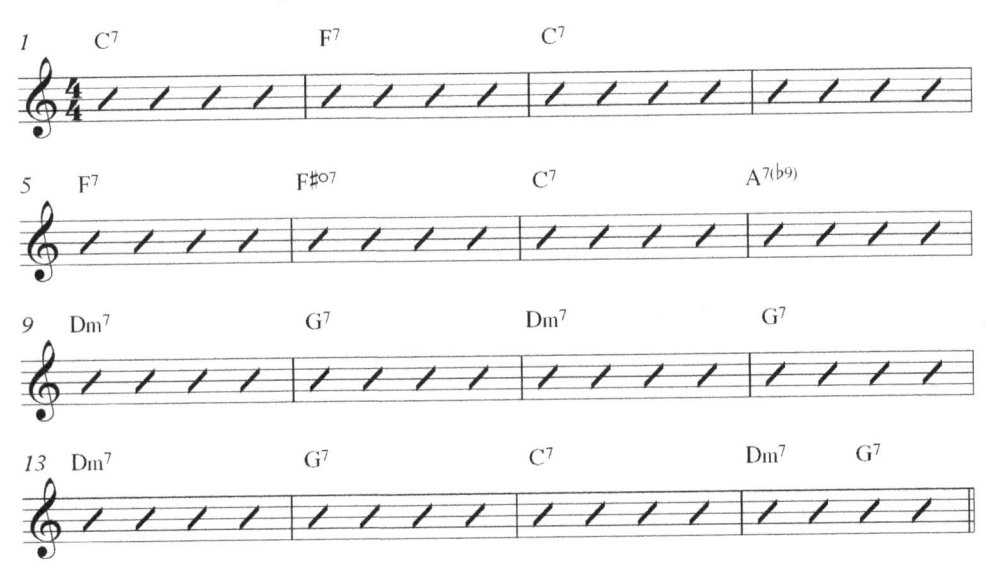

*[Bar 1:] C7 | F7 | C7 | | *
[Bar 5:] F7 | F♯°7 | C7 | A7(♭9) |
[Bar 9:] Dm7 | G7 | Dm7 | G7 |
[Bar 13:] Dm7 | G7 | C7 | Dm7 G7 |

The following eight-bar progression simply omits bars five to eight of the standard progression, whilst still strongly invoking it:

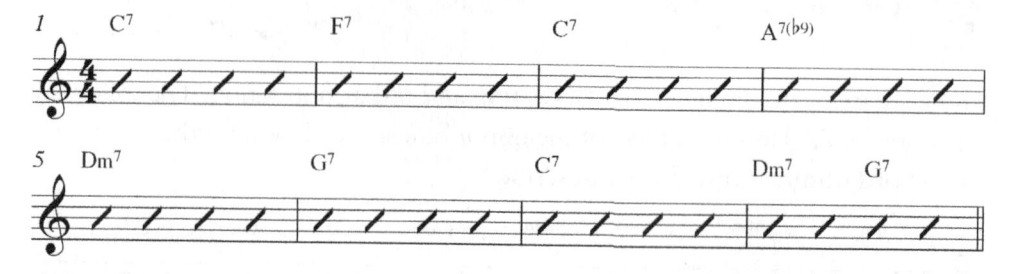

1 C^7	F^7	C^7	A$^{7(\flat 9)}$
5 Dm^7	G^7	C^7	Dm^7 G^7

The mere presence of a I^7 chord may be enough to invoke the blues aesthetic in a sequence that refers only distantly to the twelve-bar progression itself.

The first four bars of the following eight-bar passage consist of a statement and repetition of the first two bars of a C major blues. These are followed by a series of I-V progressions setting up a modulation to IV, which again appears as a seventh chord:

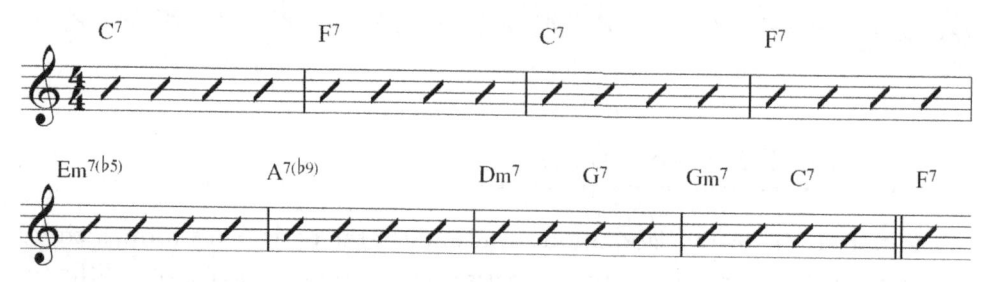

C^7	F^7	C^7	F^7
Em$^{7(\flat 5)}$ A$^{7(\flat 9)}$	Dm^7 G^7	Gm^7 C^7	F^7

The arrival of chord IV in the fifth bar of a passage is highly suggestive of the twelve-bar blues, even if the surrounding material does not particularly comply:

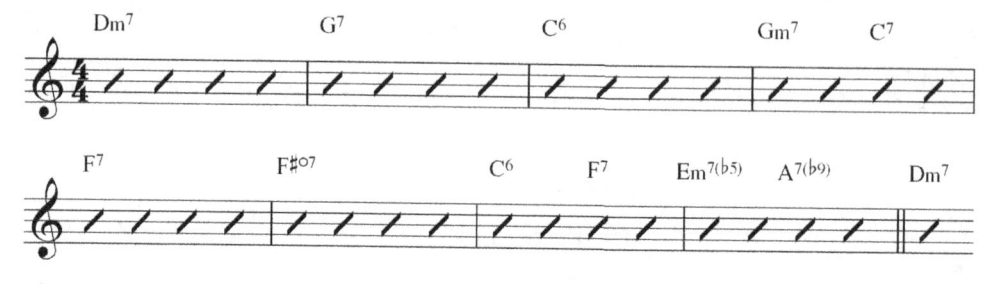

Dm^7	G^7	C^6	Gm^7 C^7
F^7	F$\sharp^{o7}$	C^6 F^7	Em$^{7(\flat 5)}$ A$^{7(\flat 9)}$ Dm^7

The following passage begins on chord IV, but the six bars that follow are so familiar that we wonder if we have not in fact turned up five bars late to a twelve-bar blues:

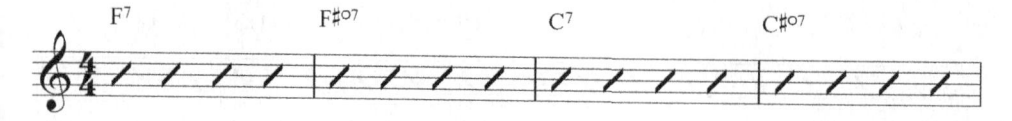

F^7	F$\sharp^{o7}$	C^7	C$\sharp^{o7}$

| Dm7 | G7 | Dm7 | G7 | C6 |

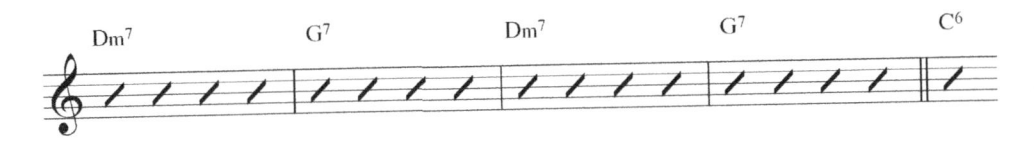

The Altered Blues

The familiarity of the twelve-bar progression makes it a highly fertile subject for chord substitutions. If a twelve-bar sequence has a chord that resembles chord IV in bar five, and chord I in bar eleven, virtually nothing can prevent us from hearing the progression as a blues variant.

A famous example of a heavily altered blues sequence comes from Charlie Parker's *Blues for Alice*, originally in the key of F. This sequence is often called a Parker Blues and begins on the tonic, before cycling around a sequence of II-Vs before arriving at IV in bar five as expected. Next, a backdoor style IV^{m7}-$^{\flat}$VII^{7} initiates a series of chromatically descending II-Vs, before the progression re-aligns with the traditional sequence in bar nine:

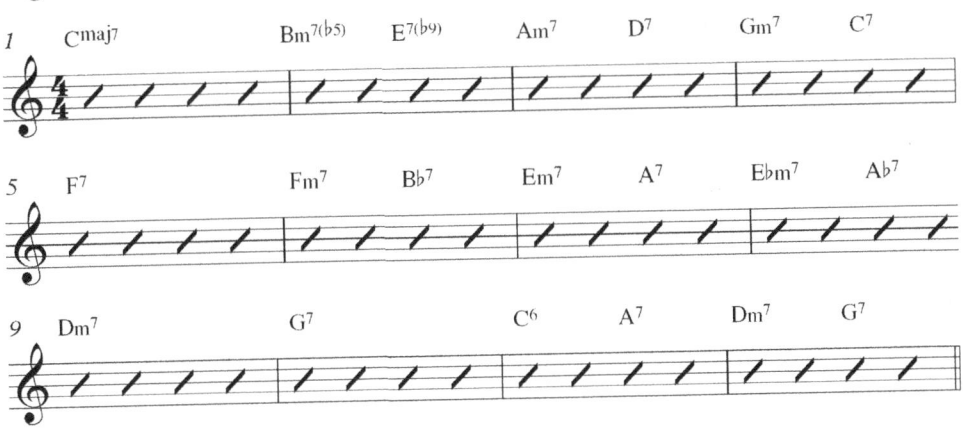

1	Cmaj7		Bm7(b5)	E7(b9)	Am7	D7	Gm7	C7
5	F7		Fm7	Bb7	Em7	A7	Ebm7	Ab7
9	Dm7		G7		C6	A7	Dm7	G7

The next excerpt features an altered blues sequence that ricochets back and forth between C major and the three-flat tonalities of E-flat major and C minor. After beginning in C, the first four bars feature a surprising modulation to the key of $^{\flat}$III major. This allows bar five to feature an F minor seventh in bar five, which functions both as the IV of C, and the II of E-flat.

Bar seven substitutes the tonic for a III^{m7} chord, which, as we have seen previously (page 71), is a close relative of I. Bars nine to twelve are lifted entirely from a standard blues progression in the parallel key of I minor:

Fundamentals of Jazz Composition •

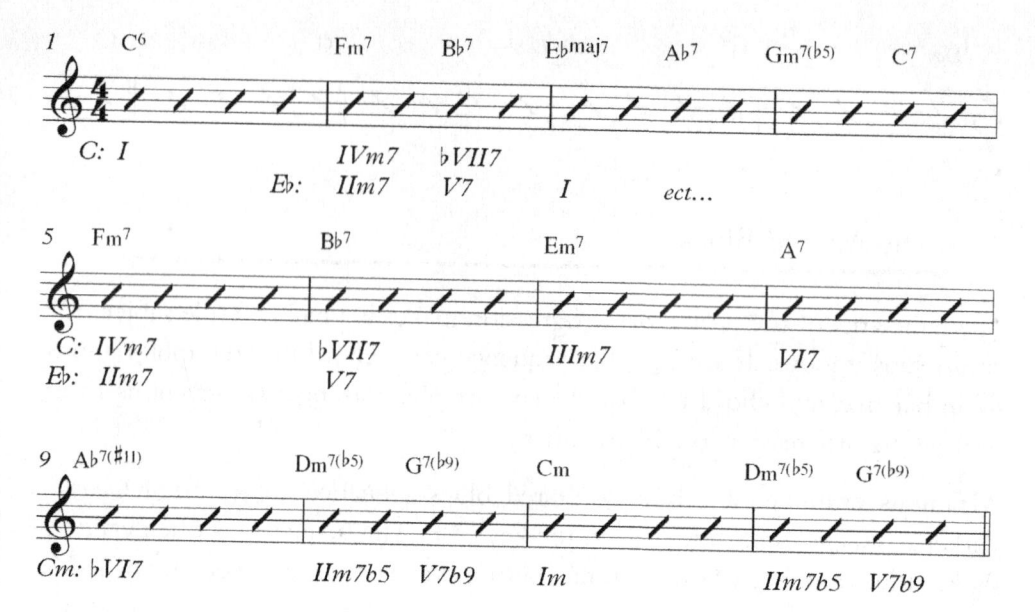

m. 1: C6 | Fm7 B♭7 | E♭maj7 A♭7 | Gm7(♭5) C7
C: I
E♭:   IIm7 V7 — IVm7 ♭VII7 — I   ect...

m. 5: Fm7 | B♭7 | Em7 | A7
C: IVm7
E♭: IIm7 — ♭VII7 / V7 — IIIm7 — VI7

m. 9: A♭7(♯11) | Dm7(♭5) G7(♭9) | Cm | Dm7(♭5) G7(♭9)
Cm: ♭VI7 — IIm7♭5 V7♭9 — Im — IIm7♭5 V7♭9

Chapter Summary

Blues music often uses dominant chord types on chords I and IV.

Blues melodies often highlight the flattened third and flattened seventh of the key.

There are numerous variations on the twelve-bar blues progression, the most significant of which is the minor blues.

The twelve-bar blues progression may be subjected to multiple alterations and substitutions, while still retaining its blues aesthetic.

Interlude I

By this stage, we have examined all of the most typical chord structures and sequences that appear in tonal jazz. Familiarity with all of this harmonic vocabulary is highly recommended, and the ability to recall, recognise, and play these chords and chord progressions in every key is an essential foundation for any jazz musician or composer.

Analysis of existing repertoire is highly recommended at this point, particularly popular jazz compositions and songbook material as played by jazz musicians. Transcriptions of this type of material are readily available in fake books, transcription books, and online, but these transcriptions must always be approached with scepticism. They often contain errors, and actual jazz performances may deviate from them significantly.

Transcribing chord progressions directly from recordings is far preferable, and though it is difficult, accuracy and speed will improve with practice. Perseverance is encouraged, because the ability to aurally interpret chord progressions is a fundamental skill for jazz musicians.

Below is a sample list of popular songbook pieces that are constructed primarily or entirely from the chord progressions already discussed. Lead sheets for these tunes are readily available, as are numerous recordings by great jazz performers.

Because musicians harmonise and re-harmonise constantly in their music, there are alternative chord progressions in use for all of these pieces. There is much to be gained from comparing recordings of these pieces with each other, and with published lead sheets:

All of Me (Marks)

All the Things You Are (Kern)

Alone Together (Schwartz)

Autumn Leaves (Kosma)

Body and Soul (Green)

But Not For Me (Gershwin)

Bye Bye Blackbird (Henderson)

Cherokee (Noble)

Days of Wine and Roses (Mancini)

Have You Met Miss Jones? (Rodgers)

How High The Moon (Lewis)

I Love You (Porter)

I Remember You (Schertzinger)

I'll Remember April (Raye/DePaul)

I'm Old Fashioned (Kern)

If I Should Lose You (Rainger)

If I Were a Bell (Loesser)

It Could Happen to You (Van Heusen)

Just Friends (Klenner)

My Funny Valentine (Rodgers)

My Shining Hour (Arlen)

Night and Day (Porter)

Oh, Lady Be Good (Gershwin)

Stella by Starlight (Young)

What's New? (Haggard)

Yesterdays (Kern)

Performances of jazz compositions tend to deviate a little less from each other in their harmonies, perhaps because for most of them there is an initial, definitive recording from which other musicians learn the piece. For the same reasons, they tend to be performed with more complex and more specific harmonies. In certain cases, even specific chord voicings may be preserved. Here are a few examples of popular jazz compositions that are primarily constructed from the functional harmonies that we have explored:

Blue Bossa (Dorham)

Cheese Cake (Gordon)

Giant Steps (Coltrane)

Good Bait (Dameron)

Jordu (Jordan)

Joy Spring (Brown)

Lazy Bird (Coltrane)

My Little Suede Shoes (Parker)

Satin Doll (Ellington)

Solitude (Ellington)

St. Thomas (Rollins)

Take the 'A' Train (Strayhorn)

Up Jumped Spring (Hubbard)

Yardbird Suite (Parker)

These pieces should be analysed in accordance with the principles so far discussed. We might ask such questions as: in which key is the passage?; does the passage modulate, and, if so, is the new key transient or firmly established?; do all of the chords have clear functionality within the key, or do some have ambiguous or dual function?; do significant harmonies such as I, IV, and II-V align with the implicit hypermeter or subvert it? In what follows, such analyses will be applied to a selection of invented chord sequences.

Example 1

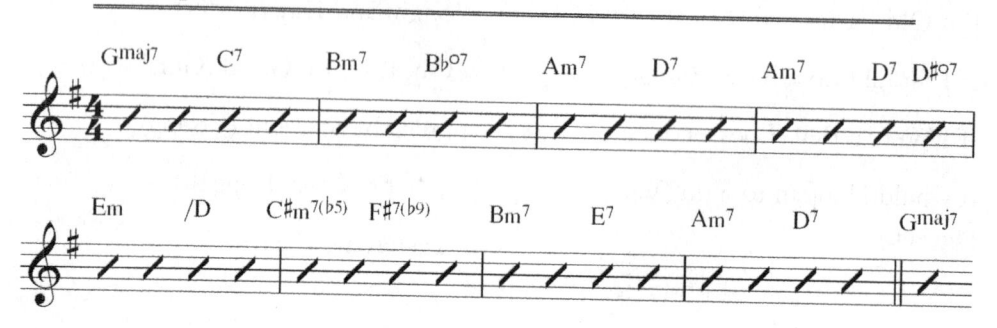

| Gmaj7 | C7 | Bm7 | B♭°7 | Am7 | D7 | Am7 | D7 D♯°7 |

| Em | /D | C♯m7(♭5) | F♯7(♭9) | Bm7 | E7 | Am7 | D7 | Gmaj7 |

This very active excerpt is primarily in the key of G major, but very briefly implies modulations to the closely related tonalities of E minor and B minor.

The passage opens with a tonic chord and cycles through III, and the common tone diminished chord to II. The II-V in bar three is repeated immediately, which delays resolution whilst maintaining the two chord per-bar harmonic rhythm.

A deceptive cadence in bar four takes us to the VI chord, E minor, which is then immediately revealed to be momentarily functioning as chord IV in the key of B minor.

By the time the B minor chord arrives, however, we are already beginning a cycle that takes us home to our initial starting point of a tonic G major chord:

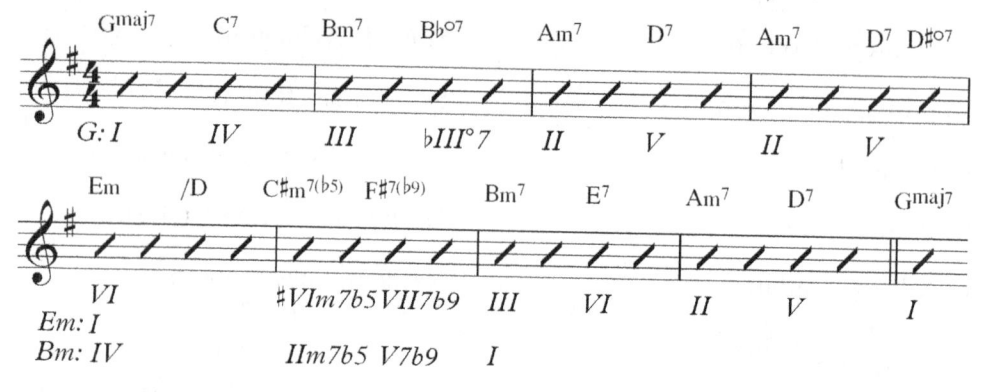

| Gmaj7 | C7 | Bm7 | B♭°7 | Am7 | D7 | Am7 | D7 D♯°7 |

G: I | IV | III | ♭III°7 | II | V | II | V

| Em | /D | C♯m7(♭5) | F♯7(♭9) | Bm7 | E7 | Am7 | D7 | Gmaj7 |

VI | | ♯VIm7♭5 VII7♭9 | III | VI | II | V | I
Em: I
Bm: IV | | IIm7♭5 V7♭9 | I

Example 2

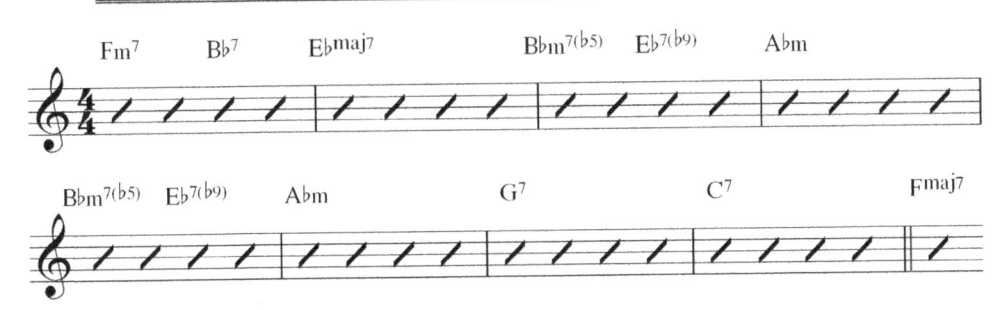

| Fm⁷ | B♭⁷ | E♭maj⁷ | B♭m⁷⁽♭⁵⁾ E♭⁷⁽♭⁹⁾ | A♭m |

| B♭m⁷⁽♭⁵⁾ E♭⁷⁽♭⁹⁾ | A♭m | G⁷ | C⁷ | Fmaj⁷ |

This passage is a little less conventional due to the modulations involved, but the lack of pivot chords make it slightly less ambiguous. A cadence into E-flat major is followed immediately by a swerve into A-flat minor. Though a rather distant tonality in terms of key signature, this could be thought of as the key of IV relative to the parallel minor. A-flat minor is closely related to E-flat minor, which in turn is closely related to E-flat major.

This A-flat minor tonality is reasserted in bars five and six, but then instantly abandoned as we modulate again, this time to a distant F major. The II chord from the key of F appears here as G⁷, the V of V, rather than G^{m7}, which ensures that it shares a pitch of B/C-flat with the preceding A-flat minor chord.

If we had moved from A-flat minor directly to G^{m7}, no pivot note would have been present, and the transition might have been a little more jarring:

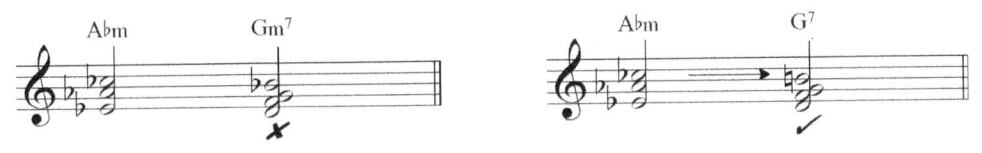

| A♭m | Gm⁷ | | A♭m | G⁷ |

This chord sequence modulates too frequently for us to discern any prevailing key, and is therefore notated without a key signature:

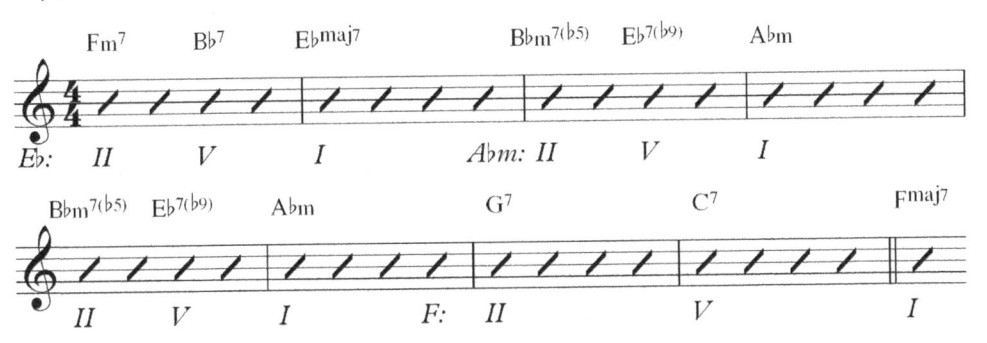

| Fm⁷ | B♭⁷ | E♭maj⁷ | B♭m⁷⁽♭⁵⁾ E♭⁷⁽♭⁹⁾ | A♭m |
E♭: II   V   I   A♭m: II   V   I

| B♭m⁷⁽♭⁵⁾ E♭⁷⁽♭⁹⁾ | A♭m | G⁷ | C⁷ | Fmaj⁷ |
   II   V   I   F: II   V   I

Example 3

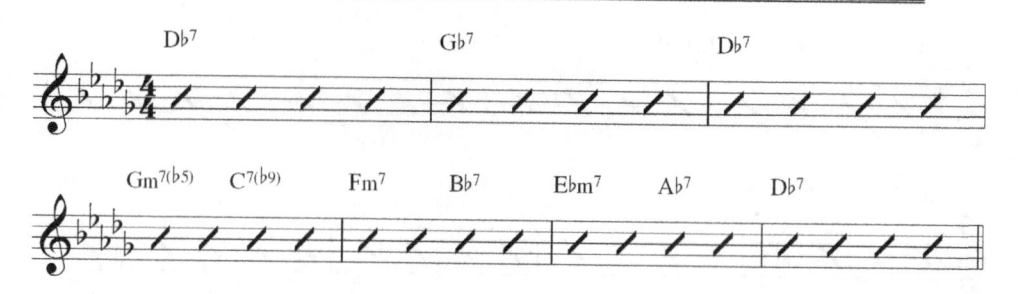

[Musical notation: Db7 | Gb7 | Db7 |]
[Gm7(b5) C7(b9) | Fm7 Bb7 | Ebm7 Ab7 | Db7 |]

The opening I^7 chord of this passage suggests the blues, a position further reinforced by the first three bars referring directly to the twelve-bar progression. The blues is quickly interrupted in favour of an asymmetrical cycle of II-Vs, which lands unexpectedly back at the tonic in bar seven.

This passage could become either a four-bar phrase followed by a three-bar phrase, or the inverse, depending on melody and rhythm section interpretation.

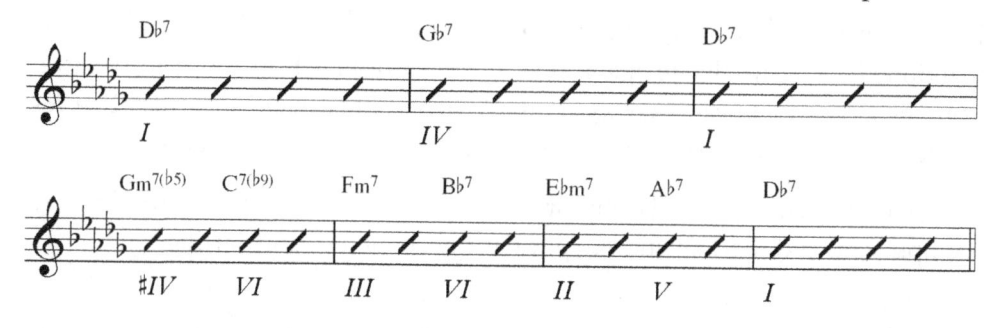

[Musical notation: Db7 | Gb7 | Db7 |]
[I   IV   I]
[Gm7(b5) C7(b9) | Fm7 Bb7 | Ebm7 Ab7 | Db7 |]
[#IV   VI   III VI   II   V   I]

Example 4

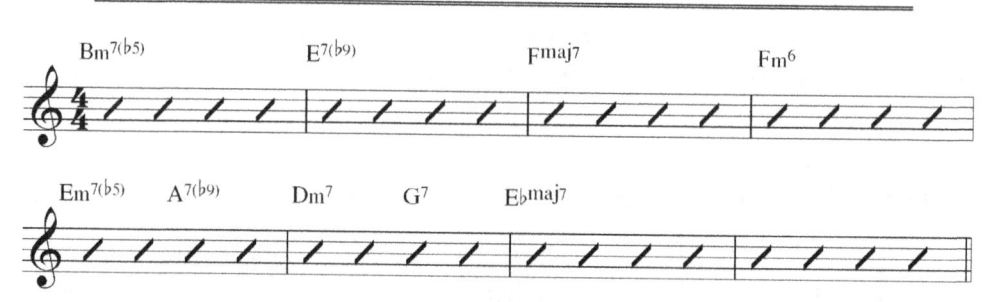

[Musical notation: Bm7(b5) | E7(b9) | Fmaj7 | Fm6 |]
[Em7(b5) A7(b9) | Dm7 G7 | Ebmaj7 |]

This chord progression makes use of unexpected cadences. The first two bars are a II-V from the key of A minor, but the V chord unexpectedly resolves up a half step to F major, rather than up a fourth to its I. This cadence suggests the key of C (page 60). The movement to F minor confirms our suspicions of a C major tonic, as do bars five and six, which appear to outline III-VI-II-V in C.

The cadence is again frustrated by a surprising shift in bar seven to a ♭III major chord. Though ostensibly an unrelated harmony to the C major that we expected, this could be analysed as a substitute for a substitute, the relative major to the parallel minor. If the tonic is C, then the parallel minor is C minor, and the relative major of that is E-flat major:

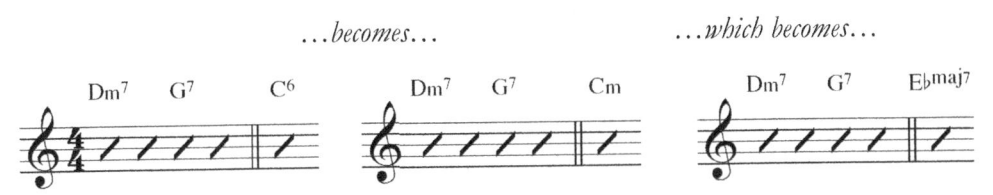

...becomes...   *...which becomes...*

| Dm⁷ G⁷ C⁶ | Dm⁷ G⁷ Cm | Dm⁷ G⁷ E♭maj7 |

Here's the whole sequence again, with Roman numeral analysis:

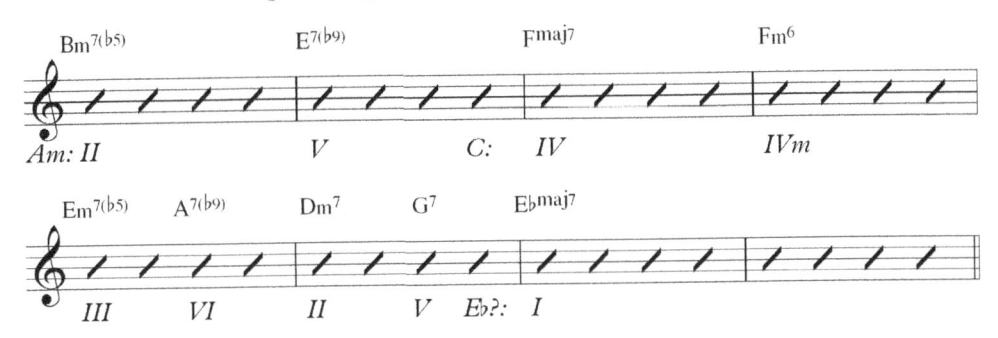

| Bm⁷⁽♭⁵⁾ | E⁷⁽♭⁹⁾ | Fmaj7 | Fm⁶ |
| Am: II | V | C: IV | IVm |

| Em⁷⁽♭⁵⁾ A⁷⁽♭⁹⁾ | Dm⁷ G⁷ | E♭maj7 | |
| III VI | II V | E♭?: I | |

Chapter 8
Melody and Song

In a certain sense, we must consider melody to be the most important element of music. The tune is often the most memorable part of a piece, and melody is, by definition, the salient component in its musical texture. We even define what constitutes a composition by its melody. Two performances might employ different orchestration, arrangement, and harmony, but if they use the same melody, we understand them to be different interpretations of the same piece.

Despite this, questions of what makes a good melody and how we might go about writing one remain difficult to answer. Successful tunes may have wildly different characteristics from one another; there are very simple melodies and very complex ones, melodies with many notes and others with very few, melodies with a great deal of repetition and others with very little.

Let us take for granted that the model of melody is song, music that is designed for performance by the human voice. Many of our favourite melodies are literally intended for performance by the human voice, but those that are not often sound lyrical and songlike anyway. It is no accident that a songbook forms so much of the backbone of language and repertoire of instrumental jazz.

Despite immense diversity, song melodies do tend to have certain attributes in common, many of which are related to the practicalities of performance by the human voice.

Tunes that adhere to all of these conventions all of the time may run the risk of being predicable or uninteresting, but most song-like melodies follow *most* of these guidelines *most* of the time. Song melodies generally have the following characteristics:

They are Divided into Phrases

Melodies consist of discrete phrases that last no more than a few seconds, and are separated by rests. Notice how quickly a long phrase begins to sound unmelodic when there are no rests:

[musical notation: phrase 1 continuing with ...!]

In song, this is a highly practical convention inspired by the limits of human lung capacity, but performed on any instrument, a melody without rests will quickly begin to sound wrong. The phrase *please take a breath* can be applied here, regardless of the instrument that is actually playing the melody.

Fortunately, this problem is very easily solved by omitting a few notes, thereby dividing the line into two distinct phrases. Note that the location of the 'breath' in the following example reinforces the hypermeter, as the second phrase now begins in the second strongest position of the passage:

[musical notation: phrase 1 ... rest / phrase 2]

They are Tonal

The pitches within a melodic phrase will typically imply a key and adhere to a single key signature. The first phrase of a song often accentuates pitches from the tonic triad, and the last pitch of a song is usually the tonic.

Pitches from outside the key signature tend only to appear in contexts where they do not undermine the sense of key. One such situation is when a chromatic passing note approaches a note in the key signature from a half step away, most typically from below, as in the following examples:

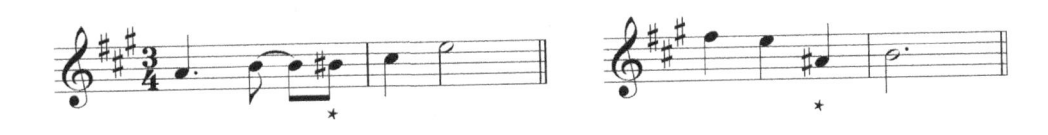

*[musical notation examples marked with *]*

Chromatic notes may connect two tones native to the key signature, either in descent or ascent:

a) descending chromatic passing note *b) ascending chromatic passing note*

Chapter 9 explores the integration of non-diatonic pitches in tonal melodies, and Chapter 10 presents a detailed discussion of how we might analyse a melody in order to write a tonal chord progression to accompany it.

They Repeat Themselves

In jazz, composed melodies are generally heard more than once in a performance, but even when they are not, they invariably include material that is repeated, either verbatim or with variation. The first five notes in this eight-bar melody are repeated four bars later:

Repeated material may be altered or disguised in some way, whether by changes in pitch content, rhythm, or both. Here, the opening phrase is repeated with variation at the start of the second line:

Like any technique, repetition must be carefully balanced: too much and our melodies may be too predictable, too little and it may sound unfocused and unintentional. Chapter 11 explores the relationships between the melodic phrases in a piece.

They Favour Smaller Intervals

As it is relatively difficult to sing wide intervallic leaps accurately, song melodies tend to move by steps or half-steps to the scale notes immediately above or below, and in thirds more frequently than in larger intervals.

Variety is necessary to create an interesting and memorable line, and in many cases, large leaps are the most interesting moments in a melody, but they should be used sparingly. The following melodies have identical rhythm and contour:

a) large intervals   *b) small intervals*

Despite the structural similarities, the melody at *(b)* is more songlike due its use of smaller, more lyrical intervals.

Broadly speaking, the smaller the interval, the more frequently it appears in song melodies. Fourths and fifths are more frequent than sixths and sevenths; seconds and thirds more frequent still, though there are exceptions to this rule.

Octaves in ascent or descent are more common than sevenths, and flattened fifths (or raised fourths) are less frequent than fifths or sixths. This is likely due to the ease of octaves to sing because of their consonance. Likewise, raised fourths/flattened fifths are more difficult due to their dissonance.

They are Limited in Range

Most untrained singers have a vocal range of one and a half to two octaves, and a far smaller comfortable range. Song melodies tend to respect this, usually not exceeding a ninth or tenth from the highest note to the lowest within a single piece.

A consequence of this is that consecutive upward leaps are likely to be followed by a change of direction, and vice versa, as to continue on the same trajectory would quickly take a melody out of normal vocal range.

These are the approximate characteristics of song melodies, but not all songs follow all of these all the time. Many of the most interesting examples break one or more of these rules at some point. The more of these guidelines we violate, the less song-like our melodies will be and, arguably, the less melodic.

Chapter Summary

Song may be considered to be the model of melody; song-like melodies are usually the most melodic.

Songlike melodies are typically divided into short phrases of sing-able length.

Songlike melodies typically have tonal implications which imply a harmonic accompaniment that resolves to a major or minor tonic.

Songlike melodies tend to derive coherency and continuity from the repetition of material.

Songlike melodies move to the next pitch in a smaller, more sing-able interval more frequently than they do in a large one. The frequency of a given melodic interval is roughly inversely proportional to the size of the interval.

Songlike melodies generally comply with the comfortable range of an untrained singer, with many not exceeding a twelfth from lowest pitch to highest.

Chapter 9
Chord Tones and Non-chord Tones

The preeminent texture of jazz and popular music is homophony, in which a single, dynamic melody line is accompanied by a succession of static chords. In a homophonic context, the pitches of a melody have varying degrees of consonance and dissonance in relation to the harmonic accompaniment, and the effect of these consonances and dissonances will vary according to the rhythmic context.

For the jazz composer, understanding these relationships is a key skill. It enables us to write chord progressions that support melodies, and melodies that fit over existing chord progressions. These tasks may be performed intuitively, but by analysing and categorising the interactions between melody and harmony we can obtain a far better understanding of how to manipulate these elements.

Chord Tones and Sevenths

A melody note that is part of the background chord is a chord tone, and is inherently consonant because it is in full agreement with its accompaniment. There are three available consonant melody notes over a given triad: the root, the third, and the fifth. Each of these has its own distinct character:

Melody note is the root of the chord: As a melody note, the root of a chord has complete stability and consonance. Many songs finish on the tonic chord with the melody on the root for a sense of total resolution:

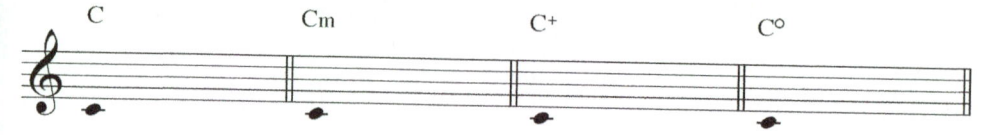

Melody note is the third of the chord: The third could be thought of as the character note of a triad, which tells us the major or minor quality of the chord, and produces a consonant major or minor third in relation to either the root or the fifth of the background harmony:

Melody note is the fifth of the chord: On major and minor triads, the fifth is related to the root by the simple ratio of 3:2, which makes it a highly consonant melody note, but also rather uninteresting. On chords with flattened or raised fifths the stability is reduced, but since there is no perfect fifth present in the chord, they still have no particular instability, and they do not demand resolution:

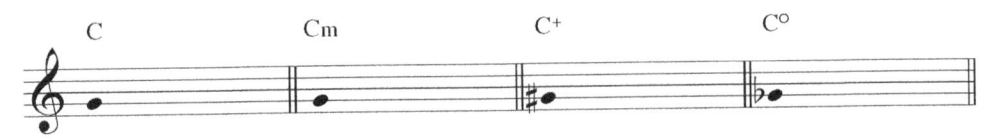

These are the normal tonal qualities of chord tones in common practice music, where the prevailing harmonic unit is the triad and most chords are either major or minor triads. Despite the fact that jazz practitioners tend to embellish accompanying chords with extensions, the three triadic chord tones remain the most stable options for melody notes in jazz. They are generally the most frequent, sustained, and rhythmically emphasised pitches of a melody in any style.

In common practice music, the flattened seventh is also available as a melody note over any dominant or minor seventh chord with, one inflexible condition: it must resolve downward into a chord tone. In a typical V-I cadence, this means that the seventh of the V chord will resolve down into the third of the I chord, as in the following examples:

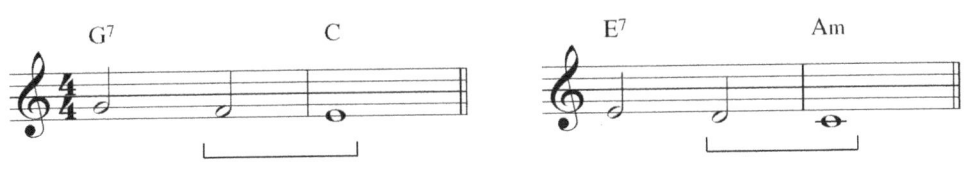

The flattened seventh of a II chord within a II-V progression functions in the same way, such that it typically resolves downward. The following example shows this movement taking place over II-V progressions in C major and A minor:

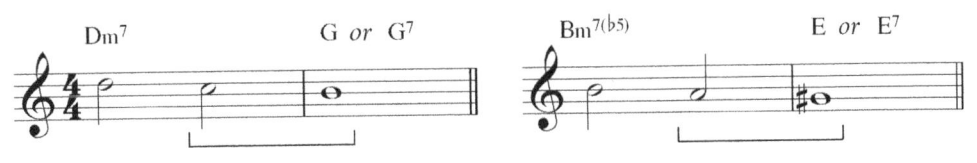

Though this tendency is not so strictly followed in jazz as it is in common practice music, stepwise downward resolution remains the normal role of the seventh in music where song-like melodies are combined with functional harmonies. Here are two fragments of melody in which sevenths resolve downward into chord tones:

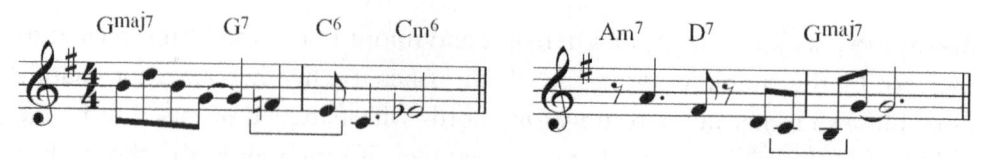

Three available stable pitches and a downwardly active seventh would be an extremely limiting palette for melody writing, though passages can be produced where the effect is not too disjointed or uninteresting:

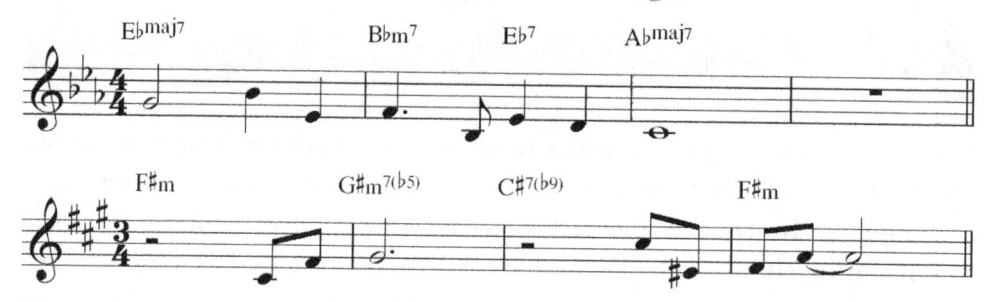

In order to increase our options, we must utilise non-chord tones in our melodies. Such pitches are inherently more dissonant than roots, thirds, and fifths, and are also less stable in the sense that they tend to suggest movement to the stability of a nearby chord tone.

In order to prevent disparity between melody and accompanying harmony, non-chord tones often appear as part of one of a number of conventional patterns.

Passing Tones

A non-chord tone may appear as a passing tone in a melodic line that ascends or descends in chromatic or diatonic steps, connecting one chord tone to another. In the following fragments, all of the non-chord tones function in this way, and the momentary dissonances that they produce are acceptable in their role as a bridge between two consonances:

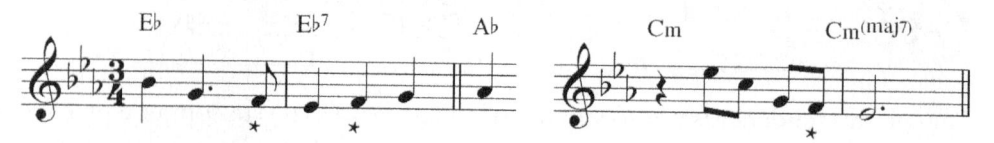

• Chapter 9: Chord Tones and Non-chord Tones

Passing tones are usually native to the key from which the current chord is drawn. The following chord sequence in the key of C begins with movement from chord I to IV via a II-V from the key of IV. This is followed by movement back again via the backdoor II-V with chords borrowed from the key of $^\flat$III.

Any diatonic non-chord tones occurring in the second or fourth bar of the passage below should be understood in relation to other keys. Bar two must use chord tones from G^{m7} and C^7, and non-chord tones from the key of F major, whilst bar four must use chord tones from F^{m7} and $B^{\flat 7}$, and non-chord tones from the key of E-flat major.

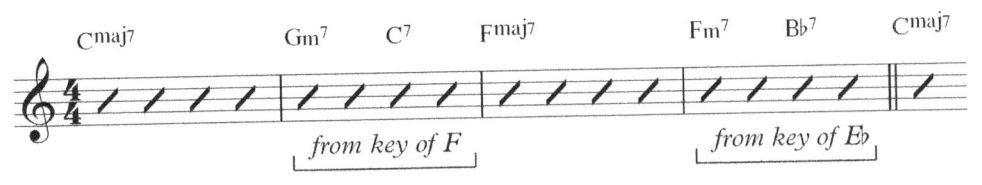

Below, a melody over the same sequence which utilises passing tones from the key of F in bar two, and the key of E-flat in bar four. All non-chord passing tones are marked with asterisks:

As we saw during our discussion of melody and song (page 111), melodies move from pitch to pitch in smaller intervals more frequently than they do in large intervals. Passing tones make scalic motion possible over static chords, and are therefore indispensable in tonal melody writing.

A line may pass stepwise through two or more non-chord tones on its way to the next consonant pitch, forming a chain of consecutive passing tones:

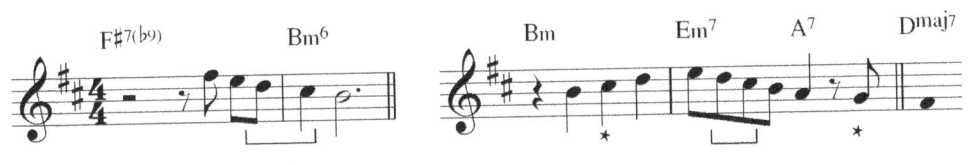

Passing tones may connect chord tones with chromatic rather than diatonic pitches:

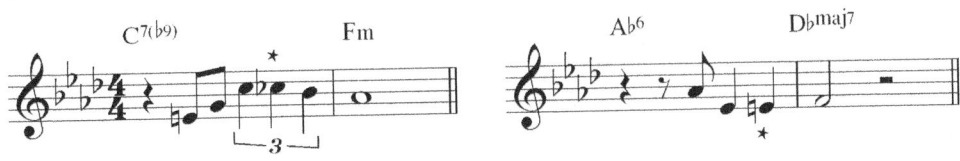

We may percieve highly chromatic phrases as consecutive passing tones. Though quite common in improvised jazz, such melodies are markedly un-songlike:

Whether chromatic or native to the key, passing tones are not particularly disruptive to the consonance of a passage because they are de-emphasised by their transience. As listeners, we intuitively understand them to be the journey between two harmonic landmarks rather than destinations in themselves.

Anticipation

An anticipated chord tone arrives before the chord to which it belongs. Anticipation by an eighth note, wherein a chord tone arrives an eighth note before the chord to which it belongs, is a very typical feature of swing-time jazz and is extremely common in all styles:

Any phrase that ends on the final eighth note of a chord's duration will be perceived as belonging to the following chord, even if that pitch does not continue into the new harmonic area. This essential idiomatic effect marks an important exception to the expected behaviours of chord tones. The anticipated pitch in each of the preceding melodies may be cut short and still maintain its sense of belonging to the following chord: F-sharp still sounds like the fifth of $B^{7\flat 9}$, and B natural still sounds like the third of G^{maj7}, even if neither pitch is actually voiced over the chord to which it belongs:

By extension, any phrase ending on the final eighth note of a chord will sound dissonant if it is not consonant with incoming harmony. We hear the pitch in relation to the following chord:

• Chapter 9: Chord Tones and Non-chord Tones

[musical example: Fm7 Bb7 Ebmaj7 | G7 Cm6]

This can be simply rectified by resolving the line onto a chord tone. Because the F in the second example below is unresolved, we perceive the subsequent E-flat as a continuation of the same phrase, despite the quarter note rest that separates the two pitches:

[musical example: Fm7 Bb7 Ebmaj7 | G7 Cm6]

Anticipation of a new harmony may also take place a quarter note before the new harmony, but any pitch anticipated by more than that risks being perceived as belonging to the current chord rather than the following one.

Below, we see two versions of the same fragment of melody. In *(a)*, the target pitch arrives a dotted quarter note before the chord that it anticipates, leading to an extended harmonic disagreement between the pitch of A and the underlying E^{7b9} harmony. If, instead, we anticipate by only a quarter note, as in *(b)*, the A is more readily percieved as belonging to the following chord.

(a) the target pitch arrives prematurely *(b) the target pitch is percieved as anticipation*

[musical examples: Bm7(b5) E7(b9) Am | Bm7(b5) E7(b9) Am]

The perceived function of a pitch is subjective, and may be affected by tempo, instrumentation, and style.

Suspension and Retardation

A suspension is a temporary dissonance caused by a chord tone that carries over into the next chord, before resolving downwards by step into a chord tone of the new harmony.

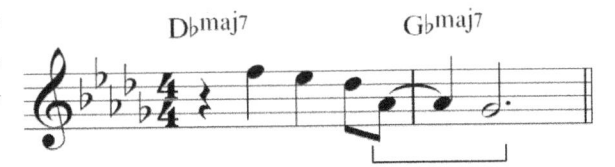

[musical example: Dbmaj7 Gbmaj7]

In the above example, the A-flat, a chord tone of the D^{bmaj7}, is sustained into the G^{bmaj7} of which it is not a chord tone before resolving downwards to the chord tone of G-flat.

We could think of this effect as the opposite of anticipation. Whereas an anticipated pitch is one that arrives too early, a suspended pitch is one that hangs on too late. The resolution of a suspension acts as a musical apology for a wrong note by justifying the dissonance of the preceding pitch. For this to work, that resolution must be by stepwise movement:

(a) suspension unresolved *(b) suspension resolved by a leap*

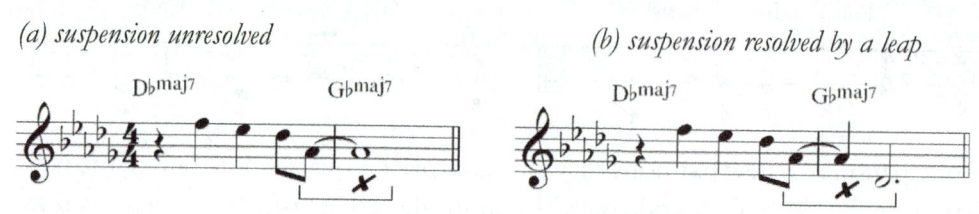

The power of the suspension to excuse dissonance is demonstrated in the following four versions of the same melody, in which a suspended D is resolved progressively later and later. Without the context of the preceding bar, and of the resolution to the chord tone of C-sharp, this pitch would be extremely conspicuous:

Suspensions are most effective when they resolve by a half step because pitches a half step above a chord tone of the prevailing chord are inherently more dissonant. Compare the strong resolution of a highly dissonant suspended F resolving into the third of a C^{bmaj7} with the weaker resolution of a suspended F-sharp:

A suspension resolving upward is traditionally called a retardation, though since the application of this effect is more or less identical, such a distinction barely seems necessary. As with suspensions, retarded pitches are resolved most effectively by half step, as in the examples below:

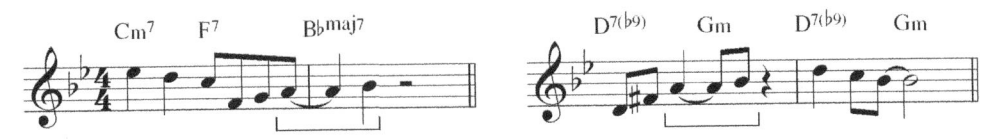

Neighbour Tones

A melody may move from a chord tone to a non-chord tone by step, and then return to it, a movement called a neighbour tone. The following passages contain examples of both upper neighbour tones, which step above their starting chord tone before returning downwards, and lower neighbouring tones, which do the inverse:

Because we begin and end in the same place, the intervening material might be omitted with minimal impact on the overall contour of the line or its harmonic relationship to the underlying chords.

Neighbour tones might be strictly diatonic, but chromatic neighbour tones are also available. Those a half step below chord tones are particularly typical of jazz lines:

Neighbour tones may also appear in pairs, approaching a chord tone with non-chord tones from above and then below, or the inverse. These can be thought of as double neighbour tones, but jazz musicians call these kinds of patterns enclosures.

In the first melody fragment below, chord tones are elaborated with double neighbour tones from above and then below. In the second, the double neighbour tone approaches from below and then above:

A non-chord tone that resolves into a chord tone by step or half step can be thought of as an incomplete neighbour tone in which the initial chord tone is absent. The second example below features an incomplete double neighbour tone, and is a very typical jazz enclosure:

Rhythm

Meter and hypermeter must always be considered in our handling of non-consonant melody notes. As we have seen in our discussion of chord progressions, musical events at the beginning of a phrase, bar, or beat are inherently emphasised relative to pitches at less significant moments.

Passing tones, neighbour tones, and any of the other preceding types of non-harmonic tones are, in effect, more dissonant when they take place at moments of metric emphasis.

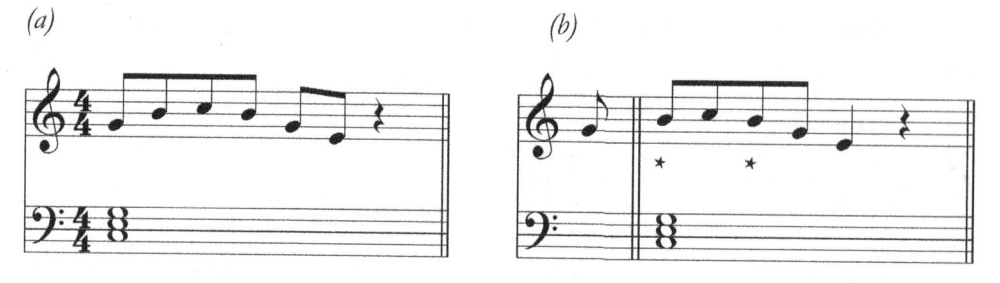

(a) *(b)*

Both of the above passages feature the same sequence of pitches, with the same rhythmic values, over the same harmony. The only difference is that that in *(b)*, the line begins an eighth note later. This has major harmonic implications: whereas *(a)* places chord tones at the beginning of each beat, *(b)* highlights an asterisked non-chord tone on both the first and second beats of the bar. This emphasis on the seventh of the chord renders the passage significantly more dissonant.

Below is another example of how rhythmic emphasis can alter the harmonic implications of a phrase:

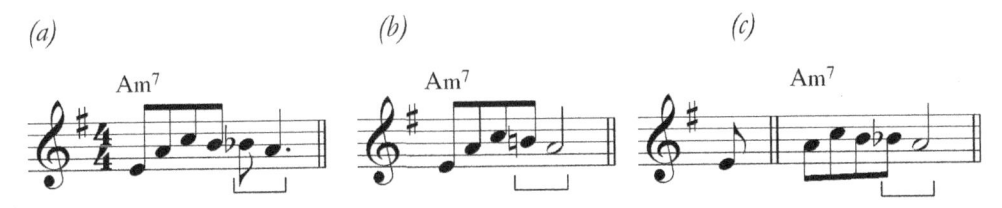

(a)   *(b)*   *(c)*

In *(a)*, B-flat appears in a melody as a chromatic passing tone. Because of its introduction on the metrically emphasised mid-point of the bar, a great deal of attention is brought to the disparity between the melody note and its underlying harmony; the meter emphasises the dissonance.

A more consonant effect might be achieved by omitting this pitch, as in *(b)*, thereby arriving at the target chord tone on the beat.

Alternatively, by beginning the entirety of phrase *(a)* an eighth earlier, as in *(c)*, the same passing B-flat is placed in a deemphasised position relative to the following chord tone, and is thereby rendered more tolerable.

Extensions

In our explorations of chord progressions, we have seen that in most jazz styles, every chord will include either a sixth or seventh, with ninths, elevenths, thirteenths, and their alterations being freely included according to the performer's interpretation. What applies to chord voicings applies also to melodies, and any pitch that might be included in an accompanying chord voicing could also be featured as a melody note.

In the example to the left, a melody appears to resolve to a non-chord tone over an E-flat major triad. A jazz musician would probably identify this as an $E^{\flat 6}$ chord, requiring no further explanation or resolution.

123

In more harmonically conservative styles, such as common practice music and most popular music, the preceding melody fragment might be heard as dissonant, with the C natural as an unresolved passing tone. This demands further downward movement to B-flat in order for the phrase to properly resolve.

That such extensions do not necessarily require resolution is a defining feature of jazz melodies. A melody may resolve to a non-chord tone, and in such circumstances, it makes sense for us to think of these pitches as chord tones of an extended chord. Consequently, extensions may be treated as chord tones in the application of any of the devices found in this chapter.

The resolution of a melody to an extension produces a less consonant effect than to the root, third, or fifth of a chord. Melodies that highlight extensions in this way can be characterised as more abstract and less grounded with regard to the background harmony.

When a non-triadic pitch is highlighted as a melody note, it can be useful to reflect it in the chord symbol that is provided for performers. This enables chordal accompanists like guitars and pianos to support the melody, either by playing a voicing with that pitch on top, or by avoiding voicings that would clash with that pitch.

What constitutes a melody note functioning as an extension rather than a non-chord tone is ultimately subjective, but obvious culprits include those that end phrases:

According to the conventions regarding anticipated notes (page 118), the B-flat that ends this first phrase above belongs to the following chord. Because no chord tone appears to resolve it, B-flat is sustained in our mind's ear, suggesting an A^{bmaj9} sonority.

Below, a diagram shows how the use of the E^{b13} chord symbol rather than the usual E^{b7} might improve a performance of the fragment above. In *(a)*, the pianist plays an E^{b7} chord with a D-flat at the top of the voicing. This is a half step above the melody pitch of C, and produces an undesirable clash. The pianist in *(b)* has been provided with a more specific E$^{♭13}$ chord symbol, encouraging them to play a voicing with a C at the top, which supports the melody far appropriately:

(a)

(b)

For the same reason, any pitch that is held for a significant portion of a chord's duration should also be reflected in that chord symbol, even if functioning according to the conventions of non-chord tones:

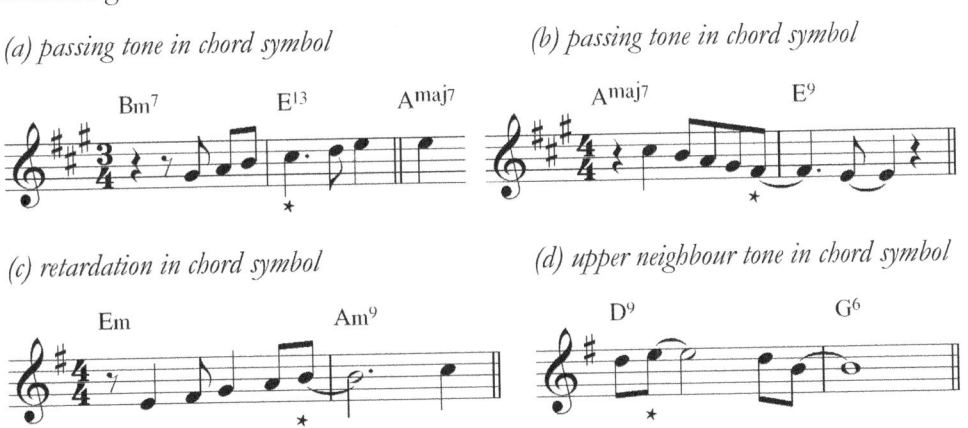

(a) passing tone in chord symbol

(b) passing tone in chord symbol

(c) retardation in chord symbol

(d) upper neighbour tone in chord symbol

Ultimately, there are no concrete rules to guide the inclusion of unaltered ninths, elevenths, and thirteenths in chord symbols. We must use our own discretion to provide enough information for performers without crowding the page with redundant details.

A large portion of our task as composers is to write melodies and chord progressions and to manage the interactions between them. We need not deliberately analyse the function of every pitch in our melodies, but having the tools to understand these relationships gives us the freedom to manipulate melody and harmony effectively and expressively.

Chapter Summary

The root, third, or fifth of the prevailing chord are the most conventional options for a sustained melody note because they do not suggest any need for resolution.

Melodies may utilise passing tones, non-chord tones that connect two chord tones by a whole step or half step. These pitches may be native to the key of the background chord, or chromatic.

A melodic note may anticipate a chord by arriving an eighth note or a quarter note before it.

A melody may depart from a chord tone by step or half step in either direction before returning its initial pitch.

Non-chord tones may be introduced by leap and resolved by step, or introduced by step and resolved by leap.

Non-chord tones in metrically emphasised positions are highlighted by the meter, drawing attention to their dissonance.

Jazz melody may treat an extension as though it were a chord tone, resolving to it without the need for resolution.

Whether or not they resolve, extensions that are sustained over a chord should be referenced in the chord symbol.

Chapter 10
Harmonising Melodies

So far, the greatest portion of this book has focused on the chords and chord progressions found in jazz repertoire. This is not intended to imply that chord progressions should be constructed prior to melodies in the compositional process. These two elements develop more or less simultaneously for most composers, and are adjusted and readjusted as a piece is honed to completion.

Melody should generally be prioritised in this process. Chord progressions are generally engineered to support melodies, rather than melodies altered to comply with chords.

For many composers, the composition of melody is an intuitive process, and the act of writing chords to fit a melody is a case of cross-referencing. Our harmonic vocabulary is scoured for the chords and chord sequences that best support the melody that we have written.

This chapter presents considerations on how we might begin to make better connections between the melodies that we have written and the chords that we have learned.

Finding the Key

Initially, identifying the key of a passage of tonal melody is a case of finding the key signature that complies most closely with the pitches present.

In both of the melodies above, the pitches E-flat and B-flat appear, but A appears un-flattened. This passage can therefore only be written without accidentals in a key signature with two flats:

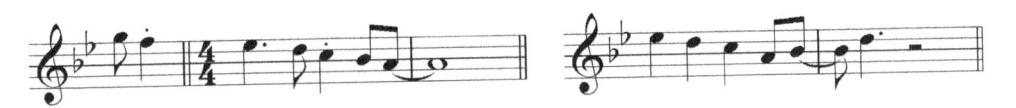

This suggests that these two fragments will fit best with chord progressions native to either B-flat major or G minor.

Below, the second phrase from the preceding example appears with a little more context, following a phrase where the only accidental is an F-sharp:

The first two bars of this passage can only be written without accidentals with a key signature of one sharp, and the second two bars only with a key signature of two flats. This suggests that a modulation has occurred:

This is not to say that the passage should necessarily be written with a change of key signature. As discussed previously (page 90), it is not necessary to notate temporary key changes with a change of key signature.

Some passages may not fully commit to a single key signature. The following melodic fragments both contain E-flat and B-flat, though neither A nor A-flat appear to cast a deciding vote upon the key signature. They are, as such, ambiguous:

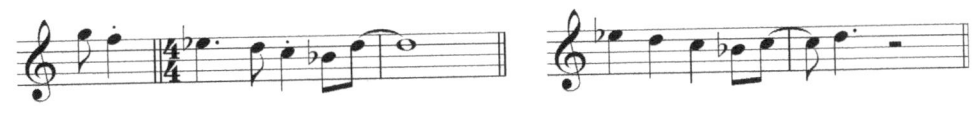

The two phrases above offer a wider range of possible harmonisations. Because all of the pitches present are diatonic to the keys of B-flat major, G minor, E-flat major, and C minor, they suggest possible harmonisations in any of those keys.

Chord Tones

The next stage in deciding upon appropriate harmonies is to determine which pitches are to be treated as chord tones, and which as non-chord tones. Sustained pitches, such as the asterisked D-natural that ends the above phrase, are obvious candidates for chord tones. This D might, for example, function as the root of some version of a D chord, the third of some variation of B chord, or the fifth of some variation of a G chord. The choices made at this juncture, such as whether these chords are major or minor and their array of extensions, will shape the harmonic contour of the piece in a significant way.

Limiting ourselves to those harmonies with conventional functions within the prevailing key gives us a far shorter and more practicable list of potential chords:

Dm7	D7(b9)	Bbmaj7	Gm	Gm7
III in Bb	V in Gm	I in Bb	I in Gm	VI in Bb

Alternatively, this sustained D-natural might be utilised as an unresolved extension: a seventh or flattened seventh, a ninth or a flattened or raised ninth, an eleventh or raised eleventh, or a thirteenth or flattened thirteenth. Limiting ourselves again to functional chords typical to this particular key gives us a shortlist of possibilities:

Ebmaj7	Cm9	Am11(b5)	F13
IV in Bb	II in Bb	II in Gm	V in Bb
bVI in Gm	IV in Gm		

Chromatic Pitches

If the majority of the pitches in a melody comply with a key signature but some do not, there are a number of ways that the latter can be managed. In both of the following examples, chromatic pitches, asterisked, connect two adjacent diatonic pitches, and thereby suggest themselves to be chromatic passing notes (page 117). They may be effectively ignored for the purposes of harmonisation:

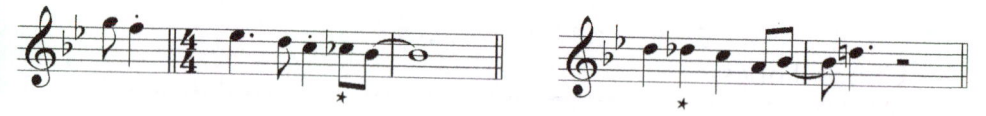

Non-diatonic pitches that approach diatonic pitches from a half step away, particularly those from below, are suggestive of chromatic, incomplete neighbour (page 122). This essentially means that these are considered to be embellishments, with negligible harmonic implications:

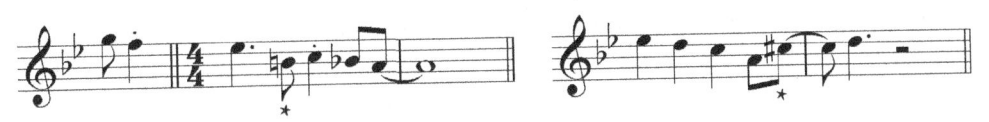

Many non-diatonic pitches can be harmonised with functional chords. We have encountered many chords already that contain non-diatonic pitches: IV⁷ (page 70) and III⁷ (Page 60), for example. Chords such as these are particularly appropriate when they support non-diatonic melody notes.

The V⁷ of a minor key is one of the most commonly occurring tonal chords to contain non-diatonic pitches. A prominent natural seventh in a minor key melody is highly suggestive of a V⁷ chord, and therefore strongly implies that chord I will follow:

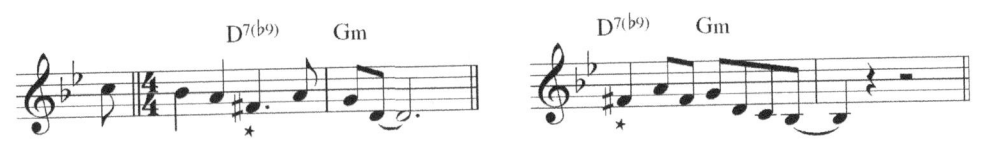

Chromatic pitches often suggest more than one harmonic possibility, and the decision that we make may be dependent upon the surrounding material.

Metric Accent

Pitches occurring in strong metric positions, such as at the beginning of a bar, are usually chord tones. In the example to the right, the E-flat that begins the phrase also falls on the most rhythmically accented point within it: beat one of the first bar. This suggests that E-flat should be treated as a chord tone for at least the beginning of this bar.

E♭⁶	Cm⁷	Am⁷⁽♭⁵⁾
IV in B♭	II in B♭	II in Gm
♭VI in Gm	IV in Gm	

Because it is followed by downward movement, this particular E-flat would also be well suited to function as the seventh of V in the key of B-flat, namely an F⁷ chord.

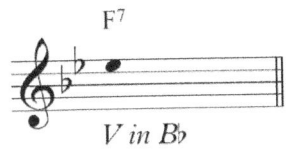

F⁷

V in B♭

Metrically accented pitches need not always be harmonised as chord tones. We could instead treat this E-flat as an accented incomplete neighbour tone that resolves to a D-natural over one of the D-supporting chords native to the key:

Dm⁷	D⁷⁽♭⁹⁾	B♭maj7	Gm	Gm⁷
III in B♭	V in Gm	I in B♭	I in Gm	VI in B♭

Phrase Endings

The final pitch in a phrase draws particular attention to itself because we perceive it to be the destination of the phrase. If the sustained D from our previous example had been followed by another pitch, that final pitch is the one that should be treated as a chord tone, and the D as an approach to this destination. In other words, the final pitch is the one that will sound resolved as a chord tone and unresolved as an extension.

If the melody were to move by step to C, a harmony containing C as a chord tone will sound resolved, and a harmony containing C as an extension will sound unresolved.

If we harmonise this passage with a C^{m7} chord, the phrase is resolved to a chord tone, and if we harmonise the passage with a B♭^{b6}, the phrase is not resolved to a chord tone:

resolved — C^{m7}

unresolved — B♭^{b6}

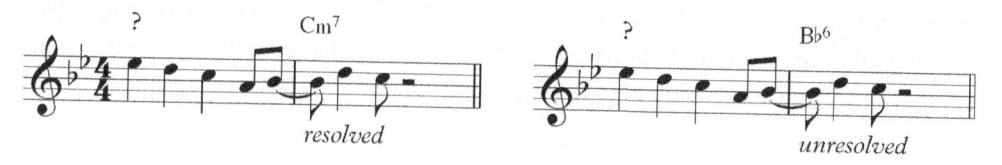

Thirds and Arpeggios

The presence of arpeggios, movement in thirds, is a particularly useful aid in harmonising a melody because, given the tertiary structure of functional harmony, such patterns limit the number of chords that can provide consonant accompaniment. One such pattern is found in the ascending major third from B-flat to D at the beginning of the second bar of this fragment.

Of the chords typical to the prevailing key, these pitches might be the root and third of a $B^{\flat maj7}$ chord, the third and fifth of G^m, or G^{m7}, the fifth and seventh of an $E^{\flat maj7}$, the seventh and ninth of a C^{m7}, or the thirteenth and root of $D^{7\flat13}$.

Because chord tones are more stable than extensions, chords containing B-flat and D as chord tones are more in agreement with this melody than those that contain these pitches only as extensions. We might sequence the list of potential chords above to reflect how closely they agree with the melodic movement from B-flat to D:

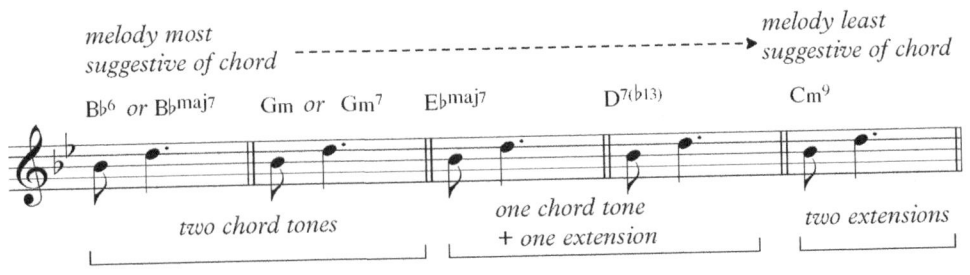

melody most suggestive of chord ---------------------------------------→ *melody least suggestive of chord*

$B^{\flat 6}$ or $B^{\flat maj7}$ — G^m or G^{m7} — $E^{\flat maj7}$ — $D^{7(\flat13)}$ — C^{m9}

two chord tones | one chord tone + one extension | two extensions

This is not a judgement on how appropriate any of the above chords are for this particular fragment of melody. Jazz harmony offers a great deal of flexibility and, depending on the context, any of these chords might be appropriate harmonisations.

A melody that leaps two or more consecutive thirds in the same direction is more prescriptive in its harmonic implications. This variation on our familiar fragment adds an F to the end of the phrase, producing a three-note ascending arpeggio. This addition makes the melody more specific in its harmonic demands. It is more descriptive of a B-flat major chord, but now has a very distant relationship with C^{m7} or D^7 chords. It precludes a tonic G^m chord entirely:

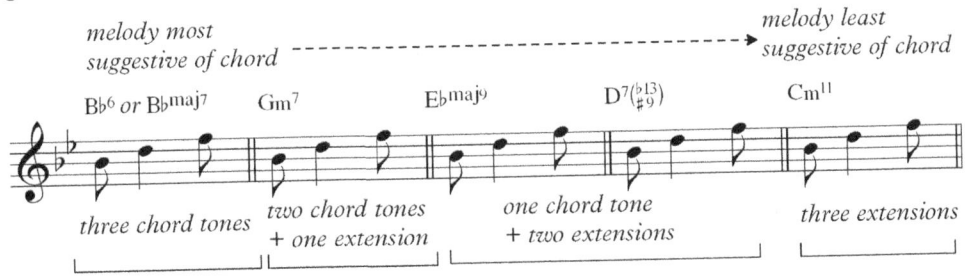

melody most suggestive of chord ---------------------------------------→ *melody least suggestive of chord*

$B^{\flat 6}$ or $B^{\flat maj7}$ — G^{m7} — $E^{\flat maj9}$ — $D^{7(\flat13)}_{(\sharp9)}$ — C^{m11}

three chord tones | two chord tones + one extension | one chord tone + two extensions | three extensions

Sometimes, arpeggios and melodic thirds might be obscured within a line. The first bar of the melody below consists primarily of scalic steps, but if we assume the first pitch to be a chord tone and the second to be a passing tone, a hidden descending arpeggio is revealed, with its first two pitches on the accented first and third beats of the bar:

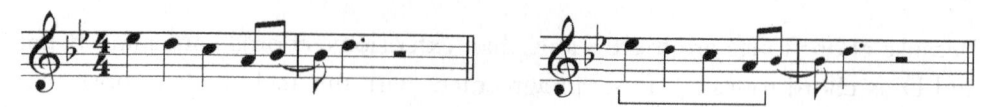

Within the tonal context, this descending arpeggio of E-flat, C, and A might be assumed to be one of the following: the flattened fifth, flattened third, and root of an A^{m7b5}, the flattened seventh, fifth, and third of an F^7, or the flattened third, root, and sixth of a C^{m6}.

Below is another example of how an arpeggio might be hidden within a passage that contains no consecutive thirds at all. Stripping away the E-naturals that function as incomplete neighbour tones, we are left with a passage consisting only of F, B-flat, and D, a B-flat major arpeggio:

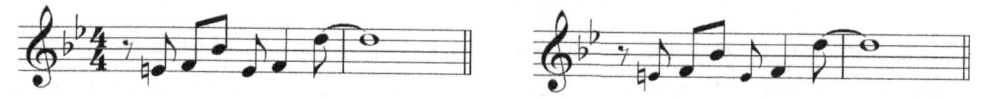

In this final example below, ignoring the unaccented pitches in this entirely scalic passage reveals a descending arpeggio of C, A, and F, which, in the prevailing key of B-flat, might suggest F^7, D^{m7}, or B^{bmaj9} as possible harmonic accompaniment:

Chord Progressions

Having examined on a pitch-by-pitch level how we might select chords to best support the individual pitches of our melody, we now consider how we might string these chords together to form larger chord progressions.

Tonal harmony places much emphasis on the use of conventional chord progressions to generate harmonic motion. In order to harmonise tonally we must constantly zoom in and out, balancing the requirements of individual pitches with the necessity for each chord to lead into the next.

The more functional applications of chords we know, the more connections and possibilities we see as we come to harmonise or re-harmonise a passage.

As an example of how this process might work, let us consider how we might harmonise the following phrase in the key of G major:

The first bar of the phrase is rather ambiguous, but the presence of the flattened third of the key, the B-flat, is quite unusual. There are several chords functional within the major key that support this pitch: $\flat\text{III}^{\circ 7}$, $\sharp\text{IV}^{\circ 7}$, and IV^7.

In order to choose between these, we must be informed by the larger context. $\sharp\text{IV}^{\circ 7}$ almost always follows IV, and the other two options, $\flat\text{III}^{\circ 7}$ and IV^7, are generally approached from I. This means that, in order to harmonise bar two of the passage, we must first determine which chord best fits the first bar:

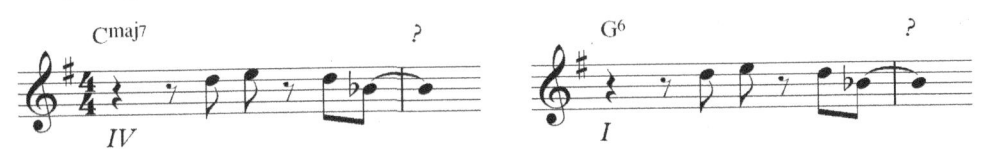

The melody of this first bar begins and ends on D, suggesting that the transient E is merely an elaborative neighbour tone. C^{maj7} could work, but G is a more appropriate harmony, since it contains D as a chord tone. The presence of G^6 in bar one renders $\sharp\text{IV}^{\circ 7}$ inappropriate for bar two, leaving $\flat\text{III}^{\circ 7}$ and IV^7 as possible harmonies:

$\flat\text{III}^{\circ 7}$ is generally followed by II^{m7}, and IV^7 most often precedes III^{m7} or I. The C that begins the melody of bar three of our excerpt is far more compatible with A^{m7} than it is with B^{m7}, which in turn suggests $\flat\text{III}^{\circ 7}$ as the best fit for bar two:

Placing the pitch of D rather than C at the beginning of bar three would have repercussions for our choice of harmony in both the second and third bars of the passage:

There are too many possible melodies and too many chord progressions that might be combined with them for this chapter to offer any kind of comprehensive method for harmonising melodies.

The style, context, and content of a melody offer clues as to the options that are available, but ultimately we must call upon our own harmonic vocabulary and aesthetic sense in order to make these decisions.

Chapter Summary

A passage of melody that conforms mostly or entirely to a single key signature suggests harmonisation in that key.

Sustained pitches and those that end phrases are particularly useful in identifying appropriate backing harmonies, which may be treated as chord tones or as extensions.

When a melody contains only occasional pitches that do not conform to a prevailing key signature, these pitches may be treated as chromatic passing tones, neighbour tones, or as chord tones of functional chords that do not wholly comply to the key signature.

Pitches in strong metric positions, such as the first beat of a bar, have particularly significant harmonic implications, and are often harmonised as consonant chord tones.

The final note in a melodic phrase is harmonically significant and must be harmonised to be a chord tone if we wish for the phrase to sound resolved.

Movements in thirds are particularly useful in identifying appropriate harmonic accompaniment. They are very specific in their requirements because they arpeggiate chords.

Context must be taken into account when producing a tonal accompaniment for a melody. The requirements of individual pitches must be balanced with the need for chords to progress in conventional sequences.

Chapter 11
Melodic Phrases

Chapter 8 examined the close relationship between melody and song and found that repetition and near-repetition are essential for writing melodies that are coherent and memorable. Melodies are arranged into short phrases (page 108), and those phrases derive continuity from repetition or near-repetition (page 110).

In this chapter we shall examine some of the relationships that consecutive fragments of melody might have with each other, and how individual phrases may be combined to form larger structures.

In order to discuss melodic phrases, we shall label them alphabetically in small case italics (*a, b, c…*). The first variation of *a* will be labelled *a'*, the second *a''* and so on. This enables us to discuss melodies in terms of the larger structures made up of combinations of individual phrases. A melody where the first phrase is repeated verbatim is notated *a-a*. If the second phrase is a variation upon the first then *a-a'*, or if the second phrase is unrelated to the first *a-b*.

Melodic Development

A melodic phrase may be repeated without the repetition being exact. We might change a few pitches, or the just the rhythm, and our revisions might be very minor or might produce a variant only distantly related to the original.

The process of altering melodies on repetition is called melodic or motivic development, and is an essential tool in ensuring that the individual phrases within a piece are coherent without being overly repetitive.

We might preserve one portion of a phrase whilst changing another. In the following example, only the second two bars are changed. *a'* preserves the rhythm of *a* exactly but changes the pitches:

• Chapter 11: Melodic Phrases

[musical notation: phrase labelled *a*]

[musical notation: phrase labelled *a'*]

In a passage such as this, the first and second phrases are sometimes labelled antecedent and consequent respectively. We might think of the first phrase as posing a musical question to be answered by the second.

In the following example, *a'* changes the pitches of the first two bars of *a*, but retains the pitches of the second two bars. Both phrases begin differently but come to the same conclusion. Again, the rhythm is identical in both phrases:

[musical notation: phrase labelled *a*]

[musical notation: phrase labelled *a'*]

Immediate and exact repetition of four bars of music is quite rare in twentieth century jazz repertoire. Most jazz melodies take place over larger-scale harmonic schemes, and developing the head or tail of a melody through repetition supports this. Here are some harmonies that might support our first idea:

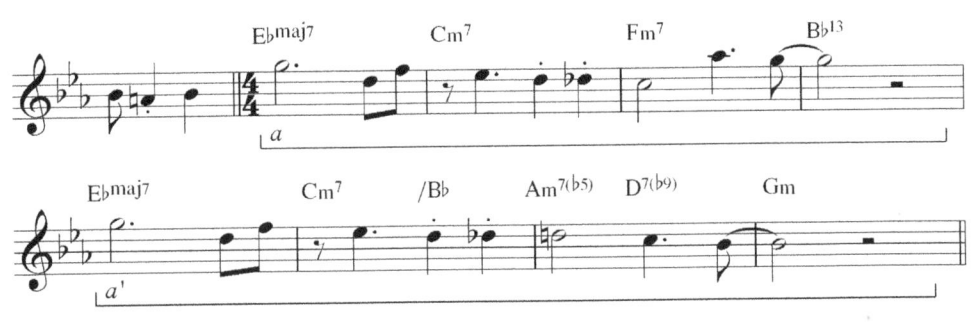

[musical notation with chords: E♭maj7, Cm7, Fm7, B♭13, labelled *a*]

[musical notation with chords: E♭maj7, Cm7, /B♭, Am7(♭5), D7(♭9), Gm, labelled *a'*]

The second example, in which the repetition changes the beginning of *a* but retains the ending, has totally different harmonic connotations. It could be harmonised thus:

[Musical notation with chord symbols: Ebmaj7, Cm7, Fm7, Gm7(b5), C7(b9), labeled *a*]

[Musical notation with chord symbols: Fm7, Gm7(b5), C7(b9), Fm7, Bb7, Ebmaj7, labeled *a'*]

We might alter more than just a few pitches. A reiteration might extend the initial phrase, reproducing it exactly and then adding new material to the beginning or end:

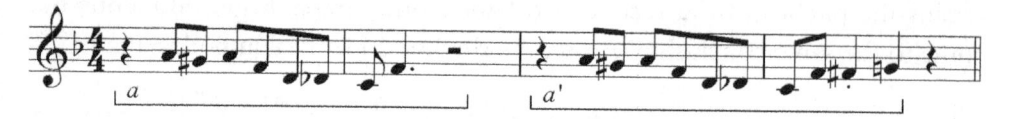

[Musical notation labeled *a* and *a'*]

Or the inverse, truncation of the initial phrase:

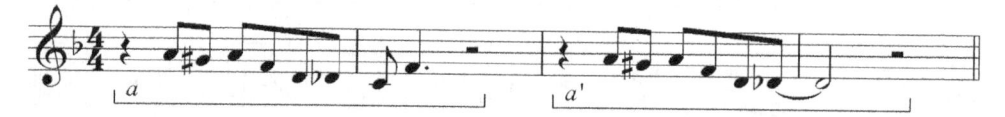

[Musical notation labeled *a* and *a'*]

A melody might be repeated, but with the duplication inexact in some way. Below, the rhythm is changed but the sequence of pitches is retained exactly:

[Musical notation labeled *a* and *a'*]

Minor ornaments might be added or removed in the repetition, but the fundamental contour of the line preserved:

[Musical notation labeled *a* and *a'*]

Any of the preceding examples of melodic developments might be combined simultaneously. Below is an example of a melody that could be described as having an *a-a'* structure, although *a'* is highly abstracted from its preceding phrase. Many of the pitches and rhythms are altered, but the general contour is retained:

Sequence

One particularly potent tool in the transformation of a melody is the use of sequence. Sequence, in the musical sense, is simply the repetition of an idea at a different pitch level. The second two-bar phrase of the following melody repeats the first exactly, but a diatonic step higher. Each pitch is shifted up to the next available within the key signature:

The same idea could be used to shift a phrase down a diatonic step, rather than up:

A line might be transposed further afield, up a diatonic third for example:

Or down a fourth:

Each of these possibilities have very different harmonic implications.

Below, a melody consisting of four two-bar phrases has the structure *a-a'-a"-b*. Each *a* is one diatonic step higher than the previous:

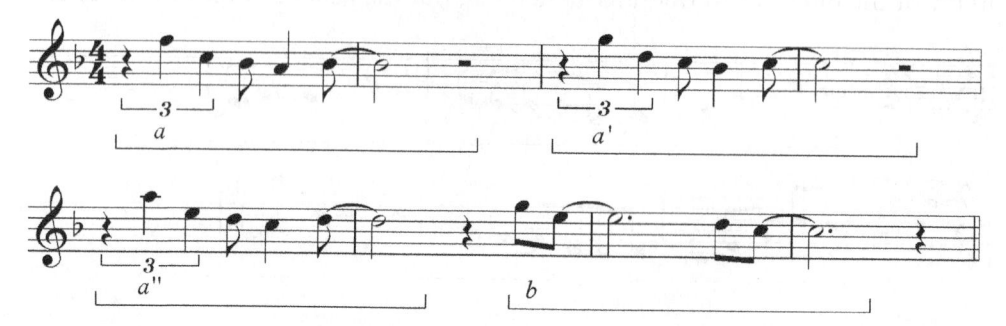

The repetitions that make up a sequence may not be literal. In fact, the previous example might be improved if subsequent *a* phrases developed upon the first rather than repeated it exactly:

All of these examples of melodic sequence have been purely diatonic, in that the transposition conforms fully to the key signature. Transpositions are also possible in which the intervals between each pitch of the melody are preserved exactly. These have specific harmonic connotations, heavily implying the need for a change of key. We may move up a half step, for example:

Sometimes composers reproduce an entire period at a different pitch level, which could be understood as a large-scale sequence. The second eight-bar period of the chorus in Jerome Kern's *All the Things You Are* is an example of this, reproducing the first eight bars an exact fourth lower. Ray Henderson's *Bye Bye Blackbird* features a large-scale diatonic sequence in which the second eight-bar period paraphrases the first a diatonic step higher. Upwardly moving sequences tend to occur more often than those that move downward, as they tend to produce a sensation of gradually building intensity.

Phrase Structure

Not all of the melodies in a piece should be motivically related, and composers must balance the interest provided by new ideas with the cohesion provided by repetition and development. The use of too many unique melodic phrases within a piece can sound random and unfocused.

Each phrase in the following excerpt is a distinct musical idea, producing a period with a melodic structure of *a-b-c-d*:

This effect is strange and un-songlike. Each phrase is valid in isolation, but they do not appear to have anything to do with each other. By reducing the number of unique phrases from four to three, we can produce a far more coherent phrase structure like *a-b-c-b*:

b might even be highly abstracted upon its repetition, as in the following *a-b-c-b'* melody. The similarity between *b* and *b'* is enough to tie the melody together motivically:

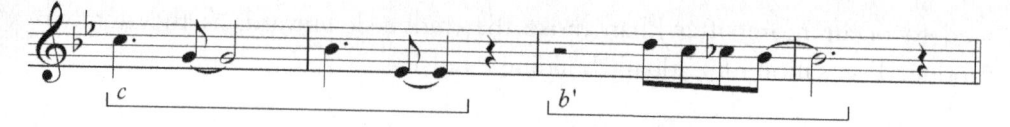

Songlike melodies tend to introduce no more than three distinct phrases before repeating one of them in some form, although there are many famous exceptions.

Melodies that introduce a great deal of new material tend to sound improvisatory, particularly in a jazz context. Slower moving tunes with non-repeating melodies sound rhapsodic, and are sometimes employed in Romantic era fantasias and impromptus. *Duke Ellington's Sound of Love* by Charles Mingus, and *Unrequited* by Brad Mehldau are two examples of music by jazz composers that approach this form.

Dense, fast-moving melodies that make little or no use of repetition and development are associated with bebop. Many composers followed in Charlie Parker's style of writing long, intense melodies that mimic the flow of his virtuosic improvisation. *Donna Lee*, credited to Parker but probably by Miles Davis, is a famous example of this. Its phrase structure could be notated as *a-b-c-d-a-e-f*.

Based on our previous example, below is an example of a sixteen-bar period with an *a-a'-b-a''* structure. It demonstrates some of the more complex interrelations that might be shared by themes within a piece:

a' begins the same as *a* but the last two bars are altered. It retains the same approximate outline of a descending scale from the pitch D, but changes the rhythm and the final pitch. Both of these endings return later in the passage however, functioning as sub-motifs that are developed within phrases. We can label them *x* and *y*:

Between them, *x* and *y* contain all of the material that appears in phrase *b*. *y* immediately becomes the basis for a sequence that descends in diatonic steps, while *x* is echoed in the rhythm and contour of the final three pitches of *b*:

Next, *a"* reproduces *a* one whole step down, implying a change of tonality, and referencing both *y* and *x* in its closing pitches:

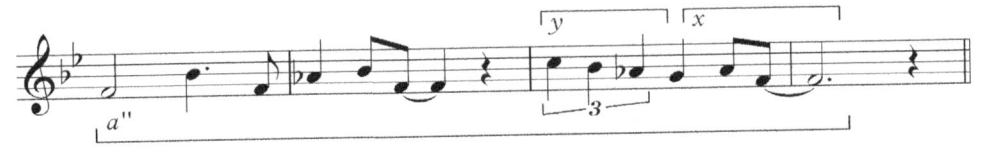

Chapter Summary

Melodies may vary upon repetition. The process of transforming a melody is called melodic or motivic development.

Some possible melodic developments of a phrase include the partial alteration of the beginning or end, truncation or extension, and the altering of rhythmic values. These techniques might be combined to produce variations that only obliquely reference the original material.

Melodic phrases may also be transformed via sequence, which is to say they may be transposed up or down to recur at different pitch levels.

We must balance exposition and repetition in order to create melodies that are both stimulating and coherent.

Interlude II

Let us now apply the analytical tools that we have developed in the preceding chapters to some musical excerpts, continuing to explore some of the commonalities of good melodies, and how we might further our understanding of them.

The following melodies are invented to fit the chord progressions introduced in Interlude I.

Example 1

This chord progression has been furnished with a highly active instrumental-style melody which chases many of the harmonic twists and turns implied by the underlying progression. For an example of a melody that describes the underlying chords, consider the first bar. On repetition of the initial three-note motif, B-natural is changed to B-flat to reflect the change in background harmony.

The final two bars of the excerpt also consist of a repeated motif, although the rhythm is transformed slightly upon repetition. The pitches in these bars are very specific to the underlying chords, consisting of the third and root of a minor seventh chord, passing downward through its seventh to the third of the following dominant chord. Even though these pitches are slightly out of sync with the suggested chord symbols, retarding the arrival of E^7 and anticipating A^{m7}, the effect is of a melody that spells out the harmony very explicitly:

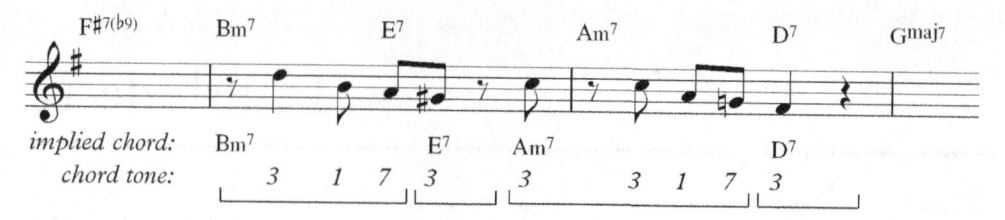

[musical notation with chord symbols: F#7(b9), Bm7, E7, Am7, D7, Gmaj7]

implied chord: Bm7   E7   Am7   D7
chord tone: 3   1 7   3   3   3 1 7 3

This final phrase is clearly related to the phrase that begins in bar three of the passage, reproducing the same contour of a descending diatonic third followed by two descending diatonic steps. Removing all rhythmic information reveals this relationship a little more clearly:

[musical notation showing bar 3 and bar 4, bar 7, bar 8]

We can describe the overall phrase structure as *a-b-c-b'*, with each phrase corresponding to roughly two bars of music:

[musical notation with chord symbols labeled with phrase markings a, b, c, b']

Example 2

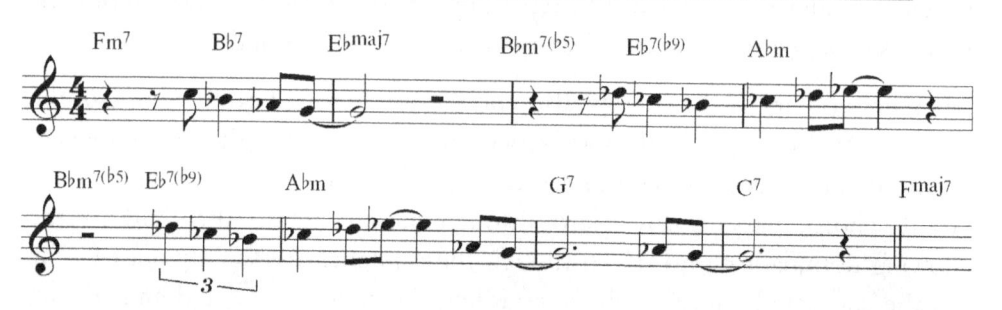

[musical notation with chord symbols: Fm7, Bb7, Ebmaj7, Bbm7(b5), Eb7(b9), Abm, Bbm7(b5), Eb7(b9), Abm, G7, C7, Fmaj7]

This single period is presented with no key signature. Without wider context, we cannot be sure whether the piece is in E-flat major, A-flat minor, or F major. The melody divides into four phrases of approximately two bars each.

The second and third phrases reflect their identical underlying harmonies in their closely related melodic content. *b'* alters only the rhythm of *b* while preserving the pitch content:

Phrases *a* and *b* are also closely related, both beginning with scalic descent. *c* consists of the same motif twice, and highlights the common tone of G-natural shared by both G^7 and C^7.

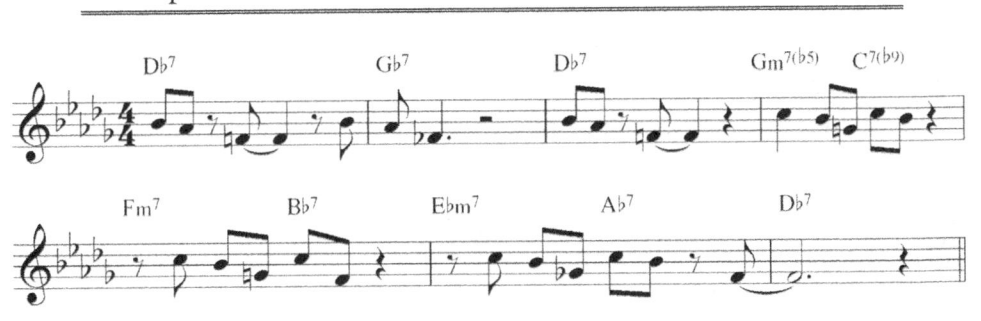

Example 3

Every motif in this bluesy, riff-like melody is related, consisting of the same repeating contour of three notes connected by descending step and then leap. Removing the rhythmic information again reveals that the underlying pattern occurs with five different pitch collections in this seven-bar passage:

Phrase delineations are somewhat subjective, but the melodic material seems to divide the seven bars more readily into three bars followed by four, than four followed by three:

Example 4

This lyrical line consists of two two-bar phrases. The second phrase lowers the pitch level by a diatonic third and abbreviates it:

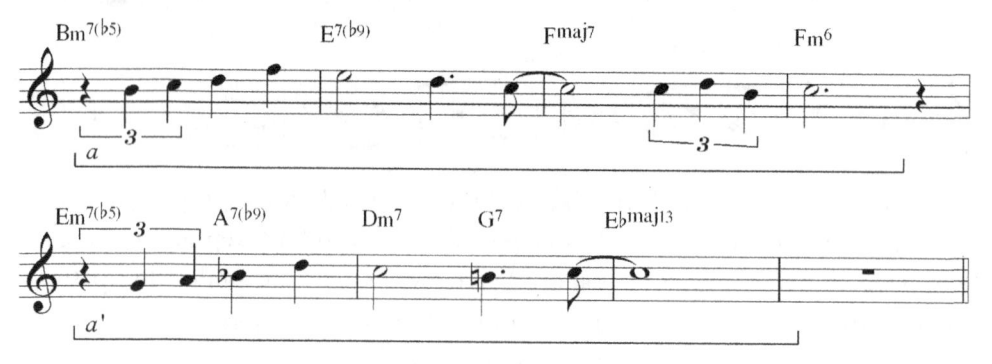

Note the characteristic use of the seventh as a descending passing note in bars two and six of the passage. In both cases, this pitch behaves as expected in common practice, resolving downward into a chord one:

When we first encountered this chord progression on page 106, we discussed the surprising cadence that takes a passage ostensibly in C major to the key of E-flat. This melody further solidifies C major as the prevailing tonality, with a penultimate seventh of the key over the V chord, B natural over G^7, resolving upwards to the tonic. We would usually expect the tonic pitch to be accompanied with chord I:

The ♭VI major chord that we receive instead supports the expected melody note, but recontextualises it, providing a far more interesting cadence to the period:

Chapter 12
The Chorus

Having explored some of the typical attributes of melodic phrases (Chapter 8), and the relationship between individual phrases (Chapter 11), let us continue to zoom out and explore the larger formal structures within jazz compositions.

Most jazz melodies and chord sequences can be subdivided into short phrases of two to four bars. These phrases are, in turn, compiled into larger passages of eight to sixteen bars. In practice, jazz musicians call such passages sections, but since this term is rather ambiguous, we will instead use the term 'period'.

In its most typical form, a period is a complete statement of both melody and harmony. It introduces melodic material and explores it to a satisfying conclusion, whilst accompanying it with a chord progression that ends either on a tonic chord, or with modulatory material that leads into the next passage.

We then combine these periods into larger structures, the most fundamental and universal of which is the chorus; repetitions of the chorus may make up the entirety of a jazz performance. The first iteration of the chorus is typically the head of the piece, a passage of perhaps twelve to sixty-four bars of melody heard over an accompanying harmonic scheme. The same chord progression is then recycled, becoming the basis for a sequence of improvised solos.

Just as the individual phrases within a period must balance the introduction of new ideas with repetition and variation, a chorus must manage the material within it in order to tell a coherent and compelling story. In discussing the sequencing of periods within a piece, we shall modify the notation that we used for phrases throughout Chapter 11, labelling them alphabetically in capital italics (*A, B, C…*). Variations are again denoted with an apostrophe: the first variation of *A* will be labelled *A'*, then *A"* and so on. Once again this allows us to discuss the form of a chorus in general terms without needing to reference the actual material of which it is composed.

Unlike the small case italics used to denote melodic phrases, the use of alphabetic designations for the periods within a chorus is very common amongst jazz musicians, and is regularly used in rehearsals and on the bandstand to communicate the structure of a piece.

The Song Form

Outside of the twelve-bar blues, the most common cyclic chord progression is undoubtedly the American songbook-style chorus, or song form. In its most typical manifestation, this is a thirty-two-bar chord sequence consisting of four eight-bar periods, structured *A-A-B-A* or *A-B-A-C*.

Repeated sections may contain minor variations, such as *A-A'-B-A"* or *A-B-A'-C*. The vast majority of Tin Pan Alley songs, as well as non-blues jazz compositions from 1930 to the mid-60s, can be understood as relating to some variation on the song form. Popular variations include *A-A-B*; *A-A-B-A*; *A-A-B-A-C*; *A-A-B-B-A*; *A-A-B-C*; *A-B-A*; and *A-B-A-C*.

Recurring periods are often not identical, perhaps having a different ending upon repeat. Furthermore, periods may be sixteen bars rather than eight, or more irregular lengths such as six, ten, or fourteen bars. The blues-with-a-bridge, for example, is a popular variation upon the *A-A-B-A* structure, in which each *A* is itself a twelve-bar blues.

The ubiquitous 'rhythm changes' deserves special mention here. After the twelve-bar blues, the chord changes of George Gershwin's 1930 song *I Got Rhythm* is by far the most popular harmonic scheme for a jazz chorus. It been the basis for countless compositions, particularly from the 1940s to 1960s, and is usually played in a swing style at medium to fast tempos.

This chord sequence epitomises the song form particularly well, and is shown here in its thirty-two-bar entirety:

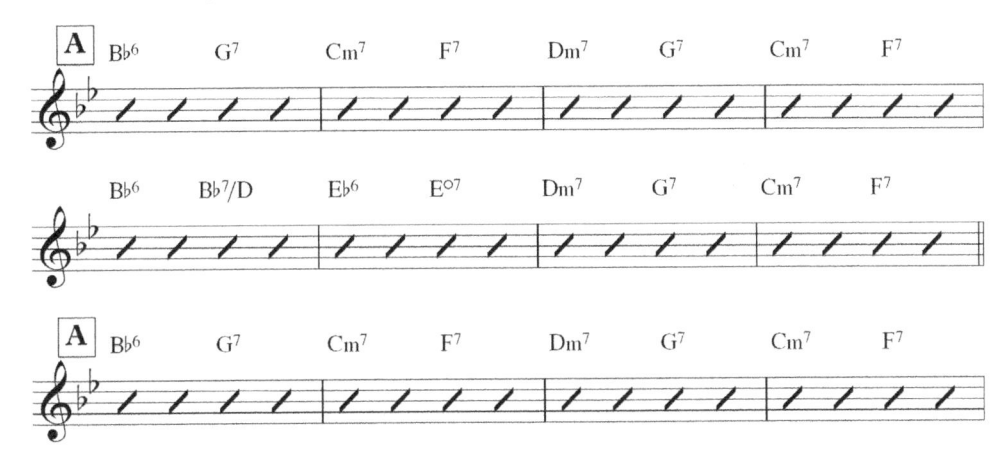

[A] Bb6 | G7 | Cm7 | F7 | Dm7 | G7 | Cm7 | F7

Bb6 | Bb7/D | Eb6 | E°7 | Dm7 | G7 | Cm7 | F7

[A] Bb6 | G7 | Cm7 | F7 | Dm7 | G7 | Cm7 | F7

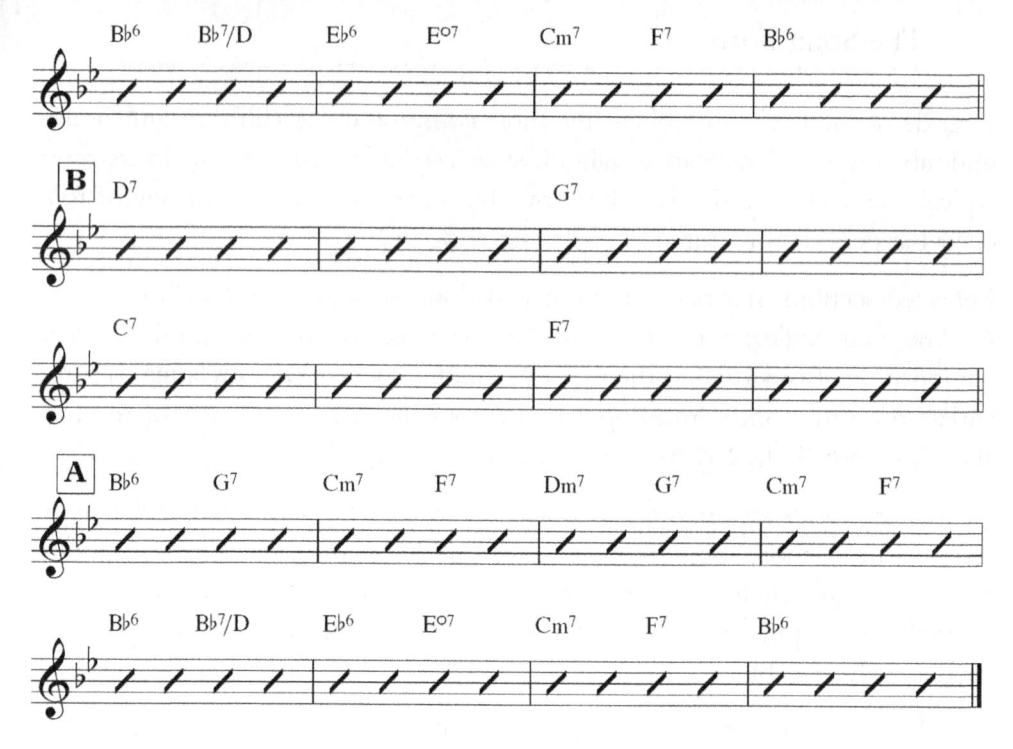

[Musical notation: Chord chart for "I Got Rhythm" in B-flat]

Section (top, unlabeled — final A):
| Bb6 Bb7/D | Eb6 E°7 | Cm7 F7 | Bb6 |

B section:
| D7 | | G7 | |

| C7 | | F7 | |

A section:
| Bb6 G7 | Cm7 F7 | Dm7 G7 | Cm7 F7 |

| Bb6 Bb7/D | Eb6 E°7 | Cm7 F7 | Bb6 |

The harmonic material of *I Got Rhythm* is simple to the point of being generic, which is perhaps the reason for its popularity. The *A* sections cycle around turnarounds in B-flat, before returning home via the IV chord.

The *B* section, the bridge in *A-A-B-A*-derived forms, is a distinctive change in mood. An extended III-VI-II-V cycle of dominant chords suggests several distant key centres. V is preceded by the V of V, and the V of V of V, and so on. The slower rate of harmonic change also helps to differentiate the bridge from the surrounding material, as we move from a chord change every two beats in the *A* sections to a leisurely change every two bars.

The Short Chorus

Early jazz compositions were often highly arranged, consisting of multiple eight- to sixteen-bar periods which might be repeated or combined in complex sequences. Other than the twelve-bar blues, these granular short forms did not generally find a place in post-1930s jazz which, as we have seen, favoured chorus formats based on popular song.

By the mid-1940s the most vital innovations in the music were being made in instrumental styles, which predictably led to a de-emphasis on the popular song as a template for jazz performance. The cyclic sixteen-bar chord progression rose to prominence once again.

Unsurprisingly, sixteen-bar forms tend to subdivide themselves most naturally into two eight-bar periods, which can be considered as either *A-B* form, or simply a single sixteen-bar *A*.

There are many strong examples of pieces based on sixteen-bar choruses from the hard bop music of the early 1950s to late 60s. Joe Henderson's *Recorda Me*, and Kenny Dorham's *Blue Bossa* are two particularly famous examples that were both initially recorded for the same album.

In the late 60s, jazz musicians began to take on influences from rock and funk, and many abandoned song forms in favour of more repetitive harmonic sequences and rhythm section ostinatos. Some of these might only be a bar or two in duration. Because it seems inappropriate to consider a one-chord funk groove to function in the same manner as a thirty-two-bar chorus, the term 'vamp' is common in such contexts. Though there is no strict definition, we might, for our current purposes, define a vamp as any repeating cycle of up to four bars.

A large factor in the undeniable potency of the classic American thirty-two-bar song is that the chord progression alone tells a story, having inherent moments of tension, resolution, climax, and recapitulation. It might tentatively be suggested that shorter forms and vamps put a little more onus upon performers to shape the structure of a piece. Both soloists and rhythm sections often intuitively demarcate eight- or sixteen-bar periods, providing some echo of the benefits of the larger scale forms found in the song form style.

Chorus Beginnings and Endings

In tonal jazz styles, choruses most commonly begin and end in the same key, which can readily be described as the key that the piece is in.

A chorus that begins in one key and ends in another is, on some level, fundamentally ambiguous, and, given the cyclic nature of the chorus form, will produce something of a harmonic see-saw effect between the tonalities present.

A tonal chorus might begin on I, but this is not a necessity. Copious examples exist of songs and jazz compositions starting on IV, II-V, V, VI, or in another key entirely. However, in order for a progression to pass as tonal, it must generally cadence into a tonic chord towards its conclusion. This is usually accompanied by a final, often sustained melody note, upon either the tonic pitch or a chord tone of the tonic triad. Sometimes this final tonic might not appear until the final bar, as in the rhythm changes shown above.

In the following example, we see the ending to an imaginary melody over rhythm changes. The final pitch of the melody's ending accompanies the final cadence to I:

*cadence into final bar

When a chorus ends on I, jazz musicians typically insert a connective harmony to link back to the beginning of the chorus. In most cases, these connective chords will either be the V of the target chord, or some variation of it:

(a) chorus ends on I and begins on I

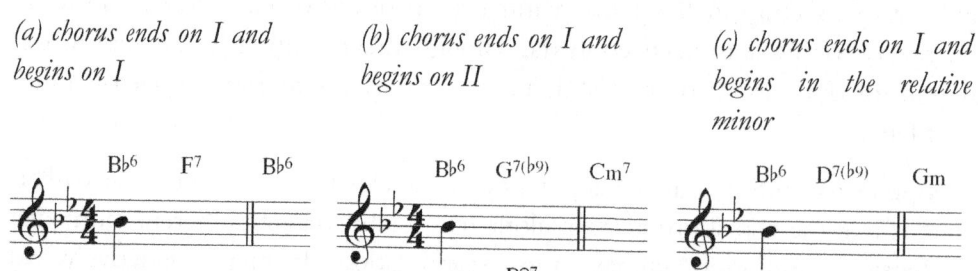

(b) chorus ends on I and begins on II

(c) chorus ends on I and begins in the relative minor

Even more frequently, the tonic arrives two bars before the end of the chorus. A thirty-two-bar chorus might end as shown in the following example, with a final tonic melody note again coinciding with a final tonic chord:

*cadence into penultimate bar

We now have two bars in which to set up our transition into the beginning of the next chorus, during which we can elaborate the connective V with a II:

(a) chorus ends on I and begins on I... or:

(b) chorus ends on I and begins on IV *(c) chorus ends on I and begins in the relative minor*

Finally, the cadence may appear four bars before the end of the chorus:

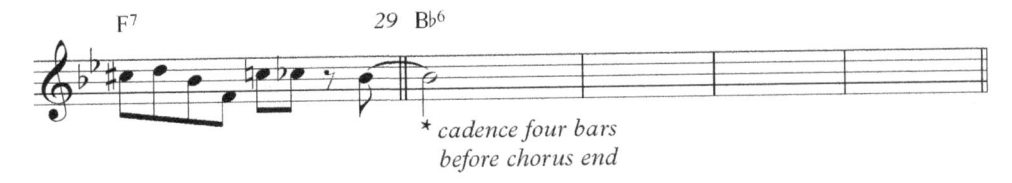

* cadence four bars before chorus end

Such areas of static tonic are often elaborated with a V, II-V, or VI-II-V:

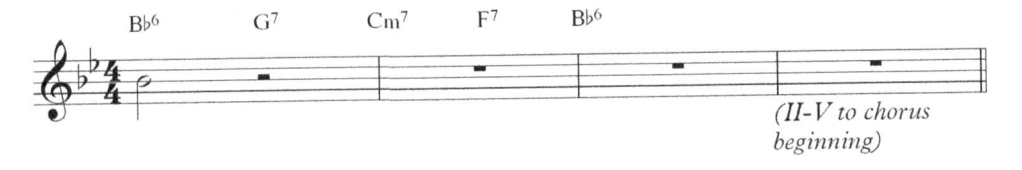

(II-V to chorus beginning)

Modulation Between Periods

The *A*, *B*, and *C* sections that make up a chorus must be distinct from one another, an effect which is often assisted by the use of distinct tonalities. Even if *B* is in the same key as *A*, it should begin on a different chord.

As we saw in Chapter 6, there are essentially two ways that modulations might be introduced in new musical periods, both of which are very common, and both of which are very effective in differentiating the periods of a piece.

Firstly, the tonic of the new key may arrive on the first beat of the new period, being preceded by a cadence, most typically a V or II-V, into the new key:

The second possibility is that the new period may begin with a V or II-V in the new key, with the new tonic only arriving later in the phrase. This is most effective when the old period ends on the tonic of the previous key, thereby tying up harmonic loose ends:

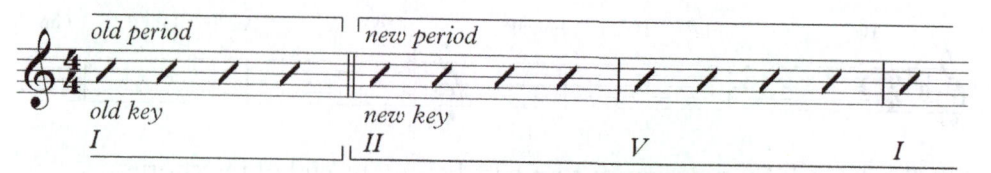

```
old period    | new period
old key       | new key
I             | II        V        I
```

With faster harmonic rhythm, the new tonic may arrive in bar two of the new period:

```
old period    | new period
old key       | new key
I             | II   V    I
```

Below shows an example of how these three options might apply in a modulation from a period in G major to a period in E major:

(a) tonic arrives in bar one:

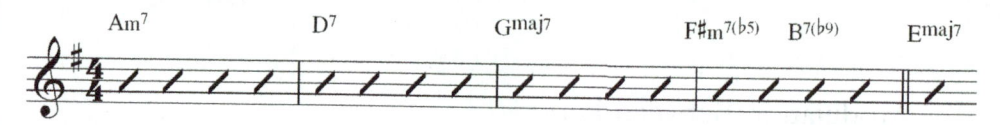

Am7   D7   Gmaj7   F#m7(b5) B7(b9)   Emaj7

(b) tonic arrives in bar two:

Gmaj7   F#m7   B7   Emaj7

(c) tonic arrives in bar three:

Gmaj7   F#m7   B7   Emaj7

There are many possible modulatory passages into a new period. Beginning the period on I, ,V, or II-V are only some of the most typical possibilities. A new period may begin on any chord of the new key.

Melodic Implications of Chorus Form

Much of the sense of narrative in the song-style chorus is provided by harmonic variation. Contrasting periods are differentiated by variations in tonality, harmonic rhythm, and harmonic style. Similarly, most compositions do not repeat or develop melodic material across the *A, B,* and *C* sections of a piece, as to do so would undermine the sense of having entered a new period.

This said, melodies are rarely different in character from period to period. Pieces with angular, intense melodies in their *A* sections usually follow them with angular and intense *B* sections, while flowing, lyrical *A* sections are usually followed by flowing and lyrical *B* sections.

The highest pitch in a song melody is a climactic moment, and should be reserved for an appropriate point relatively late in the chorus. If the highest pitch appears too early, there is a risk that the rest of the melody may sound anticlimactic. On the other hand, top notes rarely appear at the very end of the piece. We expect melodies to build to a climax and then wind down before their conclusion. In this sense, the chorus is a microcosm of the typical contours that we might expect from the performance of an entire piece.

In practical terms, this means that song-like melodies tend to start toward the bottom of their range and ascend gradually as the piece progresses, implying forward motion towards a zenith at the destination pitch. Accordingly, the highest pitch in *A-A-B-A* songs often occurs toward the end of section *B*, and in *A-B-A-C* songs near the beginning of section *C*. The conventions of song and the American songbook style inform the practice of instrumental jazz composers, who generally follow a similar contour in their large-scale melodies.

In forms where an entire period is repeated immediately, the melody is often altered upon repeat. A typical manifestation of this is that the period in question cadences to a tonic chord, which harmonises a melody note that is not the tonic the first time, and then a tonic melody note upon repeat:

[Musical notation: first example with chord changes Bm, G#m7(b5), C#m7(b9), F#7(b9), Bm, B7(b9), Em7, A7, then Dmaj7, 1. C#m7(b9), F#7(b9), Bm, G#m7(b5), C#m7(b9), F#7(b9)]

* *non-tonic melody pitch over tonic chord*

[Musical notation: 2. C#m7(b9), F#7(b9), Bm]

* *tonic melody pitch over tonic chord*

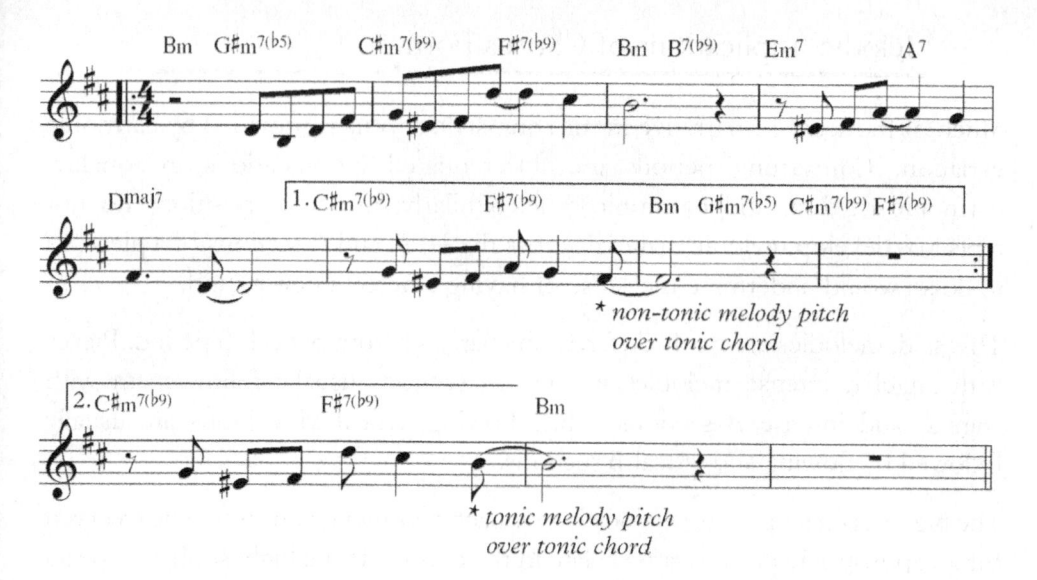

This is a good example of the antecedent/consequent structure mentioned previously (page 138). The relatively unresolved F-sharp pitch that ends the first period above is answered by the finality of the B that ends the second.

The underlying harmony could reflect the antecedent/consequent format of the melody. Below, the same melody is harmonised with a V chord, elaborated by a II, such that neither the melody nor the harmony resolve under the first-time bar:

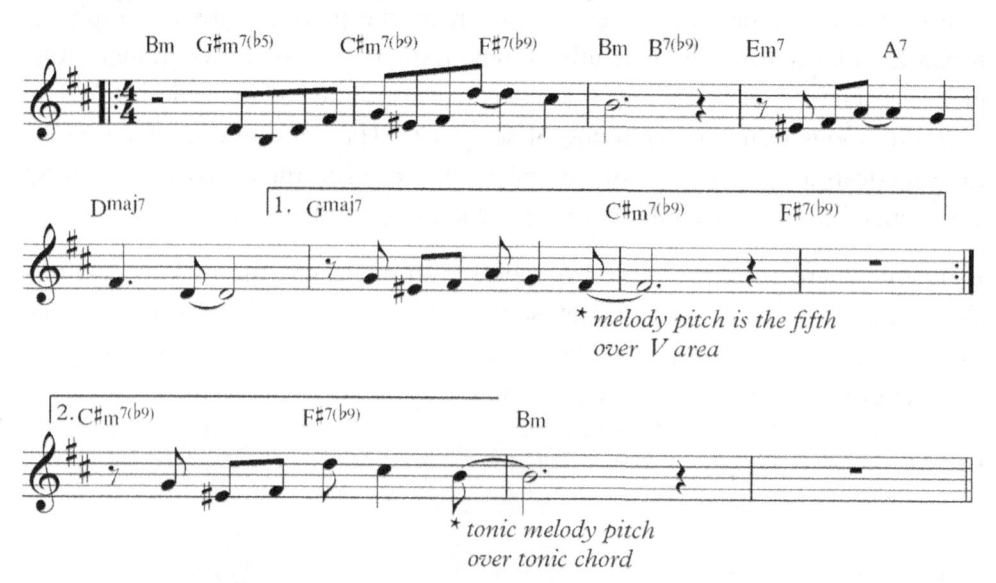

[Musical notation: Bm, G#m7(b5), C#m7(b9), F#7(b9), Bm, B7(b9), Em7, A7, then Dmaj7, 1. Gmaj7, C#m7(b9), F#7(b9)]

* *melody pitch is the fifth over V area*

[Musical notation: 2. C#m7(b9), F#7(b9), Bm]

* *tonic melody pitch over tonic chord*

A final tonic melody note is often preceded by the third of the key over the V chord. This is a highly typical appearance of the V^{13} chord:

[musical notation: Dm⁷ – G¹³ – C⁶]

third of C produces V13 harmony

A parallel effect may also occur in the minor key, where the flattened third native to the key yields $V^{7\flat 13}$ as a penultimate chord:

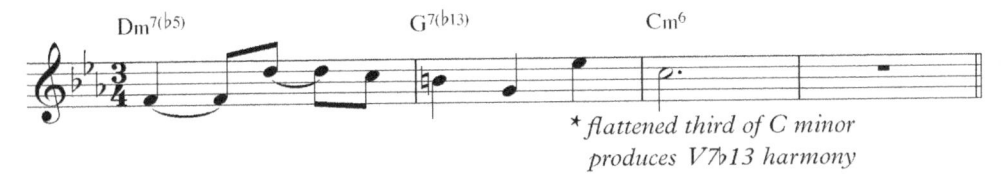

[musical notation: Dm⁷⁽♭⁵⁾ – G⁷⁽♭¹³⁾ – Cm⁶]

flattened third of C minor produces V7♭13 harmony

The finality of the tonic pitch as the last note of a melody is so potent that it can even be harmonised with a non-tonic chord. One slightly perverse example of this is in the $^{\flat}\text{II}^{maj7}$ chord that jazz musicians sometimes use to harmonise the last pitch of a song. The tonic melody note is retained, but the underlying harmony is replaced with something entirely alien to the key:

[musical notation: Dm⁷ – G¹³ – D♭maj7]

tonic of C harmonized with ♭IImaj7

Solos

In small-band jazz, the primary focus of a performance is on the spontaneous invention of soloists, the dynamic accompaniment of a rhythm section, and the interplay between the ensemble as a whole. The contribution of the composer to this is somewhat distant. Even in performing our own compositions as part of a group, we have only partial control over the execution of a piece.

The most important composed material in most jazz styles is the head and its harmonic accompaniment. The head defines a given jazz composition, the phrase structure of its melody, and the arrangement of its harmonic periods.

Jazz composers do not generally introduce new harmonic progressions as the basis for solos because the connection between the composed material of the head and the improvised solos is essential to the coherence of a jazz performance. A chord progression, particularly a long one such as a song-style chorus, tells a story. The balance of new material, repetition, and variation within such a form provides an inherent narrative structure for a solo regardless of the actual content a soloist plays.

Chapter Summary

A large proportion of jazz repertoire takes its inspiration from popular song form, particularly variations on the 32-bar *A-A-B-A* or *A-B-A-C* chorus.

Most choruses feature a conclusionary cadence into a tonic chord in the final or penultimate bar.

Modulation is a useful tool in differentiating the periods within a chorus. A new period may begin with a new tonic or a cadence into it.

Periods within a chorus tend to deviate in content rather than character or style.

The structure and harmonic scheme of chorus form has implications upon its melodic content. Melodic climaxes are generally introduced later in a chorus and melodic resolutions only at the very end.

Chapter 13
Arrangement

Once we have composed our musical material, we must prepare it for performance by creating an arrangement. This is the process of establishing the details of instrumentation and orchestration, and of the overall form of the piece. Clearly the activities of arrangement and composition overlap significantly.

This chapter will open with a discussion of some of the ways that we might instruct our rhythm sections in music that does not require specific or individual parts for them.

Most classic jazz is based on some variation of the chorus form, a cyclic chord progression that provides a backing for both composed material and improvisation. There are many ways that an arrangement might deviate from a strict chorus form, but primarily these involve additional material: introductions that take place before the first chorus or the head, codas and endings that take place after the last chorus, and interludes that are inserted in-between repetitions of the chorus.

The Rhythm Section

Since the 1930s, the jazz rhythm section has typically consisted of a piano trio: drum kit, double bass, and piano, with the possible addition of guitar or vibraphone. From the mid-1960s onwards the guitar often replaced the piano to create a guitar trio.

Piano and guitar trios are the most typical backing bands for horns, but have also been popular ensembles in their own right. In earlier styles, the rhythm section was a relatively inconspicuous unit, mostly present to provide an anonymous rhythmic and harmonic backing for brass and woodwind soloists to play over.

As the music has evolved, the rhythm section has become more expressive, and contemporary drummers, bassists, and pianists are at liberty to interact extensively both with each other and with the soloists.

The drums in a modern jazz ensemble are particularly expressive. A basic accompaniment pattern, comping, might consist of a regular rhythm on the ride cymbal, with accents and rhythmic figures on the snare. In swing and early jazz, the bass drum would generally be feathered very lightly on every beat, but one of the major revolutions of bebop-era drumming was that players began to use the bass drum more expressively, much like the snare drum.

Drummers are expected to converse spontaneously with the soloist, accenting their phrases or filling in the spaces that they leave, but they must also reference the form of the piece, emphasising formal events with fills or changes of orchestration.

The bass took over from the role of the tuba common in the jazz ensembles of early jazz, and would play primarily on the first and third beat of the 4/4 bar, perhaps alternating between the root and fifth of the underlying chords. By the end of the 1930s, this had evolved into the walking bass line, a continuous, improvised quarter note line that connects rhythmically with the drummer's ride cymbal whilst describing the harmony.

Piano accompaniment varies greatly in different styles. In early jazz, stride piano was a very common pattern, wherein a pianist plays melodically in their right hand whilst alternating low bass notes and mid-register chords in the left. As bass and drum styles became more involved, pianists were able to play more sparsely, playing percussive, syncopated patterns in the same rhythmic language as the drummer's snare drum accents.

When writing within established genres such as swing or bossa nova, jazz composers do not generally prescribe the details of the rhythm section accompaniment, preferring to merely suggest the style and approximate tempo of the accompaniment that they require. Some of these styles are outlined in more detail below.

Style and Tempo

Due to the autonomy of the rhythm section, it is neither necessary nor desirable to notate accompaniment figures. When writing within a well-established idiom such as swing, bebop, or bossa nova, the best instruction is simply a chord chart accompanied by a general instruction of style and tempo. Let us examine how a rhythm section might perform the following four-bar passage in different styles:

[Chord chart: Fm⁷ | B♭⁷ | E♭maj7 | (slashes in 4/4)]

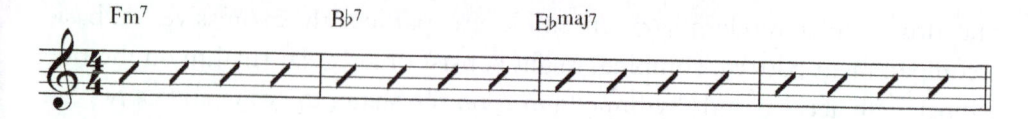

4/4 swing was the default rhythm section style for the jazz ensemble until at least the end of the 1960s. Swing is can be performed at any tempo from about 80 beats per minute (bpm) upwards; 300bpm is generally an upper limit, though one take of Dizzy Gillespie's *Bebop* was recorded at around 360bpm.

All that our rhythm section needs in order to play a swing piece is a chart showing the structure of the piece, the chords, and a tempo marking. We need not even provide a metronome mark, as an approximate instruction could be provided instead. We might simply begin our chart with an instruction such as 'Fast Swing' or 'Medium Swing' and leave the precise tempo at the discretion of our performers.

In this style, eighths are swung (page 15). The basic swing-time pattern drum pattern is as follows:

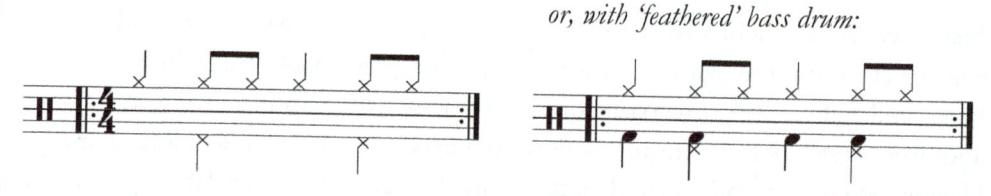

or, with 'feathered' bass drum:

[Drum notation examples]

The bass drum, snare, and toms may be used for fills and syncopated accents, or incorporated into a repeating pattern. The ride and hi-hat might be highly varied and interactive, particularly in more modern styles.

The bass usually plays a walking bass line that rhythmically underpins the ensemble whilst melodically connecting chords. Chordal roots are placed in positions of strong metric accent, and connected with a continuous quarter note line of scalic material and arpeggios:

[Bass line notation: Fm⁷ | B♭⁷ | E♭maj7, marked *8vb* ... *etc.*]

For lower intensity sections of a swing piece, the bass and drums might choose to play in a 'two feel' (or '2-feel'), with the bass primarily playing only on beats one and three, and the drummer moving the ride pattern to the hi-hat. In a more detailed arrangement, we might instruct a rhythm section to switch between a two- and a four-feel at key points.

• Chapter 13: Arrangement

To a large extent, swing-time piano accompaniment shares its rhythmic language with the drummer's snare drum. In post-1940s jazz, both instruments provide rhythmic accents that comment upon the soloist or on other musical events taking place within the ensemble:

A guitar might fulfil a similar role as the piano or, in older styles and big bands, simply play a chord on every downbeat. The following excerpt shows how an imaginary rhythm section might perform the preceding four-bar chord chart to accompany a singer or horn soloist:

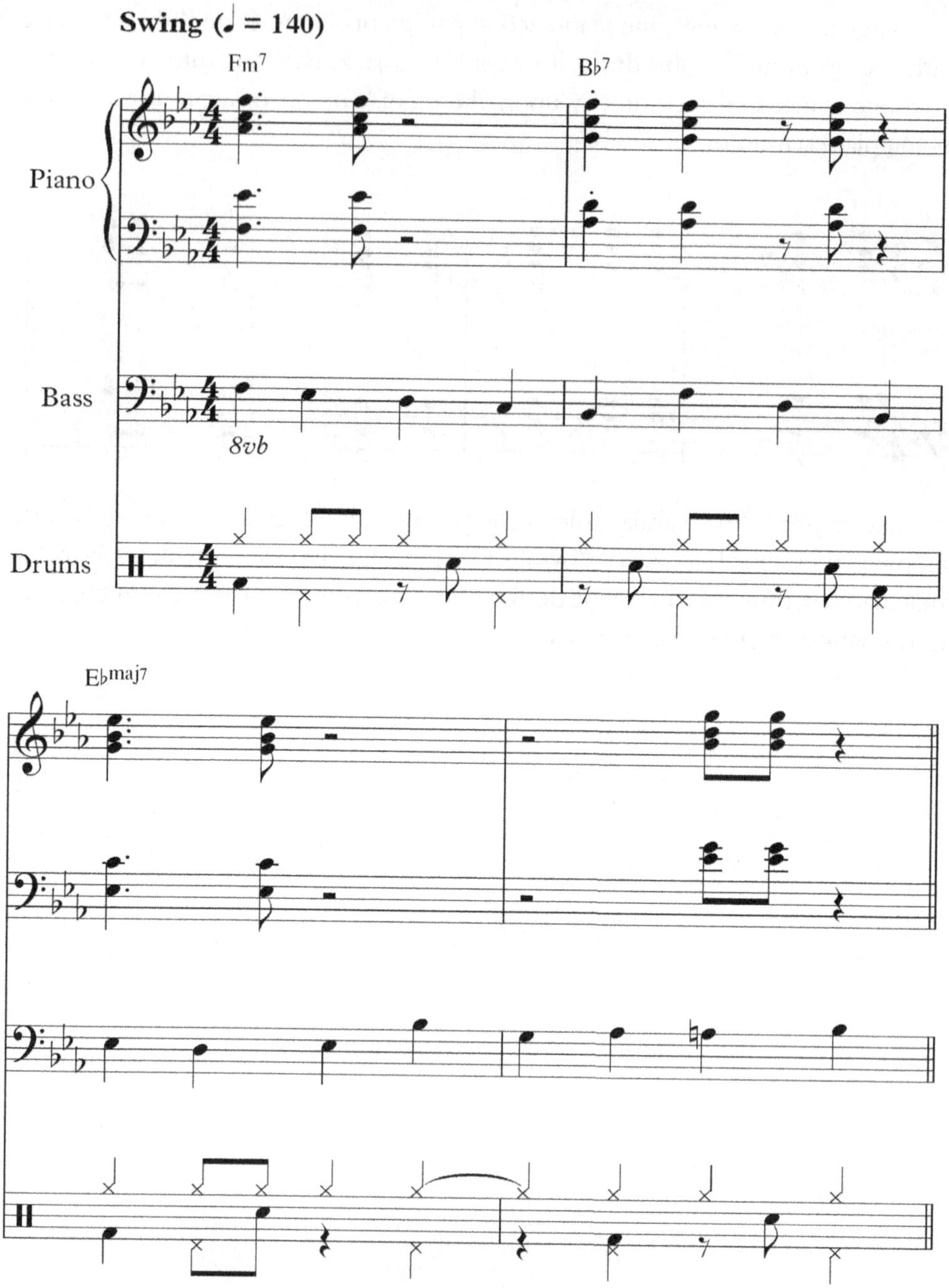
Swing (♩ = 140)
Fm7
B♭7
Piano
Bass
8vb
Drums
E♭maj7

'Latin' is a common instruction to find at the beginning of a jazz chart. At tempos between about 90 and 140bpm, this generally suggests a bossa nova, inspired by the Brazilian craze of the 1960s. A sample bossa nova drum groove is as follows:

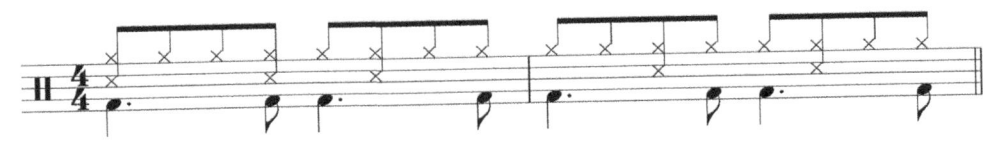

At faster tempos, 'latin' might be interpreted as something more like a samba:

In both bossa nova and samba grooves, the bass generally plays root notes and fifths on beats one and three, with occasional embellishments on two, four, or the upbeats of two and four:

Below shows how a rhythm section might perform the same four-bar chord sequence as a bossa nova. The pianist's rhythms are inspired by the bossa nova guitar style:

In casual situations, jazz composers may simply instruct their rhythm sections to play in a 'latin' style, leaving the interpretation of this to the musicians. In addition to Brazilian-inspired bossa nova and samba, Cuban-inspired styles such as the mambo are popular. The use of 'latin' as a performance direction is not particularly condoned, but may suffice in lieu of a more intimate knowledge of Brazilian and Cuban styles.

A popular arrangement technique is to begin a piece in a latin style and switch to swing for the *B* section, or the inverse. Dizzy Gillespie's *Night in Tunisia* and Lee Morgan's *Totem Pole* are examples of these.

A third essential jazz rhythm section style is the ballad. At tempos below about 80bpm, eighth notes are straightened out and the piano or guitar is free to play with greater rhythmic and harmonic freedom. Bass players play primarily on beats one and three rather than on every beat, and drummers play continuously on the snare with brushes, slightly accenting each beat:

Fundamentals of Jazz Composition •

There are many other styles that we could instruct our rhythm sections to play, but 'swing', 'latin', and 'ballad' are perhaps the most universal. Most jazz in 3/4 time is swung, for which 'jazz waltz' might be an appropriate performance direction. A 'shuffle' is a bluesy medium-tempo swing feel, usually in 4/4, with a triplet subdivision of each beat and a heavy emphasis on beats two and four. 'Straight eighths' might suggest a similar groove to a samba, but without the Brazilian implications, or might be something more closely related to rock or funk. Music with longer time signatures such as 5/4 and 7/4 might be straight or swung, and the composer should specify which is required.

Instructions such as 'rock' or 'funk' speak for themselves, although since actual rock and funk pieces tend to have specific bass lines and drum grooves, players should probably be provided with a part, the writing of which is covered in more detail in Chapter 22.

Rhythm Section Hits

As we begin to look beyond the simplified conception of jazz composition as a melody line and chord progression portrayed on a lead sheet, we might consider some of the options available to us for instructing our rhythm sections in a little more detail.

Synchronised interruptions to normal comping ('hits', or sometimes 'stabs' or 'kicks') are a useful tool. Where hits are marked on a rhythm section part, guitarists and pianists play chords in the suggested rhythms, bass players play the bass notes of those chords, and drummers mark those rhythms, interrupting their normal comping patterns.

So far we have used stem-less rhythm slashes to represent uninterrupted single beats of time-keeping. Slashes with stems can be used to denote hits, and we may instruct our rhythm section to move from standard comping patterns to hits and back again by switching between these two notation styles:

Composers usually place chord changes at metrically accented points of the bar. However, at all but the slowest tempos, jazz accompanists push and pull harmonies, initiating new chords sooner or delaying their arrival, as suggested by the asterisked notes above.

These patterns follow the same conventions as the anticipated and delayed melody pitches discussed earlier (page 118). By far the most common of these alterations to the written harmonic rhythm in both swing and the various straight eighth and Latin American styles is the anticipation of a chord by an eighth note, an effect which gives the impression of eager and active forward motion.

In the context of a lead sheet, there are a few ways that we might show hits. Firstly, we can include them above or below the stave:

If there are occasional hits in a piece, this may be the most effective way to notate them. However, if there is a lot of rhythm section information, such a notation system quickly becomes messy and confusing. Sometimes it is best to include a second clef on a lead sheet devoted to rhythm section information:

We might say that there are three primary applications of rhythm section hits behind a composed melody. Firstly, as above, they may fill the gaps between melodic phrases, creating a call and response effect between the melody line and rhythm section:

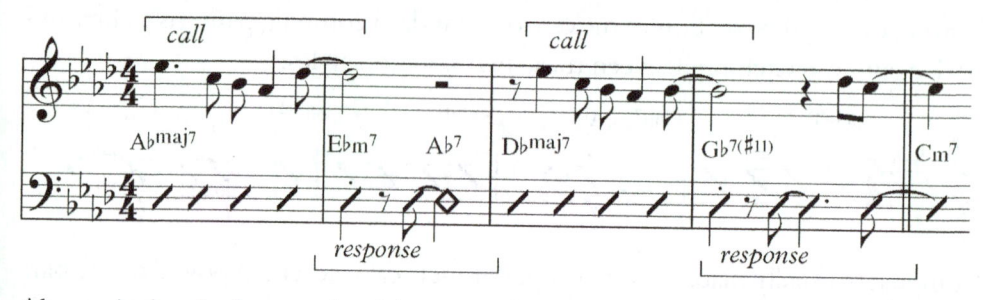

Alternatively, rhythm section hits might reinforce the melody, coinciding with prominent melody notes such as the first, last, or highest pitch in a phrase.

In the following example, hits highlight the anticipatory eighth note that ends each melodic phrase. Here the chords will also be syncopated, such that E^{bm7}, $G^{b7\#11}$, and C^{m7} will all be played on the final eighth note of the preceding bar:

[Musical notation excerpt with chords: Abmaj7 | Ebm7 Ab7 | Dbmaj7 | Gb7(#11) | Cm7]

Finally, a 'break' is a hit at which the rhythm section stops entirely for a few beats. In the head of a piece, this effect may be used to highlight a melodic phrase of particular interest or significance, as in bar three below:

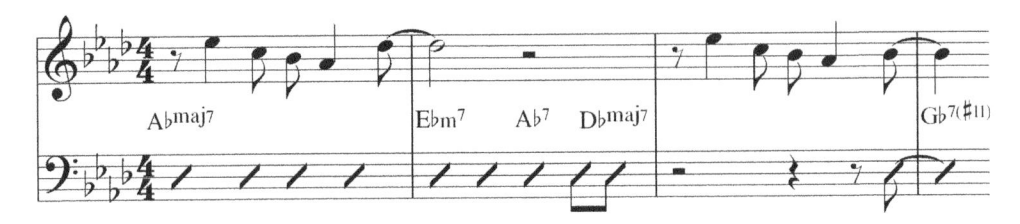

[Musical notation excerpt with chords: Abmaj7 | Ebm7 Ab7 Dbmaj7 | | Gb7(#11)]

When not used to highlight melodic material, breaks often feature the drums, or they may occur at the end of a head to highlight a soloist, who begins their solo unaccompanied before the beginning of their first chorus:

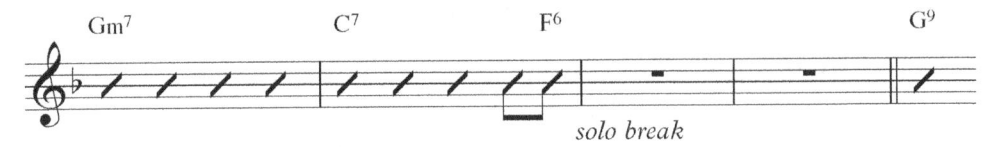

[Musical notation excerpt with chords: Gm7 | C7 | F6 | | G9]
solo break

Because hits in the head of a jazz tune usually relate directly to something that is occurring in the melody, they are often omitted for solos:

[Musical notation excerpt with chords: Abmaj7 | Ebm7 Ab7 | Dbmaj7 | Gb7(#11) | Cm7]
(head)

...becomes...

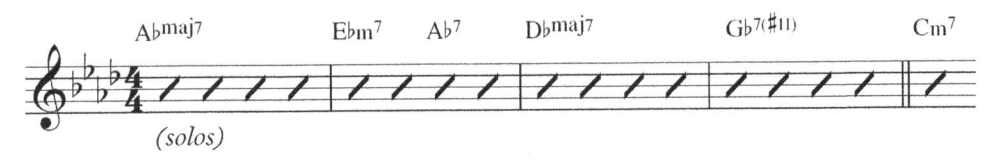

[Musical notation excerpt with chords: Abmaj7 | Ebm7 Ab7 | Dbmaj7 | Gb7(#11) | Cm7]
(solos)

This prevents too much repetition of the same rhythmic patterns, which might become tiresome if heard in every chorus. There is one popular exception to this, whereby breaks occurring at the end of a chorus might be used to highlight a changeover of soloists. A solo section might end thus, with the rhythm section playing continuously if the soloist continues, or breaking to highlight the entrance of a new soloist:

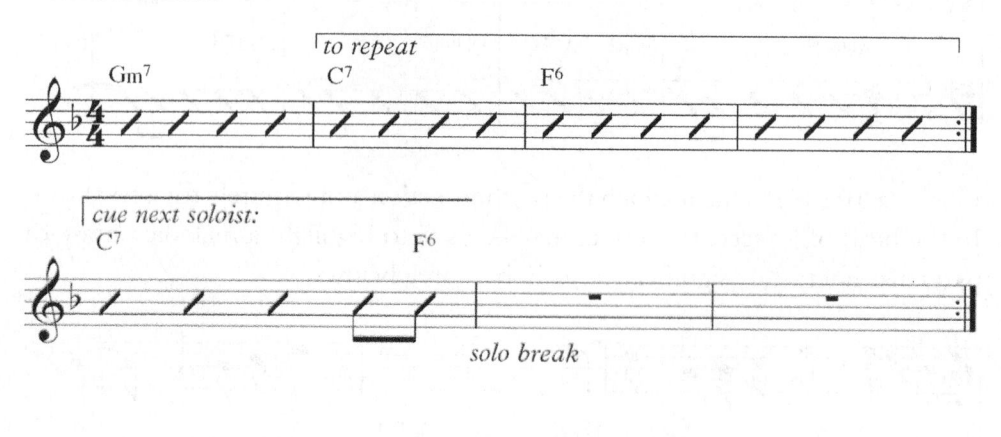

Arranging Solos

As we have seen, instrumental solos tend to be accompanied by the harmonic material presented by the head, and there is good reason for this. The melody presented at the beginning of a piece serves as the theme upon which melodic solos are variations, and the shared harmonic backing creates continuity, despite the abstracted or entirely unrelated melodic content.

In lead sheets and music for small ensembles, we usually leave the specifics of solo arrangement to the ensemble performing it, who may decide on details such as the sequence of solos at the time. In more arranged styles we may decide to dictate certain things. We may include more than one solo section, perhaps a first solo on a single period, with subsequent solos over a whole chorus, or a completely new sequence for a given soloist.

In more detailed arrangements, we may prescribe backing figures, melodic lines that accompany a soloist. Generally, this occurs towards the end of a solo late in the piece. A typical application of backing figures in a small group might be for the horns to solo first and then play backings over the final chorus of a piano solo.

Trading is another useful way to break up the sequence of solos. Players take it in turns with each other to play four- or eight-bar phrases of accompanied improvisation, or alternating with unaccompanied drum breaks. This usually takes place over the chorus, and is usually the final chorus of solos before the head out. Again, the decision to trade is usually decided by the performers at the time. One technique that has become popular in post-1990 small groups is a drum solo over a short sequence of complex hits, taking place immediately before or after the final head.

Introductions

Many jazz performances precede the head with an introduction. There is a great deal of variety in the type of material that might begin a piece, but a few general principles apply. The beginning of a head is almost always clearly demarked from introductory material, and this is often achieved with instrumentation. An introduction might be as simple as a vamp or a four-bar drum solo, but could also consist of significant unique material.

One traditional introduction to a songbook-style piece is to precede the head with the end of a chorus. A quartet of piano, bass, drums, and tenor saxophone might begin a performance of a standard with a piano improvisation accompanied by bass and drums over the harmony of the final eight bars of the chorus, before the saxophone enters with the head. This kind of introduction foreshadows the head, preparing the listener for the primary exposition of the piece.

Turnarounds and extended cadences such as those described previously (page 66) are also appropriate as an introduction to tonal material. Such progressions can serve to establish a tonality, and thus lead into the beginning of a chorus. A songbook style piece in C major might be introduced thus:

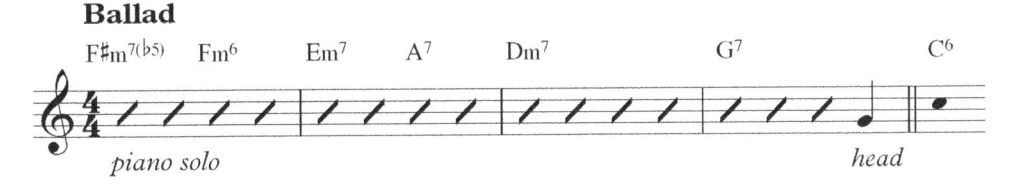

Ballad

$F\sharp m^{7(\flat 5)}$ Fm^6 Em^7 A^7 Dm^7 G^7 C^6

piano solo   *head*

Of course, many of these types of progressions can cycle, which means that they could be used as an indefinite vamp to be repeated until the soloist signals to move on. Such an introduction might be notated as follows:

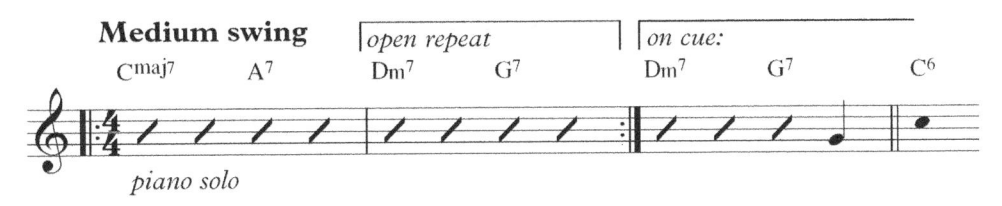

Medium swing   *open repeat*   *on cue:*

C^{maj7} A^7 Dm^7 G^7 Dm^7 G^7 C^6

piano solo

We may begin a piece with any harmonic material that forms a cadence into the beginning of the head, such the V or II-V of the head's first chord:

Bossa nova

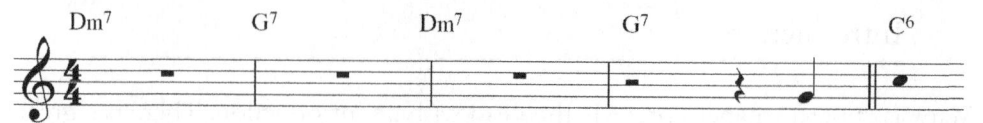

[Music notation: Dm⁷ | G⁷ | Dm⁷ | G⁷ | C⁶]

An introductory vamp is a classic application of a V^{7sus4} chord, which will be explored further later (page 207):

Bossa nova

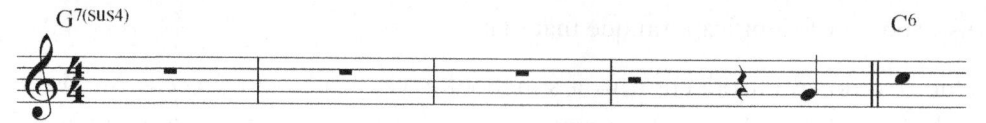

[Music notation: G⁷⁽ˢᵘˢ⁴⁾ | | | | C⁶]

Another element of the American songbook style that has influenced jazz composition is the verse. Originally, this was a sung introductory passage, perhaps sixteen or thirty-two bars long, that preceded the chorus. A verse usually consists of melodic material unrelated to the chorus, though later material may be foreshadowed at this point. Verses are sometimes a little more rhapsodic and harmonically adventurous than the chorus, and they are often performed *colla voce* or with pared back accompaniment.

All of these elements have been adopted at various times by jazz composers to create introductory passages for a chorus-based piece. The possibilities here are limitless, but introductions as diverse as the tightly arranged eight-bar ensemble passage that begins Wayne Shorter's *Witch Hunt*, and the solo piano impromptu with which Cedar Walton introduces *Holy Land* could both be seen as distant descendants of the songbook-style verse.

Endings

Most of the common techniques used in ending jazz performances exist to signpost to the listener that the piece is coming to an end. Sudden and surprising endings can sometimes be desirable, but these are somewhat rare in all styles of music.

The very final event in many pieces is a sustained chord of indefinite length, which is to say that its ending is visually cued between the performers. On a chord chart or lead sheet, this may simply be notated with a fermata over a chord symbol, followed by the final bar line showing the end of the piece:

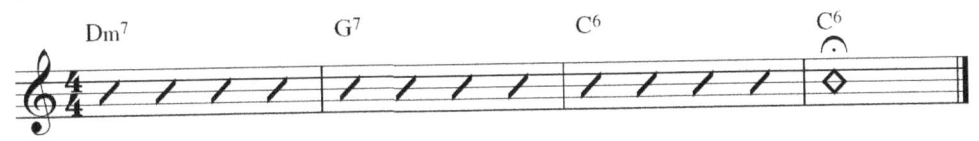

Musicians will often heavily embellish a sustained chord such as this with drum fills, arpeggios, and melodic lines according to their instrument, and the final chord of a piece is also particularly likely to be extended with a few exotic extensions. A 6/9 chord was a popular choice in pre-war jazz, a cliché that even made its way into pop music, audible in The Beatles' *No Reply*, for instance.

In more modern jazz styles, the raised eleventh is far more likely to be heard on a final I major chord than a tonic chord at any other point in a piece. Major tonics might also be transformed into seventh chords, the blues style tonic chord described previously (page 92), with a raised eleventh if desired.

Alternatively, a piece may end with a surprising twist to a distant harmony. The following are all popular enough as final chords to deserve mention, and all support the tonic pitch. Each of these chords might end a piece in the key of C, and each contains a C natural:

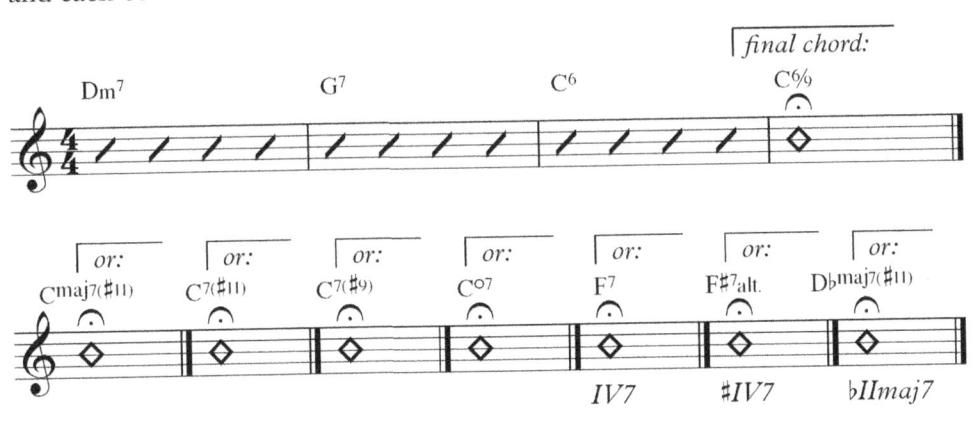

As in major keys, final tonic minor chords are likely to be more complex than those that occur in the middle of a piece. Both minor sixth or six-nine chords, and minor chords with major sevenths are popular in this position. Otherwise, the 'Picardy' I major chord (page 84) is occasionally used to end minor key pieces.

An alternative to the sustained final chord, particularly appropriate in the case of very active bebop heads, is a short ending in which the final chord coincides with a final melody note. Below, the rhythm section is represented by the bass clef, and the lead instrument represented by the treble clef:

[Musical notation: Dm⁷ | G⁷ | C⁶]

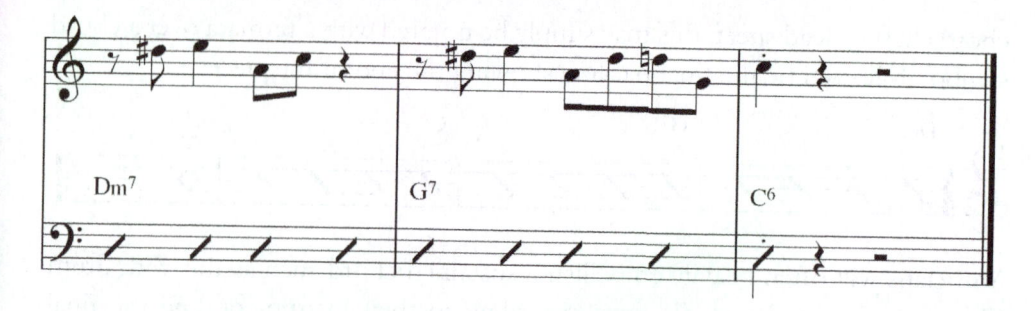

If the same melody had concluded an eighth note earlier, anticipating the final bar, the rhythm section will inevitably follow suit. An ending on the final eighth note of a bar in this manner is very common in bebop tunes:

[Musical notation: Dm⁷ | G⁷ | C⁶]

In more lyrical, songlike melodies, the end of a piece may slow down. Usually this is not an overly dramatic effect, and the deceleration rarely begins more than two or four bars before the end of the piece. In practice, jazz musicians use the directions *rallentando* and *ritardando* completely interchangeably, and passages that slow down are notated with either *rit.* or *rall.*, and a bracket or line to show the duration and position of the effect. Unsurprisingly, pieces that end with a *rit./rall.* invariably end with a sustained melody pitch over a sustained chord:

[Musical notation: **rit.** Fm⁷ | B♭⁷ | E♭maj13]

Classic, tonal, song-style choruses tend to resolve to a tonic chord in either the final bar, the penultimate bar, or four bars before the end. In either case, the listener expects the end of the hypermetric period to be played out. If, for example, a piece ends on the penultimate bar of a thirty-two-bar chorus, a silent thirty-second bar is implied:

[Musical notation: bars 29-32 with chords Dm⁷, G⁷, C⁶, !?]

Billy Strayhorn's iconic ending to *Take the 'A' Train* serves well to demonstrate how we might achieve a greater sense of finality by completing the four-bar hypermetric phrase:

[Musical notation: bars 29-32 with chords Dm⁷, G⁷, C⁶, C⁶]

Any tonic chord-compatible melodic material might be used here. Often, where the melody ends with some finality on the metrically strong first beat of bar thirty-one, a different voice within the ensemble picks up the closing phrase, as in the equally iconic 'Basie Ending':

[Musical notation: bars 29-32, trumpet and piano, with chords Dm⁷, G⁷, C⁶, Dm⁷, E♭°⁷, C⁶, C⁶]

Codas

A coda could be defined as material that extends beyond the end of the final chorus. In most styles, the introduction of significant new material at this point is relatively rare, though a coda could include new material of any kind, and might even be unrelated to the preceding piece in key, tempo, and melodic content.

One popular type of coda is an extended vamp initiated after the final head of the piece. Keith Jarrett's Standards Trio often apply this arrangement to songbook material. Their five-minute recording of the song *I Fall in Love Too Easily* concludes with an improvised one-chord vamp lasting for around nineteen minutes. A vamp might be ended by the performers on a visual cue, they might drop out one by one, or collectively decrescendo to silence.

In performances of songs, finality is often obtained by repetition of the final phrase. We can label the final phrase in a chorus 'z':

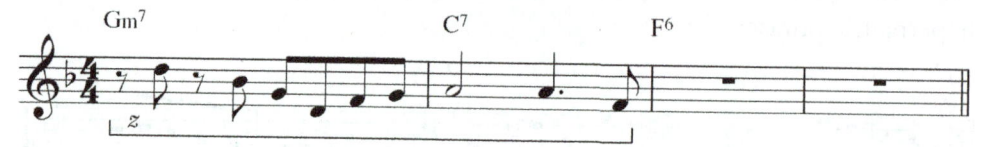

The final iteration of z might be preceded at the end of the piece with a false final phrase:

This effect signals that this really is the end of the tune, and is an effective, if clichéd, technique that produces an unambiguous sense of conclusion.

This final line might be repeated more than once, which allows for the possibility of another typical ending, in which the false final phrase is accompanied by a false harmonic cadence. Below, the II-V that accompanies the first false ending is followed not by I, but by III, delaying the arrival of the tonic and allowing for an extended III-VI-II-V turnaround to bring us home. z'' paraphrases the motif at a higher pitch level to comply with the underlying harmony:

This type of ending, often called a tag, effectively extends the length of the chorus in a manner that signposts and amplifies the sense of the finality of the last cadence.

Other Material: Interludes, Solis, and Shouts

We might define an interlude as new material that occurs between choruses. Dizzy Gillespie's *A Night in Tunisia*, and Dave Brubeck's *In Your Own Sweet Way* both contain interludes that occur after the head of the piece and after the final chorus of each solo. The former has a composed melody, and the latter consists of a static one-chord vamp. Interludes can break up the continuous cycle of the chorus form with new harmonic material and draw attention to the introduction of a new soloist.

We must be conscious of how often material will be heard throughout a performance. An interlude that ends each solo as well as the head might be heard every two minutes, and may occur more times in the piece any other material.

An interlude might also elongate the solo form, as in the tag used by Miles Davis in performances of *If I Were a Bell*. The piece is a thirty-two-bar song with a chorus ending in F major, with the following familiar harmonic phrase:

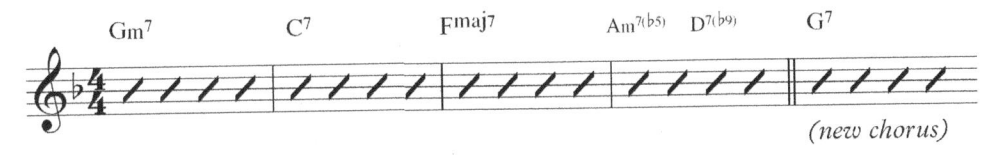

In Miles' arrangement, this closing cadence to the F major tonic is interrupted at the end of the soloist's final chorus an indefinite number of times. The soloist cues a looping four-bar chord progression, which only resolves when they hand over to the next soloist:

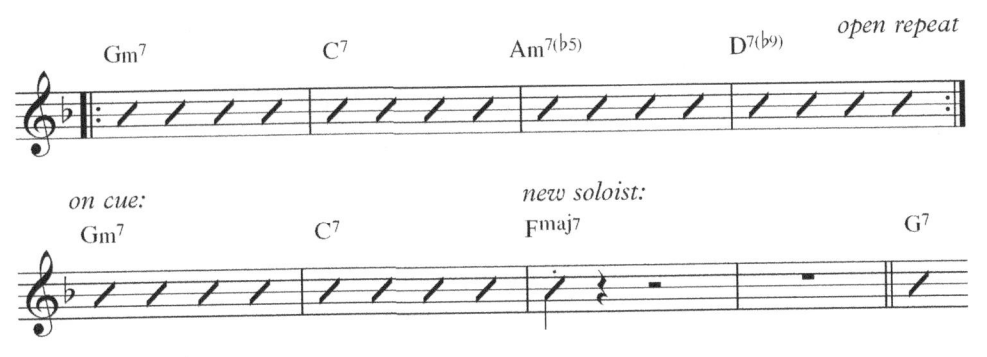

A soli is a secondary melody invariably composed over the same chord progression as the head, or some minor variation of it. This is particularly associated with big band music, where it can sometimes be referred to as an arranger's chorus.

As the name might suggest, a soli typically features more improvised or soloistic language than the head itself. In practical terms, this means a less songlike melody with a lot of notes, more complex rhythmic content, and relatively little repetition in the phrase structure.

Soli choruses usually occur towards the end of a piece, perhaps immediately before the head out, or in between solos. Solis are found in a many big band arrangements, where they feature a particular section of the band, typically the saxophones or the brass, in unison or in harmony with each other.

Solis occur occasionally in small band arrangements, but are most effective when played simultaneously on at least two instruments. The short section of unison melody that closes Chris Potter's *Wayfinder* could be considered a relative of the soli.

Like a soli, a 'shout' is a section of melody composed over the same harmony as the head. A shout chorus is an intense chorus heard before the final head, and often features a rhythmic, repetitive melodic idea. The shout is primarily a big band convention, but examples can be found of composers writing shout choruses for jazz quintets and quartets. In big band arrangements a shout chorus usually includes all of the brass and woodwinds.

The level of detail that goes into an arrangement is generally in proportion to the size of the ensemble. In conventional big band writing, the arranger is very hands-on, dictating exactly the part to be played by each instrument, the sequence and length of solos, dynamics, and form. At the other end of the spectrum, a small group can perform effectively from a single-page lead sheet consisting only of a single stave of melody with chord symbols. Ultimately, choosing which details to arrange in a piece is an aesthetic decision. Ensembles of any size might be highly arranged, completely improvised, or anywhere in between.

Chapter Summary

In order to realise a chord chart in a conventional style such as swing, bossa nova, or ballad, rhythm sections require little direction beyond an approximate tempo and a chord chart.

Hits are moments of rhythmic unison across the rhythm section, and have three main applications: they may fill gaps in a written melody, they may accentuate key pitches in a written melody, or they may initiate a break, in which the rhythm section ceases to play entirely for a few bars.

In small group music, solos usually receive very little arrangement from the composer. Larger ensembles require a little more detail in order to make full use of their instrumentation.

An introduction is material that precedes the head of a jazz piece. This may be based upon the head or chorus, might consist of a vamp or turnaround designed to cadence into the beginning of the chorus, or might contain significant unique material.

Jazz heads with very rhythmic, active melodies may end abruptly. Otherwise, many pieces end with a sustained final chord.

A coda may be added at the end of the final head. This may introduce new material, but might also be as simple as a reiteration of the final melodic phrase.

An interlude is material that interrupts repetitions of the chorus. This could be a simple vamp, or might introduce new melodic and harmonic material.

Interlude III

Interlude I introduced a number of short chord progressions based around conventional tonal sequences. In Interlude II, we added melodies to these, demonstrating a few of the many ways that melody interacts with harmonic accompaniment. We also explored how single phrases may be combined into melodies. We shall now continue to expand on these same four examples, adding secondary periods, rhythm section details, and expanding each into a fully performable lead sheet.

The lead sheet is a highly flexible form of notation which allows for a great deal of creative interpretation by performers. A basic lead sheet might consist only of a single stave showing a melody line, and chords for the chorus of a piece. This is how music is typically presented in fake books. A more detailed lead sheet might include extra-chorus material such as introductions and codas, and rhythm section details such as hits.

A lead sheet is instrumentation neutral, in the sense that it can be performed by practically any combination of instruments. If a singer or single horn is present, they will typically sing or play the written melody, accompanied by any rhythm section present. In the absence of a horn or singer, a piano, guitar, or bass might play the melody. Historically, in the majority of classic small-group jazz, horns solo first, followed by piano and guitar, bass, and then drums in that order, though this sequence should certainly be varied from piece to piece.

Two horn players may play in unison, sometimes separated by octaves, particularly on more active bebop style pieces where deviation from the composed melody is less common. On songlike tunes that lend themselves to a looser interpretation, two horns may divide the melody, with one playing the first half of a head and one taking the second, or one horn playing the bridge of an *A-A-B-A* head.

When three or more horns are available, a lead sheet is probably a missed opportunity to compose individual horn parts in harmony and counterpoint with each other. We shall discuss some of these possibilities later, particularly in Chapter 23.

The lead sheet should strive for clarity and simplicity. Complicated layouts with multiple codas, numbered repeats, and text boxes of instructions can be difficult to read, and can usually be avoided by simply adding extra pages to a chart. On the other hand, lead sheets of more than three pages bring their own problems such as impractical page turns.

A lead sheet should begin with a title and a suggested style, alongside either an approximate tempo instruction or a metronome mark. New periods should be demarked with a double bar line and, wherever practical, introduced on a new system. Each phrase should also begin a new system. As a rule, this will produce four-bar systems which are practical and easy to read.

Rehearsal marks can be useful, particularly in longer and more complex arrangements, and should be reserved for distinct sections of the piece. The first rehearsal mark might show the head, and the second the solo section. The labels that we use to describe the structure of a chorus, such as *A-A-B-A*, are not rehearsal marks. The purpose of rehearsal marks is, as the name suggests, to allow musicians to discuss passages during rehearsal. Letters that occur more than once within a part are not useful for this purpose.

Simple lead sheets such as those found in fake books often present only the head of a piece, expecting solos to take place over the same changes as the head. Where there are significant deviations between the head and solo section, such as rhythm section hits that occur only in the head, it may be clearer to write out the solo section separately from the head.

Most lead sheets are written entirely within one key signature, although if a piece changes key permanently or for an extended period, a new key signature is appropriate. Transposing instruments such as saxophones and trumpets should be provided with parts transposed appropriately to their instruments, something which will be addressed later (page 297).

If a piece is not in any particular key, or does not spend a significant amount of time in any one key, it might be best notated with no key signature. Crucially, this is not the same as writing in the keys of C major or A minor: a piece with no key signature will also have no key signature on transposed parts.

Keats Persona

S. Jackson

Fast swing (♩ = 200)

• Interlude III

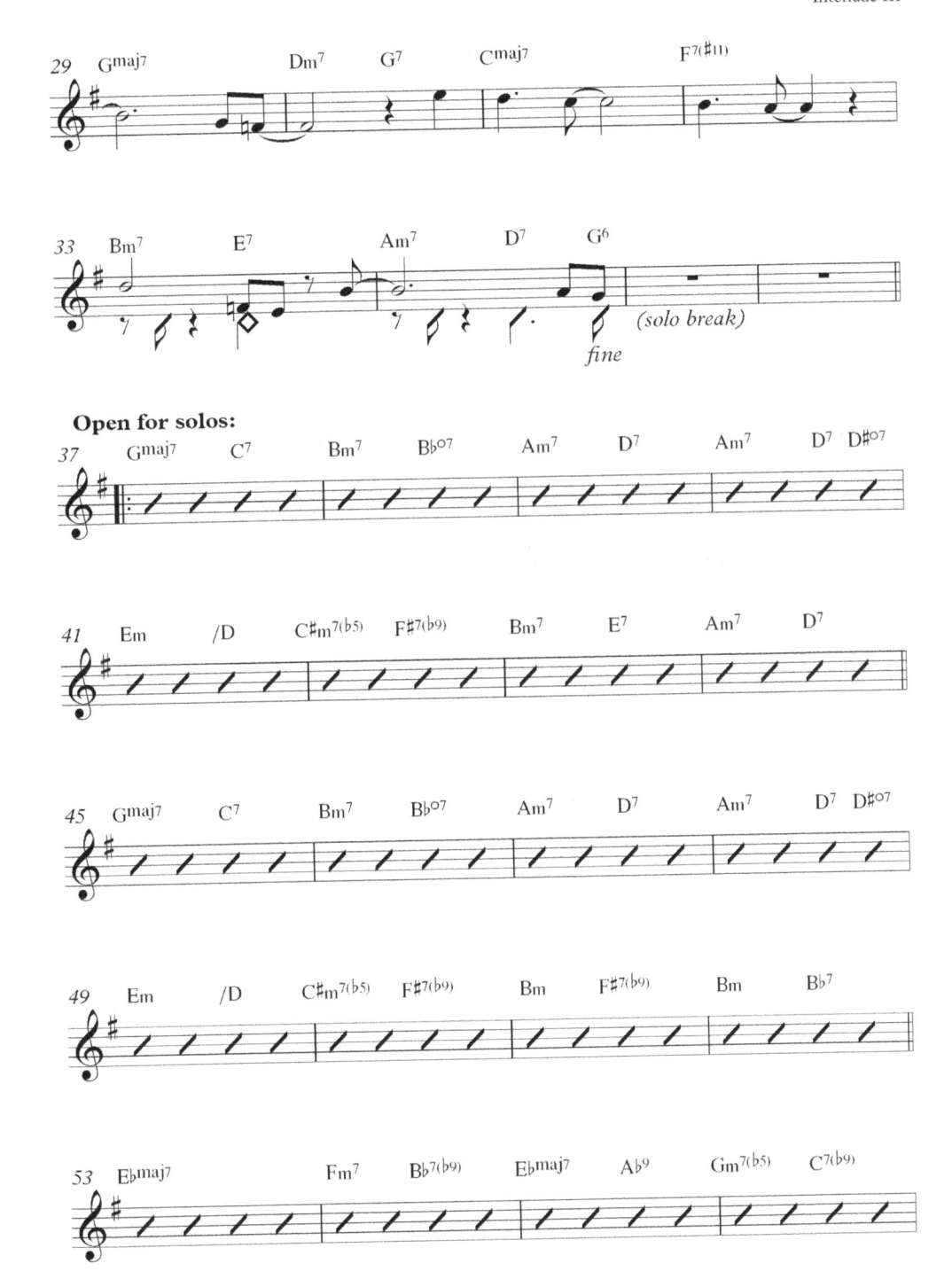

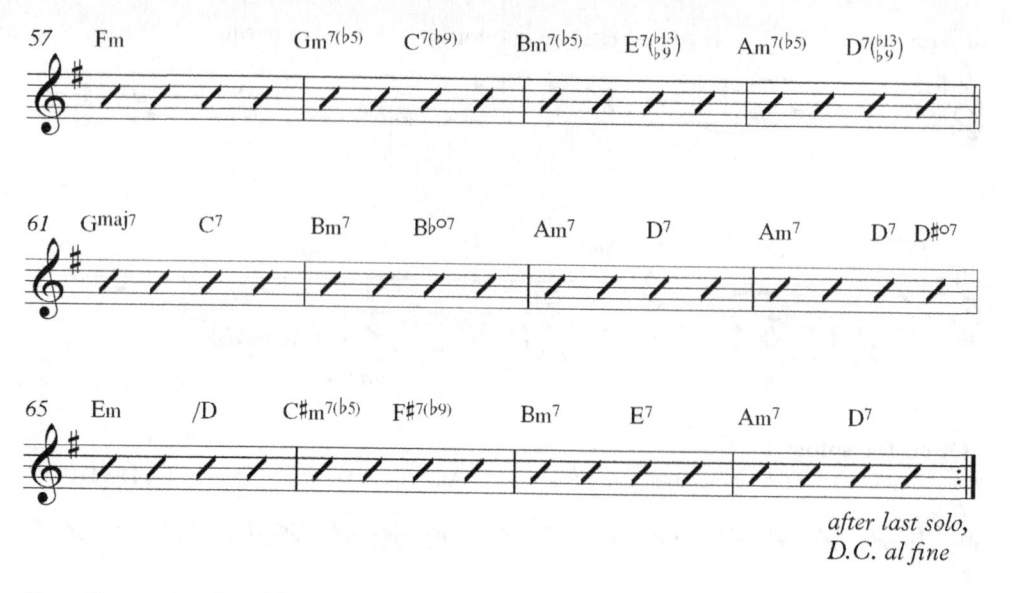

Keats Persona is a hard bop tune at a moderately fast tempo. The head is structured *A-A-B-A-C*. The first two *A*s start on bar 1, *B* at bar 13, the final *A* at bar 21, and *C* at bar 29.

Despite sharing no motivic material with *A*, the bridge at *B* is in a similar melodic style to the *A* sections, consisting of arpeggios and short scalic passages, and being essentially rhythmic rather than lyrical. *C* provides some contrast, with sustained notes and a less angular, more songlike contour.

Solos take place over a more conventional *A-A-B-A* arrangement, which has been written out separately. A shorter chart might have been constructed with a rehearsal mark 'A' at bar 1, rehearsal mark 'B' at bar 21, and the instruction '**solos over A, after last solo, D.C. al fine**'.

• Interlude III

Joy's Soul

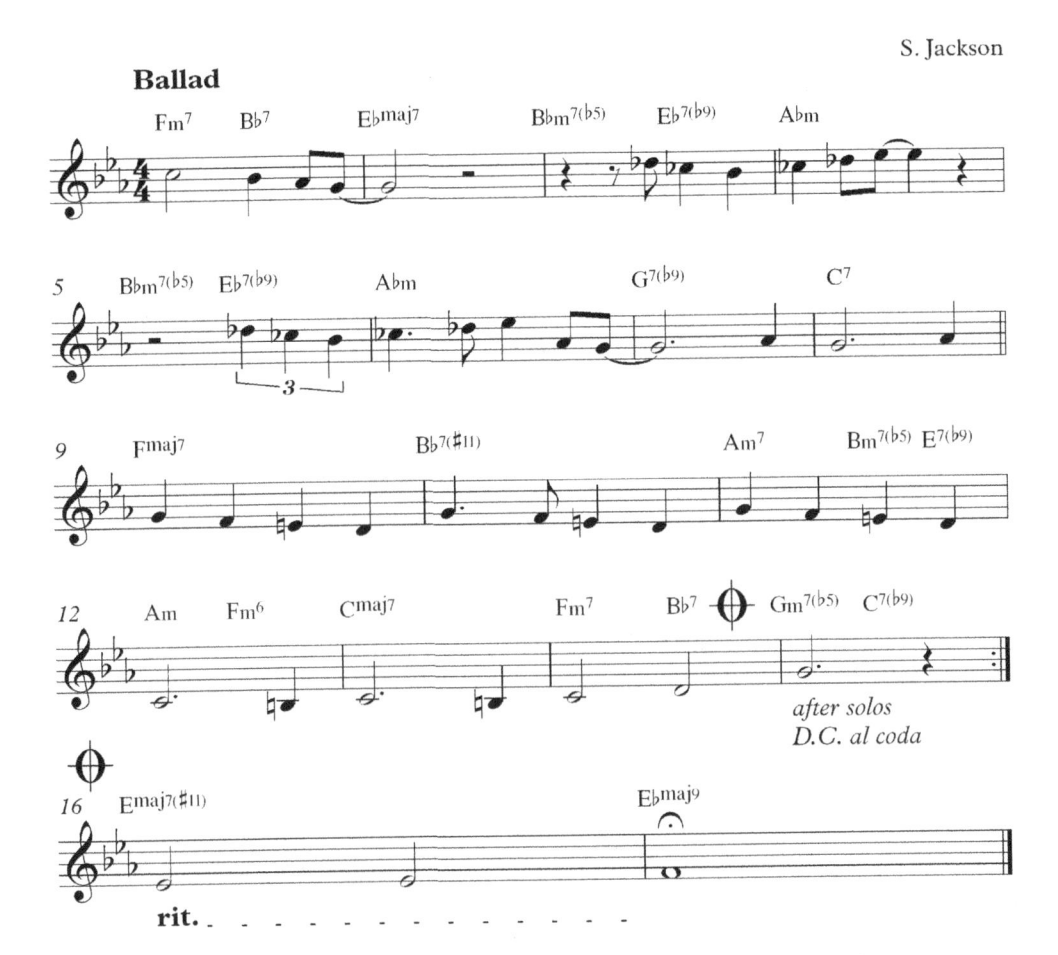

S. Jackson

[Sheet music: Ballad, 4/4 time, key signature of three flats]

Chord changes:
- Bar 1: Fm7 | Bb7
- Bar 2: Ebmaj7
- Bar 3: Bbm7(b5) | Eb7(b9)
- Bar 4: Abm
- Bar 5: Bbm7(b5) | Eb7(b9)
- Bar 6: Abm
- Bar 7: G7(b9)
- Bar 8: C7
- Bar 9: Fmaj7
- Bar 10: Bb7(#11)
- Bar 11: Am7 | Bm7(b5) E7(b9)
- Bar 12: Am | Fm6
- Bar 13: Cmaj7
- Bar 14: Fm7
- Bar 15: Bb7 ⊕ | Gm7(b5) C7(b9)

after solos
D.C. al coda

- Bar 16 (coda ⊕): Emaj7(#11)
- Bar 17: Ebmaj9

rit. _ _ _ _ _ _ _ _ _

Several elements in *Joy's Soul* suggest a more abstract harmonic style. The truncated fifteen-bar head is structured *A-B*, with an unusual seven-bar *B* section. The melody clearly divides *B* into a three-bar phrase followed by a four-bar phrase, and the layout of the chart reflects this.

A was previously presented (page 148) without key signature, but the wider context of this full chorus now suggests that, despite passing through the keys of A-flat minor, F major, and A minor, the piece can be considered to be in E-flat major.

The slower ballad tempo softens the impact of these frequent and radical modulations, and allows for a faster harmonic rhythm, such as the one-chord-per-beat changes at the end of bar 11.

191

Bar 14 of the head strongly suggests that the piece will end on the tonic chord, with the tonic pitch as a melody note as depicted here.

However, each repetition of the chorus frustrates our expectations as the melody diverts to the third, and the harmony cycles back to chord II. This keeps the chord progression rolling forward, avoiding a premature sense of finality. Even when the melody does resolve in the first bar of the coda, the underlying chord avoids resolution. When the harmony finally arrives at I in the final bar of the coda, the melody has moved again, resolving to the ninth.

• Interlude III

Sheaf Street

S. Jackson

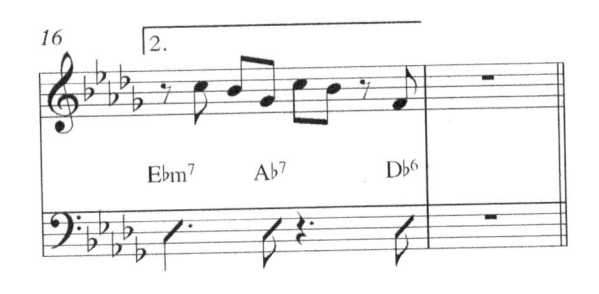

Medium swing

18
C7
F7
22
C7
F7 Bb7(b9)
Eb7 Ab7(b9)
26
Db7
Gb7
Db7
solos on 'A'
after final solo D.S. al fine
29
Gm7(b5) C7(b9)
Fm7 Bb7
Ebm7 Ab7 Db6
fine

Sheaf Street uses the seven-bar idea introduced on page 149 as the *A* section in an *A-A-B-A* chorus, adding rhythm section hits that support the melody. The piece begins with a V chord vamp, before bar 5 introduces the head with harmonies and comping figures that foreshadow bar 12.

The melody in the bridge, bars 22 to 25, incorporates a motif from earlier in the piece, serving to tie together two harmonically and melodically distinct sections. Compare bar 12 to bar 23:

Caduceus

S. Jackson

Bossa nova

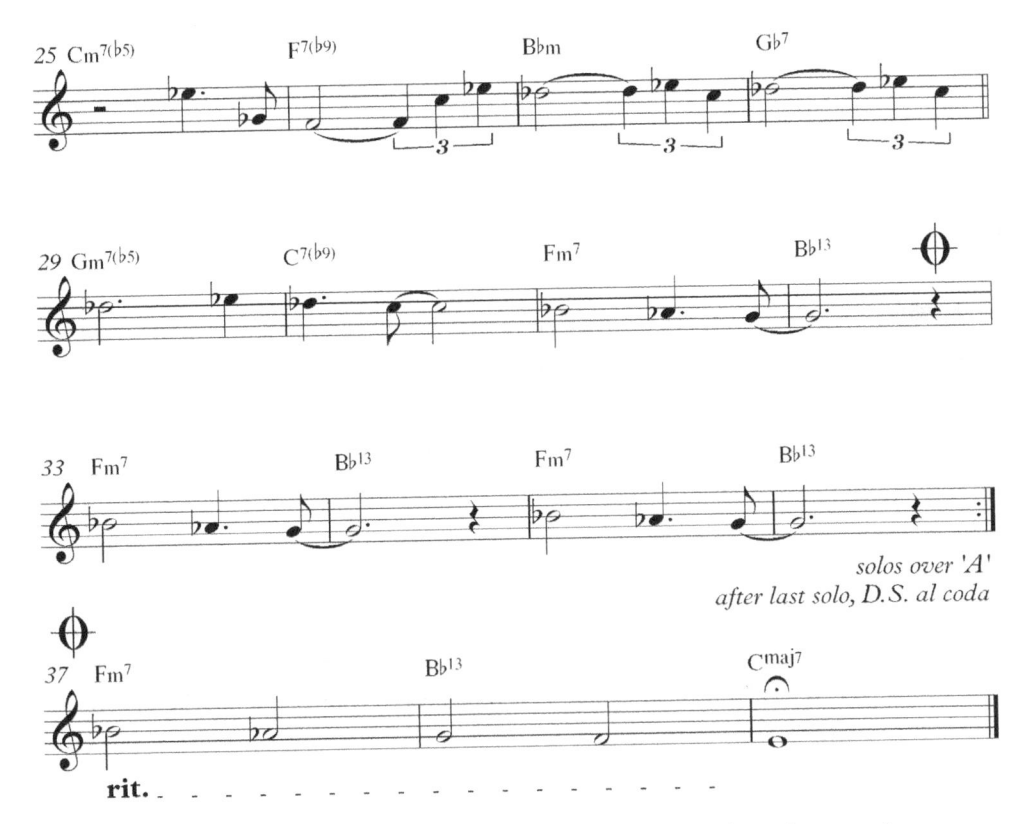

Caduceus is an *A-B-A-C* bossa nova in which section *B* is based upon the excerpt that first appeared on page 150. The melody is lyrical and songlike throughout, but has a somewhat rhapsodic and wandering feel to it. Similar motifs and rhythms are used across periods, such as this phrase from the end of the *A* section, which becomes an important motif in *B*:

Key is ambiguous in this piece. The introductory vamp suggests E-flat major as a possibility, but when the tonic chord of that key finally arrives in bar 19, it feels more like ♭III in C major.

When the piece apparently resolves in the final bar of the coda, the roles of these two keys are reversed, with a C major seventh chord emerging in an E-flat major context. Because of this ambiguity of destination and the very frequent and varied modulations throughout the thirty-two-bar chorus, this lead sheet is presented without a key signature.

Chapter 14
Substitutions for V and II-V

The next two chapters will explore some variations on the chord progressions that we have already seen. These harmonies are still functional, as they operate within contexts that establish and affirm a sense of a tonic chord and gravity towards it. The ideas in this chapter are a little more abstract and elaborate than the more common progressions so far discussed.

The V chord has central importance within tonal harmony, but there are various alternatives to it that might also serve to forecast the arrival of a tonic chord. Some of these substitutions replace more conventional chords, and some elaborate upon them by adding additional movement to areas of static harmony. They may add interest, complexity, and variation, and can support otherwise unavailable melody notes.

Tritone Substitution

The first replacement for a V chord that most jazz musicians learn is the tritone substitution. As we saw in Chapter 3, the third and seventh of a V^7 chord are dissonant with each other. The resolution of these two pitches to the nearest consonant diatonic interval produces the third and root of the I chord:

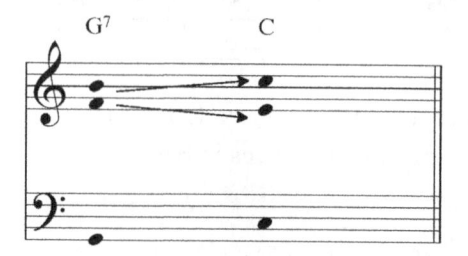

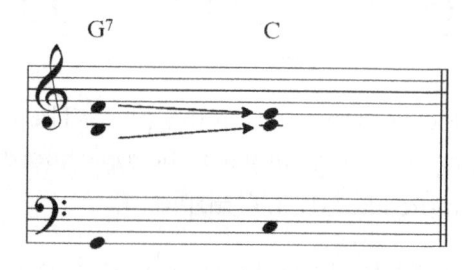

Because the intervallic distance between B-natural and F-natural is exactly half an octave (or a tritone), we can replace the root of V^7 with a pitch half an octave away to produce a transposition of the same structure, with its root on the flattened second of the key, the $\flat II^7$ chord. The respective third and seventh of V⁷ are the seventh and third of ♭II⁷ and vice versa, and the root of this new chord resolves down a half step to I. ♭II⁷ is therefore the tritone substitution of V⁷:

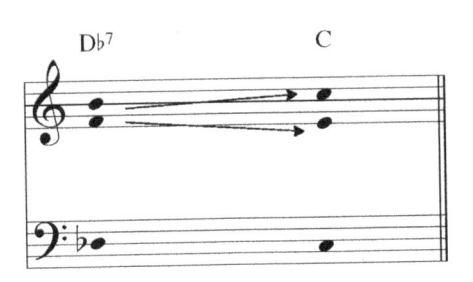

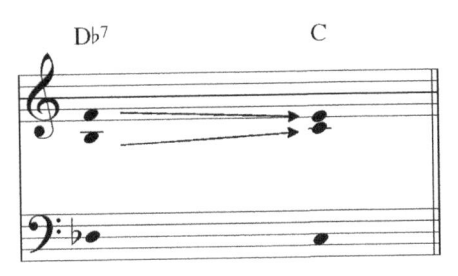

The substitution of ♭II⁷ for V⁷ is very common in both jazz composition and improvisation. ♭II⁷ might also replace V⁷ within a II-V progression:

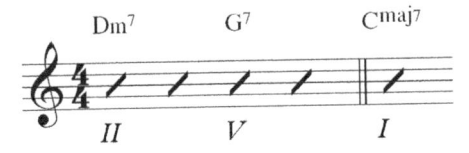

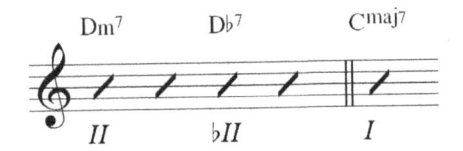

...becomes:

The tritone substitution is not available only on the V chord. Any dominant-type chord may be replaced with a dominant chord three whole steps away. In fact, the tritone substitution is more common when it replaces a seventh chord that is *not* the V of the prevailing key. This substitution is a little less disruptive to tonality when it is somewhat displaced from the tonic. Below, the VI⁷ in a II-VI-II-V progression is replaced with its tritone substitution:

...becomes:

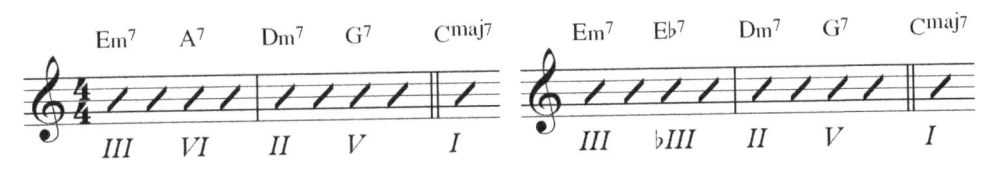

A dominant chord in its original form might be followed by its tritone substitution. The non-diatonic nature of the second chord intensifies the sense of resolution demanded by V⁷:

The inverse is possible, though a little less typical, as movement from a non-diatonic chord to a diatonic chord de-intensifies the V^7:

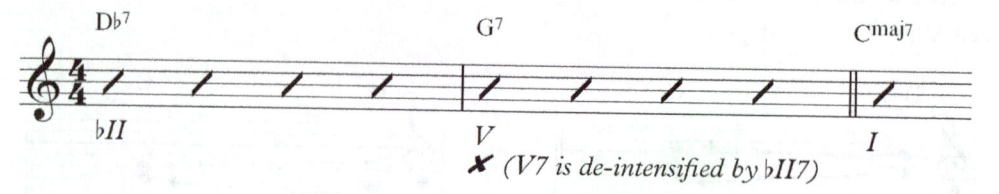

D♭⁷	G⁷	Cmaj7
♭II	V	I

✗ *(V7 is de-intensified by ♭II7)*

A tritone substitution might be elaborated with its own II. Again, this could follow a diatonic II-V:

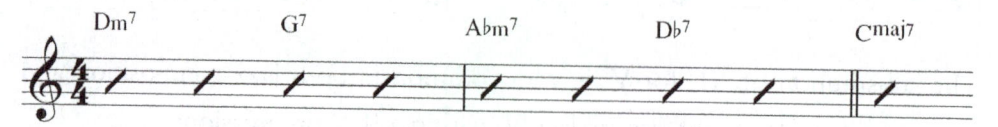

Dm⁷   G⁷   A♭m⁷   D♭⁷   Cmaj7

Alternatively, the replacement of the secondary dominants III⁷ and II⁷ with their tritones produces a chromatically descending cascade of II-Vs:

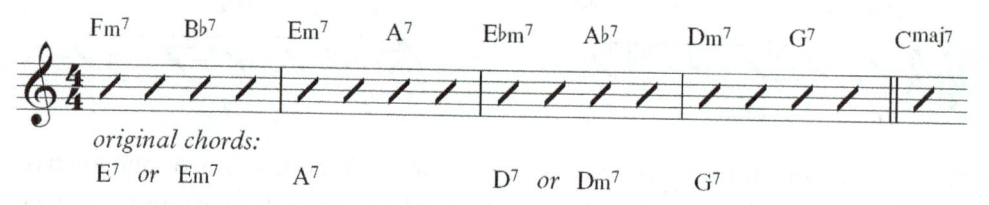

Fm⁷   B♭⁷   Em⁷   A⁷   E♭m⁷   A♭⁷   Dm⁷   G⁷   Cmaj7

original chords:
E⁷ or Em⁷   A⁷   D⁷ or Dm⁷   G⁷

Entire cadential cycles, or any components of them, can be substituted for their tritone substitutions. We can transform each chord in a major key III-VI-II-V progression into a dominant chord type:

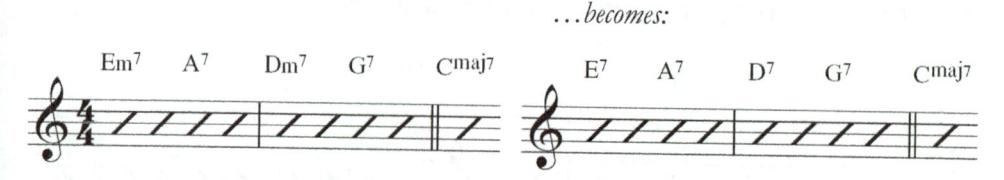

...becomes:

Em⁷   A⁷   Dm⁷   G⁷   Cmaj7   E⁷   A⁷   D⁷   G⁷   Cmaj7

III, VI, II, *and* V are now all eligible for tritone substitution:

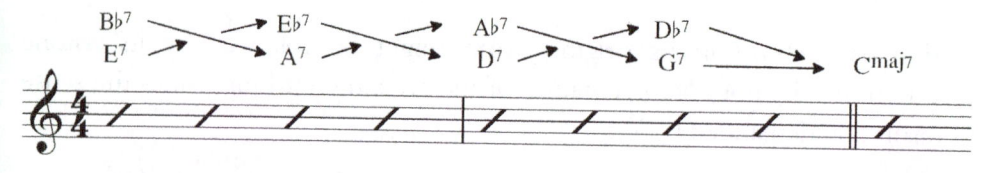

B♭⁷ → E♭⁷ → A♭⁷ → D♭⁷
E⁷ → A⁷ → D⁷ → G⁷ → Cmaj7

We can switch from the upper row of chords to the lower at any point, taking one of twenty-four possible routes to the tonic, including:

[Musical notation:
Row 1a: Bb7 | Eb7 Ab7 | Db7 | Cmaj7
Row 1b: E7 | Eb7 D7 | Db7 | Cmaj7
Row 2a: Bb7 | A7 Ab7 | G7 | Cmaj7
Row 2b: E7 | A7 Ab7 | G7 | Cmaj7]

These ideas can also be applied to other tonal progressions, such as the movements from I to II discussed earlier (page 70):

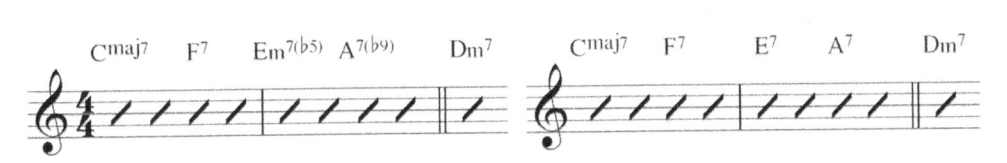

...becomes:

[Musical notation:
Cmaj7 | F7 Em7(b5) | A7(b9) | Dm7
Cmaj7 | F7 E7 | A7 | Dm7]

Again, any or all of these dominant chords might be replaced with a tritone substitution. We might cross from the upper row of chords to the lower at any point, giving us numerous functional routes from I to II:

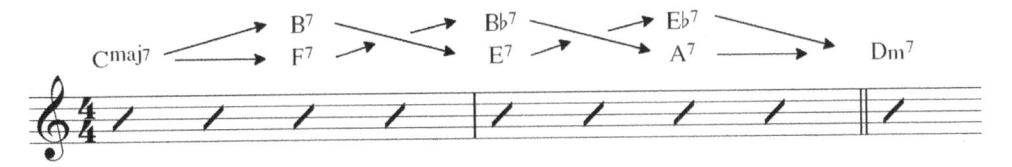

[Musical notation with crossing arrows: Cmaj7 → B7 / F7 → Bb7 / E7 → Eb7 / A7 → Dm7]

The Altered Chord

A related concept to the tritone substitution is the altered chord. Theoretically, this is a dominant chord with every possible altered extension: the flattened ninth, raised ninth, raised eleventh, and the flattened thirteenth.

In practice, the altered chord is more often voiced with either the flattened ninth or raised ninth, and either the raised eleventh or the flattened thirteenth, which prevents too many close intervals within the voicing. The fifth is usually omitted, as it would clash with either the raised eleventh a half step below, or the flattened thirteenth a half step above.

In most situations, the following harmonies are compatible and interchangeable, and may be denoted with the 'X$^{7alt.}$' chord symbol:

Although these structures are complex, the origin of the altered chord in jazz harmony is actually rather simple. This structure is a dominant seventh chord with the flattened fifth in the bass. In other words, the preceding altered structures can all be re-spelt as un-altered D-flat dominant chords:

The altered chord emerges from functional harmony whenever the bass note of a dominant chord is displaced by a tritone while the upper structure is left intact, or the inverse, when the bass note is retained and the upper structure displaced by a tritone. This tritone altered chord combines diatonic extensions with the chromatic bass movement of the tritone substitution:

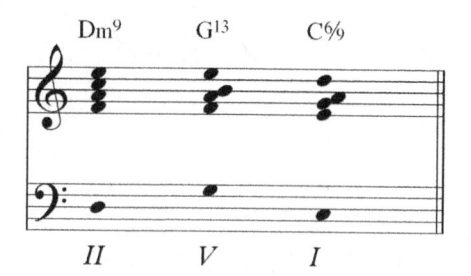

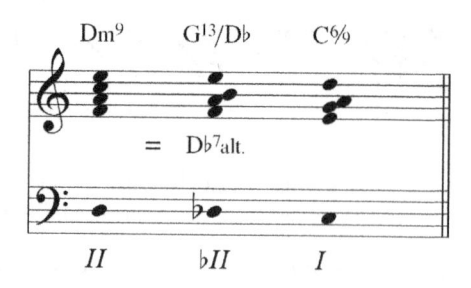

Inversely, a chord progression might combine the upper structure of a tritone substitution with the bass note of V^7 to produce $V^{7alt.}$:

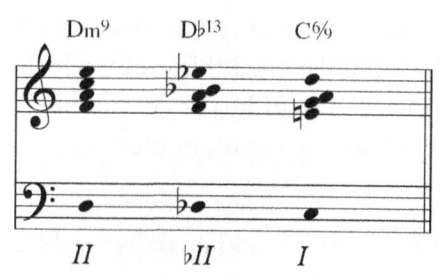

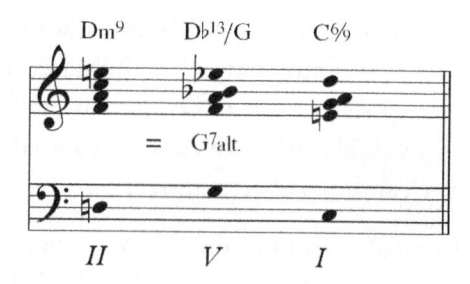

Like the tritone substitution, the altered chord type can be applied to any dominant harmony, and is more typical on dominant chords that are not the V of the key.

Because the altered chord, like the tritone dominant, contains non-diatonic pitches, it intensifies an unaltered dominant chord, and can be used after it. Moving from an altered to an unaltered dominant chord de-intensifies, weakening the urgency of resolution, and is therefore less common:

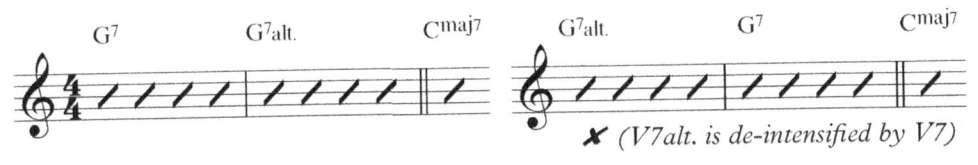

(V7alt. is de-intensified by V7)

Between them, the tritone substitution and altered chord give us three alternatives to V^7 in a cadence to I.

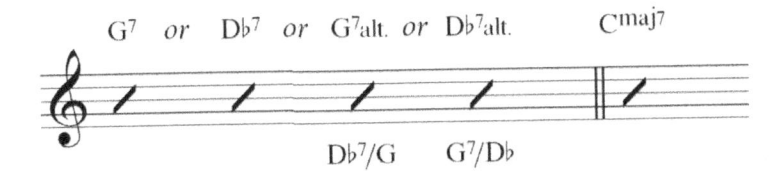

More Alternatives to V and II-V

As we discussed at length in Chapter 3, II-V is an elaboration of V. It can replace V whilst providing an increase in complexity, and in the rate of harmonic change:

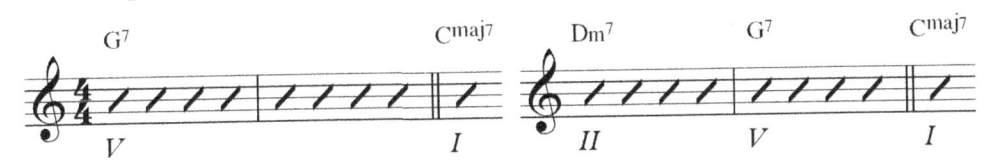

There are numerous alternative elaborations available for V and II-V. Firstly, a long II-V in which each chord lasts one bar might be replaced by two short II-Vs *(a)*, or by a bar of chord IV followed by a short II-V *(b)*:

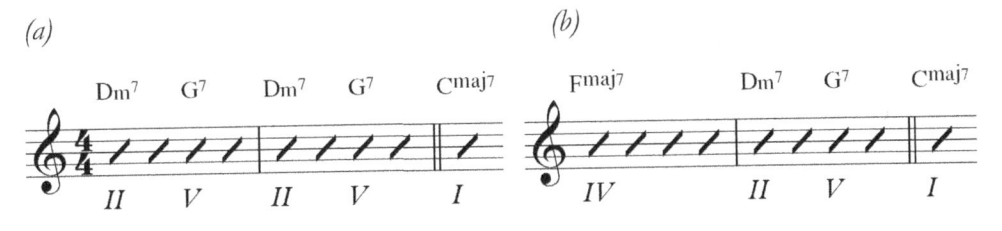

A long passage with a V chord might be replaced with a chord progression that climbs up to the tonic through II with a ♭VII° passing chord and V/3, as in *(c)*.

A similar effect comes from moving each pitch of the voicing up to the next diatonic pitch, such that the structure shifts diatonically from II^{m7}, through III^{m7} and IV^{maj7} to V^7, as in *(d)*. Both progressions build a sense of tension as the bass line ascends towards its destination:

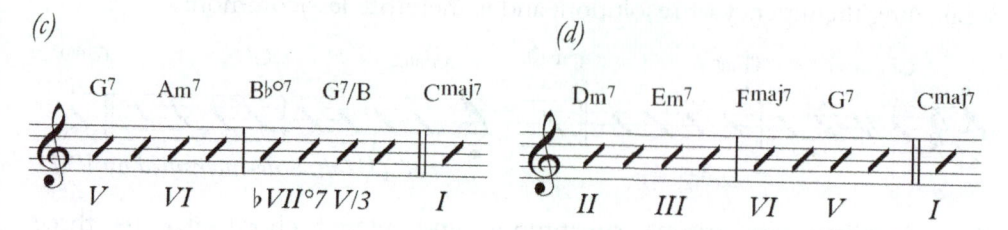

(c) G^7 Am^7 B♭^{o7} G^7/B Cmaj7
       V   VI   ♭VII°7 V/3   I

(d) Dm^7 Em^7 Fmaj7 G^7 Cmaj7
       II   III   VI   V   I

The voice leading implications of such progressions are obvious. Each pitch in the chord voicing simply moves upwards into an available pitch within the next chord:

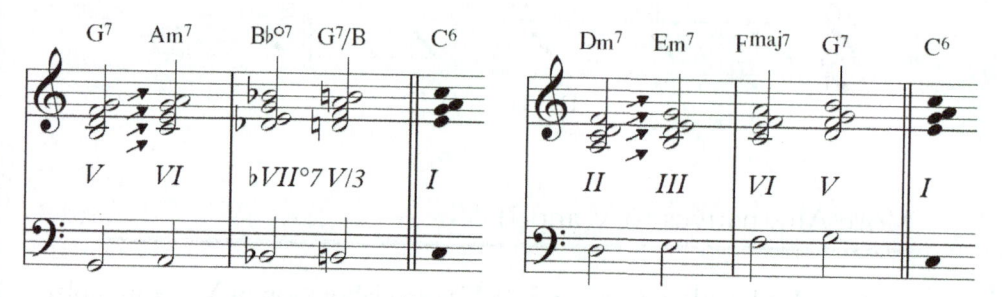

Below here are some of ways that we use the secondary dominant to elaborate a major II-V progression. II^{m7} may be transformed into II^7 *(e)*, V^7 elaborated into II-V *(f)*, and II7 elaborated into II-V *(g)*:

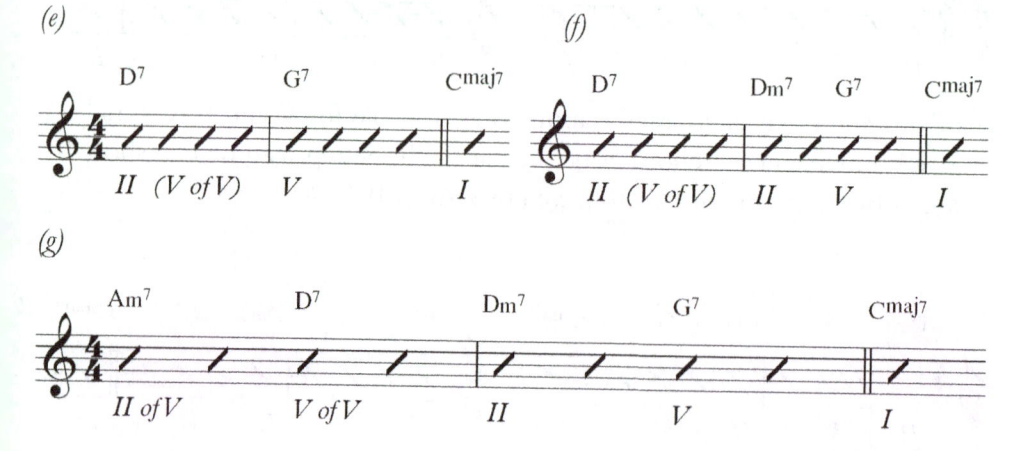

(e) D^7 G^7 Cmaj7
      II (V of V) V   I

(f) D^7 Dm^7 G^7 Cmaj7
      II (V of V) II   V   I

(g) Am^7 D^7 Dm^7 G^7 Cmaj7
      II of V   V of V   II   V   I

Another popular variation on the major II-V is to replace it with chords from the parallel minor. A major tonic might be preceded with a full minor-style II-V, as in *(h)*, or a major II and a minor V, as in *(i)*:

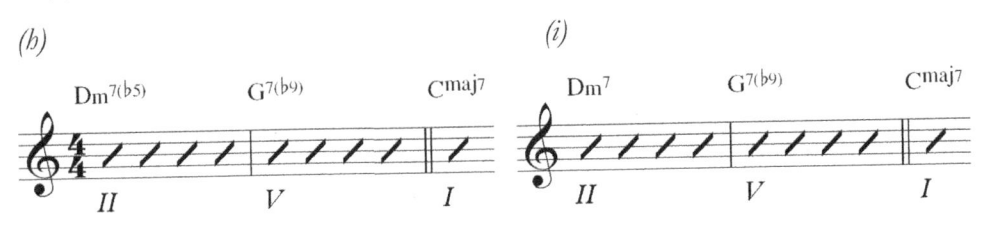

(h)   *(i)*

On page 77 we saw the application of $^\flat VI^7$ in minor keys, where only its seventh is foreign to the key signature. This harmony is also available in major keys, as in *(j)*, and its elaboration *(k)*. $^\flat VII^7$ can be understood as a tritone substitution for II^7.

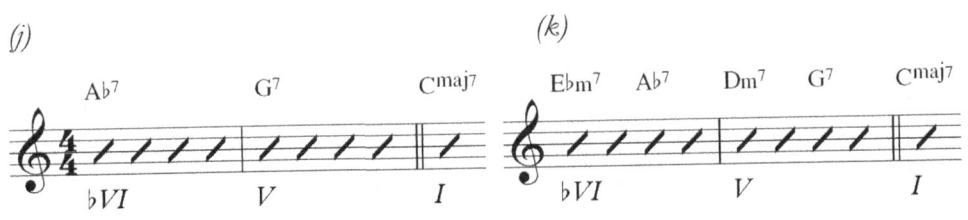

(j)   *(k)*

II^{m7} might be elaborated with a detour to its own dominant, as shown in *(l)*, pushing back the arrival of V. *(m)* is a similar elaboration of II. Both *(l)* and *(m)* imply a descending chromatic line in either melody or accompaniment:

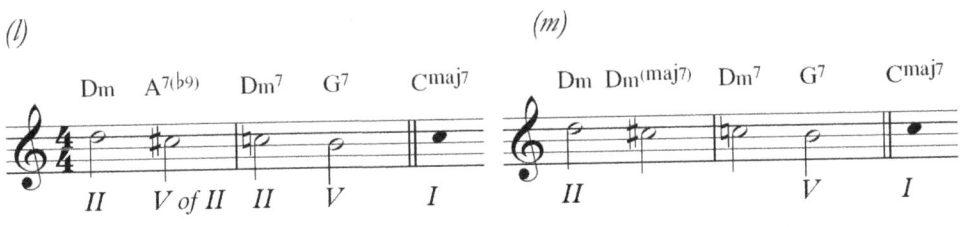

(l)   *(m)*

Finally, V^7 may be replaced with a V augmented triad, V^{+7}, in order to support the flattened third/raised second of the key as a melody note. It generally occurs as a lower neighbour to the third. This popular melodic movement is disguised by elaboration in the second example:

Minor Key Alternatives to V and II-V

Owing perhaps to a less consonant tonic chord, the minor key is less secure in its tonality than the major, and has a tendency to avoid anything that might suggest the parallel major. Consequently, there are fewer conventional alternatives to V and II-V in minor keys.

Although the minor style II-V is often used to cadence into a major tonic, major II-Vs are rarely used to approach tonic minor chords. As discussed on page 56, II^7 appears occasionally in minor keys as an alternative to II^{m7b5}. Extensions from within the key signature yield an altered chord in this position:

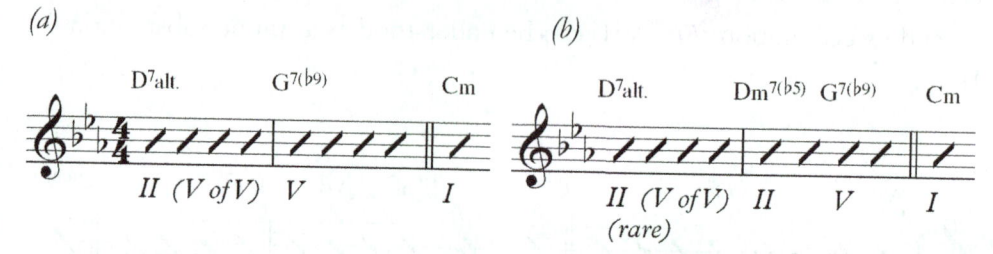

(a) D7alt. G7(b9) Cm
II (V of V) V I

(b) D7alt. Dm7(b5) G7(b9) Cm
II (V of V) II V I
(rare)

Doubling up the II and V chords is as common in minor as it is in major, as in *(c)*. Also common is the delaying of II by preceding it with IV, as in *(d)*. In minor keys, IV tends to move to II through IV/7:

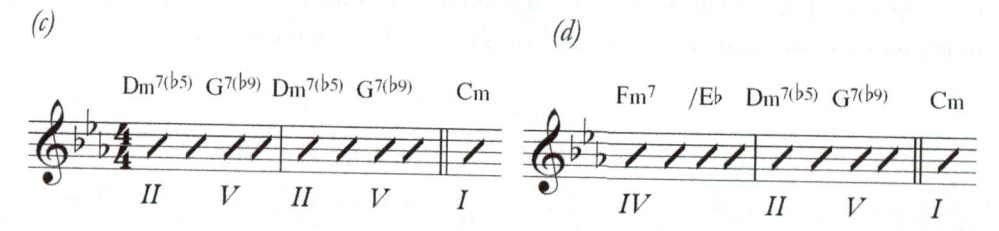

(c) Dm7(b5) G7(b9) Dm7(b5) G7(b9) Cm
II V II V I

(d) Fm7 /Eb Dm7(b5) G7(b9) Cm
IV II V I

Finally, the $^bVI^7$ chord that is so typical in minor keys *(e)*, may be elaborated with a II, as in *(f)*:

(e) Ab7 G7(b9) Cm
bVI V I

(f) Ebm7 Ab7 Dm7(b5) G7(b9) Cm
bVI V I

Suspended V

The suspended chord is a dominant chord in which the third is replaced with a fourth. In tonal jazz, this usually functions as a V chord, appearing with its root on the fifth of the key. It includes a flattened seventh, as well as those extensions available within the key signature. In C:

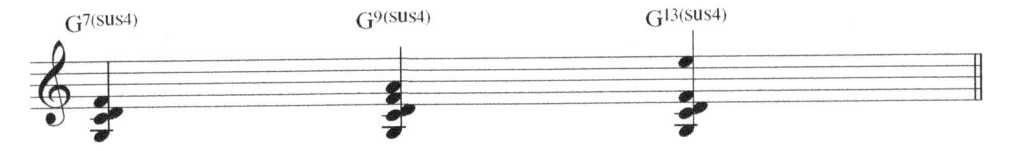

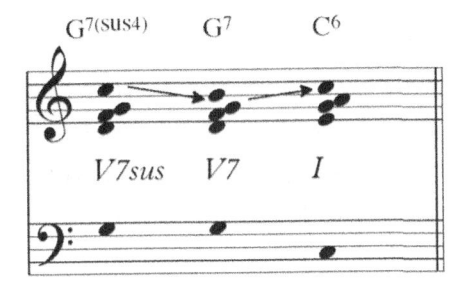

Extensions are optional, and G^{7sus4} is a suitable chord symbol for any of the pitch collections above. In its most typical form, the fourth of the V^{7sus4} resolves to its third, and the resulting V^7 resolves to I.

V^{7sus4} is often written as a slash chord II/4, or IV/2, which is to say G^{7sus4} may be written as D^{m7}/G or F^{maj7}/G. The former is a particularly useful way to conceptualise the chord. This effect may arise serendipitously in jazz performance if, for example, a bass player plays V whilst a pianist plays II-V:

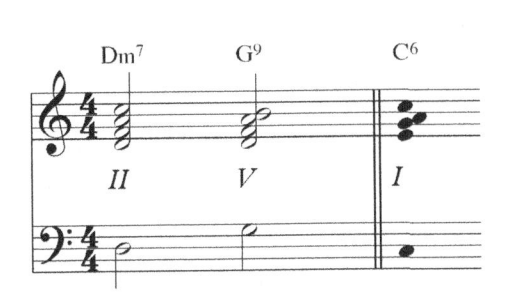

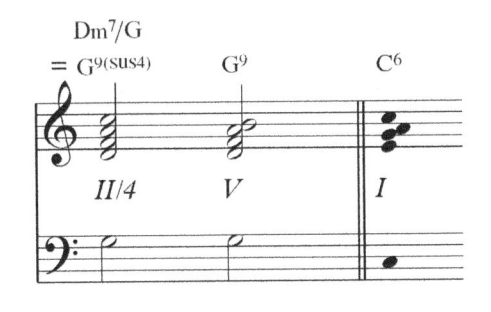

In minor keys, V^{7sus4} is elaborated with extensions native to the key signature, namely the flattened ninth and the flattened thirteenth:

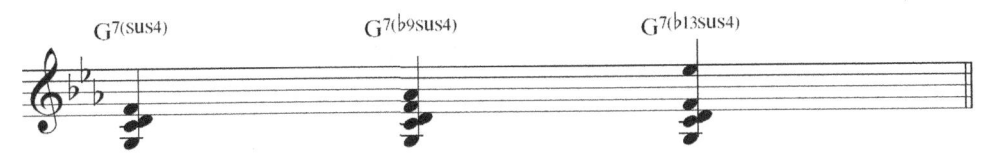

As in major, this minor version of the V^{7sus4} structure is typically followed by V^7, and can be thought of as II over the bass note of V:

Other Routes to the Tonic

A few miscellaneous alternatives to V or II-V remain. The backdoor II-V was introduced on page 61 as a connective harmony between IV to I. This cadence can approach I from anywhere, but it is particularly common in connecting II to I (note the similarity between II^{m7} and IV^{maj7}). In this situation, the backdoor cadence could be said to be replacing the V of a II-V progression:

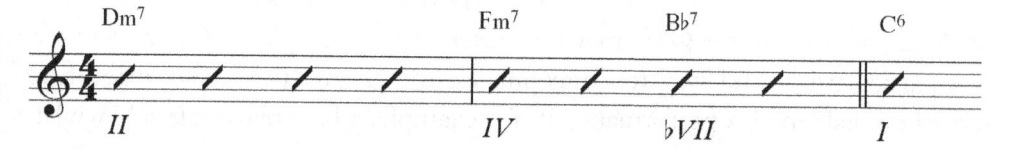

Another interesting alternative that can precede I is $I^{°7}$. We have already encountered two inversions of this chord: $\sharp IV^{°7}$ (page 62), which tends to resolve to I over its fifth, and $\flat III^{°7}$ (page 72), which usually resolves to II^{m7}.

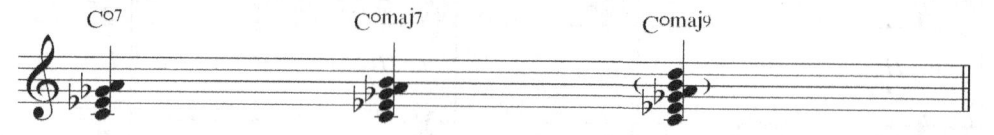

The movement from $I^{°7}$ to I derives its functionality from a resolution of dissonance entirely unrelated to the V-I cadence.

The voice leading becomes a little more explicit if we again conceptualise $I^{°7}$ as a major triad on VII, with I in the bass:

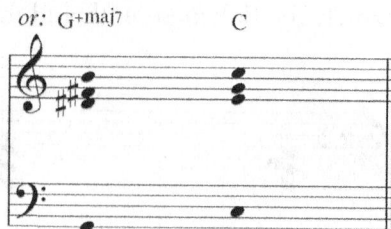

The same upper structure can also be combined with a V bass to produce a V^{+maj7} chord, a rather strange harmony which combines an upwardly resolving triad with bass movement suggestive of the V-I cadence:

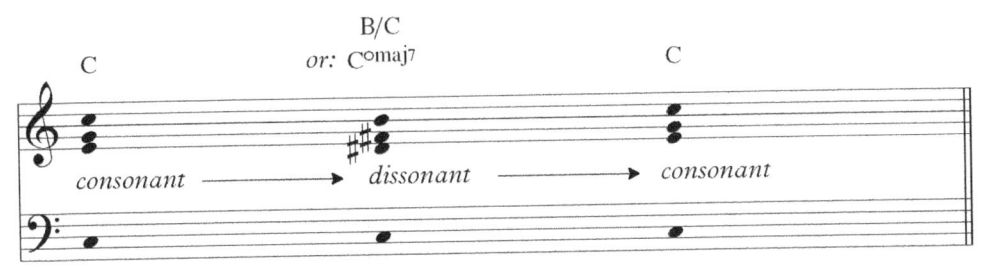

I^{o7} supports the flattened third and raised fourth of the key, both of which have a very strong tendency to resolve upward by a half step. In the first example below, the asterisked raised fourth resolves upward directly into the fifth. In the second, this happens indirectly through a short scalic elaboration. Both melodies are supported perfectly by the I^{o7} to I cadence:

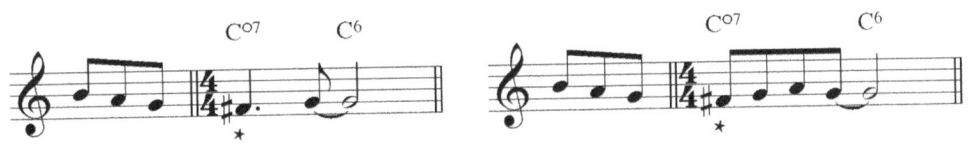

Alternatively, I^{o7} can elaborate static I harmony in situations where the tonic or sixth is sustained. This may happen literally, as in the first example below, or it may be obscured by melodic elaboration, as in the second:

In either case, I^{o7} may occur after a cadence to I, particularly from V, delaying the arrival of the tonic:

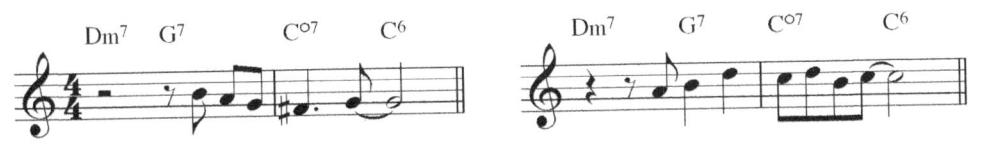

We have seen the resolution of a dominant up a half step to IV on page 60, and the same cadence may occur in the movement of VII^7 to I. VII is most typically voiced as a minor V-style seven flat 9 chord, which complies better with the prevailing key, and may be preceded by its II:

B7(♭9)
C6
VII
I

F♯m7(♭5)
B7(♭9)
C6
♯IV
VII
I

Notice the similarity of this cadence to the $I^{\circ 7}$-I cadence discussed above. $I^{\circ 7}$ and $VII^{7\flat 9}$ are exactly the same structure over different bass notes:

C°7
C6
I°
I

B7(♭9)
C6
VII
I

F♯m7(♭5)
B7(♭9)
C6
♯IV
VII
I

None of these variations are common in minor keys, where the upward half step voice leading does not lead as surely to the tonic triad.

Chapter Summary

Melody line permitting, any dominant-type chord may be replaced with a dominant chord a tritone away.

Melody line permitting, any dominant-type chord may be replaced with an altered dominant chord, which is effectively a dominant chord with its root displaced by a tritone.

There are numerous substitutions and elaborations in use that might replace the V chord in a V-I progression.

V^7 might be replaced or preceded by V^{7sus4} which is, in effect, chord II over the bass note of V.

Although entirely unrelated to the V chord, $I^{\circ 7}$ resolves satisfactorily to a tonic major chord.

Chapter 15
Elaborations of I

This chapter covers a number of miscellaneous chord progressions that we might use to elaborate static tonic harmony. The most common progression with this function, the I-VI-II-V turnaround and its variations, has already been covered extensively in Chapter 5, but there are other significant progressions that jazz musicians use to avoid the stasis of an extended period of chord I.

As with the V chord substitutions discussed previously, these progressions can support or suggest different melodic ideas, and provide variation and interest.

Elaborations of the Major Tonic

On page 204 we saw two progressions that move upwards in parallel from chord to chord, rather than moving in the more common pattern of ascending fourths/descending fifths. Similar effects may elaborate a tonic chord:

The logic of such a progression becomes clear when we consider the voice leading. The pitches within each voicing simply move up and down in parallel with each other. This effect is so powerful that we might even retain the tonic bass note throughout. The relatively dissonant $II^{m7}/^{b}7$ chord that results, asterisked below, is wholly justified by the context:

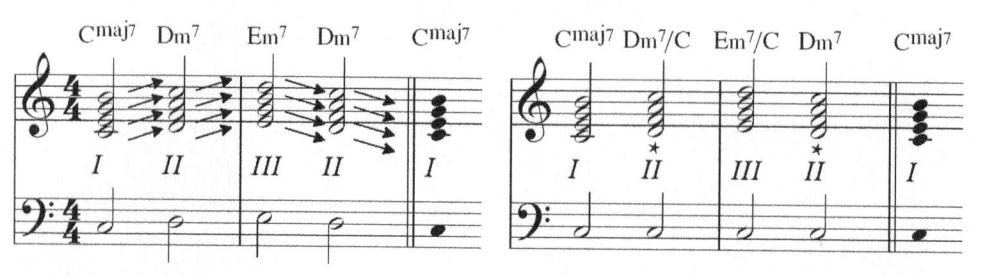

We might also elaborate I by moving to I⁶ and back again through a connective augmented triad:

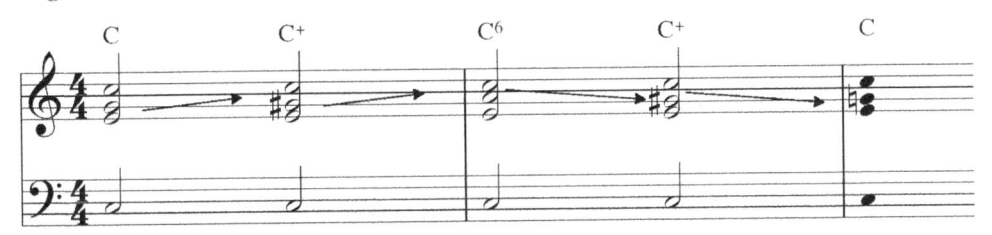

The I diminished chord, introduced in the previously (page 209), can be used to elaborate a tonic major as well as precede it, such that I may move to I^{o7} and back again. This can support a melody that highlights either the root or sixth *(a)*, or resolves either the flattened third or flattened fifth into a chord tone of I *(b)*.

(a)

(b)

We have already discussed chord IV as a destination in tonal passages, but in some sense IV is interchangeable with I. Any melody that fits over the tonic chord of a major key fits over the IV chord, and movement back and forth between these two harmonies causes minimal tonal disruption.

For this reason, extended periods of tonic harmony can be replaced with movement to IV and back again. This effect is not typical of classic pre-60s tonal jazz, and might even be suggestive of a folk or rock sound:

213

Fundamentals of Jazz Composition

...becomes:

Cmaj7	Cmaj7	Cmaj7	Fmaj7	Cmaj7
I	I	I	IV	I

...or:

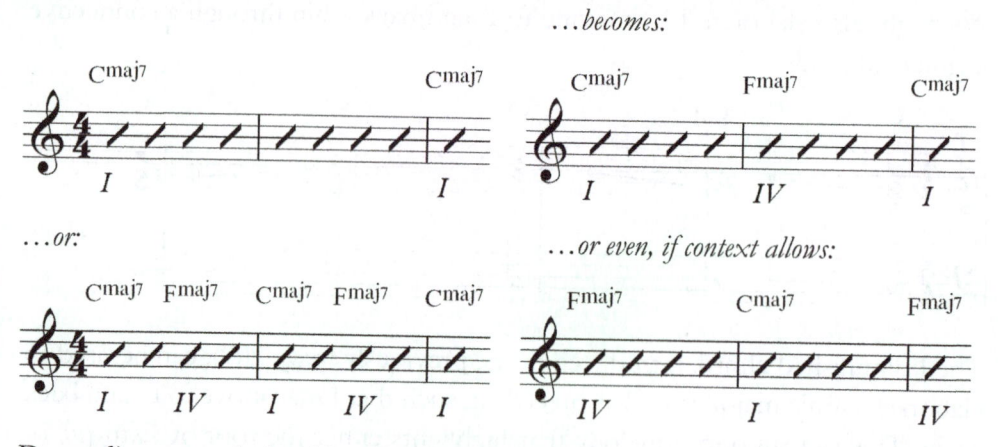

Cmaj7 Fmaj7	Cmaj7 Fmaj7	Cmaj7
I IV	I IV	I

...or even, if context allows:

Fmaj7	Cmaj7	Fmaj7
IV	I	IV

Depending on melody, this effect is also possible if we use IV^7, which supports any chord tone but the third of I, or IV^{m6}, which supports any chord tone but the sixth of I:

Cmaj7	F7	Cmaj7	Cmaj7	Fm6	Cmaj7
I	IV	I	I	IV	I

These new chords also support new pitches which would not have otherwise been consonant. IV^7 enables us to use the flattened third of the key, as in *(a)*, and IV^{m6} allows the flattened sixth, as in *(b)*:

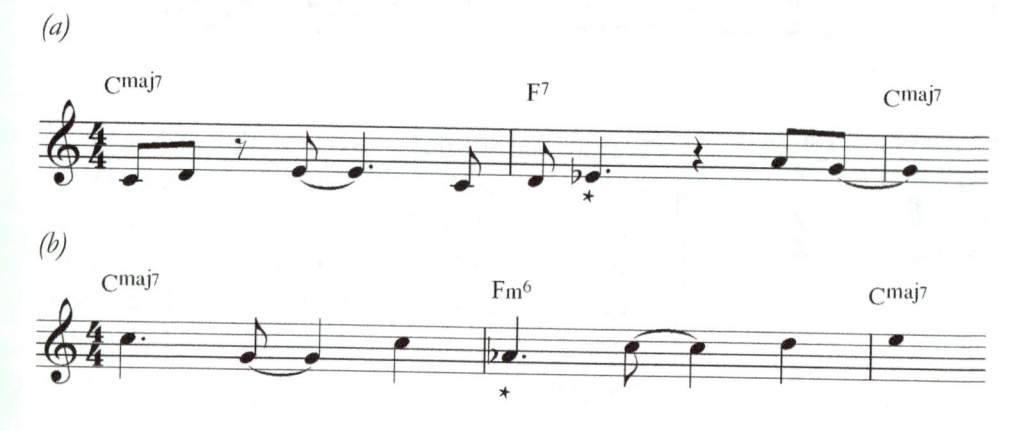

(a)

| Cmaj7 | F7 | Cmaj7 |

(b)

| Cmaj7 | Fm6 | Cmaj7 |

Elaborations of the Minor Tonic

Many analogous elaborations are also available on minor tonic harmony. As with major, we have the option of moving one inner voice of the chord, such as in the following, which is used in the famous theme from James Bond:

[musical example: Cm – Cm(♭6) – Cm6 – Cm(♭6) – Cm]

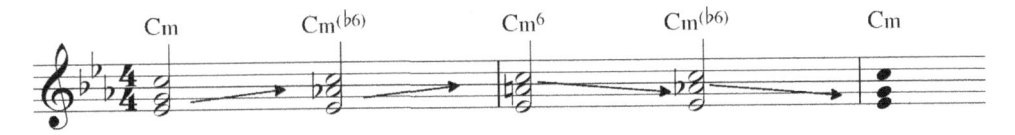

In minor keys, a similar option is produced by moving a single voice of the chord chromatically downward from the root to the sixth. This is particularly fitting when I is followed by a chord that includes the flattened sixth of the key as a chord tone, allowing the chromatic movement to continue into the next chord:

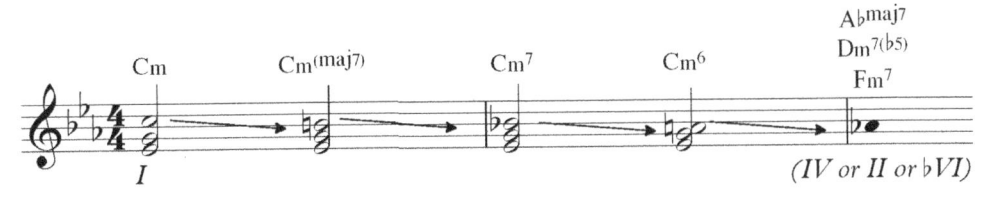

[musical example: Cm – Cm(maj7) – Cm7 – Cm6 – A♭maj7 / Dm7(♭5) / Fm7; I ... (IV or II or ♭VI)]

We also have the option of moving from I to I over its third through a passing diminished chord. This type of minor chord vamp is perhaps most typical of the swing era, and was replaced by II-V turnarounds in later styles:

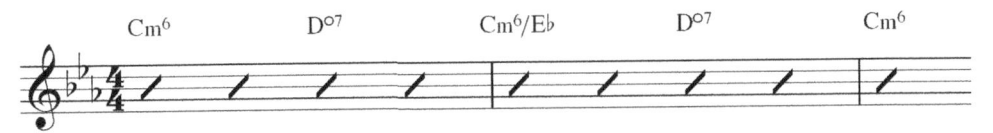

[musical example: Cm6 – D°7 – Cm6/E♭ – D°7 – Cm6]

The II°7 in this example is essentially a V7♭9 over its fifth. The passage above is simply a chain of I to V to I movements, and could be respelled thus:

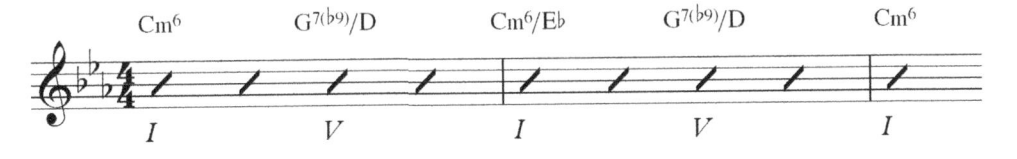

[musical example: Cm6 – G7(♭9)/D – Cm6/E♭ – G7(♭9)/D – Cm6; I V I V I]

Hypermetric Considerations

The tension and release provided by most of the progressions in this chapter are relatively weak, and are invariably used when a tonic chord is sustained within a period. In other words, they do not span a moment of greater hypermetric emphasis than their starting point.

Double bar lines in the examples below represent the boundaries between periods. Here, the first elaborative pattern from this chapter (page 212) is shown crossing into a new period *(a)*. Problematically, this means that the new period begins on the weak, mid-progression chord III. The passage would be better served with *(b)*, in which a stronger V-I cadence broadcasts the arrival of the new period:

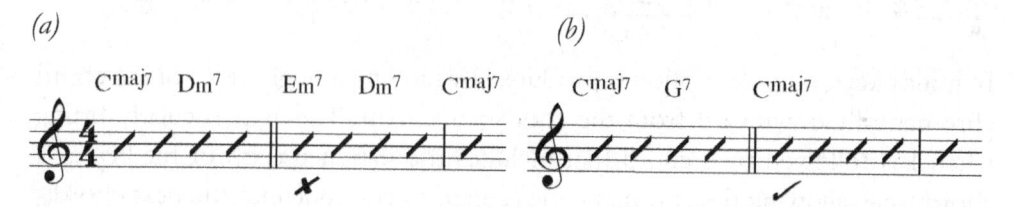

(a)   *(b)*

| Cmaj7 Dm7 Em7 Dm7 Cmaj7 | Cmaj7 G7 Cmaj7 |

Likewise, the II chord that ends the period in *(c)* resolves too weakly to the tonic to properly demark the new period. A V-I movement would be better suited in this position, as in *(d)*.

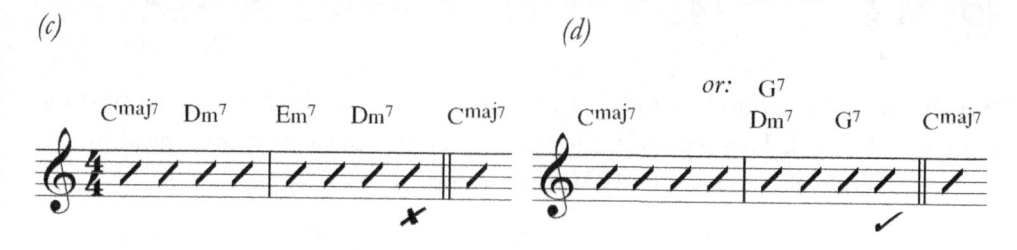

(c)   *(d)*

                                                           or: G7

| Cmaj7 Dm7 Em7 Dm7 Cmaj7 | Cmaj7 Dm7 G7 Cmaj7 |

Chapter Summary

Extended periods of tonic harmony are usually elaborated with movement. This may include planing effects, the I^{o7} chord, or movement to IV and back again.

These effects must not overlap a point of greater hypermetric emphasis than their starting point as this would highlight a weak mid-progression harmony.

Chapter 16
Modes and Modal Jazz

Throughout the latter half of the nineteenth century, European music began to look back to an idea that had gradually been abandoned in the late Renaissance. Rather than the primary engine of motion being the chord progression, music may simply consist of the interaction of a melody, or melodies, with a single static pitch or chord.

Music that functions in this way is said to be modal. Modal music still has a tonic in the sense that it resolves around a central pitch. As in tonal music, this central pitch may be elaborated with a chord, and modal music may still move between different chords. It does not, however, use conventional voice leading patterns such as the V-I cadence to construct large-scale chord sequences. Modal music might, therefore, be defined as music that does not use conventional voice leading patterns to construct large-scale chord sequences.

This essentially means that virtually all music that does not use common practice-style tonal harmony falls into the wastebasket taxon of modal, including any style with its harmonic origins outside of Europe.

A mode is a specific collection of pitches that is used within a given modal passage. In common parlance, the terms 'mode' and 'scale' are largely interchangeable. Both are used in their most general sense to describe a set of pitches, but 'mode' is often reserved for pitch collections that are not traditionally found in tonic harmony in major or minor keys. These are often generated from permutations of diatonic major and minor scales, which will be explored fully in this chapter.

Modal Jazz

Jazz musicians have always found inspiration in the modal harmony of early twentieth century Old World composers, as well as in folk music traditions from around the world. The idea of modal jazz truly emerged under the influence of George Russell's seminal 1953 book *The Lydian Chromatic Concept of Tonal Organization*, and its most famous realisation in the Miles Davis' 1959 sextet album *Kind of Blue*.

Modal harmony in jazz is not so much a genre as a harmonic technique. A piece of music may contain a modal passage surrounded by more traditionally tonal context, and there is no clear delineation between what is or is not tonal as opposed to modal in a jazz context.

Different pieces or passages may be debatably modal, or modal to varying degrees, but generalisations can be made about what constitutes modal jazz. It often involves harmonies of extended duration, perhaps four to eight bars, and harmonies that do not resolve in predictable or established ways.

The following eight-bar excerpt is certainly modal. It consists of two relatively long stretches of static harmony, the second chord does not follow conventionally from the first, and the passage does not suggest any particular tonic destination:

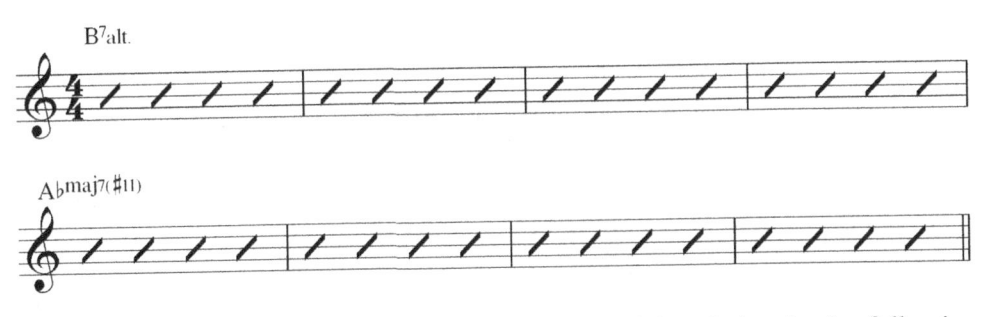

B7alt.

A♭maj7(♯11)

Other situations may be more ambiguous. Most of the pitches in the following sequence are available within the key of D minor, but the presence of a seventh in the apparent tonic chord hints at other tonalities. This sequence lacks any V to I movement that would fully eliminate this ambiguity of key:

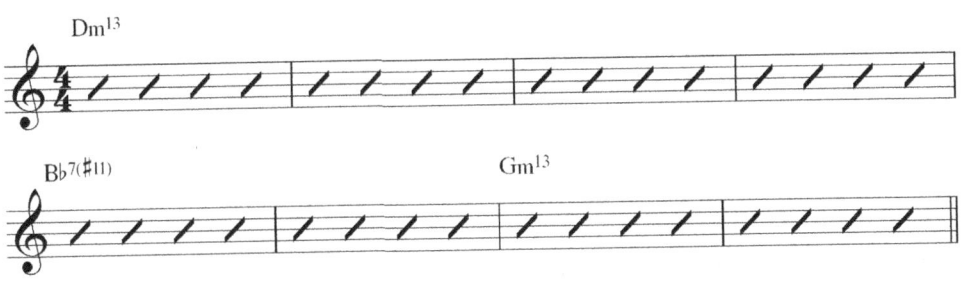

Dm13

B♭7(♯11)   Gm13

Some ideas that might help us to organise and compose modal chord sequences will be explored in Chapter 17, but first we must examine the available materials in more detail.

Constructing Modes

Much of the modal music used in the western traditions is based upon one of the seven permutations of the major scale. In tonal contexts, the following pitches are most associated with tonal music in the key of C major, and as such are named the C major scale:

Using this collection of pitches in a context where the tonal centre is something other than C recontextualises all seven pitches. What was 1, 2, 3, 4, 5, 6, and 7 relative to C becomes 1, 2, ♭3, 4, 5, 6 and ♭7 relative to D, or 1, ♭2, ♭3, 4, 5, ♭6 and ♭7 relative to E, and so on.

Any of these pitches could be the tonal centre of a modal passage, and each has its own distinct sound and name. A passage that uses these pitches alongside a tonal centre of D is in the D Dorian mode, and a passage which uses the same pitches alongside a tonal centre of F is in the F Lydian mode. We shall return to these terms shortly.

Chords in modal passages may be embellished with extensions, just as we would expect in tonal contexts. Because each mode contains a unique collection of pitches relative to the root, a chord symbol alone can specify a required mode.

For example, a minor seventh flat thirteen chord can only be constructed from the Dorian mode, and a major thirteenth raised eleven only from the Lydian mode. The use of those particular chord symbols effectively instructs our performers to use those modes.

The seven modes of the major scale are traditionally named after regions of ancient Greece. Some permutations of other scales have nicknames that relate them to major scale modes, though these titles are not in universal use.

The Ionian Mode - The Major Scale

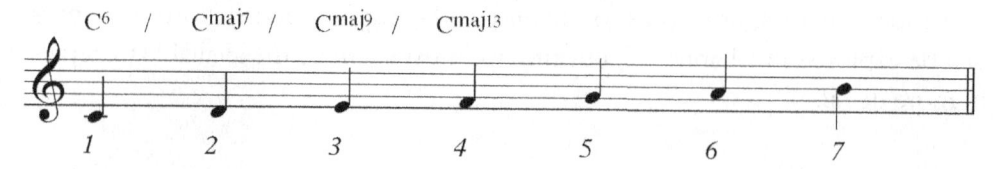

C6 / Cmaj7 / Cmaj9 / Cmaj13

1 2 3 4 5 6 7

Modal Ionian material is rather rare. Long passages of major seventh harmony tend more often toward the Lydian mode, whose raised eleventh is more consonant with the tonic triad than the natural eleventh found here. The difference between a modal Ionian passage and one simply in C major is not well defined, but harmonic stasis and the absence of a V chord could be considered indications of modality.

Much contemporary pop music cycles triads constructed from these pitches – I-V-VI^m-IV is very common – in a manner that, due to the complete absence of the V-I cadence, might be considered modal.

The Dorian Mode

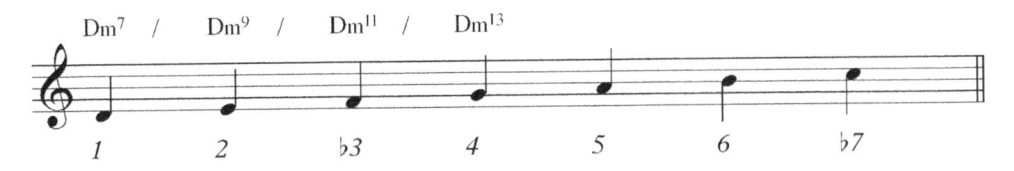

All of the pitches of the Dorian mode are reasonably consonant with the home triad, making this a default choice for extended passages of minor harmony. Jazz musicians since the 1960s have used used these pitches on the tonic of minor key pieces.

Movement between a tonicised minor triad and the major triad a fourth above, D minor to G major, and back again is highly typical of modal dorian music, as is the use of the minor triad a whole step above the tonic, D minor to E minor. Miles Davis' *So What* is a famous example of the use of modal harmony in jazz. It comprises a thirty two-bar *A-A-B-A* arrangement in which the *A* section consists of a D Dorian chord and the *B* of E-flat Dorian.

The Phrygian Mode

The Phrygian mode is frequently used to evoke Spain or the middle east. Melodic resolution of the flattened second to the root, and the flattened sixth to the fifth are highly characteristic of this mode, as is the movement between the tonic minor triad and a major triad one half step above, such as between E minor and F major in the E Phrygian mode shown.

The Lydian Mode

Fmaj7(#11) / Fmaj9(#11) / Fmaj13(#11)

1 2 3 #4 5 6 7

The Lydian mode is the least dissonant pitch collection that supports a major chord. Any of its seven pitches are viable extensions. This makes this mode the default for static major harmony in jazz, just as the Dorian is to a static minor chord. Movement from an F major to a G major chord and back is typical of the F Lydian mode.

The Mixolydian Mode

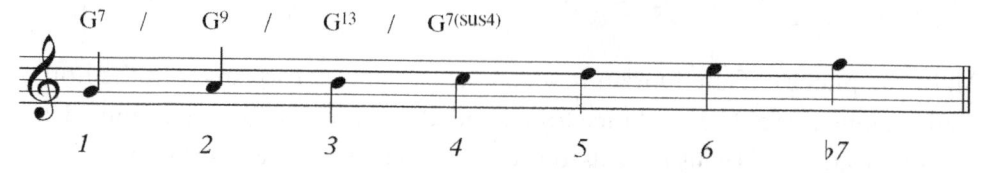

G7 / G9 / G13 / G7(sus4)

1 2 3 4 5 6 b7

A home seventh chord inevitably evokes a bluesy sound, although blues tonality usually has too many tonal implications – V chords, for example – to be considered truly modal. Music that resolves from a major triad up one whole step to a major triad, F to G major in this transposition, could be considered to be modal Mixolydian. This is a common sound in rock music.

The Aeolian Mode - The Natural Minor Scale

Am7(b13) / Am9(b13) / Am11(b13)

1 2 b3 4 5 b6 b7

The Aeolian mode is often suggested by the presence of a minor triad alongside the minor triad a fifth above, or the major triad a whole step below, such as E minor or G major relative to A minor. These sounds are common combinations in pop and rock music, but the dissonance of the flattened thirteenth makes extended Aeolian harmony uncommon in jazz, where extended chords are preferred to triads.

The Locrian Mode

Bm$^{7(\flat 5)}$ / Bm$^{11(\flat 5)}$

1 ♭2 ♭3 4 ♭5 ♭6 ♭7

The Locrian mode, with its unstable diminished target triad, has found little application. Its most notable use is the four bars of F♯$^{m7\flat 5}$, F-sharp Locrian, that begins the chorus of Joe Henderson's *Inner Urge*.

An alternative way to conceptualise these seven pitch modes is to align them all parallel to each other, relative to the same tonal centre. This allows for a direct comparison between the intervallic structures of each mode. We may now sequence them from Lydian to Locrian, lowering one pitch by a half step each time. Here the seven modes of the major scale are shown relative to C:

The Lydian Mode

1 2 3 ♯4 5 6 7

The Ionian Mode - The Major Scale

1 2 3 4 5 6 7

The Mixolydian Mode

1 2 3 4 5 6 ♭7

The Dorian Mode

1 2 ♭3 4 5 6 ♭7

The Aeolian Mode - The Natural Minor Scale

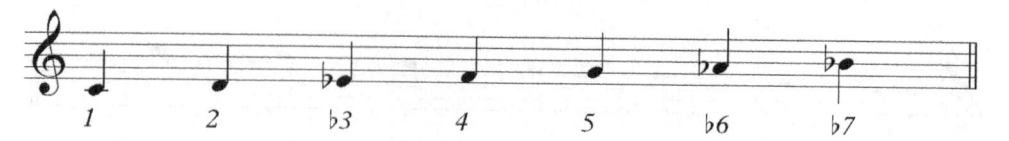

1, 2, ♭3, 4, 5, ♭6, ♭7

The Phrygian Mode

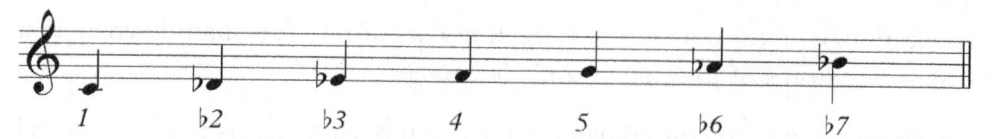

1, ♭2, ♭3, 4, 5, ♭6, ♭7

The Locrian Mode

1, ♭2, ♭3, 4, ♭5, ♭6, ♭7

The Melodic Minor Scale and its Modes

The seven modes listed above are all permutations of the major scale, retaining its basic structure of step, step, half-step, step, step, step, over different harmonies. This same concept may be applied to scales with different intervallic structures, producing new modes and chords, many of which are rather uncommon. The remainder of this chapter catalogues the modes that can be constructed from the four diatonic scales. These are all of the pitch collections that can be written with seven alphabetic letters A to G.

The melodic minor scale, whose dubious pedagogical origin is explained on page 33, has been adopted by jazz musicians as an alternative source of harmonic material. The descending form of the melodic minor scale correlates to the Aeolian mode, but the ascending form is commonly used harmonically and melodically in both tonal and modal jazz. Some of the modes below are encountered only very rarely, and most do not have established names.

First Mode of the Melodic Minor - The Melodic Minor Scale

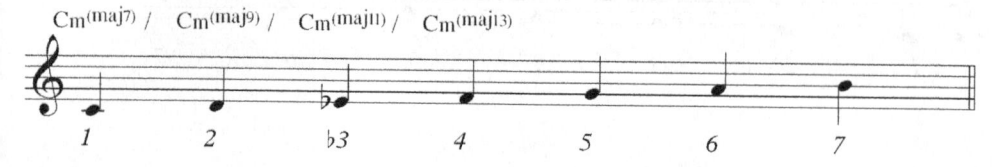

Cm(maj7) / Cm(maj9) / Cm(maj11) / Cm(maj13)

1, 2, ♭3, 4, 5, 6, 7

The melodic minor scale itself is a possibility for an extended minor triad with a natural seventh. The chorus of Horace Silver's *Nica's Dream* begins with a cycle between C$^{m(maj7)}$ and B$^{bm(maj7)}$, each of which could be interpreted as a modal melodic minor chord.

Second Mode of the Melodic Minor

Dm7($^{b9}_{b5}$) / Dm11($^{b9}_{b5}$) / Dm13($^{b9}_{b5}$)

1, b2, b3, 4, 5, 6, b7

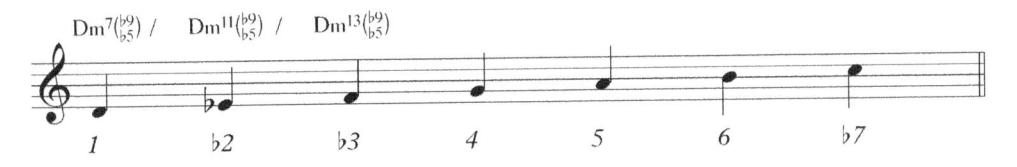

Third Mode of the Melodic Minor

Eb+maj7 / Eb+maj9 / Ebmaj7($^{\#11}_{\#5}$) / Ebmaj13($^{\#11}_{\#5}$)

1, 2, 3, #4, #5, 6, 7

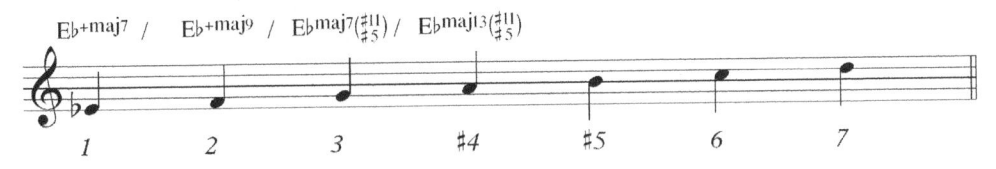

Modes that produce neither a major or minor triad from their tonic are rather unstable. Like the Locrian chord, extended periods of augmented triad harmony are rather uncommon.

Fourth Mode of the Melodic Minor - The Lydian Dominant Scale

F7(#11) / F9(#11) / F13(#11)

1, 2, 3, #4, 5, 6, b7

Like the Dorian and Lydian scales, none of the pitches in the Lydian Dominant are particularly dissonant with the tonic triad, making this mode something of a default for extended periods of dominant harmony. This is particularly so when the chord does not resolve up a fourth/down a fifth.

Fifth Mode of the Melodic Minor

G7(b13) / G9(b13)

1, 2, 3, 4, 5, b6, b7

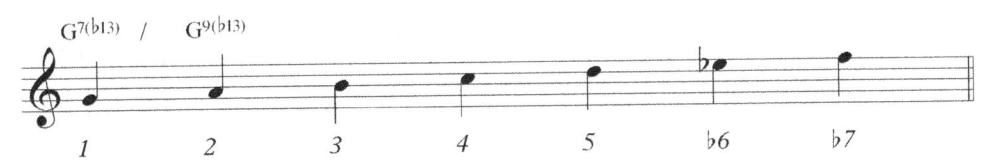

Sixth Mode of the Melodic Minor

Am9(b5) / Am11(b5)

1   2   b3   4   b5   b6   b7

Seventh Mode of the Melodic Minor - The Altered Scale

B7alt. / B7(b13/b9) / B7(#11/b9) / B7(b13/#9) / B7(#11/#9)

1   b2   b3   b4   b5   b6   b7

Supporting all of the altered extensions possible on a seventh chord, the pitch collection of the seventh mode is associated with altered dominant chords.

The Harmonic Minor Scale and its Modes

The harmonic minor, as introduced on page 33, is another potential source of modal material. The interval of three half-steps between the flattened sixth and natural seventh of the parent scale is highly conspicuous, particularly when used in melodies. It is likely that this reason accounts for the fact that extended passages based upon the harmonic minor and its modes are reasonably uncommon.

First Mode of the Harmonic Minor - The Harmonic Minor Scale

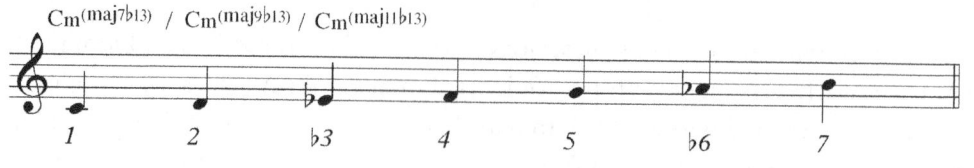

Cm(maj7b13) / Cm(maj9b13) / Cm(maj11b13)

1   2   b3   4   5   b6   7

The harmonic minor itself is an alternative to the melodic minor scale on minor chords with natural sevenths, albeit a far less popular one. The dissonance of a flattened thirteenth against the tonic triad (A-flat relative to C minor), and the awkward augmented second between that pitch and the natural seventh (A-flat to B-natural) are perhaps the reasons that this scale is far less popular than the melodic minor scale over tonic minor chords. The presence of both a consonant tonic triad and a dominant chord on the fifth degree mean that music made from this pitch collection tends toward tonal rather than modal.

• Chapter 16: Modes and Modal Jazz

Second Mode of the Harmonic Minor

Dm13(b5)

1 — b2 — b3 — 4 — b5 — 6 — b7

Third Mode of the Harmonic Minor

Eb+maj7 / Eb+maj9 / Ebmaj13(#5)

1 — 2 — 3 — 4 — #5 — 6 — 7

Fourth Mode of the Harmonic Minor

Fm7(#11) / Fm9(#11) / Fm13(#11)

1 — 2 — b3 — #4 — 5 — 6 — b7

Fifth Mode of the Harmonic Minor

G7(b9) / G7(b13, b9)

1 — b2 — 3 — 4 — 5 — b6 — b7

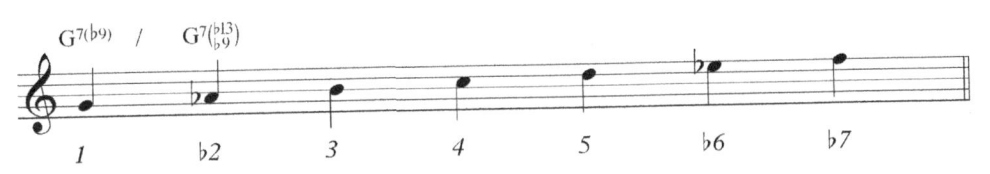

Sixth Mode of the Harmonic Minor

Abmaj7(#9) / Abmaj7(#11, #9) / Abmaj13(#11, #9)

1 — 2 — 3 — #4 — 5 — 6 — 7

Seventh Mode of the Harmonic Minor

B°7

1 — b2 — b3 — b4 — b5 — b6 — bb7

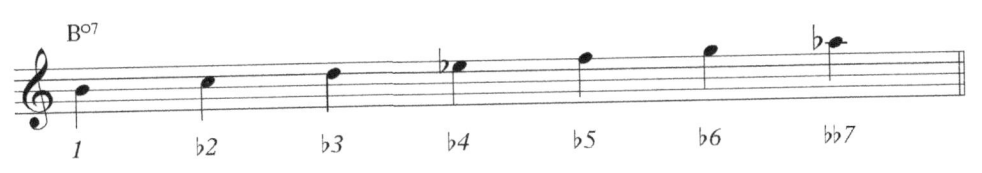

The Harmonic Major Scale and its Modes

All three of the parent scales explored so far in this chapter contain a root, and a natural second, fourth, fifth, and seventh. In the major scale, the remaining third and sixth are both natural. In the melodic minor scale, the third is flattened and the sixth is natural. In the harmonic minor scale, both the third and sixth are flattened. In a sense, these three pitch collections imply the existence of a fourth in which the third is natural and the sixth flattened.

This scale is most often called the harmonic major scale, as it combines the sixth of a harmonic minor with the third of a major scale. This is the only remaining seven-note diatonic scale possible that has a tonic triad and a V^7 chord.

Though the harmonic major modes do have musical applications, none of them are prevalent enough to have widely accepted names.

First Mode of the Harmonic Major - The Harmonic Major Scale

Cmaj7(b13) / Cmaj9(b13)

1 2 3 4 5 b6 7

Uniquely, this scale supports both a tonic major chord and a minor triad a fourth above, namely the C major seventh and F minor, a common pairing which often occurs in tonal contexts.

Second Mode of the Harmonic Major

Dm13(b5)

1 2 b3 4 b5 6 b7

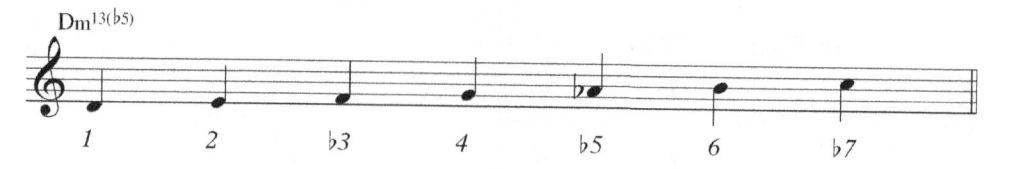

Third Mode of the Harmonic Major

E7(#9) / E7(b13, #9)

1 b2 b3 b4 5 b6 b7

Fourth Mode of the Harmonic Major

Fm(maj7♯11) / Fm(maj9♯11) / Fm(maj13♯11)

1, 2, ♭3, ♯4, 5, 6, 7

Fifth Mode of the Harmonic Major

G13(♭9)

1, ♭2, 3, 4, 5, 6, ♭7

Sixth Mode of the Harmonic Major

A♭maj7(♯9) / A♭maj7($^{\sharp 11}_{\sharp 9}$) / A♭maj13($^{\sharp 11}_{\sharp 9}$)

1, ♯2, 3, ♯4, ♯5, 6, 7

Seventh Mode of the Harmonic Major

B°7

1, ♭2, ♭3, 4, ♭5, ♭6, ♭♭7

The diatonic nature of the pitch collections listed in this chapter make them well suited to use as modes in modal writing, because they allow us to build tertiary chords made up of stacked thirds. Our modal passages may consist of non-harmonic pitches and extensions over a triadic base. Other modal sounds are possible, but rather rare. The remaining scalic materials in common usage are the subject of Chapter 18.

Chapter Summary

Music that does not use conventional harmonic progressions such as the V-I cadence to establish a tonal centre may be described as modal.

What constitutes modal harmony in jazz is ambiguous and ill-defined. Passages with harmonic stasis and the absence of V-I movement are the best indicators.

Diatonic scales are defined, ,for our purposes, as seven-note scales in which a major or minor triad can be constructed from the tonic, and a dominant seventh chord from the fifth. Four such scales may be constructed: the major scale, the melodic minor scale, the harmonic minor scale, and the harmonic major scale.

Most modal passages are based on permutations, modes, of diatonic scales because these pitch collections support consonant triads and seventh chords that use the tonal centre as their root.

Chapter 17
Non-Functional Harmony

Functional harmony describes the set of conventions where musical information implies the existence of a destination tonic. Non-functional harmony, therefore, must simply be everything else. Jazz nomenclature makes no strict or widely accepted delineations between non-functional and modal harmony, although pieces with slow harmonic rhythm, such as single chords lasting for four bars or more, are particularly likely to be described as modal rather than non-functional.

Similarly, the delineation between tonal and non-functional/modal harmony is often unclear. We might best understand chords and chord progressions in terms of a subjective continuum from functional to non-functional.

The 'everything else' nature of the non-functional category means that there can be no rules or conventions to non-functional harmony. Freed from the necessity to establish key or tonal centre, we may utilise any chords we wish in our compositions, and in any order. This chapter aims to suggest a few interrelated analytical tools that we might use to understand some of the ways that unconventional chords might relate to one another.

Substitutions and Secondary Substitutions

Unorthodox harmonic progressions can often be related to functional ones. In the following excerpt, a simple melody is harmonised with a II-V-I progression in the key of E-flat:

Fm^7 B♭^{7} E♭^{6}

We can re-harmonise this passage in a non-functional style:

A♭maj^7 E^{7}alt.   Cm^7

A closer inspection reveals that these new chords are actually identical structures over new bass notes. This particular re-harmonisation abandons the characteristic ascending fourth/descending fifth bass movement of the II-V-I, but keeps the upper structures of those chords intact:

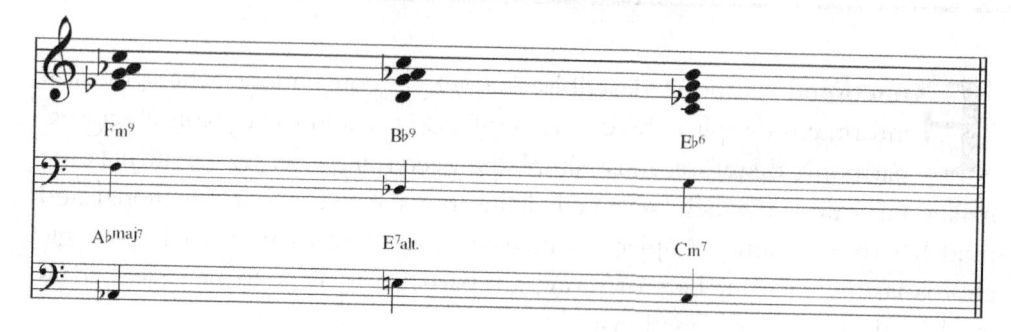

[Musical notation: Fm⁹ / A♭maj7, B♭⁹ / E⁷alt., E♭⁶ / Cm⁷]

The same melody could be harmonised with an even more abstract progression. Below, our first re-harmonisation is itself re-harmonised. This time chord qualities are altered but the bass notes are retained. We could conceptualise of these chords as secondary substitutions, as they are substitutions of substitutions:

[Musical notation: A♭+maj7, Em7(♭5), Cm(maj7)]

The resulting sequence is highly abstracted, and appears to bear very little resemblance to the original II-V-I. Nevertheless, melody is still well supported, and many of the same pitches within the chords are retained. Such non-functional re-harmonisation can allow for different interpretations of the same underlying melody.

Common Tones and Voice Leading

A melody may use common tones to connect a string of apparently unrelated chords. The following chords are all very different in terms of harmonic proximity, but all share E-flat/D-sharp as a common tone:

[Musical notation: Cm7(♭5), A♭m⁶, G♭13(♯11), Emaj7(♯11/♯5)]

This means that we may use E-flat as an adhesive, attaching these harmonies together and disguising their discontinuity. The pitch is restated in each bar of this melody:

The example below shows how the repetition of the C-natural in the melody excuses an otherwise abstract chord progression:

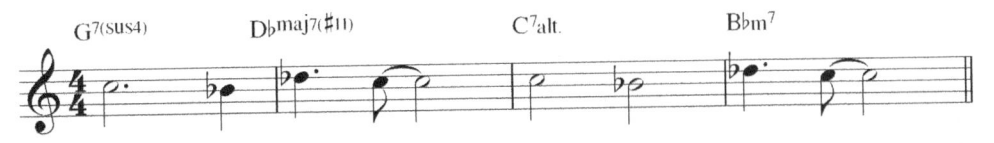

Another expression of this idea is that chords might move over a consistent bass note, often called a 'pedal' because of the origin of this technique in organ music in which the bass notes are operated with the feet.

Below, both melody and harmony are anchored by the stability of an F pedal, with even the highly dissonant $E^{maj7\sharp11}/F$ being aurally permissible as an interstitial harmony:

Rather than a single, static pitch, we might use an active melodic voice to connect chords. We might progress through the following four chords with a chromatically descending sequence of pitches:

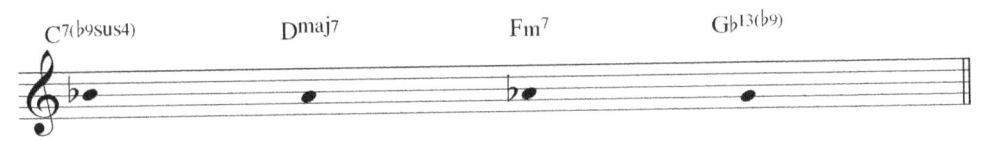

Again, a florid melody can obscure this hidden structure, bringing adhesive logic to otherwise strange sequence of harmonies:

Such a melody highlights the voice leading possible within a harmonic sequence. A voice leading line might ascend through a progression rather than descend, and might do so by whole step rather than by half step movement. Movement of more than a whole step compromises the effect, as our ear will begin to lose the thread. The example below suggests a line over the same chord progression that ascends in a mixture of whole and half steps:

[Musical notation: C7(b9sus4) — Dmaj7 — Fm11 — Gb13(#11,b9)]

And the same idea, hidden within a melody:

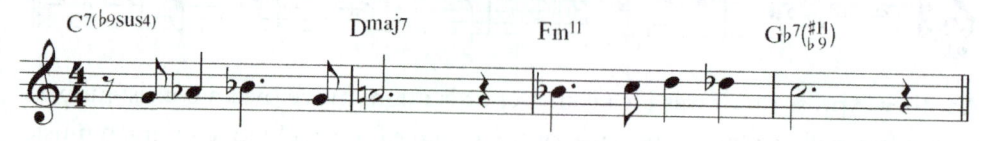

[Musical notation: C7(b9sus4) — Dmaj7 — Fm11 — Gb7(#11,b9)]

As with common tones, stepwise voice leading may occur in the bass voice. Unrelated harmonies may be justified by logical bass movement. Below, the bass ascends in half steps while the melody descends:

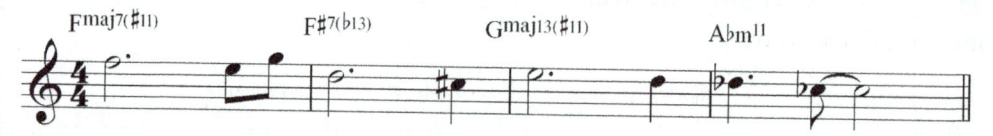

[Musical notation: Fmaj7(#11) — F#7(b13) — Gmaj13(#11) — Abm11]

Below, the bass movement descends in a mixture of whole steps and half steps, as with the pedal point idea above. The logic of a stepwise bass allows for unusual and dissonant harmonies, such as the D^{maj7}/F in the third bar:

[Musical notation: Gmaj13(#11) — F#m9 — Dmaj7/F — Eb7(sus4)]

Pedal points and voice leading lines such as these are also essential to tonal melody writing, and are explored in greater detail in the 'Implicit Counterpoint' section on page 250. The slash chords produced by the use of static or stepwise-moving bass notes also have application in tonal writing, and are explored further in Chapter 20.

Non-functional harmony is essentially harmony in the absence of conventions. The ideas in this chapter are necessarily rather vague and subjective. They attempt to provide some possible frameworks by which we might understand harmonic movements that are without established precedent.

The introduction of the ideas present here into the jazz composer's vocabulary marks a well-defined watershed in the history of the music. Following the modal innovations of George Russell, Miles Davis, and Bill Evans in the late 50s, non-functional harmonies in the music of Herbie Hancock, Wayne Shorter, Joe Henderson, and their peers were massively influential on future jazz styles.

Chapter Summary

Chord progressions that do not move in conventional ways do not establish or confirm tonality. As such, we understand them to be non-functional. There are no secure boundaries between these two types of chord progression, and in many passages the presence of functionality is nebulous or subjective.

Chords may be replaced by structures that resemble them, and those may in turn be substituted to form secondary substitutions.

Common pitches between chords have an adhesive effect and may be utilised in chord voicings or melodies to tie together otherwise unrelated harmonies. A similar adhesive effect is produced when a line ascends or descents in steps and half steps through a progression.

A common bass note might similarly unite disparate chords, as might a bass line that ascends or descents predictably in steps and half steps.

Chapter 18
More Scales

Diatonic scales and their modes represent most of the scalic material in frequent usage by jazz musicians, with a few significant exceptions. Two of these, the whole tone scale and the diminished scale, are derived synthetically from simple patterns, and can suggest both harmonic and melodic material.

Bebop scales are generated by adding a chromatic note to a diatonic scale to produce an eight-note scale. We can add chromatic passing notes to scalic melodies, or entire passing chords to functional passages.

The other two types of scale discussed here are the pentatonic scale and the so-called blues scales derived from it. Unlike other scales that we have explored, these are essentially used only as the basis of melodies, as they do not produce useable harmonic material.

Whole-Tone Scale

Ascending or descending in whole steps from a given pitch produces a hexatonic (six-note) scale that is symmetrical in the sense that each mode has an identical structure: 1, 2, 3, #4/♭5, #5/♭6, ♭7.

Because this scale contains half of the available twelve pitches, there are only two possible pitch collections that can make up whole-tone scales. This can be seen in the following diagram, which shows a chromatic scale, where the pitches with upward note stems belong to C whole-tone scale or any of its modes, and pitches with downward note stems belong to C-sharp whole-tone scale or any of its modes:

Because of its perfect symmetry, the whole-tone scale produces the same chord structure from each bass note: an augmented triad with a flattened seventh, a natural ninth, and a raised eleventh. As a harmonic device, this has never been particularly fertile ground for jazz composers, but the scale is sometimes employed by soloists over a dominant chords.

Two of the most famous examples of this type of harmony in jazz composition are Wayne Shorter's *JuJu,* and Lee Morgan's *Our Man Higgins,* recorded in 1964 and 1965 respectively. Both pieces make use of long stretches of whole-tone harmony, the former in eight consecutive bars over a B-natural bass, and the latter in the form of a double length twenty-four-bar blues in which each chord is replaced with a whole-tone chord.

Otherwise, the scale is associated with Thelonious Monk, who often superimposed it over dominant-type chords in patterns such as that shown below, which alternates inversions of B-flat augmented and C augmented triads over a B^{b7} chord:

Diminished Scale

Another scale synthesised from a simple pattern is the diminished or octatonic scale, which is produced by ascending or descending from a given pitch in alternating steps and half steps, or alternating half steps and steps. Like the whole-tone scale, the diminished scale has symmetry; some of its modes are transpositions of each other.

In the case of the diminished scale, there are two possible modes, one of which begins with ascent of a half step followed by a whole step, and one that does the inverse. All other modes are transpositions of one of these two structures:

C Half-whole Diminished Scale

C Whole-half Diminished Scale

Because there are eight pitches, diatonic spelling of diminished scales is impossible. This means that diminished scale melodies and harmonies may be written with various enharmonic spellings, and the composer must use their discretion to choose the notation that is the most conducive to easy interpretation.

There are exactly three sets of pitches that constitute diminished scales. Because the structure of the scale repeats in minor third intervals, the pitches of the C half-whole diminished scale are shared by the E-flat, G-flat, and A half-whole diminished scales, as well as the D-flat, E, G, and B-flat whole-half diminished scales.

Likewise, the following set of pitches constitute the C-sharp, E, G, and B-flat half-whole, and D, F, A-flat, and B whole-half diminished scales:

Finally, the D, F, A-flat, and B half-whole, and E-flat, G-flat, A, and C whole-half diminished scales:

European composers began to experiment with octatonic scales in the latter half of the nineteenth century, but it is particularly associated with the early twentieth century works of Igor Stravinsky, Alexander Scriabin, and Béla Bartók. One of its primary uses in a jazz context is in the chord generated from its half-whole iteration, namely a seventh chord with a flattened ninth, raised eleventh, and natural thirteenth:

Because of the symmetry of the diminished scale, $X^{13b9\sharp11}$ remains structurally unchanged when its bass note is displaced by a tritone. Replacing the bass note of $G^{13b9\sharp11}$ with D-flat produces $D^{b13b9\sharp11}$. This chord became popular in jazz from the bebop era onwards, and numerous examples can be found in the music of Thelonious Monk, where it often functions as a secondary dominant.

Melodic material may also be derived from the scale, as in the following example, in which a diminished scale line is heard over the V of II in the key of C:

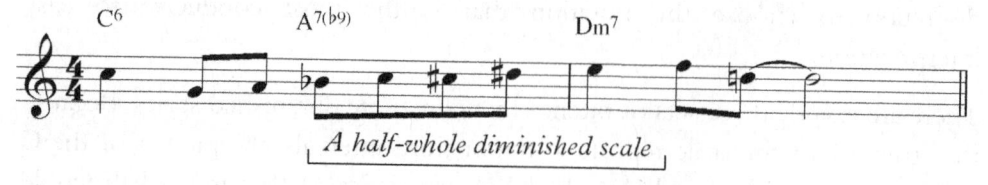

A half-whole diminished scale

The diminished scale produces a diminished seventh chord from every pitch of the structure. The C half-whole diminished scale can be used to construct a C, E-flat, G-flat, A, D-flat, E, G, *and* B-flat diminished seventh. This makes it an option for scalic melodies over diminished chords, even in a functional context. A slight re-harmonisation of the secondary dominant above can be seen here, renamed in relation to the new root note:

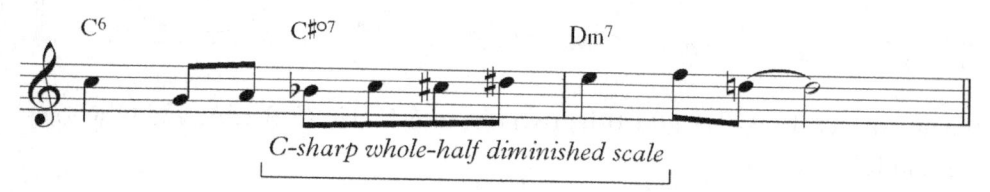

C-sharp whole-half diminished scale

Or over $I^{\circ 7}$:

C whole-half diminished scale

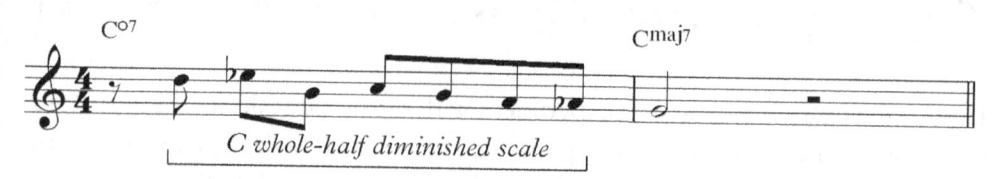

The same line fits over $I^{\circ 7}$'s inversion $^{b}III^{\circ 7}$:

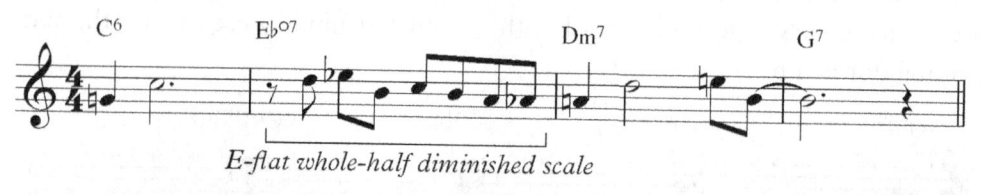

E-flat whole-half diminished scale

When adding extensions to diminished seventh chords, we find that pitches a whole step above one of the four chord tones are the most consonant, particularly when those pitches are available within the prevailing key. Taken to its logical conclusion, this implies the possibility of an eight-note double diminished chord featuring all of the pitches of the whole-half diminished scale.

Such a structure is of course rather dense and highly dissonant, but practical applications can be found with open voicings and the omission of a few pitches. The asterisked chords in both of the following passages are essentially this. Here, an incomplete diminished chord is shown beneath an incomplete diminished chord a step higher, with the chord symbols simplified:

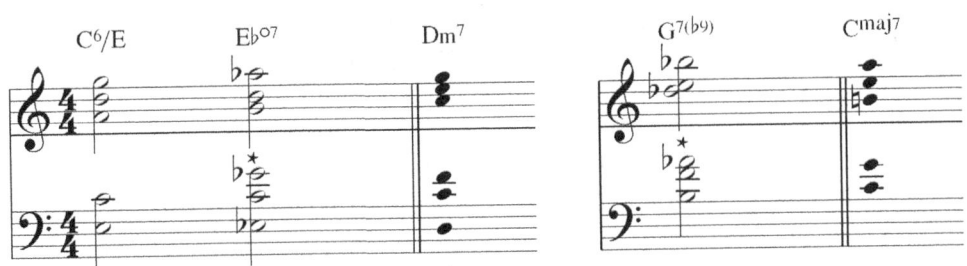

Due to its symmetry, any melody or harmony constructed from the pitches of the diminished scale can be transposed up or down three, six, or nine half steps and remain within the same diminished scale. Below, the same melodic fragment appears three times in descending flattened thirds. The entire sequence is available within the diminished scale:

Bebop Scales

The use of chromatic passing tones by soloists has led jazz educators and theorists to formalize a system of bebop scales, although it seems unlikely that Charlie Parker, Bud Powell *et al* actually conceived of their music in these terms. Advocates of the bebop scale assert that when a diatonic scale is played as eighth notes over a bar of 4/4, a chromatic passing tone should be added in order that each beat of the bar may receive a consonant chord tone.

For example, a bebop scale might be constructed to fit a C^6 chord by the addition of a passing A-flat/G-sharp between the fifth and sixth degrees of the scale. The emphasised on-beat pitches C, E, G, and A now spell out the underlying C^6 chord:

[C6 musical example]

This produces a melody in better alignment with the harmony than a diatonic major scale, which places non-chord tones on strong beats, asterisked:

[C6 musical example with asterisks]

Bebop scales can also be constructed to fit any chord with a flattened seventh by inserting a chromatic pitch between the flattened seventh and the root. On the G^7 chord below, a chromatic pitch between the flattened seventh and the root ensures that the root, third, fifth, and flattened seventh of the chord all fall on the beat:

[G7 musical example]

Below, a bebop scale is constructed to align with a minor seventh flat five chord. Passing through a natural seventh allows both the flattened seventh and the root to both fall on emphasised beats:

[Bm7(b5) musical example]

Ultimately, the practicality of these scales in melodic writing is somewhat debateable, as composed and improvised melody often places non-chord tones on downbeats. An understanding of the use of chromatic passing tones (page 117), and the importance of the metric position of melody notes (page 122), negates the need for us think in terms of an inflexible bebop scale. There is, however, a significant harmonic application of these types of pitch collections in the writing of thickened line harmonies, which is discussed more fully from page 283.

Pentatonic Scales

Pentatonic scales are extremely common in folk music all around the world, having been developed apparently independently by several cultures. Although numerous five-note scales are possible even within equal temperament, we usually reserve the pentatonic label for scales that do not contain any consecutive half steps, in particular, the so-called major pentatonic and one of its permutations, the minor pentatonic.

Below, the C major pentatonic is shown, consisting of the pitches 1, 2, 3, 5, and 6 relative to the root:

This can be understood as a major scale with the fourth and seventh degrees removed. These pitches, B and F relative to C, are the only ones in the major scale that lie a half step from a chord tone of the C major triad, which means that their omission removes any real potential for dissonance over that harmony. We may even sound all five pitches of a pentatonic scale at same time to produce the fairly consonant $C^{6/9}$ chord.

The same collection of pitches is also associated with a modal A minor context, where it may be called the A minor pentatonic. This is a familiar sound from blues and rock. Again, no dissonances are possible:

Melodies constructed from the pentatonic scale may be simple, powerful, and memorable, with a folky or even nursery-rhyme quality. A few songbook tunes utilise this effect. Ray Noble's largely pentatonic *Cherokee* is a familiar example to jazz musicians. The example below shows a song-like melody that utilises the G major pentatonic scale over functional, songbook-style harmony:

And here, a pentatonic phrase is followed by a more typical phrase that combines diatonic and chromatic material:

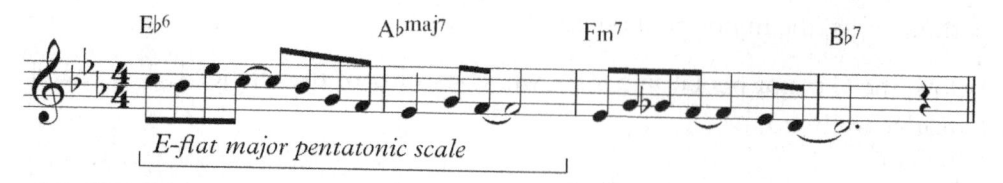

Pentatonic melodies are often associated with blues music, in which a minor pentatonic is often superimposed over a major key progression (see page 256). It may also be used to evoke the 'far east', as in Wayne Shorter's *Oriental Folk Song*, or Aaron Parks' *Peaceful Warrior*.

The harmonic ambiguity of pentatonic scales also made them popular in the intense modal jazz of the 60s and early 70s. A particular trope of that style is the harmonisation of a modal pentatonic melody in parallel fourths.

Despite the D root, the top line of the passage above is actually derived from the pitches of the C major pentatonic scale. This brings our attention to another important property: the tonal ambiguity of a pitch set with only five notes means that each pentatonic scale is consonant with a large number of chords. The C major/A minor pentatonic scale is compatible with any of the following harmonies:

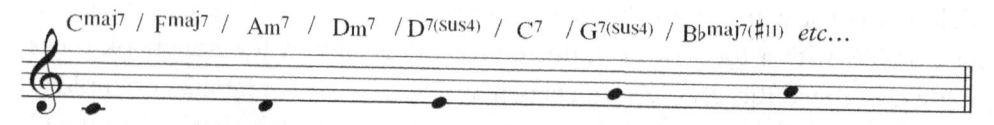

When superimposing a C pentatonic melody over any of these chords we find no real disagreements, but also no true concurrence. We might say that pentatonic scales fail to truly commit to any particular harmonic context.

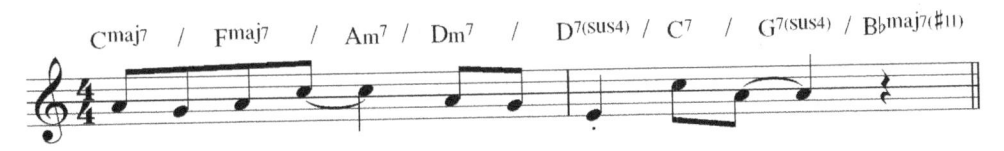

[Musical notation: Cmaj7 / Fmaj7 / Am7 / Dm7 / D7(sus4) / C7 / G7(sus4) / B♭maj7(♯11)]

There is exactly one other pentatonic scale possible within equal temperament that is not a permutation of the major pentatonic scale and that does not include consecutive half steps. This set does, however, contain a tritone, shown between F natural and B natural in the scale below, making it particularly suitable over minor sixth, dominant seventh, and minor seven flat five chords. This scale is in occasional use, and is sometimes called the minor sixth pentatonic scale:

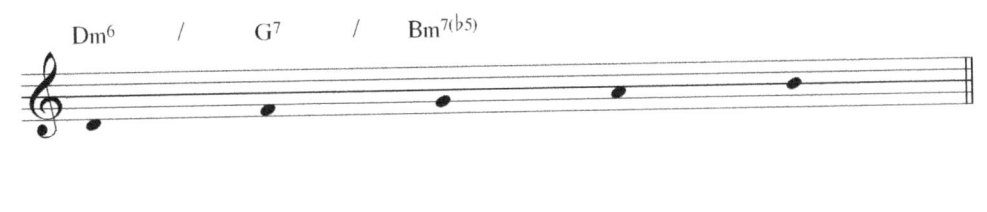

[Musical notation: Dm6 / G7 / Bm7(♭5)]

Blues Scales

The idea of a blues scale as a basis of melodic content in African-American music has been around since the late 1930s, but has been particularly prevalent in music education in the last four decades. The most common blues scale variant consists of six pitches: 1, ♭3, 4, ♯4, 5, and ♭7. Here is the C blues scale:

[Musical notation: C blues scale]

This is, in essence, a minor pentatonic scale with a chromatic passing tone inserted between the fourth and fifth degrees, and is generally associated with both modal minor harmony and blues harmony. Despite its flattened third, the pitches shown are often heard over the C major blues (see page 256). The same scale is also associated with E-flat major, relative to which it constitutes a major pentatonic with a chromatic pitch between the second and third: 1, 2, ♭3, 3, 5, and 6.

By combining the power and simplicity of a pentatonic scale with a hint of chromatic colour, the blues scale attempts to suggest a single pitch set as the basis for idiomatic blues language.

If there is something to be learned from the enduring popularity of this scalic sound, it is that we might insert chromatic passing notes in between the steps in a pentatonic scale, and that this is an effect often used in blues-style pieces and blues music.

The following passage, which consists entirely of pentatonic ideas and (asterisked) chromaticism, lands a lot closer to the language used by great blues and jazz musicians than the material that is typically produced from a blues scale:

The material outlined in both this chapter and Chapter 16 is a more or less comprehensive list of those scales in popular enough usage by jazz musicians to have any particular conventions associated with them. However, there is no reason that we cannot use others, or simply invent our own. There is a long and distinguished history of jazz musicians deriving and generating material from prescribed collections of pitches. George Russell's *Lydian Chromatic Concept of Tonal Organization* is a famous example of a theory of music-making based upon scales, and the chord-scale system espoused by Jamey Aebersold's *How to Play Jazz & Improvise* series is one of the most pervasive ideas in jazz education.

A pitch collection alone is not a compositional method, and must be accompanied by a technique or series of techniques that can be used to create music from it. This said, the connections between scale and melody or scale and harmony have often been overemphasised: the idea that music is derived from scales is overly simplistic, and not always useful to composers or performers. In most cases, these connections are analytical tools made after the fact, and many music makers do not conceive of their music in terms of scales.

Chapter Summary

The whole tone scale may be constructed by ascending or descending in whole steps from a given pitch. All modes of this scale are identical, and an augmented triad with a flattened seventh, a natural ninth, and a raised eleventh is produced from any root.

The eight-note diminished scale has two modal iterations, one that alternates whole steps and half steps and one that does the inverse. As well as producing a diminished seventh chord with its root on any pitch, the scale also yields a seventh chord with a flattened ninth, raised eleventh, and natural thirteenth, which is often used as a secondary dominant in tonal contexts.

The addition of a single chromatic tone to a diatonic scale allows us to create a bebop scale which, when played as eighth notes in 4/4 time, places a chord tone on every beat of a bar.

The omission of the fourth and seventh of a major scale produces a pentatonic scale. The simplicity of this pitch collection makes it compatible with a wide range of harmonic contexts.

Many pedagogical sources mention the blues scale, which is constructed by adding a chromatic passing tone to a pentatonic scale. Scalic passages produced from these pitches are often idiomatically dubious.

Chapter 19
More Melodic Techniques

This chapter is intended as a miscellany of melodic devices that have not already been covered in previous chapters. The ideas discussed here are compatible with those found earlier, and provide additional tools that we might use in melody writing, as well as new analytical angles that might provide insight into the melodies that we encounter.

Rhythmic Displacement and Hemiola

Rhythmic displacement is the reiteration of an idea into a different rhythmic position, which changes the patterns of emphasis within the phrase. De-emphasised pitches become emphasised, and vice versa. In the following example, the initial iteration *a* is followed immediately by the same phrase displaced by two beats (*a'*). Where *a* begins on beat one of the bar, *a'* begins on beat three:

The rhythmic displacement of the melody shifts its emphasis from the pitch E on the first beat of bar one, to the C-sharp on the first beat of bar three.

This is an extremely common effect in both composed and improvised jazz melody. Thelonious Monk's *Straight, No Chaser* is a particularly famous and explicit example of this technique.

Rhythmic displacement might be combined with any of the melodic developments described on page 138. Below, a tail is added to the previous example, which expands upon, varies, and concludes the original phrase.:

A phrase might be repeated at a different pitch level as well as in a different rhythmic position, combining sequence (page 141) with displacement. Here, *a'* is displaced by two beats from the initial phrase, placed a diatonic step higher in pitch, *and* has a tail ending:

The contour of the line might change completely, displacing only rhythmic content:

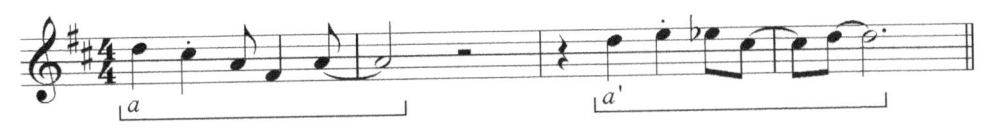

One particular type of rhythmic displacement occurs when the repetition of a fragment suggests an alternative time signature. An extremely common manifestation of this in jazz language occurs in 4/4 time, when a fragment with a duration of three eighth notes repeats in 4/4 time; we hear 3/8 superimposed over 4/4.

Below, a pattern consisting of two eighth notes and an eighth rest repeats three times, repeatedly recontextualising the fragment before resolving it with a consequent phrase:

This effect is a mainstay of jazz language. It occurs in many well-known tunes, such as Duke Ellington's *It Don't Mean a Thing*, specifically on the lyrics "do-ah do-ah do-ah do-ah do-ah …".

The effect is retained even when pitch content does not repeat. The rhythmic pattern below follows a group of three eighth notes, the second of which is a rest:

This polyrhythmic technique is often called a hemiola. Within the jazz idiom, the word 'hemiola' might be used to describe any instance of a polyrhythm with a time signature superimposed over any other, though the same word carries a far more restricted meaning in the context of common practice music. For the purposes within this book, the word 'hemiola' will be retained in favour of 'polyrhythm', in keeping with jazz parlance.

A two-beat phrase might cycle over a 3/4 time signature, as in the following example:

Or:

A hemiola may include longer phrases such as a three-beat cycle over 5/4 time. The displaced repetition of the melody repeatedly recontextualizes the pitches, as the melody falls out of sync with the primary time signature:

A cycle five eighth notes in length which implies simultaneous 5/8 over a prevailing 4/4 is shown below:

These longer and more complex hemiola examples are certainly less songlike and are associated with contemporary instrumental styles, although the chorus of Irving Berlin's 1927 song *Puttin' on the Ritz* begins with a seven-beat hemiola in 4/4 time.

Implicit Counterpoint

As mentioned on page 233, a pedal originally meant a sustained bass note under active harmonies and melodies. In a wider sense, a pitch to which a melody repeatedly returns is often called a pedal point or pedal pitch. This pitch is usually either the lowest in the phrase or the highest (a high pedal is sometimes referred to as an inverted pedal). Below, the repeated F-natural frames the top of the melody:

Here, the melody repeatedly bounces off the floor of a low C:

Such melodies have contrapuntal implications that suggest two simultaneous voices, one of which sustains a drone or pedal, whilst the other performs a more active line. The two examples above could be parsed into two voices:

The harmonic implications of such melodies must be noted, as the underlying harmony must relate to two melodies rather than just one. This generally means that the pedal tone is common to each underlying chord, thus highlighting the continuity between harmonies.

A similar idea was discussed on page 232, where we saw that this is particularly effective as an adhesive for more abstract progressions. Below, a top E-flat highlights commonalities between chords plucked from very different tonal palettes:

Inverting this idea, the repetition of a pedal may legitimise it over harmonies where it would otherwise feel very foreign and dissonant.

In the following phrase, C-natural appears in the melody first as a consonant major third before, being recontextualised as a flattened ninth, a raised fifth, and a raised ninth over $B^{7alt.}$, E^{+maj7}, and $A^{7alt.}$ respectively. Despite functioning as a rather distant altered extension over each of these chords, the repetition of this pitch as part of a simple, diatonic melody excuses its presence:

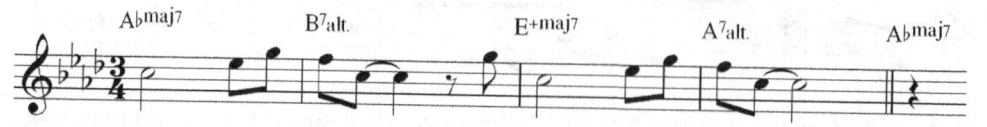

Rather than staying as a static repeated pitch, a pedal might move. The following phrase again implies two voices, an active upper voice over a lower voice that descends in semitones:

We might again parse this melody, expressing it on two staves to reflect its contrapuntal implications:

A secondary line such as this is typically discerned by its range. It appears either above a more active melody or below it. It may descend, as in the example above, or may ascend, and typically does so by either whole steps, half steps, or a combination of the two. Intervals larger than a whole step impair the continuity and perceptibility of the line.

Below are two more examples, both melodies of which imply an active voice beneath an upper line, asterisked, that ascends diatonically:

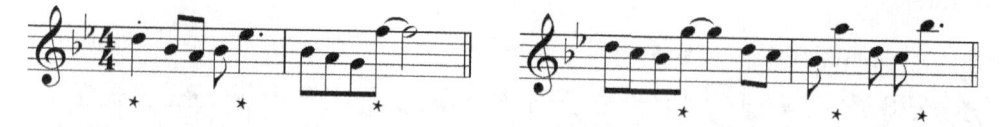

There are, as ever, harmonic implications. Moving pedal points can follow harmonies, highlighting their implicit voice leading, as in the ideas discussed on page 234 in the context of non-functional progressions. Below, a lower voice marked with asterisks spells out chromatic descent through a functional chord progression:

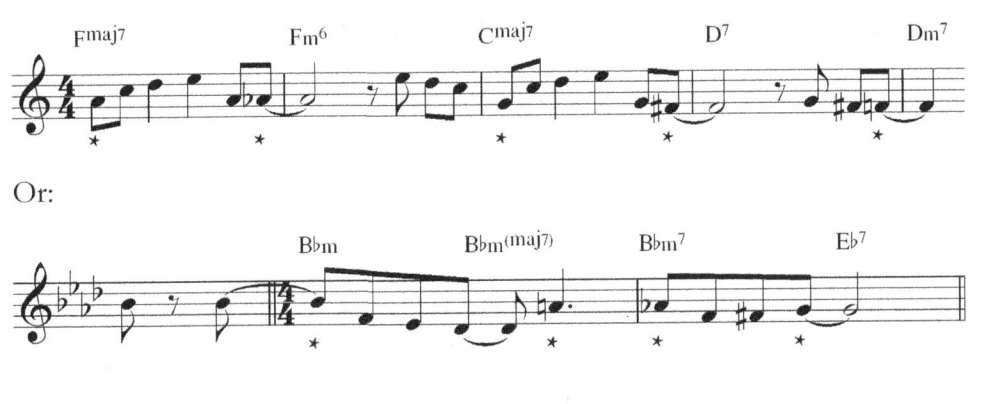

Or:

Harmonic Divergence

Melodies might disagree with underlying harmonies to varying degrees. As we have just seen, a melody with such inbuilt logic as a repeated pedal tone, a sequence, or a chromatic or whole step voice has the authority to disregard an underlying chord progression. The chromatic passing notes discussed on page 117 are an example of this, but the effect can also work on a larger scale.

In the melody below, the initial cell a is simply repeated a half step lower. This melody essentially ignores the underlying harmony of C^7 and takes an alternative route from G^{m7} to F^{maj7}. Whilst this is undeniably dissonant, the logic of the passage overrides the harmonic discrepancy:

In many cases, such effects can be understood as a suggestion of an alternative, simultaneous harmony. The bracketed section of the melody below has a very abstract relationship to the accompanying A^7 chord. It begins on its flattened ninth, then progresses through the natural thirteenth to the flattened thirteenth, ending on the raised eleventh.

Whilst this could be understood as a complex altered dominant structure, there is an alternative analysis, in which the melody is seen as simply descending chromatically through the E^{bm7} chord on its own private route from E^{m7} to D^{m7}:

This effect is rather dissonant and certainly un-songlike, but because the dissonance is paid for by the repetitive logic of the line, the overall effect is coherent.

The examples below contain two more invented excerpts. In both cases, bizarre and dissonant pitches are heard over G^{maj7} chords, and both can be understood as substitutions that are present in the melody but not the backing.

In the first example, a series of pitches arpeggiate a dominant chord a half step below the target harmony, achieving a similar effect to I^{o7}. In the second example, tension is created over a static major seventh chord with material that seems to suggest $^bII^7$, a tritone substitution for the V chord:

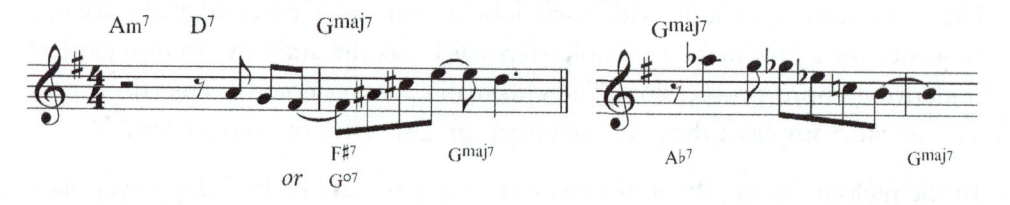

Both of these are functional chord progressions superimposed over other functional chord progressions. These melodic fragments imply a harmonic duality.

Another option is to side-step the underlying chord by a half step. We might move out of a chord and then back into it, as in the following fragments. Both are highly dissonant and have a high degree of disparity with their accompaniment, but the logic of stepping in and out of consonance sells the effect:

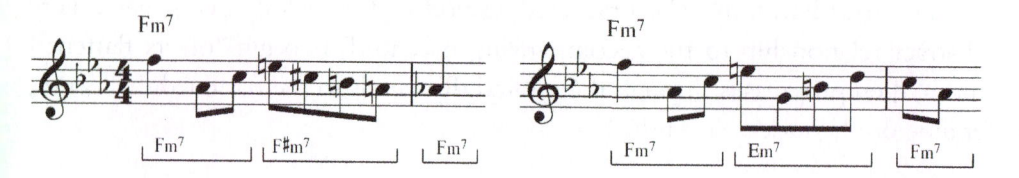

All of the preceding examples are highly dissonant and un-songlike. This degree of harmonic divergence usually only occurs as an occasional effect. Furthermore, all of these examples have two things in common that help to aurally sell the dissonance. Firstly, they all rely upon implying a logical alternative harmony to that of the accompaniment, whether that is an alternative functional progression or a chromatic side-step. Secondly, each of these melodies resolve by step or half-step into a chord tone of the accompanying harmony.

Part of the lesson here is that we can get away with extreme chromaticism and dissonance, provided that it is resolved satisfactorily. None of these phrases would be nearly as acceptable if they did not resolve.

Instances of divergence between melody and accompaniment are found in more conservative contexts. These are often in the form of idiomatic blues language, which shall be discussed later in the chapter. Other examples are found in highly diatonic melodies that ignore some of the details of their accompaniment.

The asterisked A-natural in the passage below looks, on paper, to be in strong disagreement with the A-flat in the prevailing $B^{\flat}7$ chord, but the songlike pentatonic nature of the melody overrides the disparity to some extent, and the pitch does not stand out as much as we might expect:

We might say that the melody suggests an alternative chord progression that does not pass through the elaborative $B^{\flat}7$ on its way from I to $IIIm^{7\flat5}$:

Same Melody, Different Chords

In Chapter 11 we explored various techniques that can be used to transform melodic motifs, which enables us to maintain continuity without the tedium of literal repetition. By examining melody in isolation, we missed out a very simple and essential technique: a change of an underlying harmony can recontextualise a repeated phrase.

This effect can even render the immediate and exact repetition of a phrase palatable. Below, a new harmonic setting disguises the fact that the second phrase is melodically identical to the first:

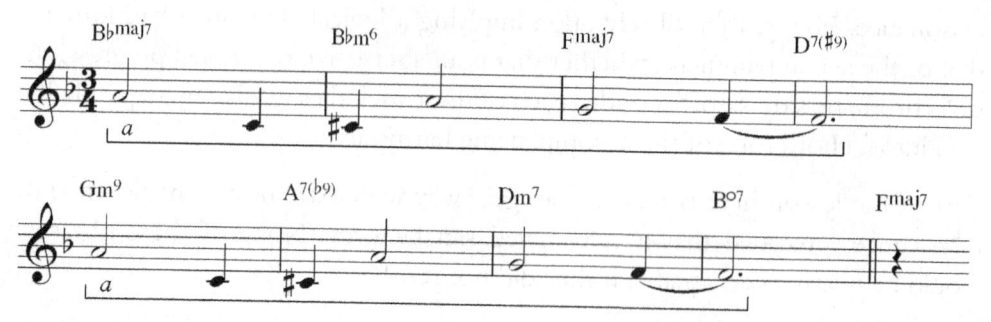

Blues Melody

Many elements of jazz language that do not align with the European harmonic tradition are associated with The Blues. Blues music as a genre shares a common ancestor with jazz, and the blues is present within jazz as an essential part of its aesthetic. The Blues is certainly undefinable, and though any attempt to describe it must defer first to the performances and recordings of great musicians, there are a few features of blues melody tangible enough to be discussed here.

As we know from Chapter 7, the tonic chord in a blues piece might appear as a major triad or sixth chord, but may also include a flattened seventh, making it a dominant chord type with little suggestion of V functionality. It does not imply resolution to a chord with a root a fifth lower or a fourth higher.

Many typical blues melodies superimpose pentatonic pitch collections over this harmony, either the major pentatonic, every pitch of which is consonant with I^7, or the minor pentatonic, which includes the fourth and a surprising flattened third:

As is generally the case with melodies, these pitch collections tend to appear in short, motivic fragments rather than in long scalic sequences. Below are two melody fragments that utilise the pitches of the major pentatonic scale:

[musical notation: two fragments with C⁷ chord]

Below, we see two fragments that use only pitches from the minor pentatonic scale. Both contain an E-flat in prominent positions, the rather dissonant raised ninth of the underlying chord. The harmonic potency of this pitch is lessened by its pentatonic context.

Chromatic alterations to pentatonic pitch sets are typical in blues language, such as the flattened third/raised second as a lower neighbour tone to the natural third (page 121). The appearance of this pitch as a grace note, as in the second example, is very typical:

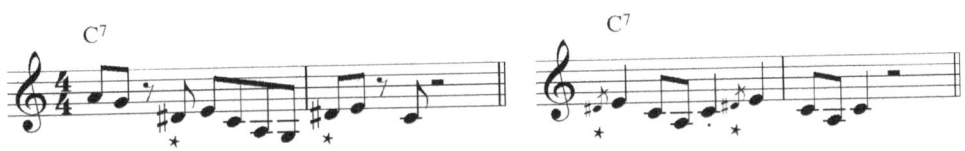

[musical notation: two fragments with C⁷ chord]

A very popular chromatic alteration to minor pentatonic material is the use of a raised fourth/flattened fifth as a lower neighbour tone to the fifth, or an upper neighbour tone to the fourth. This is the pitch that produces the blues scale (p. 245), and it often appears as a grace note:

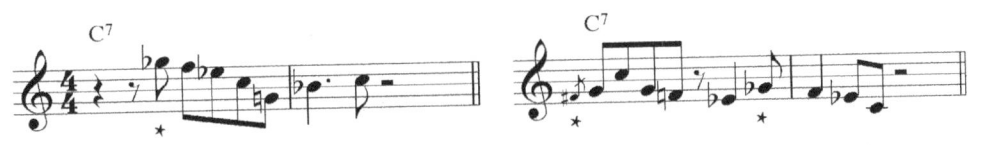

[musical notation: two fragments with C⁷ chord]

Other chromatic pitches are used to connect pentatonic tones. In the first example below, the natural seventh appears as a chromatic passing tone between the root and flattened seventh of a minor pentatonic line.

In the second example, a flattened sixth appears between the natural sixth and fifth of a major pentatonic line:

[musical notation: two fragments with C⁷ chord]

Major and minor pentatonic may be combined. The first example below shows a line that begins with major pentatonic pitches and ends with minor pentatonic pitches. The second example shows the reverse:

[musical notation: two examples labeled C7 showing minor pentatonic and major pentatonic phrases]

The repetition of a short phrase, perhaps with minor variations or rhythmic displacement, is a typical blues effect. This effect is often called a riff. Below, a three-note motif is rhythmically displaced as it repeats:

[musical notation: C7 riff example]

This blues riff receives a different tail upon repetition, suggesting a call-and-response in miniature:

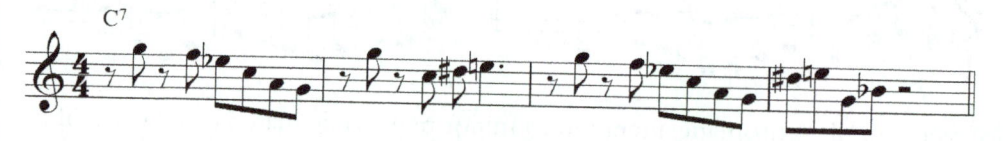

[musical notation: C7 call-and-response example]

Melody over Twelve-bar Blues

The twelve-bar blues progression has always accounted for a significant proportion of jazz repertoire, and there are a number of specific conventions associated with the writing of a jazz head over this form. As we saw in Chapter 7, the twelve bars of a blues chorus are subdivided into three four-bar phrases, with the first, fifth, and ninth bar receiving the most hypermetric accent.

Traditionally, these three phrases consist of a call, its repetition (or a variation on the call), and a response. The lyrics to Robert Johnson's *Kindhearted Woman* provide a classic example, reproduced here with approximate bar numbers in superscript:

> [1]"I got a kind-hearted woman, do anything in this world for me,
>
> [5]I got a kind-hearted woman, do anything in this world for me,
>
> [9]But these evil-hearted women, man, they will not let me be."

This *a-a-b* phrase structure is extremely common in blues music, but is also preserved in much of the instrumental jazz that uses this form. Jazz blues compositions often consist of a phrase, its repetition, and a final antecedent phrase.

Below is a twelve-bar blues head with this structure. The phrase beginning in the fifth bar is an example of the 'same melody, different harmony' technique discussed earlier in the chapter:

A common variation on this concept has the second phrase following the harmony, beginning a fourth higher:

Sometimes, a melody that works over the first four bars of a blues is incompatible with the IV chord of bar 5. This generally occurs when the third of the tonic chord appears prominently in the first bar, because that pitch becomes the natural seventh of IV:

[Musical notation: G7 – C7 – G7 phrase labeled *a*]

[Musical notation: C7 – G7 phrase labeled *a*, with an *x* marking, ending "etc..."]

Such a situation suggests two possible situations. Firstly, as suggested above, the second phase of the head may follow the harmony, beginning a fourth higher:

[Musical notation: C7 – G7 phrase labeled *a'*, ending "etc..."]

Alternatively, we can maintain the same pitch level, modifying only those pitches necessary to allow the line to agree with IV^7. Modified pitches are asterisked, below:

[Musical notation: C7 – G7 phrase labeled *a'* with three asterisks below modified pitches, ending "etc..."]

One final type of blues head is common enough to be worthy of mention: a very simple riff might repeat three times to form an *a-a-a* phrase structure. Sonny Rollins' *Sonnymoon for Two*, and Duke Ellington's extremely minimalist *C-Jam Blues* are famous examples, but for our example below, we will use an invented one.

There is a notable lack of agreement between melody and harmony by the time we get to bars 9 and 10, but the simplicity of the pentatonic line and the predictability of its repetition legitimises a line that would otherwise be unacceptable:

Actual Counterpoint

Contrapuntal textures have always been present in jazz performance. Early jazz would often feature simultaneous improvisation by several wind instruments, but the growth in the popularity of big bands decreased emphasis on such effects.

The thread of simultaneous improvisation was not wholly lost in post-war jazz, and was retained by musicians such as Warne Marsh, Lee Konitz, and Lennie Tristano, the Tristano School. Charlie Parker also wrote contrapuntal pieces such as *Ah-Leu-Cha* and *Chasin' the Bird*, both of which consist of two simultaneous melodies over rhythm changes.

One manifestation of counterpoint in jazz is the repetition of a passage with the cumulative addition of melodies. Benny Goodman's famous recording of *Sing, Sing, Sing* uses this effect, but it is also present in smaller ensembles. Charles Mingus' twelve-bar blues piece *E's Flat Ah's Flat Too* begins with a wonderful example. As well as being a highly effective way to build intensity, this effect enables the listener to become familiar with each melody before the next is introduced, which ultimately allows us to introduce extremely dense textures in an accessible manner.

Contrapuntal practice in common practice music places strong emphasis on the avoidance of voice crossing. A melodic voice that begins below another must stay there. This is considerably less important in the more freewheeling and improvisational texture of jazz counterpoint. Although much of the best contrapuntal jazz melody is riff-based, improvised, or deliberately evocative of improvisational style, there is much to be gained from a brief glance into the minutiae of how simultaneous melodies might interact. When two melodic lines move separately, they may do so in one of three ways:

Similar or parallel motion – as one melody moves from pitch to pitch, its counterpoint moves in the same direction at a different pitch level. The two lines ascend and descend together. Similar motion reduces the contrapuntal effect, and is used sparingly when a sense of separate voices is required.

Contrary motion – as one melody moves, its counterpoint moves in the opposite direction. When one line ascends in pitch, a contrary counterpoint descends, and vice versa.

Oblique motion – as a melody moves from pitch to pitch, its counterpoint remains static, and when it remains static its counterpoint moves.

In practice, contrapuntal melodies combine all three relationships, moving between similar, contrary, and oblique motion as they progress:

similar --> oblique --------------------------> similar --> contrary

In order to be perceived as consonant, a melody must agree with underlying harmony at points of hypermetric emphasis. Contrapuntal melodies performed with rhythm section accompaniment must agree not only with underlying harmony, but with each other. In fact, the latter relationship is perhaps more significant. A dissonance between melody and countermelody is more pronounced than one between melody and underlying harmony.

Open thirds, flattened thirds, sixths, and flattened sixths between two melody lines produce warm consonances. Octaves, unisons, and fifths are consonant but colourless, and all other intervals are dissonant to varying degrees.

Below is a short melodic phrase which interacts as we would expect with the harmony. The rhythmically significant beginnings of bars coincide with chord tones of the underlying chords:

Below, a lower stave is added with a countermelody that harmonises each emphasised chord tone with a pitch that produces a consonant interval against it. These melodies are in agreement with both the background chords and with each other:

This is not the only option. We might choose to highlight these key points with dissonances:

Simultaneous melodies generally keep out of each other's way, with one voice becoming more active as the other retreats into a role of melodic accompaniment. When more than two voices are involved, it may become practically impossible (and undesirable) to maintain equality between voices.

Below is a passage consisting of three simultaneous melodies which pass the baton of activity as they progress:

Chapter Summary

A melodic phrase or fragment may be repeated or paraphrased with a change of rhythmic position, which changes the relative emphasis of its pitches.

Rhythmic displacement might be used to suggest an alternative time signature. This effect is known within the jazz idiom as a hemiola.

A melody may return repeatedly to a single pedal pitch. This has contrapuntal implications which suggest the presence of two simultaneous lines.

A melody might imply two active voices. In most cases, one of these will be extremely simple, ascending or descending in a combination of steps and half steps.

Melody and harmony may diverge. This is most acceptable and effective when used occasionally and judiciously, when both parts have a logic of their own, and when the resolution is explicit.

Blues melodies often use the major pentatonic scale, the minor pentatonic scale, or a mixture of both, combined with additional chromaticism.

Melodies written over the twelve-bar blues progression often feature *a-a-b* phrase structure, but *a-a-a* is also common.

Contrapuntal melodies are constructed by combining the three types of intermelodic relationship: similar, contrary and oblique motion.

Chapter 20
More Harmonic Techniques

Parallel to the previous chapter's melodic miscellany, this chapter is a discussion of two types of harmonic structure that haven't been directly or thoroughly addressed elsewhere: slash chords and polychords.

Slash Chords

Several specific usages of slash chords have been covered in our discussions of harmony, but a few general points may be made.

A given chord may appear over any of twelve bass notes. In the tertial language of common practice music, triads or seventh chords with a chord tone in the bass are referred to as inversions:

C	C/E	C/G
root position	first inversion	second inversion

Inversions are the most stable slash chords, because the upper pitches are consonant with the bass. This principal holds true even in the relatively dense harmonic structures typical of jazz. Extended chords are elaborations of the underlying triad and are still most stable and consonant when they appear over one of the pitches of that triad.

Slash chords generally occur for one of three reasons. Firstly, a bass line might ascend and/or descend in steps and/or half steps, thereby connecting the harmonies within a progression. We saw in our discussion on page 234 that this technique can be used to marry distant harmonies, but the same holds true in functional chord progressions.

Both of the following excerpts are completely functional, with the slash chords only highlighting the voice leading within the conventional movement above. Such progressions are extremely common:

[Musical notation: Ab6 | C7(b9)/G | Fm | F7(b9)/A | Bbm7]

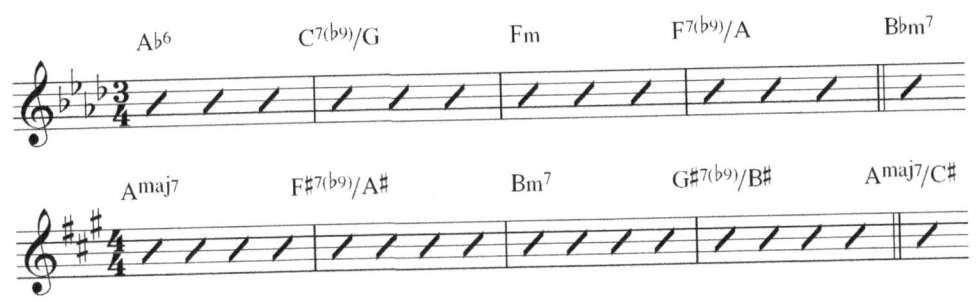

[Musical notation: Amaj7 | F#7(b9)/A# | Bm7 | G#7(b9)/B# | Amaj7/C#]

We find that the aural logic of linear bass movement can excuse some rather dissonant harmonies, even within a wholly functional context. The chords in the second and third bars below are, in isolation, rather dissonant, and in another context might be very conspicuous:

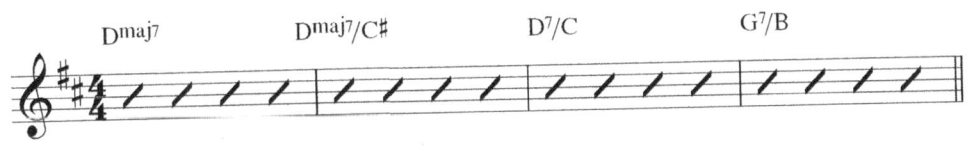

[Musical notation: Dmaj7 | Dmaj7/C# | D7/C | G7/B]

The second common usage of slash chords was also discussed on page 234 in reference to non-functional harmony: structures may move over a constant bass note. Again, this has applications in functional contexts, where it may allow strange and dissonant slash chords that would otherwise be jarring. Below, a consistent pedal on the fifth of the key justifies a bizarre $E^{b\circ7}/B^b$ chord:

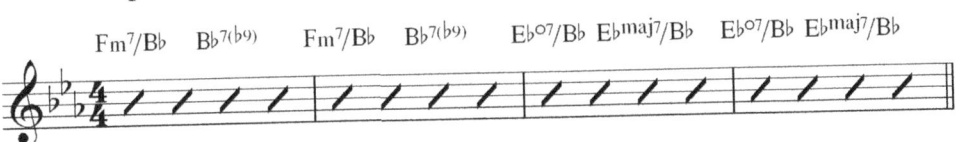

[Musical notation: Fm7/Bb Bb7(b9) | Fm7/Bb Bb7(b9) | Ebo7/Bb Ebmaj7/Bb | Ebo7/Bb Ebmaj7/Bb]

As a further example, a consistent tonic bass note here allows V^7 to appear over its fourth:

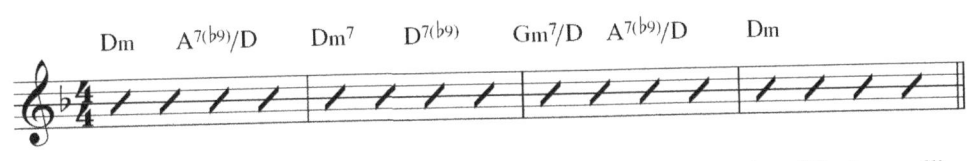

[Musical notation: Dm A7(b9)/D | Dm7 D7(b9) | Gm7/D A7(b9)/D | Dm]

The final common usage of the slash chords is that they may simplify the spelling of a particular chord or sequence of chords.

Below, a structure that would usually be spelled as $C\#^{m7b5}$ appears as $E^m/C\#$. Although this is a more complicated chord symbol, it better reflects the functionality of the sequence as a static structure above a shifting bass:

Fundamentals of Jazz Composition •

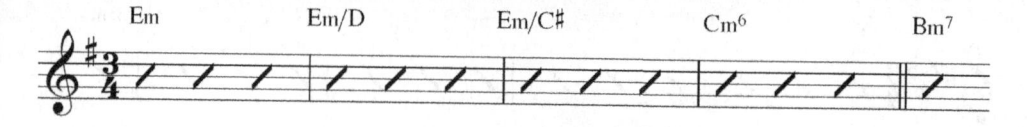

[Musical notation: Em | Em/D | Em/C# | Cm6 | Bm7]

The second chord in this passage could be written as $C^{7sus4b9}$, but the unusual B^{bm6}/C chord symbol allows us to understand its true function; this passage is simply a case of static harmony over an active bass:

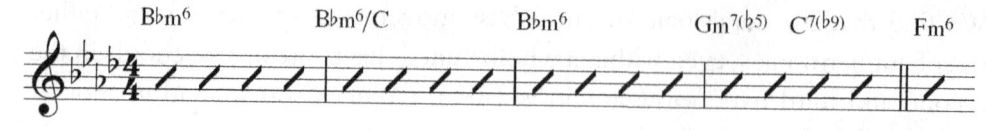

[Musical notation: Bbm6 | Bbm6/C | Bbm6 | Gm7(b5) C7(b9) | Fm6]

Polychords

A polychord consists of two chords sounded simultaneously, usually one above the other. The upper structure of a polychord is usually a triad, and the lower portion may be a triad or a seventh chord. Polychords are usually written as two chord symbols, one directly above the other, and separated by a horizontal line.

Like slash chords, polychords are often alternate spellings for structures that can also be described with conventional chord symbols. Here are few examples:

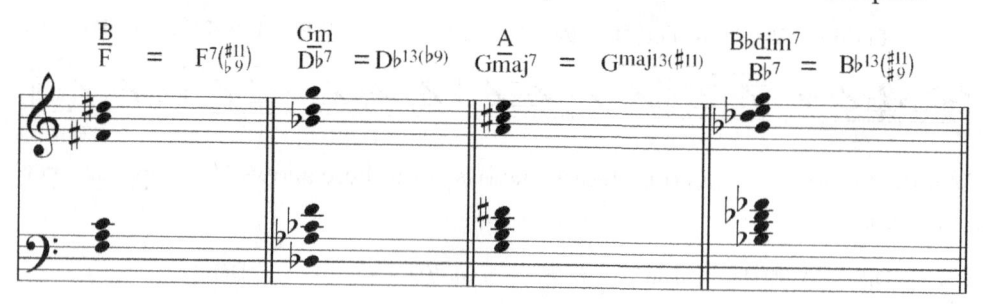

[Musical notation: B/F = F7(#11,b9) | Gm/Db7 = Db13(b9) | A/Gmaj7 = Gmaj13(#11) | Bbdim7/Bb7 = Bb13(#11,#9)]

The simple, familiar consonance of the major or minor triad makes it particularly suitable for appearance at the top of a chord voicing. It can legitimise some rather strange harmonic moments.

The following is a simple triadic chord progression with the simple twist that the tonic triad appears at the top of each voicing. Once again, the unusual and dissonant structures that this produces are made permissible only by the context:

[Musical notation: A | A/G | A/D/F# | A/E | A]

Inverting this idea, a lower structure may remain constant beneath shifting upper structures. In a different context, the C triad over B-flat triad in the fourth bar might be spelled as B♭$^{bmaj13\sharp11}$:

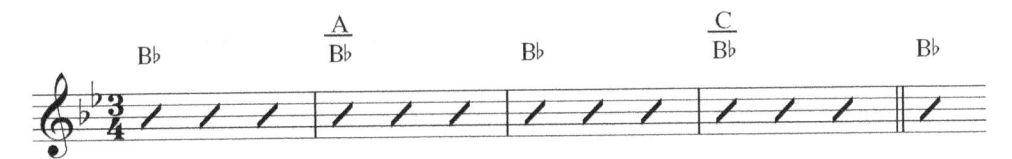

[musical example: Bb | A/Bb | Bb | C/Bb | Bb, in 3/4]

Just as a static upper triad can legitimise unusual harmonies, chromatic or whole step movement of an upper structure might connect the chords within a progression. The following is a III-VI-II-V-I progression in F major, where the first four chords are all re-harmonised as dominant sevenths with a major triad at the top. This produces a sequence that suggests two simultaneous chord progressions: a series of dominant chords that cycles in fifths beneath a series of major triads that descends in half steps. Each of these dominant chords conform to the diminished scale discussed on page 238:

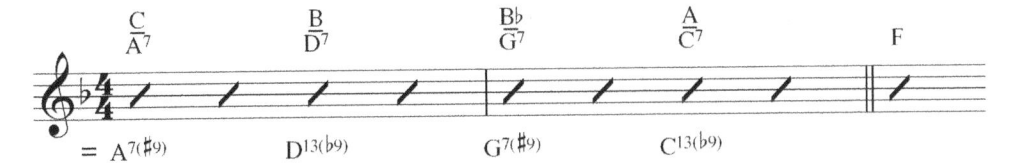

[musical example: C/A7 | B/D7 | Bb/G7 | A/C7 | F, in 4/4]
= A7(♯9)   D13(♭9)   G7(♯9)   C13(♭9)

We can also invert the idea, placing the fourths cycle in the upper triads and the descending half steps in the dominant chords beneath. This gives us a dual chord progression that works on two levels:

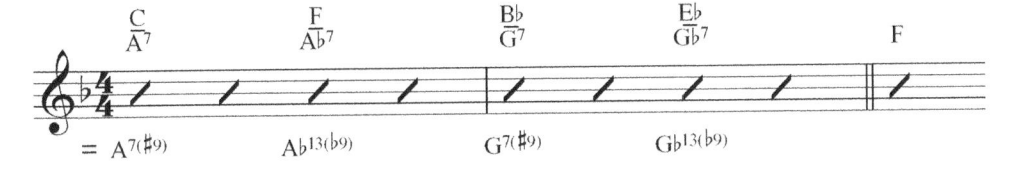

[musical example: C/A7 | F/Ab7 | Bb/G7 | Eb/Gb7 | F, in 4/4]
= A7(♯9)   Ab13(♭9)   G7(♯9)   Gb13(♭9)

Chapter Summary

Any chord may appear over any bass note, but slash chords typically function in one of three ways: they connect harmonies via step-wise bass movement, they connect harmonies via a constant bass note, or they simplify the spelling of unconventional structures.

A polychord is the presence of two simultaneous chords. This usually takes the form of a triad over another triad or seventh chord. Logical polychord sequences can excuse very dissonant and unconventional structures, even within functional contexts.

Chapter 21
Chord Voicings

We have thus far conceptualised chords as abstract collections of simultaneous pitches. When writing a lead sheet or chord chart, this is an entirely appropriate model for the jazz composer. "However, as we add more detail to a composition, moving from a lead sheet towards an arrangement with specific parts for a set instrumentation, we may encounter situations where we wish to specify the spacing and exact pitch content of harmonic structures.

It is usually unnecessary to specify chord voicings for our harmonic instrumentalists such as the guitars, pianos, and vibraphones, but there are exceptions. A chord might have an unusual structure that cannot be expressed accurately with a symbol. A specific voicing might have some importance to a composition, perhaps as a recurring central motif or in unison across an ensemble. As we come to orchestrate passages of melody across multiple instruments, we may wish to harmonise each pitch of a melody with its own chord, creating a so-called thickened line.

Register

One element that we must consider when voicing a chord is the registral position and spacing of its pitches. The notes within a chord might be spaced in large intervals, or cramped in a close clusters, and may occur in the bass, high in the upper register, or spread over many octaves.

As a very general rule, we tend to use wider, more consonant intervals lower in a voicing, and closer and more dissonant intervals higher up in a chord, a convention for which there are very good reasons based on the physical properties of sound.

A sound that we perceive as having pitch is one in which a single frequency dominates. This is called the fundamental, and is usually the lowest frequency present. Above the fundamental, a sound source also produces a series of low-amplitude overtones in a pattern called the harmonic series or overtone series. The following diagram shows the harmonics produced when a low C is sounded.

Some of these frequencies will be significantly out of tune with the equal tempered pitches notated:

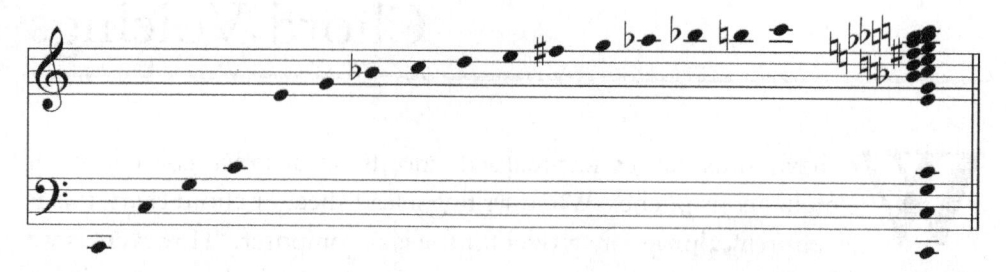

When we sound pitches simultaneously as a chord, we hear not only the combination of the fundamental pitches present, but also the combination of all of their harmonics. The lower a pitch is, the more harmonics are produced within the audible range, which means that, even in a theoretically consonant chord sounded in a low register, upper harmonics will be dissonant with each other. Intervals and chords are therefore more dissonant the lower they are in pitch.

Octaves will always sound consonant because their harmonics are exact octaves apart. However, even a perfect fifth, which sounds very consonant in the middle or high register, becomes rather dissonant if voiced in a very low octave:

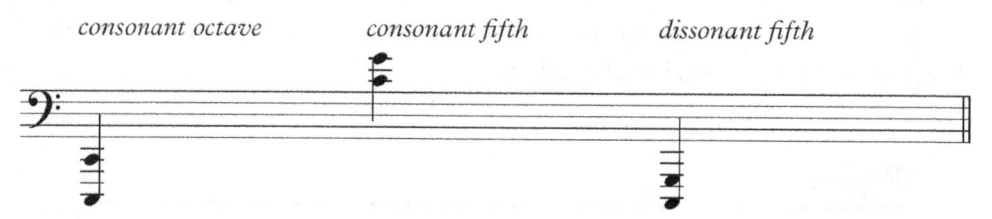

consonant octave   *consonant fifth*   *dissonant fifth*

As we can see from the harmonic series of C shown above, a rough rule is that the higher we ascend in the harmonic series, the closer the intervals are grouped together. This effect is approximately mirrored in how we tend to voice chords. By mimicking the tendencies of physical sound, we create stable structures that are easier for our ear to understand.

The two chord voicings on the right demonstrate this. They both contain the same six pitches displaced into different octaves. The first voicing closely mimics the harmonic series of its lowest pitch, producing a practicable and consonant voicing of $C^{maj9\#11}$. The second voicing deviates far more from the harmonic series of its bass F-sharp, featuring a dense cluster at the bottom and wider intervals higher up. This produces a far more dissonant structure with far less general application, despite containing the exact same pitches as the first voicing.

Pitch Content

One issue to consider in voicing chords is the question of which pitches to include and which to omit. Although a thirteenth chord symbol such as C^{maj13} would seem to imply the presence of seven discrete pitches voiced in thirds, such a structure is practically non-existent in real music.

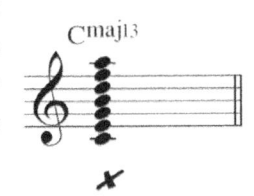

The reality is that jazz composers and performers strategically omit certain theoretically available notes from their chord voicings in order to create more open structures that are more in line with the registral considerations discussed above.

All chord symbols designate a root note, but in certain circumstances the root may be omitted from the upper voicing of a chord. Whenever a voicing appears over a rhythm section that includes a bass instrument, the bass may be considered to be playing the root.

The excerpt below shows a series of four-part harmonies appearing over a rhythm section. At no point does a root note appear in any of the upper structures. The lower stave might represent any combination of rhythm section instruments, and the upper might be performed on a piano or any combination of four melodic instruments:

(rhythm section)

Because the relationship between the perfect fifth and the root is such a simple interval, and because the perfect fifth is such a prominent pitch in the harmonic series produced by the root, a root note can be considered to imply the presence of a fifth. The perfect fifth need not therefore be included in a voicing. It serves only to thicken the texture without adding colour. On the other hand, if a thick sounding voicing is required, a low root and fifth at the bottom of a voicing might be the perfect choice.

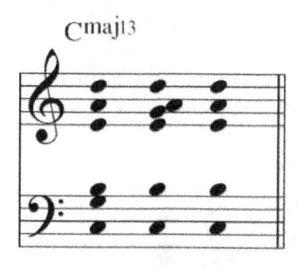

Here are three very similar voicings of C^{maj13}. The first includes a low fifth, G in this case, in the bottom octave of the structure. Its removal lightens the latter two voicings considerably. The second voicing includes the G one octave higher. Here it increases the density of the middle of the chord, producing a dissonant second against the natural thirteenth, in this case the A.

In the third voicing above, the omission of the fifth produces a lighter and more open sonority with no loss of colour or functionality. Each of these voicings may be applicable in certain contexts.

As a rule, the third is included in any chord where it is available, such as within any tertiary structure other than a suspended chord. The third is the most descriptive of a chord's quality, and describes the basic tonality of the underlying triad, whilst harmonising both consonantly and colourfully with the root.

In suspended chords, the fourth theoretically replaces the third, although in practice both pitches are sometimes included in a dominant chord. We could call such a chord as a dominant eleventh, and notate it as $X^{7sus(add10)}$.

Unadorned triads were used in early jazz, particularly on IV and I chords, but most styles include a diatonic seventh on IV and a natural seventh or sixth on tonic major chords. Between the 1940s and the incursion of rock's influence, the tonic minor was the only position in which a triad was regularly heard. This means that most chord voicings include at least two pitches over a root: a third or flattened third, and a seventh, flattened seventh, or sixth.

As an example of how this might be applied, let us imagine how we might write chordal backing figures for two horns of the kind that might appear behind a soloist or written melody in a swing piece. In the passage below, the two melodic voices cover the thirds and sevenths, fully describing the harmony by including all of its essential pitches. Root notes and extensions are left to discretion of the rhythm section:

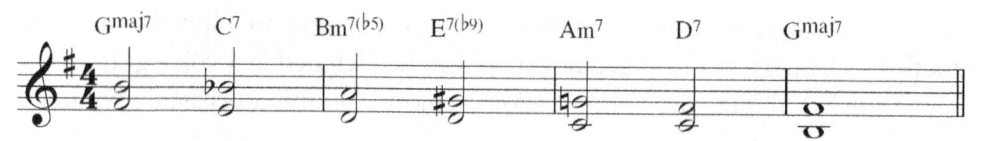

With the respective third and seventh/sixth of a chord is in place, extensions, roots, and fifths are optional extras. If a third horn were available, roots and fifths can thicken the line without adding colour. They also create exposed dissonances, asterisked, whenever the root is voiced immediately above the seventh at the top of a voicing:

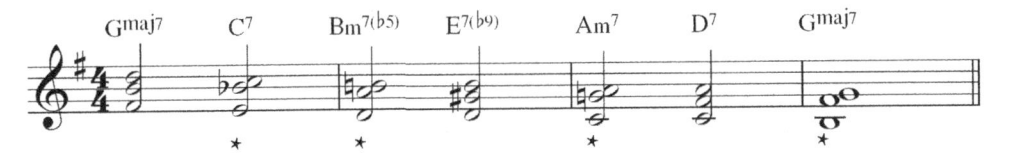

Upper extensions such as ninths and thirteenths are more colourful, and the wider intervals now available produce a more open sound:

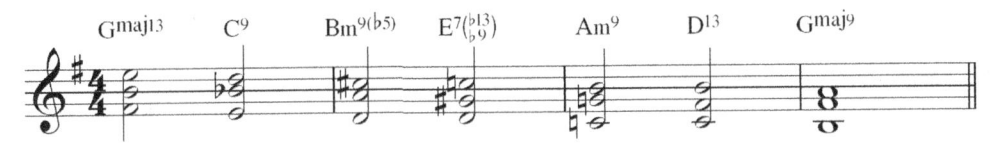

With four voices our options increase again. Two are taken up with the essential third and seventh/sixth, leaving us with two voices remaining to cover the root/ninth and fifth/thirteenth. One possible harmonisation of this passage in four parts might opt for extensions:

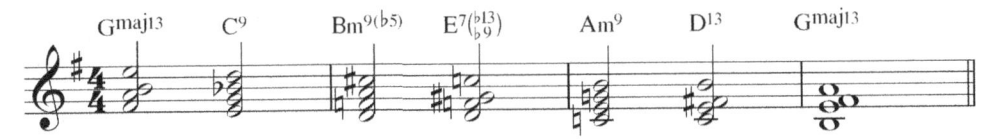

…Whilst another might thicken, preferring roots and fifths:

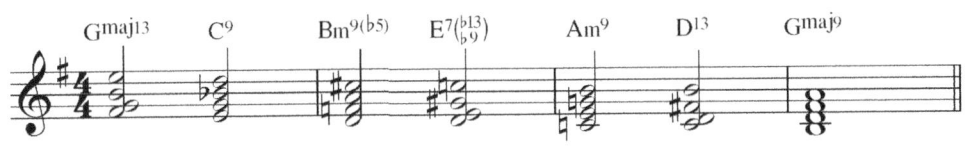

Sometimes, orchestration demands that pitches within a voicing are doubled, which is to say that the same pitch may occur in more than one octave. This is most frequently the bass of a chord or its root, though in slash chords the root is not the bass note.

The doubling of higher extensions draws attention to them that may be undesirable in a background texture. The avoidance of doubled notes is a relatively minor concern in jazz harmony, and is generally overruled by the demands of voice leading.

Voice Leading

The human voice is not only the archetypal melodic instrument, but also, in a sense, the archetypal harmonic instrument. We hear in a chord progression not only a sequence of harmonic structures, but also a series of simultaneous melodies, analogous to a chorus of voices. This effect is most potent when each pitch in a chord is a step or half step from a pitch in the preceding and following chords. Let us return to the sequence featured above, which clearly implies two distinct voices that descend through the passage:

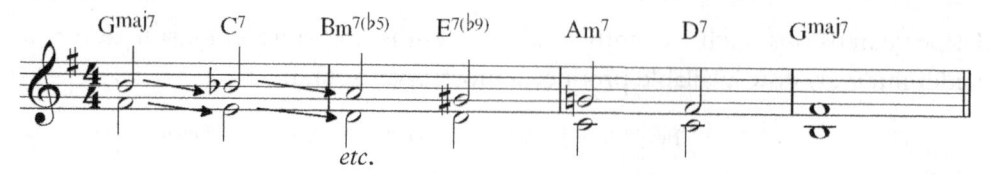

The essence of this effect is that each pitch moves to the closest available pitch in the next harmony. In contrast, the following passage, which consists of the same pitch collections re-voiced, sounds disjoint and random:

Chords generally occur in the background of a homophonic texture. Their role is to add colour and context to the melody that they accompany without drawing attention away from it. It is for this reason that smooth and economic voice leading is a solid rule. Large intervallic leaps bring a background texture to the foreground.

Below is another example which shows two contrasting routes that a pianist might take through a simple chord progression. In *(a)*, consecutive voicings are very different from each other in structure and register, with the top note of each leaping in large intervals. In *(b)*, conventional voice leading is applied.

Each chord contains four pitches over a bass note, and each pitch of the upper structure moves by the shortest possible distance into an available pitch of the next chord:

(a) *(b)*

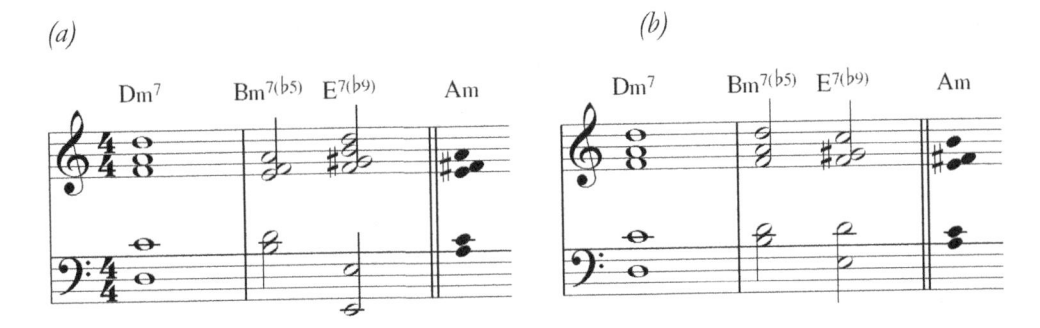

[Musical notation: Dm⁷ Bm⁷(♭5) E⁷(♭9) Am | Dm⁷ Bm⁷(♭5) E⁷(♭9) Am]

Example *(b)* produces a far smoother and less disruptive texture than *(a)* as it navigates the given chord progression. In cases where chord voicings are intended to provide a background texture, *(b)* is more appropriate.

Intervals

The intervallic relationships between the vertically adjacent pitches in a voicing account for much of their distinctive character. In most jazz voicings, vertically adjacent pitches are separated by thirds and fourths, with some seconds and fifths. When wider intervals do occur, they are most often between the bass and the next pitch up, in compliance with the principles of the harmonic series discussed earlier in this chapter.

Although most voicings use a combination of interval types, the flexibility of jazz harmony is such that we can even produce useable voicings consisting entirely of one type of interval. All of the following are voicings for C^{maj13}, consisting entirely of a single interval type over a bass note:

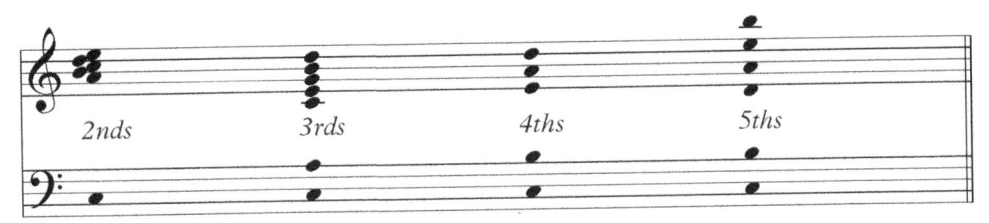

[Musical notation: 2nds 3rds 4ths 5ths]

Stacked seconds, particularly flattened seconds, are dissonant, and are rarely found at the bottom of a voicing, especially in a low register. At the top of a voicing, seconds and flattened seconds are very conspicuous and are often avoided, particularly when we require the top note to be perceived as the melody. This idea is discussed in more detail later in this chapter (p. 280).

Adjacent seconds are at their least conspicuous in the core of a voicing. Every voicing in the following passage consists of a step or half step cluster, which is sonically cushioned by the more obvious outer pitches of the chord:

Thirds are both consonant and colourful, which is why they are at the heart of our harmonic language. As was noted in Chapter 2, major and minor triads are the largest harmonic structures possible in which every pitch is consonant with every other. This is why they are such an essential element of our harmonic language, even in very complex examples such as the slash chords and polychords.

Much has been made of the use of fourths in jazz harmony, but in reality so-called quartal harmony does not exist as an alternative to the nominally tertiary system at the heart of the music. Quartal structures are employed to voice chords that have conventional tertiary names and functions. Even a II-V-I progression might be voiced entirely in diatonic fourths, as shown here.

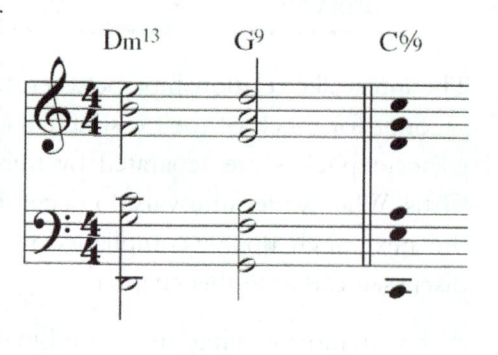

The interval between the bass note of a voicing and the next pitch up may be as large as a tenth or twelfth, but anything larger than a vertical fifth between two pitches in the upper structure is texturally rather disruptive, and relatively rare.

Density

One tool that jazz musicians use to manipulate the vertical spacing of a voicing is the idea that we might drop the pitches of a closed voicing by an octave in order to create an open voicing.

Let us return to the passage introduced on page 275. Each chord here is in a closed position, meaning that all pitches occur within the same octave. The pitches are as closely clustered as is possible without changing the top note.

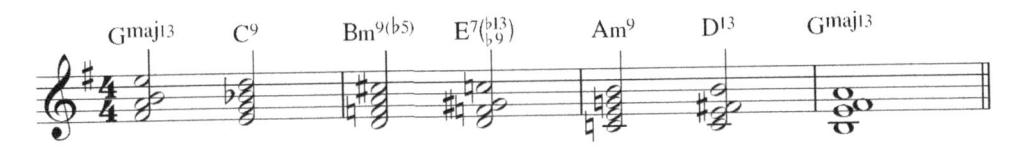

[Musical notation: Gmaj13, C9, Bm9(b5), E7(b13,b9), Am9, D13, Gmaj13]

This creates a dense texture that covers a small range and contains dissonant whole step and half step clashes between adjacent voices. In order to cover a wider range to better mimic the structure of the harmonic series, and to avoid close dissonances, we may choose to displace one or more of the pitches in one of these voicings into a different octave. In chords voiced across an ensemble, this has the added benefit of allowing us to place each instrument in a comfortable range.

In order to create a drop voicing from a closed position chord, we designate a number to each according to its vertical position in the chord. The highest note is 1, the next one down 2, and so on. By displacing or dropping pitch 2 by an octave, we create a drop 2 voicing; dropping pitch 3 by an octave, gives us a drop 3 voicing, and so on. Drop 2 and drop 3 voicings are the most common because they most closely mimic the harmonic series.

Drop 2 and 4 chords have a relatively even spacing and cover a huge range. Other spacing patterns, such as drop 4 and drop 2 and 3 are less practicable, since they yield unbalanced, bottom-heavy structures:

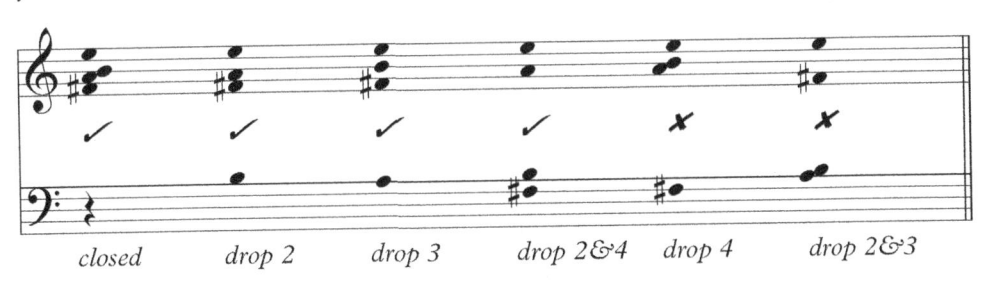

[Musical notation showing: closed ✓, drop 2 ✓, drop 3 ✓, drop 2&4 ✓, drop 4 ✗, drop 2&3 ✗]

Below is the entire passage from above, re-voiced in drop 2 voicings:

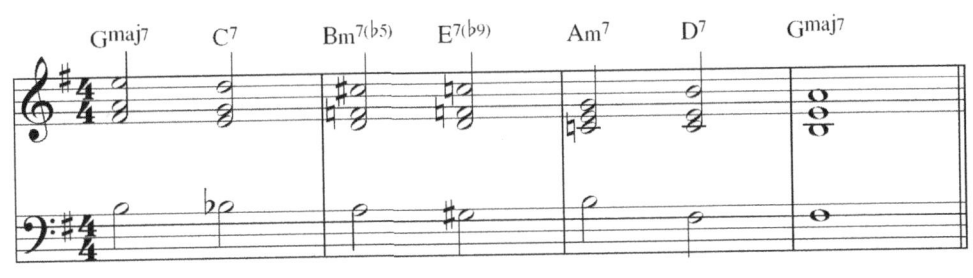

[Musical notation: Gmaj7, C7, Bm7(b5), E7(b9), Am7, D7, Gmaj7]

…and the same in drop 2 and 4:

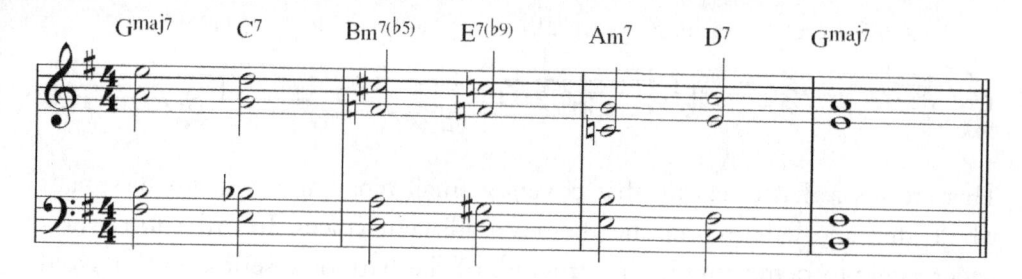

[Musical notation: Gmaj7 | C7 | Bm7(b5) E7(b9) | Am7 D7 | Gmaj7]

Instruments sound their best when operating in the middle of their range. This can often dictate the density of the voicings that we use when writing harmonies across the ensemble.

In closed position, the passage used throughout this section might suit four trumpets. Drop 2 voicings would be appropriate for two alto saxophones and two tenors, as it would place each instrument comfortably in its middle range. Drop 2 and 4 voicings would be a good choice for a brass ensemble of two trumpets and two trombones, making most of the lower range available from the trombones. Ultimately, the most appropriate voicing will depend on instrumentation and context.

Thickened Line

As jazz bands of the 1920s and 30s began to play to larger audiences, they encountered a need for greater volume. This was primarily achieved by the addition of extra horns to ensembles, which in turn created a necessity for a greater level of detail in arrangements. With ten or more brass and woodwind instruments, collective group improvisation becomes riotous, and unison melody becomes strident and difficult to intone.

The answer came in the form of a new textural technique, later called the thickened line. A melody could be harmonised across a horn section so that a chord hangs down from each melody note. The original melody line becomes the top note of a series of chords. In its most typical application, this technique is used to harmonise a melody in four parts for four trumpets, saxophones, or trombones. We can begin with a simple melody in A major:

[Musical notation in 3/4 A major: A6 | F#m9 | Bm7 | E7]

Because each pitch of this melody is a chord tone, we can simply hang a voicing of the current chord below each note. The melody note must remain at the top of each voicing in order to preserve its function. If another pitch were higher, we would hear that as the melody note:

We may now distribute the four pitches in each of these chords across an ensemble, with one performer playing the original melody, another playing the next note down from each voicing, and so on. Each voice always moves at the same time as the original melody and in the same direction, creating four individually coherent melodies, each of which preserves the contour of the original line whilst supporting it harmonically and complying with the background chords:

We examined on page 276 the principles of smooth and efficient voice leading in chordal textures for accompaniment, such that each voice moves to the nearest available pitch as we move from chord to chord. In a thickened line, our intention is the opposite. Parallel movement is the rule because we require the four voices to blend into one thickened voice.

So long as the top note of each chord remains at least a whole step above the second voice down in the chord, we will still perceive it as the primary melodic line within the passage. Despite using chords functionally identical to the voicings shown above, the following example contains two problematic moments where the second voice crowds the melody line, thereby obscuring it:

Fundamentals of Jazz Composition

In order for the thickened line to be consonant with itself, non-chord tones in a melody must be harmonised with a voicing that disagrees with the prevailing harmony, thus producing a momentary discrepancy between the thickened line and the rhythm section. We are effectively expanding melodic non-chord tones into entire chords, and justifying the resulting dissonance with the melodic logic of parallel movement.

In the following passage, a highly chromatic melody is harmonised with a thickened line, producing a fast-moving sequence of chords that are superimposed over the rhythm section's harmony:

There are various methods that may be used alone or in combination to harmonise non-chord tones in this manner. In the following fragment, the first and third pitches are chord tones and are harmonised as such, with a voicing that agrees with the prevailing C^6 harmony:

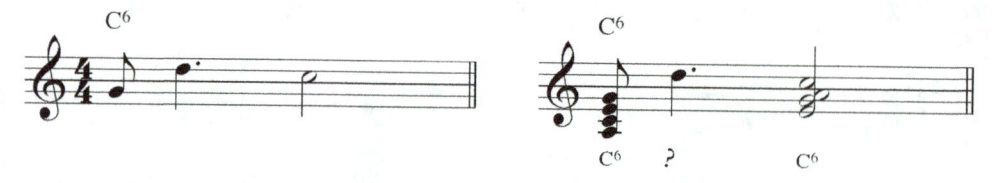

Analysing the remaining D-natural as a non-chord allows us to treat the C that follows it as our target pitch, and its C^6 chord harmonisation as our target chord. The preceding D-natural must be harmonised with a chord that resolves into C^6. The main options are as follows:

Diatonic planing: because the melody approaches the target pitch of C from a diatonic step below, we may do the same with every pitch in the harmony. This creates a temporary B^{m7b5} or D^{m6} passing chord.

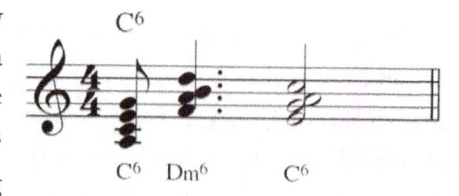

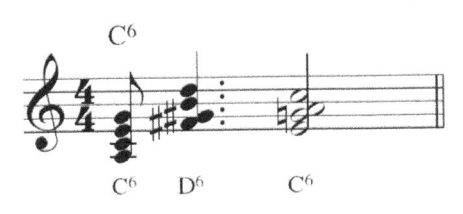

Parallel planing: here the non-chord tone is harmonised with an identical structure to the target pitch, which is to say that each voice moves into the target chord by the same interval, a descending whole step in this case.

Parallel planing is particularly effective when a non-chord tone resolves by a half step into a chord tone, whether from above or below. Disagreement with the underlying harmony is more severe, and the resolution more powerful:

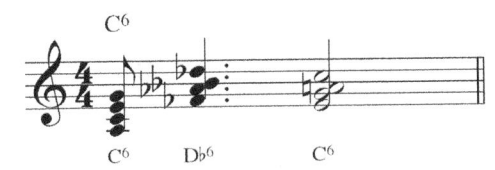

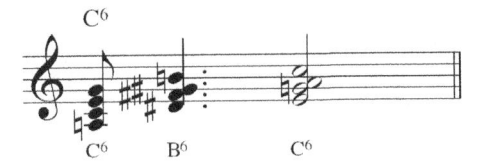

With regard to tension and resolution, another option is to harmonise the non-chord tone with the V of the prevailing chord, in this case a G^7. The passing dominant is a poor choice here because, as the top voice moves from D to C, the third voice repeats the pitch G, violating the principal that underlying parts follow the contour of the melody.

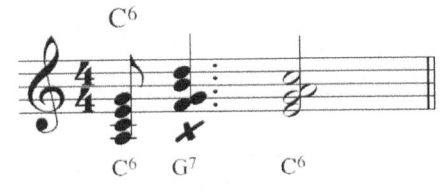

Because V and I share a chord tone, this is often a problem with V chord harmonisation of a non-chord tone, although some situations do allow it:

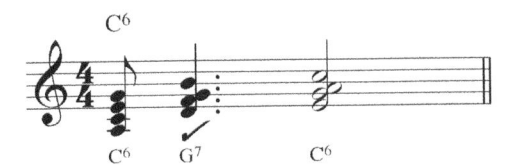

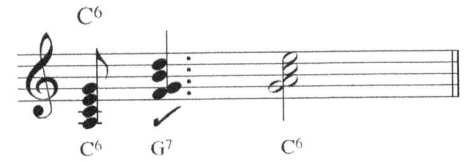

Passing diminished chord: A more flexible alternative to the V chord harmonisation is to replace the root of the V chord with its flattened ninth, thus creating a diminished seventh structure that is effectively a rootless V^{7b9}. Now, the tonic sixth chord and the V do not contain any common pitches, so there is no possibility of repeated notes when moving from $II^{\circ 7}$ to I.

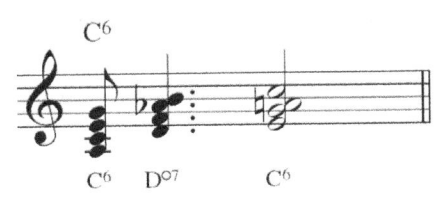

Fundamentals of Jazz Composition

Diminished passing chords are extremely popular, especially in older styles and over tonic harmony. In scalic passages, we might think of each voice as adhering to the bebop scale introduced on page 241:

Each pitch of the eight-note bebop scale may be harmonised with either an inversion of chord I, or with a diminished seventh chord:

$C^6 \quad D^{o7} \quad C^6/E \quad F^{o7} \quad C^6/G \quad G\sharp^{o7} \quad C^6/A \quad B^{o7}$

We might thereby ascend or descend the bebop scale in four parallel voices, each of which adds a chromatic pitch between the fifth and sixth degree of the scale:

In the following passage, every non-chord tone is harmonised with a diminished seventh chord. Each of these passing chords is a rootless $V^{7\flat 9}$ relative to the current harmony, which means that every time the melody moves from a non-chord tone to a chord tone we hear a miniature V-I resolution. The entire passage is voiced in drop 2:

Thickened line voicings need not include the root. The passage below is a re-harmonisation of the preceding passage which integrates rootless voicings. The lower chord symbols express this by analysing the voicings at face value:

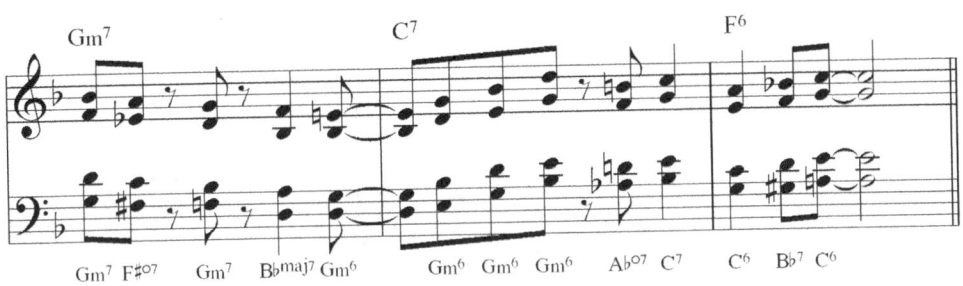

When writing thickened line orchestration for fewer than four voices, we are forced to make decisions about which pitches are the most important. In general, the principles outlined under the Pitch Content heading of this chapter apply. We should generally include thirds and sevenths/sixths wherever possible.

Sometimes, a three-part thickened line must break these rules in order to maintain the integrity of the lower voices. Below is a reduction of the previous excerpt for three voices. Asterisked chords omit either the third or seventh of the prevailing harmony when doing so would force a lower voice to take a different contour to the melody:

When five instruments are available to thicken a melody line, we have two options. Firstly, we may voice the passage in five true voices, such that each instrument plays its own pitch in each chord. The result is a very dense, complex harmony:

Five-note voicings have their place, but are best used sparingly, perhaps when they are heard for longer durations and at slower tempos, giving us the time to register the complex sounds. More often, the solution in five-voice writing is to double the lead voice an octave lower, thus strengthening the melody and simplifying the harmony. Here is the same harmonisation in drop 2, with the lead doubled in the fourth voice:

Chapter Summary

Intervals are more dissonant in lower registers due to the series of harmonic overtones produced by pitched sound.

The largest internal interval within a chord is most typically found between the bass note and the next pitch up, with clusters occurring higher in the voicing. This approximately mimics the structure of the harmonic series.

The theoretical content of a chord symbol does not always reflect how a chord is voiced. The root and fifth of a chord are the least harmonically descriptive, and are most likely to be omitted from the upper structure of a voicing, whilst the third and sixth/seventh are usually mandatory.

The various pitches within a chord imply the presence of several discrete voices, each of which must move by whole step or half step in order to maintain coherency as they move from chord to chord.

Voicings may appear in closed position with all of their pitches within a single octave. By displacing select pitches by an octave, we may create open positions with different sonic attributes and orchestrational applications.

When orchestrating melodies for multiple melodic instruments, we typically use a thickened line, whereby each melody note receives an entire chord. The first stage in harmonising a melody in this style is to identify and harmonise chord tones before finding appropriate harmonies for non-chord tones.

Chapter 22
Writing for Rhythm Section

As has already been noted, the rhythm section is traditionally fairly autonomous, and is at its best when competent musicians are provided with just enough information and the freedom to make a part their own. Much of the great music composed within the jazz tradition does not have specific parts assigned to the bass, drums, piano, and guitar.

Generally speaking, rhythm sections need only be provided with formal and harmonic information in the form of a lead sheet or chord chart, along with a general indication of style and tempo, but there may be times when we require something more specific. This chapter contains a few guidelines for writing reasonably conventional parts for the most common instruments of the rhythm section. This is a recommended starting point for rhythm section writing, as we must be familiar with the traditional functions of these instruments before utilising them in more innovative roles.

Writing for Drums

Drum notation is a relatively modern discipline, and though its conventions are well defined, it is still somewhat unstandardised. The following notation key represents relatively accepted array:

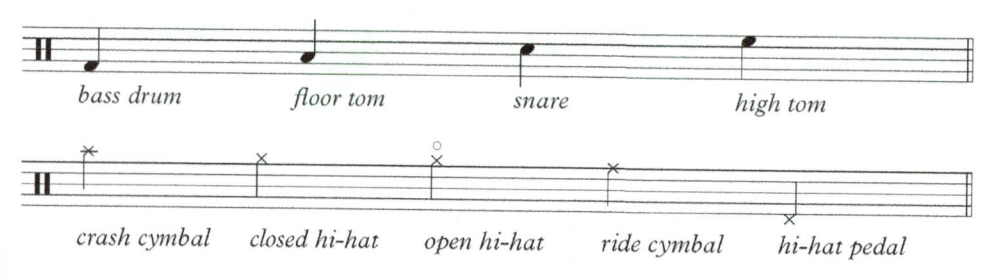

bass drum   *floor tom*   *snare*   *high tom*

crash cymbal   *closed hi-hat*   *open hi-hat*   *ride cymbal*   *hi-hat pedal*

Here are two examples of typical drum grooves:

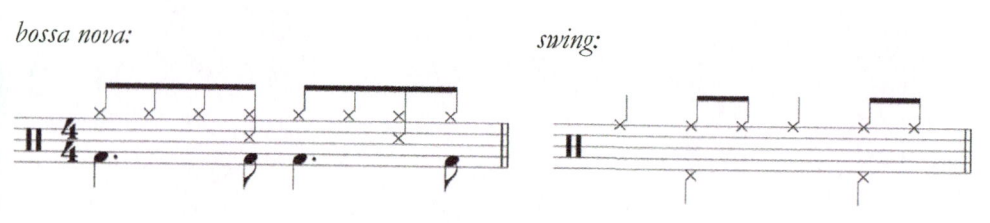

bossa nova: *swing:*

Very few jazz composers provide their musicians with specific drum parts. Usually, a drum part simply states the style of the piece, and the drummer is provided with the freedom to create their own part.

The following is typical of how a drum part for a bossa nova piece might begin. Stemless rhythm slashes count out the beats in the bar, with the addition of stems highlighting passages where specific hits are required. It is left to the drummer to orchestrate these rhythms as they see fit:

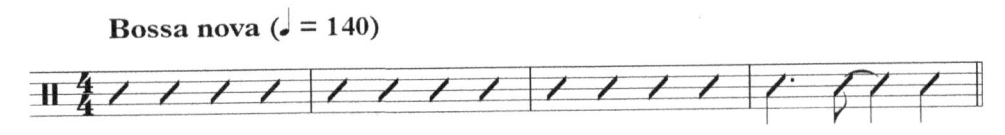

Bossa nova (♩ = 140)

When a specific drum part is required, it is not necessary to write out every bar of the piece. A single bar of the suggested pattern is a far tidier solution:

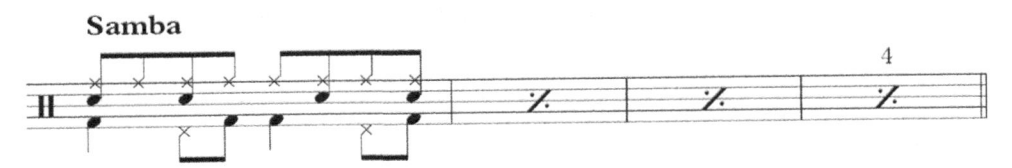

Samba

In this context, rhythm slashes may be preferred, indicating that the drummer can improvise their own similar time keeping pattern:

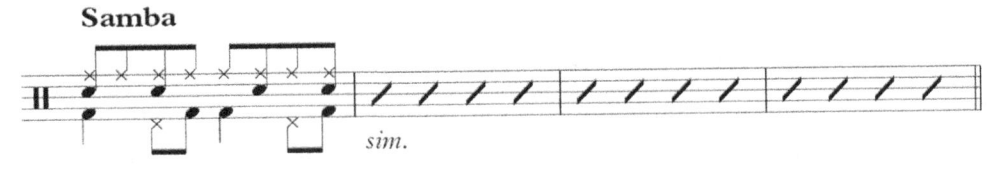

Samba

sim.

The above example is relatively unusual, as a composer will rarely write a specific drum pattern unless it is absolutely pivotal to the arrangement.

Lead sheets more often mimic the bossa nova example above, where simple rhythm slashes indicate that a relevant time feel is to be maintained for the duration.

Writing for Double Bass and Bass Guitar

As with drums, there is often no reason to write any specific material for the bass, particularly if the rhythm section is playing in an established idiom such as swing or bossa nova.

The two most common string bass instruments, the bass guitar and the double bass, have essentially the same range, and both are written an octave higher than they sound. In order to produce middle C, we must write the pitch one octave above that in a bass guitar or double bass part.

This diagram shows the practical range of both instruments. Some bass guitars have a lower fifth string that enables them to play a low B below the E, and some double basses have an extension that enables them to play a low C, although these are very rare in jazz.

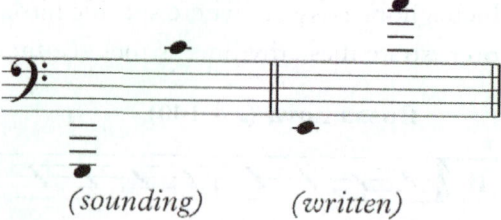

(sounding)   (written)

Both instruments have enough fingerboard to play higher than the C suggested, but anything above the written G above the bass clef is atypical of the instrument's normal usage. Most bass guitars are able to play the E-flat above this suggested range, and double basses can play considerably higher, although the sound has very little sustain in higher registers and intonation can be very difficult to control.

The bass can be used to double melodic passages, or may play melodies on its own. As with most instruments, the middle of the range is the most characteristic and expressive. The double bass in particular is a somewhat unwieldy instrument, and not particularly well suited to fast passages and large leaps, which can be difficult to intone accurately and articulate cleanly.

Both instruments have some limited ability to play harmonic intervals, but due to the range and the challenges of fingering and intonation, and the low register of the instrument, fifths in the middle range are the only frequently employed example.

Most double bass players have access to a bow which provides a new sound palette and practically infinite sustain. Most jazz bassists are not bow specialists, and as a general rule bowed (*arco*) bass parts should be even more conservative than plucked *pizzicato* ones. We must be sure to give players time to put the bow down and pick it up when switching back and forth between arco and pizzicato passages:

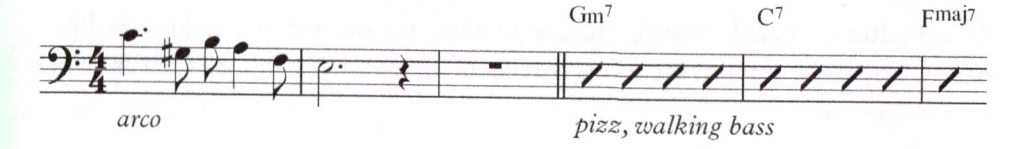

arco   *pizz, walking bass*

Most styles occasionally incorporate passages with a repeating bass line ostinato. This is one of the most frequent situations in which specific bass parts may be written. A bass ostinato has important harmonic implications, and usually relates very closely to the prevailing chord, often transposing to follow chord changes:

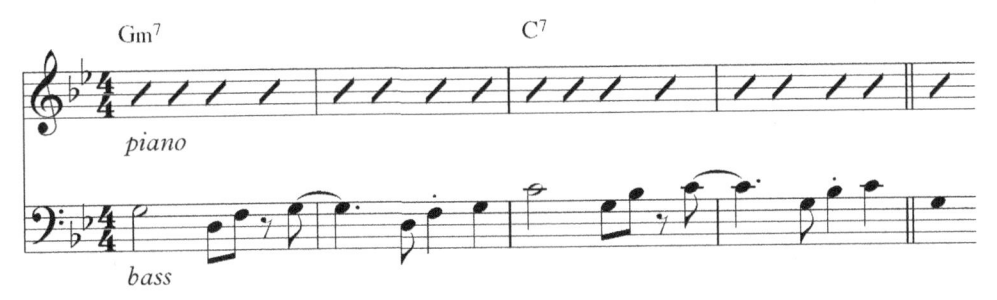

Sometimes, a bass ostinato might remain static beneath shifting harmony, in which case it essentially functions as an elaborated pedal point. Because the bass line below accentuates the pitch G, C⁷ is transformed into a slash chord. The stasis of the bass line excuses its disparity with the chord above:

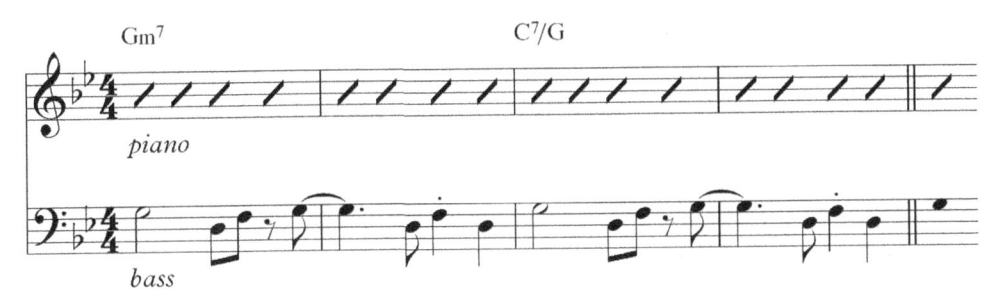

Many styles use bass ostinato throughout the entirety of a piece, but the effect may also be used intermittently.

Writing for Piano

The piano is the most versatile instrument in the jazz ensemble, able to play complex harmonies and melodies anywhere in its enormous range with equal and considerable ease, as well as having unique textural capacities. A pianist can simultaneously produce melody and harmony, melody and bass line, or bass line and harmony.

Like all rhythm section players, the pianist is typically left to their own devices. A chord chart and some stylistic direction is all that is

Fundamentals of Jazz Composition •

necessary to cover the normal roles of the instrument within a jazz ensemble. When the pianist is to accompany a melodic instrument, a single stave showing chord symbols and slashes/hits is sufficient:

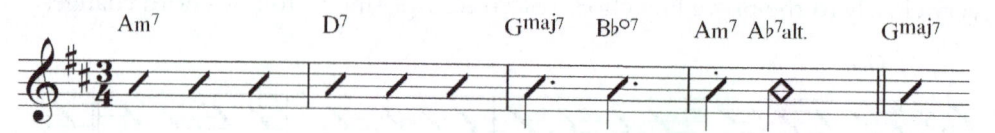

If we require a melody and chords, we might use two staves:

The extensive registers of an 88-key piano or keyboard are highly impractical for reading, and for passages that would need to be written many ledger lines above or below the stave, 8va and 8vb are useful to transpose the music either an octave above or below where it is written. The second rendering of the passage below is far more legible:

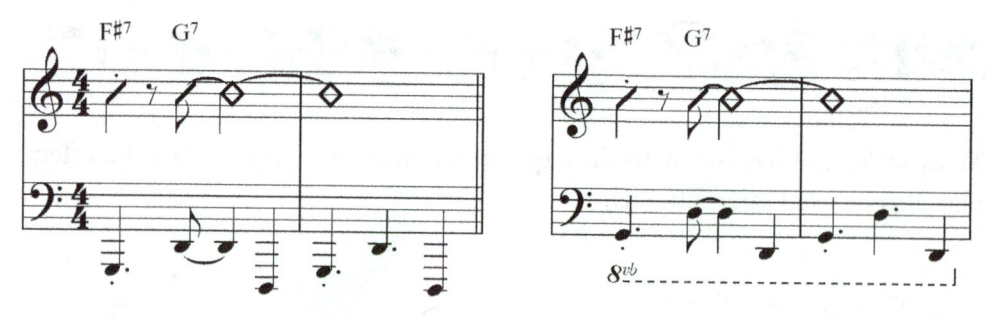

Writing for Guitar

A typical guitar part shows little more than the style, form, and harmony of a piece. Because the instruments often fulfil such similar roles, guitar and piano parts may even be interchangeable. The guitar is rather more likely to behave as an exclusively melodic instrument than the piano, and often functions as a horn, particularly where a piano is also present or if there are no actual wind instruments.

More than any other instrument in jazz, the electric guitar is capable of massive sonic variety through the use of effects units. Most composers leave the sound of the guitar to the discretion of guitarists.

Like the double bass and bass guitar, the guitar is written an octave higher than it sounds. Most guitars used in jazz have access to the high D shown, although the top fifth or so of this range is not often utilised, even in solos. As with the piano, 8va notation is recommended for passages that stray more than a few ledger lines above the stave.

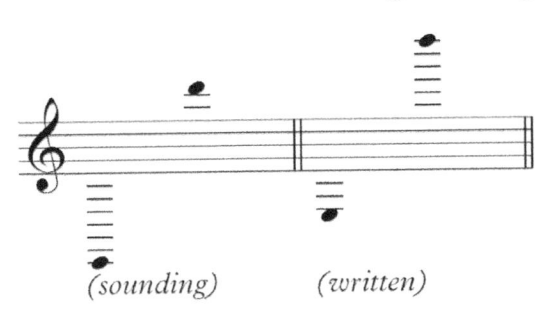

(sounding) *(written)*

Unlike the piano where practically any chord with up to ten notes within a reasonable span may be executed, the guitar is actually fairly limited in terms of the chord voicings it can produce. Most guitar voicings contain only four or five pitches, and there are further limits within these restrictions. Many structures are impractical or impossible, particularly those involving whole step and half step clusters.

The guitar, piano, bass, and drums are certainly the best-established members of the jazz rhythm section, but a few other non-wind instruments have established strong traditions within the idiom. In particular, there have been many great vibraphonists since the 1930s. The instrument is capable of harmonic comping and is melodically agile. The vibraphone is often paired with the guitar in unison passages.

There is a long tradition of the use of auxiliary percussion within jazz ensembles alongside a conventional drum kit. Cuban instruments such as the conga and bongo drums, timbales, and cowbells are particularly popular, as are tambourines, maracas, shakers and the like. Similar to a drum kit player, a percussionist is generally at their best when given the bare necessities of information about style and form and left to their own devices.

Rhythm Section Orchestration

Although excellent music has been made with highly arranged and prescribed rhythm section parts, most of the best jazz is undoubtedly made when expert musicians are given the freedom to accompany as they see fit. Jazz as an art form places enormous emphasis on personal expression and the development of an idiosyncratic artistic voice. This emphasis on the need for creative freedom extends even to a musician in their capacity as accompanist. It is simply not the role of the composer to instruct accompanists how to accompany.

When rhythm sections are instructed, it tends to be in passages that have motivic importance to a composition. Ostinato basslines, hits, or drum grooves should be included when it is felt that they are essential to the essence of a piece, supporting a melody perhaps, providing a countermelody, or providing a memorable hook that reinforces the structure of a chorus.

When one instrument within a rhythm section has a specific part, others are more likely to require something complementary. Hits, for example, are usually applied across the whole band. In the following excerpt, the bass risks sounding out of place as it ploughs on obliviously through the piano and drum hits:

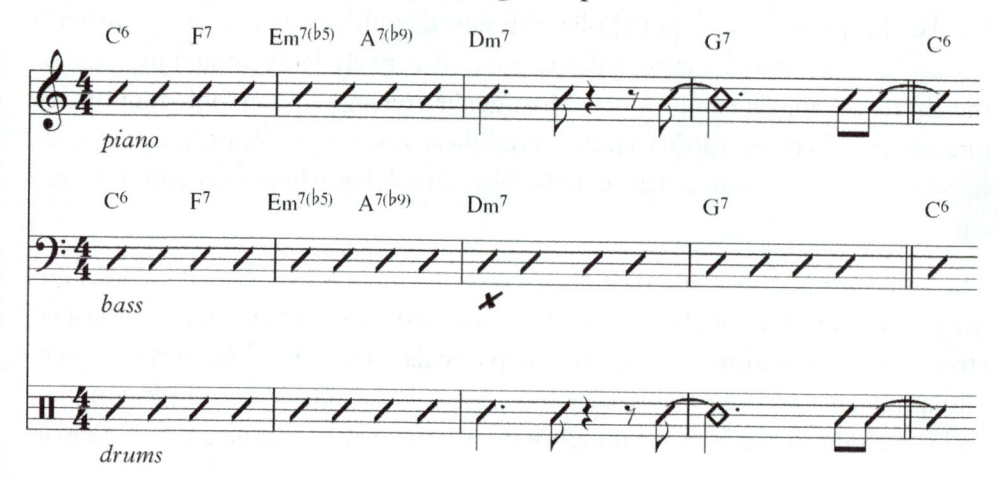

Another example of the importance of rhythm section parity is found in the regularity of a written bass pattern, such as the one found on page 291. This demands not only doubling in the pianist's left hand, but a complementary right-hand figure for the piano:

Highly orchestrated passages such as the excerpt above are generally only utilised in swing feel and latin jazz for short sections of a performance, perhaps as a vamp or a section of the chorus. They may last for the entirety of a rock or funk piece.

Chapter Summary

Rhythm sections are at their best when given the freedom to extemporise. Composers write for them only when specific effects are desired.

Written rhythm section material usually emphasises uniformity. When one rhythm section instrument receives a specific part, others are more likely to demand written material that either duplicates or compliments it.

Chapter 23
Writing for Melodic Instruments

Instruments that play a primarily melodic role within the ensemble are often referred to as the front line, as opposed to back line of the rhythm section. This usually includes wind instruments of the brass (trumpet and trombone) and woodwind (saxophone, clarinet, and flute) families. Although these horns are the instruments most characteristically used in melodic roles, the guitar in particular is sometimes promoted to the front line, particularly when a piano is also present.

Numerous configurations are possible. The piano might perform a melodic counterpoint to a horn melody rather than a conventional chordal accompaniment, or the bass might play a melody with horns in a supporting role, as in Miles Davis' *So What*.

Since brass and woodwind play such an important role in all styles, let us begin our exploration of the front line by considering the capabilities, strengths, and weaknesses of these instruments. The most reliable effects are produced when we primarily utilise the ensemble in a broadly conventional manner, so familiarity with the normal roles of these instruments is recommended as a starting point.

As a general rule, instruments do not produce their most characteristic or expressive sound in the extremes of their register. We endeavour to write so that most instruments are in their comfortable middle range most of the time. Furthermore, when multiple horns are available within an ensemble, we usually orchestrate them such that they do not swap registral roles. The trombone part is invariably lower than the trumpet, for instance, and the tenor saxophone below the alto, and so on.

Transposition

In the previous chapter, we saw that music must be written for double basses, guitars, and bass guitars an octave higher than their true pitch. This makes them transposing instruments, because their parts must be transposed by an octave relative to standard or concert pitch.

Saxophones, clarinets, and trumpets are also transposing instruments, although they do not transpose by exact octaves, which means that music written for them will appear in a different key and at a different pitch level to concert pitch.

A trumpet's middle C, for example, is a whole step below a concert middle C. When a trumpet player plays their C, we hear the B-flat a whole step below it. A trumpet is therefore said to be in B-flat. All music written for the B-flat trumpet must be written a whole step above where it is to sound: C must be written as D, C-sharp as D-sharp, and so on. By extension, a piece in the concert key of C must be written in the key of D.

There are a number of interconnected historical and pragmatic reasons for this convention, many of which are not at all relevant to our current discussion, but the advantages are particularly visible in the saxophone family. Sopranino, soprano, alto, tenor, baritone, and bass saxophones all have exactly the same written range, meaning that a saxophonist may switch from one to the other, reading music in radically different registers but finding each written note in the same place on each instrument.

Writing for Saxophones

(written range of all saxophones)

Soprano, alto, tenor, and baritone saxophones are all regularly used in jazz. In theory, all saxophones have a written range spanning from the B-flat below the treble stave to the F an octave above it. The soprano saxophone is a transposing instrument in B-flat, and sounds a whole step lower than it is written. The alto is in E-flat, a fifth below the soprano and a sixth below concert pitch. The tenor saxophone is a full octave below the soprano, transposing down a natural ninth:

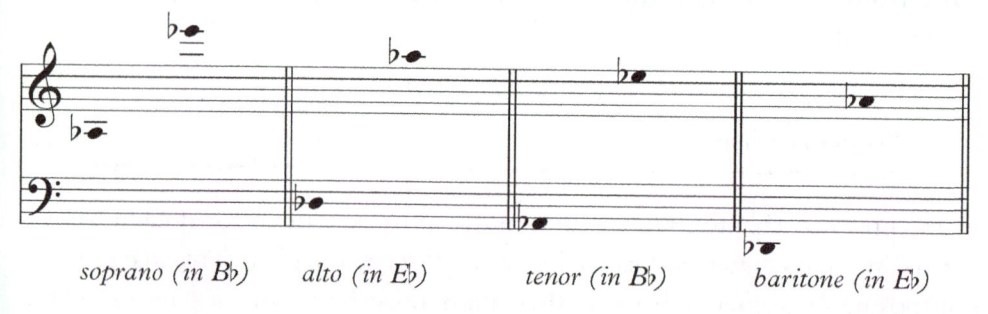

soprano (in B♭)   alto (in E♭)   tenor (in B♭)   baritone (in E♭)

Although initially a little confusing, this is actually a rather elegant system because it allows saxophonists to switch between instruments without the need to relearn fingering. Middle C is found on the same place on each instrument, whether it sounds a step, sixth, ninth, or thirteenth below concert pitch. This enables saxophonists to become proficient on multiple instruments, although most do tend to specialise on either the tenor or alto horn.

Many saxophonists are able to play pitches significantly higher than their keyed top F. Almost all modern instruments have a high F-sharp pitch, which increases the standard range by a half step. Pitches significantly higher than this are available in the altissimo range, which is accessed by manipulating the overtone series with embouchure, throat position, and oral cavity. Writing in the altissimo register is dissuaded unless the composer knows exactly what their saxophonist is capable of, because the abilities of musicians vary a great deal.

Other Woodwinds

Clarinets were practically mandatory in early jazz groups, being more or less replaced by the saxophone by the end of the swing era. They are still used a little in big band music and small groups, particularly when the intention is to invoke older music, but have also been applied to more contemporary styles. The clarinet is a transposing instrument in B-flat, sounding a whole step lower than it is written.

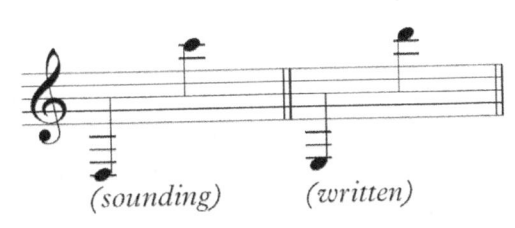

When writing for the clarinet we should be aware of the so-called break between the B-flat and B-natural in the middle of the staff. Fast passages that repeatedly cross this position are very awkward to finger. The upper range shown above is again rather conservative, showing a practical limit for written material rather than the highest pitch possible on the instrument.

The bass clarinet is also popular in jazz, occupying a similar range and role to the baritone saxophone. It has the same written range and is in B-flat, but sounds a ninth lower than written, making it one octave below the clarinet.

The flute was rare in jazz ensembles until the 1960s, when it increased in popularity as an alternative instrument for saxophonists in small groups and big bands. The flute is not a transposing instrument, and has a lowest pitch of middle C. The high F suggested is not a hard upper limit, but notes above this become very shrill.

Though very few contemporary jazz musicians are clarinet and flute specialists, many saxophonists play one or both of these in addition to their primary horn, and a lot of modern big band music requires its saxophonists to double on the flute and/or clarinet.

Writing for Trumpets

The trumpet is a transposing instrument in B-flat, written a whole step higher than it sounds. The bottom fifth of the range suggested here is rather weak and difficult to control, but anything between middle C and the top of the stave is loud and projecting.

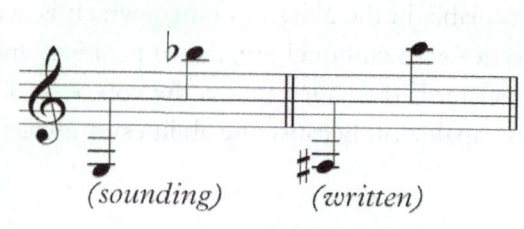

(sounding)   *(written)*

The high B-flat suggested as an upper range limit is rather dependant on context, and many trumpet players are able to play pitches significantly higher than this. The upper register of the trumpet is extremely strident and piercing, and is rarely used for composed melodies in a small group context. It is far more useful in big band writing, where a first trumpet may be supported with up to four others in harmony beneath it.

Composers should be aware of a musician's endurance. Playing the trumpet in the upper register is physically demanding for even the most experienced professionals. High notes should be used sparingly throughout a tune or performance. The trumpet is at its most agile and expressive in its comfortable middle register. Passages that require large leaps are also very difficult to execute accurately.

The trumpet can also increase its sonic versatility through the use of mutes, which attach to the bell of the instrument and obstruct air flow in various ways. The most common are the straight mute, cup mute, harmon mute, and plunger mute, each of which has its own distinctive sound, and each of which is in widespread use, particularly in big band settings.

Many trumpet players also play the flugelhorn, which has a softer sound but a weaker high register. The flugelhorn is often used in mellow and lyrical contexts such as ballads.

The cornet was popular in early jazz, and is used by a few modern players. It has a similar range to the trumpet but with a broader, softer sound and a less pronounced upper register.

Writing for Trombones

The trombone is notated at pitch in the bass clef. Most modern trombones have an attachment that extends the range, allowing them to play the C below the stave, a third below the low E depicted here. When writing for trombone, composers must be aware of the nature of the slide. This not only means that fast, complex passages will be difficult, but also that any slurred movement will sound as a glissando.

As with all brass instruments, the upper range is theoretically open-ended, but the G above this stave is a practical limit for most situations. All of the mutes available to trumpets are also available and commonly used by trombonists.

Small Group Orchestration

An ensemble consisting of a rhythm section and one or two horns may produce excellent music from a lead sheet, but the more front line melodic instruments we have, the more we have to gain from involved arranging.

A lot of classic jazz has been made by a rhythm section fronted by a single horn or two-horn combinations, such as trumpet and alto saxophone or trumpet and tenor saxophone. With two horns, melodies may be played in exact unison or octaves, which is particularly suitable for complex and involved melodies such as bebop. Charlie Parker's small group music is almost all orchestrated in octaves, with the trumpet and alto saxophone playing in unison:

Below is how this passage would actually appear on the musician's parts. For the trumpet, the passage is written in B-flat, a whole step higher than it sounds:

(trumpet)

For the alto, the same passage is written a natural sixth higher than concert pitch, in F major:

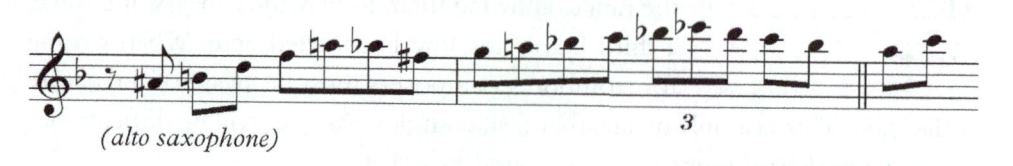

(alto saxophone)

If our ensemble included a trombone rather than an alto saxophone, we would need to accommodate for the instrument's lower range, orchestrating the same passage in octaves rather than in unison:

(trumpet)

(trombone)

Even with two front line voices, we have a great many textural options beyond unison and octaves. A unison melody might split into harmony at key points, which is most effective on sustained notes. In the following passage, each phrase ends with a sustained pitch, upon which our two melodic instruments deviate:

Harmonising occasional short notes within a primarily unison passage is confusing and it tends to sound like an error. We might say that the orchestration here is at odds with the music because it emphasises pitches that the line does not:

[musical notation: Gmaj7, C7(#11)]

A melody might, however, be harmonised note-for note in a lower voice. With two voices, this is most effective on lyrical, song-like melodies, and is an example of the thickened line texture explored earlier (page 280). Typically, the harmonising voice is heard beneath the melody, and follows its contour as closely as possible, whilst conforming to the prevailing harmony:

[musical notation: Dm6, Gm7, Em7(b5), A7(b9), Dm6]

A note-for-note harmonisation such as this should not draw our attention away from the primary melody. It must be clear to the listener which line is the melody and which the accompaniment.

Below is an alternative of the preceding passage, with a cross marking every time the lower voice moves in a larger interval than its master. The resulting lower line is both ugly and distracting, and fights the original melody for our attention:

[musical notation: Dm6, Gm7, Em7(b5), A7(b9), Dm6]

Counterpoint (page 261) is an option with two horns. This might mean two voices of equal activity and significance:

[Musical notation: Bm6 | F#m7(b5) B7(b9) | Em7 | A7 | Dmaj7]

The effect need not be so egalitarian. The passage below shows a variation of the preceding excerpt with a far less active lower line. The long tones provide harmonic accompaniment rather than melodic interest:

[Musical notation: Bm6 | F#m7(b5) B7(b9) | Em7 | A7 | Dmaj7]

A line such as the one below is uninteresting enough that it may appear above a melody without stealing the attention. We still hear the lower, more active voice as the primary melody:

[Musical notation: Bm6 | F#m7(b5) B7(b9) | Em7 | A7 | Dmaj7]

Below, an ostinato pattern in the lower voice performs a similar effect. Despite being considerably more active than the melody that it accompanies, the repetitive nature of the pattern allows it to blend into the background, causing us to hear the lower line as an accompaniment rather than melody:

[Musical notation: Bm6 | F#m7(b5) B7(b9) | Em7 | A7 | Dmaj7]

• Chapter 23: Writing for Melodic Instruments

With three horns, the textural possibilities increase. Below, the lower two melodic instruments provide a harmonic pad beneath the melody:

In a re-orchestration of the same material, the melody appears beneath the pad in a register that might be suitable for trombone, double bass, or baritone saxophone. Despite appearing in the low register, this line asserts itself as the primary melody through its rhythmic activity and larger intervallic movement:

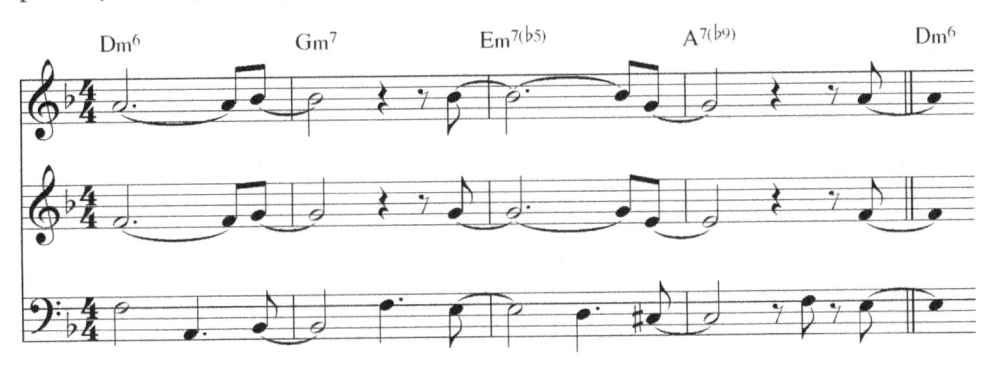

Three-voice thickened line is also an option:

Alternatively, we may simply choose to orchestrate our three voices in unison/octaves, perhaps occasionally splitting into harmony at key points. This approach is particularly appropriate for fast tempos and active melodies:

The Big Band

In a classic big band instrumentation, a rhythm section accompanies four trombones, four or five trumpets, and a saxophone section of two altos, two tenors, and a baritone. Although passages for solo instruments are included in most arrangements, each section is typically deployed as a unit.

The trombone, trumpet, and saxophone sections can be thought of as three discrete melodic voices, any of which might be orchestrated either in unison or octaves, or as a thickened line. There are numerous possible configurations; the saxophone section might play a melody in octaves, whilst trombones back them with rhythmic stabs:

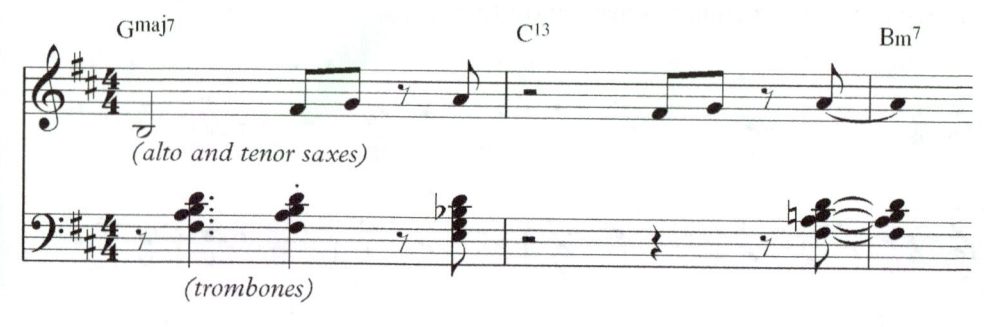

Below, trumpets play the same melody in thickened line while saxophones accompany with a pad:

• Chapter 23: Writing for Melodic Instruments

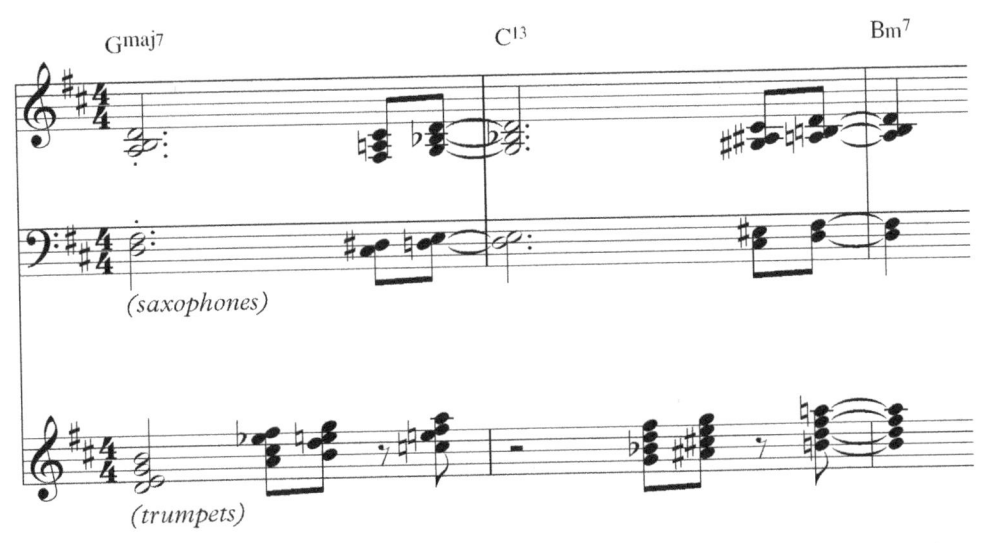

[musical example with saxophones and trumpets, chords Gmaj7, C13, Bm7]

The trumpet and trombone sections, sonically the most similar pair of the three sections, are often used together. One possible technique is to voice the entire trombone section an octave below the trumpets:

[musical example with trumpets and trombones, chords Gmaj7, C13, Bm7]

The saxophone section might be added to this passage so that all of the horns are playing at once, in *tutti*. The excerpt below adds five saxophones to the preceding example in drop 2 and 4, and with the lead doubled:

In the middle ground between the quintet and the big band, a jazz ensemble may employ any number and configuration of horns. A dectet might be assembled from a rhythm section plus two trumpets, one trombone, an alto, two tenors, and a baritone saxophone. Such a front line still suggests numerous textural possibilities that might be formed from various configurations of unison, octaves, thickened line melody, pads and solo voices.

Chapter Summary

Melodic instruments are often referred to collectively as 'horns' or 'the front line'. This usually comprises the wind instruments, but sometimes we may wish to use other instruments in melodic roles.

We may choose to orchestrate a front line of two or three instruments in unison/octaves, unison/octaves with occasional harmony, melody and pad, parallel harmony like thickened line, counterpoint, or any combination of the above.

Big band orchestration treats the trumpet, trombone, and saxophone sections as three distinct instruments that can be deployed either in unison or thickened line. This gives us access to an enormous array of orchestrational textures.

Closing Thoughts

This concludes our overview of the fundamentals of jazz language. As was remarked in the introduction, the intention of this book has been to describe and catalogue the common compositional vocabulary that underpins the writing of jazz music.

The working processes of individual composers vary too greatly for any kind of universal method to be suggested here. Any element might form the initial seed of a piece, be it a chord, a fragment of melody, a formal concept, or an extra-musical stimulus. From the original zygote, it is our knowledge and command of the musical language that carries a piece to completion.

As they are assimilated, the numerous ideas explored in the preceding chapters and subheadings become interconnected and adaptable elements in an ever-expanding musical vocabulary.

A piece may reach a point where it feels finished, but many artists feel as though they never truly complete a work, and may present the same piece in different iterations over the course of many years. Indeed, a famous cliché states that a work of art is never completed, only abandoned. Regardless, a pivotal part of the composer's method is the art of knowing when to stop. This is often connected to the need for an economy of expression; the longer we work on a piece, the more we are likely to add to it.

Pieces that are sweated over for too long are liable to accumulate details, and we must be wary of becoming too attached to elements that may later need to be removed. Another classic aphorism of creative practice states that it is easier to add elements than to remove them.

The editorial scalpel must be close at hand as we work towards the completion of a piece. A composer must constantly ask whether there is a simpler way to achieve the desired effect. Good jazz musicians are, by definition, capable of creating great music from very little material, and the composer's hand has often been relatively light in the creation of great jazz.

Consciously or unconsciously, all music is written within limitations. The composer is limited by the time in which that they have to write, the performers for whom they are writing, the requirements of the commission, or simply the confines of their own musical vocabulary. Such limitations must be embraced. Indeed, artists have often used the imposition of arbitrary limitations as a creative stimulus.

A deep familiarity with jazz is necessary for anyone that wishes to write within the tradition. We return repeatedly to our favourite pieces and recordings whilst fostering a hunger for new music. As we explore the canon of great music, we do so with a critical and analytic ear. Our aesthetic sense – what we like or dislike, which elements we wish to assimilate or reject – is as unique as a fingerprint, and is nurtured and explored as part of the process of developing a compositional voice. Because this aesthetic identity is inherently unique, there is no need to deliberately contrive a personal style. With time, study and practice a style will develop.

Of course, the only guaranteed path to development and improvement is continued and deliberate practice. It could be said that the greatest obstacle standing in the way of most potential composers is that they simply do not start; a musician who sets aside half an hour with a sharpened pencil and a blank page is already leading the pack. In a sense, the only actual compositional method suggested here is to start composing immediately, and to persist.

Index

♭II⁷, 198
♭VI, 78
♭VI⁷, 205
♭VII⁷, 62
♯IV°⁷, 63
altered blues, 99
altered chord, 38, 201
altered scale, 226
antecedent phrase, 139
anticipation, 118
augmented triad, 28
backdoor cadence, 61, 208
backing figures, 176
bass, 165, 289
bebop, 8
bebop scale, 241
blues, 256
bossa nova, 169
break, 175
bridge, 154
chord, 28
chord progressions, 40
chord symbols, 36
chord tone, 114
chorus, 21
chromatic scale, 23
circle of fifths, 80
clarinet, 299
classical music, 23

coda, 181
common practice music, 23
consequent phrase, 139
consonance, 23
contrafact, 8
counterpoint, 251, 261
Cuba (the music of), 8
diatonic, 32
diminished scale, 238
diminished triad, 29
dissonance, 23
dominant, 46
drop voicing, 279
drums, 165, 288
early jazz, 7
eleventh, 35
extensions, 35, 275
flat, 24
flute, 299
free jazz, 10
functional harmony, 30
half-diminished chord, 53
hard bop, 9
harmonic major, 228
harmonic minor, 226
harmonic minor scale, 33

harmonic series, 271
harmony, 28
head, 21
hemiola, 249
hits, 173
hypermeter, 19
I, 45
I (in minor), 51
I°⁷, 208
I⁷, 92
II, 47
II (in minor), 53
III⁷, 60
III^m7, 71
II-V-I, 48
II-V-I (in minor), 51
interlude, 183
intervals, 23, 277
IV, 59
IV^m, 62
IV^m6, 214
jazz fusion, 10
jazz standards, 11
key, 30
key signature (changing), 90
latin (performance style), 169
lead sheet, 5, 186
major scale, 24, 220
major triad, 28
melodic minor scale, 33, 224

312

minor blues, 96
minor triad, 28
mixed meter, 18
modal jazz, 9, 218
modulation, 80
natural, 24
ninth, 35
non-chord tone, 116
non-functional harmony, 30, 231
octave, 23
odd meters, 16
pad, 305
parts, 5
passing tone, 116
pedal, 233, 250
pedal point, 250
pentatonic scale, 243, 256
period, 21, 152
phrase, 20
phrase (melody), 108
piano, 165
pitch, 23
pivot, 82, 89
polychord, 268
rhythm changes, 153
rhythm section, 164
rhythmic displacement, 248
riff, 258
Roman numerals, 41
saxophones, 298
score, 5
section, 21
sequence (melody), 141
seventh, 34
sharp, 24
slash chords, 40, 266
soli, 184
solos, 161, 176
song form, 153
songbook, 8
suspended chord, 207
suspension, 119
swing (musical style), 7
swing (performance style), 166
swing (rhythmic effect), 15
tag', 183
tempo, 14
tertiary harmony, 29
thickened line, 280
tonal, 24
Trading, 176
transposing instruments, 297
triad, 28
tritone, 198
tritone substitution, 198
turnaround, 68
twelve-bar blues, 92
V, 46
V (in minor), 52
V^7, 70, 214
VI^7, 69
$VI^{7alt.}$, 77
VII^7, 209
VI^{m7}, 67
VIm7b5, 75
voice leading, 41, 234, 276
whole-tone scale, 237

313

Artificer Productions

Drum Kit Methodology

Linear Freedom: *A Complete Concept for the Development of Linear Drumming*

- Jonathan Curtis
- 978-0-9957273-0-4

Broken Time Drumming: *A Complete Concept for the Development of Broken Time Drumming*

- Jonathan Curtis
- 978-0-9957273-3-5

Snare Drum Methodology

The Snare Drum Virtuoso: *Technical Studies for the Development of Snare Drum Technique*

- Jonathan Curtis
- 978-0-9957273-5-9

Compositions

Snare Drum Compositions: *Volume 1*

- Jonathan Curtis
- 978-0-9957273-2-8

The Music Box Suite: *Duets for Snare Drum and Marimba*

- Jonathan Curtis
- 978-0-9957273-6-6

www.JonathanCurtis.co.uk

Made in the USA
Middletown, DE
22 September 2024